# THIS DATE IN

# PITTSBURGH

# PIRATES

# HISTORY

# THIS DATE IN

# PITTSBURGH

# PIRATES

## HISTORY

**Morris Eckhouse**
**Carl Mastrocola**

𝔖𝔅

A SCARBOROUGH BOOK

STEIN AND DAY/*Publishers*/ New York

FIRST SCARBOROUGH BOOKS EDITION 1980
Copyright © 1980 by Morris Eckhouse and Carl Mastrocola
All rights reserved
Designed by Louis Ditizio
Printed in the United States of America
Stein and Day/ *Publishers*/ Scarborough House
Briarcliff Manor, N.Y. 10510

**Library of Congress Cataloging in Publication Data**

Eckhouse, Morris, 1959—
    This date in Pittsburgh Pirates history.

    1.   Pittsburgh.   Baseball Club (National League)
—History.   I.   Mastrocola, Carl, 1957-        joint
author.   II.   Title.
GV875.P5E25    796.357′64′0974886    79-3801
ISBN  0-8128-6052-7 (pbk.)

To my father Carl, who never gets tired of telling stories to a son who never gets tired of listening.

To my mother June, for her understanding, patience, and encouragement.

To my sweetie Julie, who is trying to teach me that the world is not all white with red stitches.

CM

This book is dedicated to my parents Melvin and Eleanor, and my sister Ellen. Without them this project would never have been completed.

ME

# ACKNOWLEDGMENTS

We would like to thank the following people and organizations for contributing to the contents of this book.

The Pittsburgh Pirates' publicity department: Joe Safety, director, and Sally O'Leary, administrative assistant, for putting all their material at our disposal.

Joe O'Toole, Pirates' vice president, for his cooperation and interest in our project.

Jean Donatelli, secretary to Mr. Peterson, for her help on the trade section and always brightening up the day with her friendly smile.

*The Sporting News,* publishers of *The National League Green Book, The Official Baseball Register, The Official World Series Records, The Official Baseball Record Book, The Baseball Dope Book, Baseball Daguerreotypes* and *100 Years of National League Baseball.* We would also like to thank *The Sporting News* for allowing us the use of their resources. We would especially like to thank Larry Wiggie and Paul McFarland for giving of their time to help us and make us feel welcome in St. Louis.

Nellie King for spending an afternoon to give us his remembrances of the Pirates. Nellie King is a gentleman and a professional, and will always have our respect and admiration.

The Chilton Book Company, publishers of the *Great No-Hitters* by Glenn Dickey, from which comes all the no-hit box scores (except John Candelaria's).

The Elias Sports Bureau for their help with the statistics of the early 1900s. We would like to thank the Elias Sports Bureau for their help throughout the entire season.

Theresa Mandula and Lila Omaits for typing part of the manuscript.

The authors' photographs were taken by Seymour Hofstetter.

Space does not permit us to list all the friends that have helped us during the season and the writing of this book, and any list that we could put together would not include all the first-class people in the Pirate organization and the people associated with the ballclub. However, there are some special people that we want to thank here while we have the chance.

Jon Neiderer, Pirates' assistant director of scouting, the leader of the five man task force to Baltimore for the last two games of the series and a guy who never forgets the frosty.

Richard "Pro" Probola, super-scout, a small man with a big heart.

The guys at 308 Miltenberger: Jim Valenti, the landlord; Herman Kinzler, the man in the freezer; and Bill "Skunk" Strunk, a true friend and the Pirates' good luck charm.

Lou Bucci and his magic trumpet.

Steve Schanwald, Pirates' promotions director, who sometimes calls 'em like he sees 'em.

John Hallahan, Pirates' equipment manager, for his help and patience during the last month of the season.

Ying and Kris, wherever you are.

Art McKennan, the Pirate PA announcer, one of the most knowledgeable baseball men we have ever had the pleasure to work with.

Vince Lascheid who is always ready with his organ (I'll say).

And especially, the best receptionist in baseball, Bettyann Pecovish (regards to Bonnie Cashdollar).

# CONTENTS

*Illustrations between pages* 136 *and* 137.

# INTRODUCTION

There has been a Pittsburgh club in the National League since 1887. Pittsburgh's team was originally known as the Alleghenies. The Alleghenies played in the American Association from 1882–86. They remained the Alleghenies in the National League until 1891 when they signed second baseman Lou Bierbauer as a free agent. Bierbauer had jumped to the Players League from Philadelphia of the American Association in 1890. When the league disbanded, the Athletics expected Bierbauer to return to them. When he signed with Pittsburgh, the signing was called "Piratical" and the team has been known as Pirates ever since.

In their 93 National League seasons, Pittsburgh has had some good teams, and some bad teams but rarely dull teams. When almost all the Alleghenies jumped to the Players League in 1890, a rag-tag collection of has beens and never-weres managed to win just 23 games. In 1900 Barney Dreyfuss bought the Pirates and brought along Honus Wagner and Fred Clarke from his old Louisville club. The Pirates improved dramatically in 1900 and won pennants in 1901, 1902, 1903, and 1909. They had to wait another 16 years before reaching the World Series in 1925. The Pirates became the first team in history to rebound from a 3–1 deficit as they defeated Washington in the seventh game of the series for their second World Championship, their last for 35 years. After winning another National League pennant in 1927, the team slowly declined and was sold to a syndicate including John Galbreath and singer-actor Bing Crosby. The Pirates reached rock bottom in 1952, losing 112 games with what some experts believe was the worst team in baseball history. When Joe L. Brown became General Manager in 1955, the Pirates began moving back toward the top. Brown's trades built the 1960 World Champions. There was another drought, marked by great hitting and not so great pitching. In 1970 the Pirates won a divisional title and became the World Champions again in 1971, beating Baltimore in a seven game series marked by the brilliant play of Roberto Clemente. The Pirates were the National League's most successful team in the seventies and capped the decade with another World Championship. They became the only team to come back from a 3–1 deficit twice in the series, led by the inspirational play of Willie Stargell.

In this mini-history, the great moments in Pittsburgh's National League history are listed. When the date of birth of a player is the event, his name is listed, followed by the letter "B," then (in parentheses) by his position and the years he appeared in an Alleghenies or Pirates uniform. The managers and coaches are also listed along with their years in Pittsburgh. The team's All-Time roster is included to provide an alphabetical listing of all the players and includes the number of games each participated in with Pittsburgh. The pitchers are listed separately with their won-lost records as members of the Pittsburgh National League club. The Pirates' yearly leaders are listed to acknowledge the performances of the great players in the team's history. Separate sections on trades and the Pirates' post-season competition are also included.

*This Date in Pittsburgh Pirates History* is hoped to bring back fond memories of past events and players remembered by long time Pirates' fans. It is also hoped to entertain and enlighten newer Pirates fans and baseball fans in general to the club's long, usually successful, history and rich heritage.

# THIS DATE IN

# PITTSBURGH

# PIRATES

# HISTORY

# 1. DATE SECTION

## JANUARY 1

1855 — Bill McGunnigle — B (Manager 1891)

1884 — Ham Hyatt — B (OF–IB 1909–10, 12–14)

1911 — Hank Greenberg — B (IB 1947)

### January 2

1854 — Sam Crane — B (2B 1890)

1892 — George Boehler — B (P 1923)

1895 — Jesse Altenberg — B (OF 1916–17)

### January 3

1884 — Kirby White — B (P 1910–11)

1906 — Gus Suhr — B (IB 1930-39)

1920 — Ben Guintini — B (OF 1946)

1926 — Harry Fisher — B (P 1952)

1944 — Dick Colpaert — B (P 1970)

### January 4

1872 — Bill Gray — B (OF 1903)

### January 5

1880 — Fred Hunter — B (IB 1911

1914 — John Salvesor — B (P 1935)

1928 — Bob Oldis — B (C 1960–61)

1946 — Pirates purchase infielder Jimmy Brown from the Cardinals

1954 — Hall of Famer Walter "Rabbit" Maranville dies at age 63.

### January 6

1903 — George Grant — B (P 1931)

1917 — Phil Masi — B (C 1949)

1922 — Lee Walls — B (OF 1952, 56–57)

1935 — Dick Schofield — B (SS 1958–65)

1955 — Dorian Boyland — B (IB–OF 1978–present)

## January 7

1875 — Kitty Bransfield — B (1B 1901–04)

1889 — Leo Murphy — B (C 1915)

1902 — Cliff Knox — B (C 1924)

1904 — Al Todd — B (C 1936–38)

1921 — Ted Beard — B (OF 1948–52)

1924 — Jim Pendleton — B (OF 1957–58)

## January 8

1864 — John Gilbert — B (SS 1890)

1915 — Walker Cooper — B (C 1954)

1921 — Marv Rickert — B (OF 1950)

1934 — Gene Freese — B (3B 1955–58, 64–65)

## January 9

1886 — Harley Payne — B (P 1899)

1918 — The Pirates trade shortstop Chuck Ward, pitcher Al Mamaux, and pitcher Burleigh Grimes to Brooklyn for second baseman George Cutshaw and outfielder Casey Stengel.

## January 10

1908 — Bill Swift — B (P 1932–39)

1922 — Cliff Chambers — B (P 1949–51)

1926 — George Strickland — B (SS 1950–52)

1933 — Billy O'Dell — B (P 1966–67)

## January 11

1868 — Charles King — B (P 1891)

1890 — Maurice Keliher — B (1B 1911-12)
       Max Carey — B (OF 1910–26, coach 1930)

1955 — Pirates trade pitcher Paul LaPalme to the Cardinals for pitcher Ben Wade and cash.

## January 12

1859 — Ed Swartwood — B (OF 1892)

1866 — Tom Kinslow — B (C 1895)

1925 — Ed Stevens — B (1B 1948–50)

1951 — Bill Madlock — B (3B 1979–present)

## January 13

1869 — Judson Smith — B (3B 1896, 01)

1880 — Goat Anderson — B (OF 1907)

1901 — Fred Schulte — B (OF 1936–37)

1909 — Spades Wood — B (P 1930–31)

1940 — Ron Brand — B (C 1963)

1949 — Jim Foor — B (P 1973)

1953 — Odell Jones — B (P 1975, 77–78)

1954 — The Pirates trade pitcher Murray Dickson to the Phillies for pitcher Andy Hansen, third baseman Jack Lohrke, and cash. Neither Hansen nor Lohrke played a regular season game for Pittsburgh.

## January 14

1868 — John Newell — B (3B 1891)

1871 — Art Madison — B (INF 1899)

1891 — John Shovlin — B (1911–no position listed as he only appeared in two games)

1892 — Billy Meyer — B (Manager 1948–52)

1911 — Hank Gornicki — B (P 1942–43, 46)

1952 — Terry Forster — B (P 1977)

## January 15

1882 — Ed Kinsella — B (P 1905)

1948 — Third baseman Eddie Bockman is purchased from Cleveland.

## January 16

1858 — Art Whitney — B (3B 1887)

1891 — Erskine Mayer — B (P 1918–19)

## January 17

1922 — Jack Merson — B (2B 1951–52)

## January 18

1899 — Eddie Moore — B (2B 1923–26)

1929 — Cal Neeman — B (C 1962)

1931 — Laurin Pepper — B (P 1954–57)

1936 — Larry Foss — B (P 1961)

1947 — Pirates purchase first baseman Hank Greenberg from Detroit. His acquisition is in large part responsible for an attendance increase of over 500,000 in 1947.

## January 19

1872 — Ed Spurney — B (SS 1891)

## January 20

1873 — Tom O'Brien — B (OF–1B 1898–1900)

1880 — Otis Clymer — B (OF 1905–07)

1904 — Denny Southern — B (OF 1930)

1922 — Sam Jethroe — B (OF 1954)

1936 — Jesse Gonder — B (C 1966–67)

1944 — Carl Taylor — B (C–OF 1968–69, 71)

## January 21

1868 — Jocko Menefee — B (P 1892, 94–95)

1913 — Fern Bell — B (OF 1939–40)

1918 — Ken Gables — B (P 1945–47)

1927 — Danny O'Connell — B (INF 1950, 53)

## January 22

1876 — Warren McLaughlin — B (P 1902)

1917 — Gene Geary — B (SS 1942–43)

1919 — Diomedes Olivo — B (P 1960, 62)

1940 — Pirates acquire pitcher Ray Harrell from the Phillies on waivers.

1948 — Fred Cambria — B (P 1970)

## January 23

1890 — Ed Barney — B (OF 1915–16)

1899 — William Regan — B (2B 1931)

1905 — Jack Saltzgaver — B (2B 1945)

1947 — Kurt Bevacqua — B (INF 1974)

## January 24

1874 — Dave Brain — B (INF 1905)

1907 — Bill Clarke — B (INF 1929–30)

1910 — Johnny Dickshot — B (OF 1936–38)

1917 — Walt Judnich — B (OF 1949)

1954 — Tim Jones — B (P 1977)

## January 25

1936 — Hal Pritchard — B (INF 1957)

1947 — Pirates claim pitcher Hi Bithorn from the Cubs on waivers. Bithorn never played for the Pirates in the regular season.

## January 26

1847 — Kaiser Wilhelm — B (P 1903)

1915 — Chuck Workman — B (OF 1946)

1930 — Vic Janowicz — B (C–3B 1953–54)

1956 — Former Pirates Joe Cronin and Hank Greenberg are elected to Baseball's Hall of Fame.

## January 27

Nothing of importance happened on this date.

## January 28

1898 — Chief Yellowhorse — B (P 1921–22)

1900 — Emil Yde — B (P 1924–27)

1914 — Alf Anderson — B (SS 1941–42, 46)

1916 — Bob Muncrief — B (P 1949)

1929 — Carlos Bernier — B (OF 1953)

7

## January 29

1949 — Pirates purchase Murray Dickson from the Cardinals. (Dickson pitched 40 or more games in each of his five years with Pittsburgh before being traded to the Phillies.)

1971 — Pirates trade outfielder Matty Alou and pitcher George Brunet to the Cardinals for pitcher Nelson Briles and outfielder Vic Davalillo.

## January 30

1872 — Charlie Heard — B (P–OF 1890)

1888 — Vin Campbell — B (OF 1910–11)

1936 — Pirates acquire outfielder Fred Schulte from Washington.

1947 — Matt Alexander — B (OF–INF 1978–present)

1959 — Pirates traded outfielder–third baseman Frank Thomas, outfielder Johnny Powers, outfielder Jim Pendleton, pitcher Ron Blackburn, and cash to Cincinnati for catcher Smokey Burgess, pitcher Harvey Haddix and third baseman Don Hoak. (This trade turned the Pirates from contenders to champions.)

## January 31

1861 — Al Buckenberger — B (MGR 1892–94)

1870 — Jot Goar — B (P 1896)

1894 — John Stewart — B (2B 1922)

1895 — Jimmy Zinn — B (P 1920–22)

1899 — Don Songer — B (P 1924–27)

1950 — Pirates sign high school star pitcher Paul Petit for a $100,000 bonus. (Petit won one regular season game for Pittsburgh.)

1974 — Pirates trade shortstop Jackie Hernandez to the Phillies for catcher Mike Ryan.

## FEBRUARY 1

1890 — Jim Kelly — B (OF 1914)

1892 — Dixie McArthur — B (P 1914)

1930 — Chuck Churn — B (P 1957)

1931 — Bob Smith — B (P 1957–59)

1947 — Jim McKee — B (P 1972–73)

## February 2

1885 — Bill Abstein — B (1B 1906, 09)

1906 — Johnny Welch — B (P 1936)

1918 — Arthur "Cookie" Cuccurullo — B (P 1943–45)

1927 — Fred Waters — B (P 1955–56)

1929 — Ed Wolfe — B (P 1952)

## February 3

1912 — Abrey Epps — B (C 1935)

1947 — Joe Coleman — B (P 1979–present)

## February 4

1875 — Al "Lefty" Davis — B (OF 1901–02)

1890 — George "Possum" Whitted — B (OF–3B 1919–21)

1949 — Steve Brye — B (OF 1978)

## February 5

1897 — Jake Miller — B (OF 1922)

1925 — Jack Maguire — B (OF 1951)

1928 — Don Hoak — B (3B 1959–62)

1932 — Owner Barney Dreyfuss dies of pneumonia at age 66.

## February 6

1901 — Glenn Wright — B (SS 1924–28)

1926 — Dale Long — B (1B 1951, 55–57)

1927 — Smokey Burgess — B (C 1959–64)

1932 — Bill Koski — B (P 1951)

1949 — Richie Zisk — B (OF 1971–76)

## February 7

1878 — William "Spike" Shannon — B (OF 1908)

1894 — Charles Jackson — B (OF 1917)

1907 — William Steinecke — B (C 1931)

1927 — Joe Lonnett — B (Coach 1977–present)

1930 — Felipe Montemayor — B (OF 1953, 55)

1938 — Juan Pizzaro — B (P 1967–68, 74)

## February 8

1886 — Roy Ellam — B (SS 1918)

1922 — Monty Basgall — B (2B 1948–49, 51)

1949 — Pirates claim outfielder Walt Judnich from Cleveland on waivers.

1973 — Former manager Frankie Frisch dies in an auto accident at age 74.

## February 9

1867 — Sumner Bowman — B (P 1890)

1870 — Hi Ladd — B (OF 1898)

1895 — Wally Hood — B (OF 1920)

1903 — Roy Mahaffey — B (P 1926–27)

1944 — Jim Campanis — B (C 1973)

1950 — Pirates sell catcher Phil Masi to the Chicago White Sox.

## February 10

1868 — Fred Roat — B (3B 1890)

1893 — Bill Evans — B (P 1890, 92)

1894 — Cotton Tierney — B (2B 1920–23)

1947 — Pirates purchase pitcher Jim Bagby, Jr. from the Red Sox.

## February 11

1924 — Hal Rice — B (OF 1953–54)

1965 — Pirates trade pitcher Bob Priddy, outfielder–first baseman Bob Burda, and cash to San Francisco for catcher Del Crandall. (Burda went from the Columbus AAA farm club to Tacoma.)

## February 12

1893 — Earl Sheely — B (1B 1906–07)

1912 — Lloyd "Dutch" Dietz — B (P 1940–43)

## February 13

1866 — Fred "Crazy" Schmidt — B (P 1890)

1883 — Harl Maggert — B (OF 1907)

1901 — Herman Layne — B (OF 1927)

1915 — Oad Swigart — B (P 1939–40)

1919 — Bobby Rhawn — B (INF 1949)

1921 — Pete Castiglione — B (3B 1947–53)

1930 — Al Grunwald — B (P 1955)

## February 14

1867 — Morgan Murphy — B (C 1898)

1897 — Earl S. Smith — B (C 1924–28)

## February 15

Nothing of importance happened on this date.

## February 16

1873 — John Sullivan — B (C 1908)

1889 — Jim "Skip" Dowd — B (P 1910)

1912 — Ray Harrell — B (P 1940)

1952 — Jerry Hairston — B (OF 1977)

## February 17

1890 — Rivington Bisland — B (SS 1912)

1901 — Eddie Phillips — B (C 1931)

1905 — Ed Brandt — B (P 1937–38)

1935 — Whammy Douglas — B (P 1957)

1941 — Dave Wissman — B (OF 1964)

## February 18

1891 — Sherrod "Sherry" Smith — B (P 1911–12)

1927 — Luis Arroyo — B (P 1956–57)

1938 — Manny Mota — B (OF 1963–68)

1926 — Joe Garagiola — B (C 1951-53)

1939 — Dal Maxvill — B (SS 1973–74)

Bob Miller — B (P 1971–72)

1950 — Bruce Kison — B (P 1971–79)

## February 19

1944 — Chris Zachery — B (P 1973)

## February 20

1866 — Harry Raymond — B (3B 1892)

1875 — Jack Rafter — B (C 1904)

1882 — Tom Stankard — B (INF 1904)

1920 — Frankie Gustine — B (2B, 3B 1939–48)

1928 — Elroy Face — B (P 1953, 55-68)

## February 21

1867 — Jouett Meekin — B (P 1900)

1937 — Ted Savage — B (OF 1963)

## February 22

1862 — Connie Mack — B (C 1891–96, manager 1894-96)

1900 — Roy Spencer — B (C 1925–27)

1911 — Billy Baker — B (C 1941–43, 46)

1922 — Frankie Zak — B (SS 1944–46)

Forrest "Woody" Main — B (P 1948, 50, 52–53)

## February 23

Nothing of significance happened on this date.

## February 24

1874 — Honus Wagner — B (SS 1900–17, manager 1917, coach 1933–35)

1892 — Wilbur Cooper — B (P 1912–24)

1907 — Earl Grace — B (C 1931–35)

1909 — Clarence Struss — B (P 1934)

1915 — Pirates send pitcher George McQuillan to the Phillies on waivers.

## February 25

1893 — Phil Slattery — B (P 1915)

1931 — Jim Dunn — B (P 1952)

## February 26

1864 — Sam LaRoque — B (2B 1890–91)

1892 — Jack Hammond — B (2B 1922)

1915 — Preacher Roe — B (P 1944–47)

1941 — George Kopacz — B (1B 1970)

1963 — Bill Mazeroski named team captain.

## February 27

Nothing of importance happened on this date.

## February 28

1881 — Harry McCormick — B (OF 1904)

1899 — Ulysses "Lil" Stoner — B (P 1930)

1915 — Pirates send outfielder–first baseman Ham Hyatt to the Cardinals on waivers.

1921 — Terry Turner — B (3B 1901)

1943 — Bob Oliver — B (C 1960–61)

## February 29

Nothing of significance happened on this date.

## MARCH 1

1852 — Paul Hines — B (OF 1890)

1885 — Cleon "Lefty" Webb — B (P 1910)

1915 — Nick Strincevich — B (P 1941–42, 44–48)

## March 2

1879 — Anthony "Chick" Robertaille — B (P 1904–05)

1891 — Bill Fischer — B (C 1916–17)

## March 2 (continued)

1898 — Floyd "Rip" Wheeler — B (P 1921–22)

1918 — Frank Colman — B (OF 1942–46)

1924 — Cal Abrams — B (OF 1953–54)

1936 — Don Schwall — B (P 1963–66)

## March 3

1879 — Edward "Babe" Phelps — B (C 1902–04, 06–08)

1910 — Bill Brenzel — B (C 1932)

## March 4

1888 — Jeff Pfeffer — B (P 1924)

1891 — Dazzy Vance — B (P 1915)

1917 — Clyde McCullough — B (C 1949–52)

1918 — Mel Queen Sr. — B (P 1947–48, 50-52)

1952 — Pirates sell pitcher Jim Suchecki to the St. Louis Browns.

## March 5

1911 — Earl Browne — B (1B-OF 1935–36)

1916 — Harry Shuman — B (P 1942–43)

1930 — Del Crandall — B (C 1965)

1938 — Larry Elliott — B (OF 1962–63)

1947 — Kent Tekulve — B (P 1974–present)

## March 6

1863 — John Coleman — B (OF–P 1887–88, 90)

1869 — Jim Hughey — B (P 1896–97)

1878 — Bert Husting — B (P 1900)

1940 — Willie Stargell — B (OF, 1B 1962–present)

## March 7

1881 — Doc Scanlan — B (P 1903–04)

1931 — Dick Rand — B (C 1957)

## March 8

1912 — Ray Mueller — B (C 1939–40, 50)

1915 — Kirby Higbe — B (P 1947–49)

1917 — Bill Salkeld — B (C 1945–47)

1922 — Al Gionfriddo — B (OF 1944–47)

1924 — Toby Atwell — B (C 1953–56)

1949 — Juan Jimenez — B (P 1974)

## March 9

1872 — Tom Delahanty — B (3B 1896)

1893 — Billy Southworth — B (OF 1918–20)

1898 — Joe Dawson — B (P 1927–29)

1912 — Arky Vaughan — B (SS 1932–41)

1932 — Ron Kline — B (P 1952, 55–59, 68–69)

1944 — Ed Acosta — B (P 1970)

1954 — Outfielder Bob Skinner called-up from AAA farm club at New Orleans.

## March 10

1862 — Edward "Pop" Lytle — B (OF 1890)

1880 — Walt Nagle — B (P 1911)

1907 — Art Herring — B (P 1947)

1932 — Paul Martin — B (P 1955)

## March 11

1893 — Ralph Capron — B (OF 1912)

1918 — Ed Fernandes — B (C 1940)

1945 — Dock Ellis — B (P 1968–75, 79–present)

## March 12

1866 — Dennis Lyons — B (3B 1893–94, 96–97)

1930 — Vern Law — B (P 1950–51, 54–67, coach 1967–69)

## March 13

1886 — Frank Miller — B (P 1916–19)

1918 — Ed Pellagrini — B (INF 1953–54)

1939 — Al Luplow — B (OF 1967)

1940 — Gary Kolb — B (OF–C 1968–69)

## March 14

1869 — Billy Rhines — B (P 1898–99)

1928 — Earl C. Smith — B (OF 1955)

## March 15

1876 — Bill Hallman — B (OF 1906–07)

1902 — Fred Bennett — B (OF 1931)

1919 — Whitey Wietelmann — B (INF 1947)

1928 — Nellie King — B (P 1954–57)

1977 — Pirates traded pitchers Dave Giusti, Doc Medich, Doug Bair, Rick Langford, and outfielders Tony Armas and Mitchell Page to Oakland for second baseman Phil Garner, infielder Tommy Helms, and pitcher Chris Batton. Garner replaced free agent loss Richie Hebner at third base.

1978 — Pirates sign pitcher Jim Bibby, who had been declared a free agent following a contract dispute with Cleveland.

## March 16

1865 — Patsy Donovan — B (OF 1892–99)

1902 — D'Arcy "Jake" Flowers — B (Coach 1940–45)

1906 — Lloyd Waner — B (OF 1927–41, 44-45)

1972 — Pie Traynor dies at age 72.

## March 17

1871 — Charles "Chick" Fraser — B (Coach 1921–23)

1874 — Bill Duggleby — B (P 1907)

1883 — Oscar Stange — B (Coach 1927–30)

1894 — Ralph Shafer — B (P 1914)

Hal Carlson — B (P 1917–23)

1897 — Harry Riconda — B (SS 1929)

1919 — Pete Reiser — B (OF 1951)

James G. Walsh — B (P 1946, 48–51)

1944 — Clarence Gaston — B (OF 1978)

## March 18

1874 — Nixey Callahan — B (Manager 1916–17)

1916 — Elbie Fletcher — B (1B 1939–43, 46–47)

1926 — Dick Littlefield — B (P 1954–56)

1978 — Pirates release pitcher Carl Morton. (Morton had been invited to spring training but never played for Pittsburgh during the regular season.)

## March 19

1931 — Paul Smith — B (1B–OF 1953, 57–58)

1947 — Angel Mangual — B (OF 1969)

## March 20

1864 — Pete McShannic — B (3B 1888)

1887 — Walter Schmidt — B (C 1916–24)

1940 — Pirates release catcher George Susce.

1952 — Rick Langford — B (P 1976)

## March 21

1918 — Bill Brandt — B (P 1941-43)

1941 — Manny Sanguillen — B (C–1B 1967, 69–76, 78–present)

1951 — Dale Long dons the "tools of ignorance" in an exhibition game against San Diego, becoming the Pirates' first left-handed catcher in half a century.

## March 22

1947 — Pirates send pitcher Hi Bithorn to the Chicago White Sox on waivers. Bithorn was an 18–game winner with the Cubs in 1943, but never won with the Pirates and only once with the Sox.

1965 — Pittsburgh claimed Quinton Willingham from San Francisco.

## March 23

1865 — William "Farmer" Weaver — B (OF 1894)

## March 23 (continued)

1885 — Danny Moeller — B (OF 1907–08)

1886 — Cy Slapnicka — B (P 1918). (Following an undistinguished major league career, Slapnicka became a scout for the Cleveland Indians and is responsible for signing Bob Feller.)

1893 — Ray Kremer — B (P 1924–33)

1927 — Johnny Logan — B (INF 1961–63)

## March 24

1874 — Roy Thomas — B (OF 1908)

1884 — Mike Mowrey — B (3B 1914)

1906 — Art Veltman — B (C 1934)

1907 — Gus Dugas — B (OF 1930–32)

1965 — Pirates purchase outfielder John Jeter from Baltimore.

## March 25

1882 — Jimmy Sebring — B (OF 1902–04)

1947 — Pirates purchase pitcher Lou Tost from the Boston Braves.

## March 26

1869 — Jack McCarthy — B (OF 1898–99)

1874 — Gene DeMontreville — B (SS 1894)

1947 — Pirates purchase John Christensen from the Braves.

1948 — Bucs purchase infielder Don Gutteridge from the Red Sox.

## March 27

1895 — Billy Burwell — B (P 1928 Coach 1947–48, 58–62, Manager 1947)

1975 — Pirates release pitcher Steve Blass. (After two years of hoping for a return to form, the Bucs were no longer able to make room for their former ace.)

1978 — Pitcher Larry Demery is sold to the Toronto Blue Jays.

## March 28

1868 — Elmer Smith — B (OF-P 1892–97, 1901)

1929 — Bill MacDonald — B (P 1950, 53)

1969 — Pirates trade catcher Chris Cannizzaro and pitcher Tommy Sisk to San Diego for outfielder Ron Davis.

1974 — Pittsburgh acquires pitcher Wayne Simpson from Kansas City in exchange for pitcher Jim Foor. (Simpson never regained the brilliance he displayed with Cincinnati and went to Philadelphia for Bill Robinson in 1975.)

## March 29

1865 — Hank Gastright — B (P 1893)

1873 — Duff Cooley — B (OF 1900)

1894 — Robert Steele — B (P 1917–18)

## March 30

1857 — Tom Burns — B (3B 1892, Manager 1892)

1866 — George Van Haltren — B (OF 1892–93)

1879 — Art Meier — B (OF 1906)

1897 — Ed Sicking — B (2B 1927)

1899 — Hal Rhyne — B (INF 1926–27)

1904 — James "Ripper" Collins — B (1B 1941)

## March 31

1886 — Fred Kommers — B (OF 1913)

1887 — Chester "Chick" Brandom — B (P 1908–09)

1894 — Tom Sheehan — B (3B 1906–07)

1895 — Carson Bigbee — B (OF 1916–26)

1945 — Pirates trade outfielder Vince DiMaggio to the Phillies for pitcher Al Gerhauser. (Gerhauser won only five games in '45 while the eldest DiMaggio drove in 84 runs in Philadelphia. He also led the league in strikeouts for the fourth consecutive season with 91.)

1977 — First baseman Bob Robertson is released. (Pegged for stardom by the *Baseball Digest* after the 1971 World Series, he fell to a .193 average the next year and never recovered. He caught on with the Seattle Mariners in 1978.)

## APRIL 1

1884 — Hugo Bezdek — B (Manager 1917–19)

1926 — Vernon "Jake" Thies — B (P 1954–55)

1974 — Pirates trade pitcher Tom Dettore and cash to the Cubs for infielder Paul Popovich. (Dettore was assigned to the Cubs AAA farm club at Wichita.)

## April 2

1963 — The Bucs acquire outfielder Manny Mota and cash from the Houston Colt 45s for outfielder Howie Goss. (Goss played just one season for Houston while Mota established himself as one of the game's top pinch hitters before going to Montreal in the 1968 expansion draft.)

1973 — Pirates trade catcher Charlie Sands to Detroit for pitcher Chris Zachery.

## April 3

1856 — Guy Hecker — B (1B–P 1890, Manager 1890)

1919 — Larry Shepard — B (Manager 1968–69)

1921 — Dick Conger — B (P 1941–42)

1927 — Alex Grammas — B (Coach 1965–69, Interim Manager 1969)

## April 4

1883 — Billy Hinchman — B (OF 1915–18, 20 Coach 1921–23)

1903 — Les Bartholomew — B (P 1928)

1942 — Jim Fregosi — B (INF 1977 — 78)

1977 — Outfielder Mike Easler is acquired from California for pitcher Randy Sealy. Easler is assigned to Columbus where he won the batting title in 1978.

1978 — The day before leaving Bradenton, the Pirates send outfielder Miguel Dilone, pitcher Elias Sosa, and a player to be named later to Oakland for Manny Sanguillen. (The Bucs paid a high price to reacquire the popular catcher. Sosa is now the ace reliever of the Montreal Expos. Mike Edwards was assigned to Oakland April 10th to complete the deal.)

## April 5

1877 — Wid Conroy — B (SS 1889)

1948 — Pirates claim shortstop Grady Wilson from the Phillies on waivers.

1951 — Rennie Stennett — B (2B 1971–79)

1975 — Pirates trade pitcher Wayne Simpson to Philadelphia for outfielder–infielder Bill Robinson. (Robinson became the Bucs "super-sub," while Simpson won only one game for the Phillies.)

## April 6

1931 — Emanuel "Sonny" Senerchia — B (3B 1952)

1951 — Bert Blyleven — B (P 1978–present)

1973 — A record crowd of 51,695 jams Three Rivers Stadium to honor the late Roberto Clemente. Clemente's jersey is retired in a pregame ceremony, then the Bucs rally in the ninth for a 7–5 victory over St. Louis.

## April 7

1875 — John Ganzel — B (1B 1898)

1879 — Art Weaver — B (C 1903)

1887 — John Ferry — B (P 1910–13)

1933 — Bobby Del Grecco — B (OF 1952, 56)

1966 — Pirates purchase pitcher Bob Purkey from St. Louis.

1967 — Catcher Jimmie Price sold to Detroit.

## April 8

1864 — Pete Daniels — B (P 1890)

1938 — Tom Butters — B (P 1962–65)

1969 — Pirates win opener in 14 innings, 6–2 at St. Louis. Bruce Dal Canton gets the victory.

## April 9

1909 — Claude Passeau — B (P 1935)

1930 — Pirates trade pitcher Burleigh Grimes to the Braves for pitcher Percy Lee Jones and cash. (Grimes went from Boston to St. Louis and helped the Cardinals to pennants in '30 and '31. Jones was 0–1 with the Bucs in 1930.)

1952 — Pitcher Clarence "Hooks" Iott is sold to Cincinnati.

## April 10

1908 — Howie Grosskloss — B (2B 1930–32)

1911 — Roger Wolff — B (P 1947)

1936 — Joe Gibbon — B (P 1960–65, 69–70)

1948 — Lee Lacy — B (OF 1979–present)

1957 — Pirates trade infielder Dick Cole to Milwaukee for outfielder Jim Pendleton and cash.

1971 — Willie Stargell hits three home runs against the Braves but Pirates lose 5–4 in Atlanta.

1975 — Stargell hits two homers in 8–4 opening day victory at Chicago.

## April 10 (continued)

1976 — Dave Parker scores deciding run in a violent collision with the Phillies' Johnny Oates, giving the Pirates a 5–4 opening day victory. Oates suffered a broken collar bone and missed two months of the season.

## April 11

1858 — John "Pop" Corkhill — B (OF 1891–92)

1892 — Willard "Red" Smith — B (C 1917–18)

1919 — Hank Schenz — B (2B 1950–51)

## April 12

1876 — Vic Willis — B (P 1906–09)

1878 — Bill Clancey — B (1B 1905)

1908 — Joe Vitelli — B (P 1944–45)

1933 — Cliff Latimer — B (C 1900)

1940 — Woody Fryman — B (P 1966–67)

1942 — Tommie Sisk — B (P 1962–68)

1966 — The Braves host Pittsburgh in their first game in Atlanta. Willie Stargell's two-run homer in the 13th gave the Bucs a 3–2 win.

## April 13

1870 — Able Lezotte — B (1B 1896)

1889 — Claude Hendrix — B (P 1911–13)

1959 — Pirates claim pitcher Paul Giel from San Francisco on waivers.

1963 — Bob Friend balks four times, but the Bucs pound Cincinnati 12–4 at Crosley Field.

## April 14

1880 — George Merritt — B (OF-P 1901–03)

1884 — Bill Luhrsen — B (P 1913)

1976 — Pirates sign pitcher Tom Hilgendorf, released by Philadelphia.

## April 15

1871 — Bill Grey — B (3B 1898)

1877 — Ed Abbaticchio — B (INF 1907–10)

1886 — Leonard "King" Cole — B (P 1912)

1926 — Bill Pierro — B (P 1950)

1933 — Pie Traynor's diving stab with bases loaded in ninth inning enables Pirates to beat the Cubs in extra innings.

1958 — Pirates open the season with a 4–3 victory in fourteen innings at Milwaukee.

### April 16

1903 — Paul Waner — B (OF 1926–40)

1912 — The Pirates turn an unusual 5–3–7 doubleplay with Max Carey coming in from leftfield to make the second putout at second base. Pittsburgh beat Cincinnati 8–2.

1937 — Pitcher Joe Bowman comes to Pittsburgh from the Phillies for infielder-out-fielder Earl Browne.

### April 17

1903 — Bob Osborne — B (P 1931)

1953 — Pirates purchase infielder Ed Pellagrini from the Reds.

1955 — Roberto Clemente makes his major league debut against the Dodgers in Forbes Field.

1964 — Pirates defeat New York 4–3 in the first game ever played at Shea Stadium.

### April 18

1872 — John Rothfuss — B (1B 1897)

1877 — Tully Sparks — B (P 1899)

1892 — John Scott — B (P 1916)

1902 — Claud Linton — B (C 1929)

1942 — Steve Blass — B (P 1964, 66–74)

1960 — Bob Skinner's two-run homer caps a six run, ninth inning rally to beat Cincinnati 6–5 at Forbes Field.

### April 19

1908 — Ernest "Babe" Phelps — B (C 1942)

1935 — Cy Blanton pitches a one-hitter to defeat St. Louis, 3–0.

### April 20

1881 — Jim Flanagan — B (OF 1905)

1909 — Barney Dreyfuss chooses Forbes Field as the name for the Pirates' new home, in honor of General John Forbes, one of the founders of Pittsburgh. Dreyfuss received 100,000 suggestions in a poll to determine the new stadium's name.

1936 — Gus Suhr's two-out, three-run, ninth inning homer defeats Chicago 9–8.

1970 — Willie Stargell homers over the right field roof at Forbes Field off the Astros' Jim Bouton, as the Pirates beat Houston 3–1.

## April 21

1913 — Eight hits and a sacrifice fly in succession give the Pirates a seven-run eighth inning and an 8–5 win over the Cardinals.

1919 — Stan Rojek — B (SS 1948–51)

1964 — Bucs and Cubs combine for nine home runs in 8–5 Pirates win at Wrigley Field.

1971 — Stargell hits three homers against Atlanta for the second time in April, as the Bucs top the Braves 10–2 in Pittsburgh.

## April 22

1894 — Jake Pitler — B (2B 1917–18)

1898 — Cincinnati's Ted Breitenstein pitches a no-hitter, defeating Pittsburgh 11–0.

1918 — James "Mickey" Vernon — B (1B 1960, Coach 1960, 64)

1941 — Pirates sell pitcher Mace Brown to Brooklyn. Brown had some good years left and led the American League in appearances with the Red Sox in 1943.

1962 — Pirates defeat the Mets for their tenth straight victory, equaling the all time record for consecutive victories at the start of a season.

## April 23

1875 — Bob Ganley — B (OF 1905–06)

1885 — Connie Walsh — B (P 1907)

1906 — Ray Starr — B (P 1944–45)

1935 — Ron Blackburn — B (P 1958–59)

1946 — Babe Dahlgren is sold to the St. Louis Browns. He played only 28 games for St. Louis.

1974 — Pirates reacquire shortstop Jackie Hernandez, previously released by the Phillies. He was assigned to Charleston and was never recalled.

## April 24

1891 — Pete Falsey — B (1914)

1898 — Fred Haney — B (Manager 1953–55)

1919 — Homer Howell — B (C 1947)

1949 — Pirates use 20 players, putting Frankie Gustine behind the plate in the process, before dropping a 9–5 decision to Cincinnati.

1970 — Bucs sign pitcher Al McBean, released by the Dodgers. (He appeared in seven games before being released on May 18th.)

## April 25

1868 — Fred Hartman — B (3B 1894)

1910 — Jimmy Brown — B (INF 1946)

1911 — Fred Clarke makes 10 catches in leftfield during 9–4 win against the Cardinals.

1943 — Bob Johnson — B (P 1971–73)

## April 26

1919 — Virgil Trucks — B (Coach 1963)

1920 — Ron Northey — B (Coach 1961–63)

1947 — Shortstop Billy Cox, second baseman Eddie Basinski, and first baseman Hank Greenberg team up on a triple play against Cincinnati.

## April 27

1955 — Statue of Honus Wagner is dedicated in Schenley Park outside Forbes Field. The statue is now located in front of Gate C at Three Rivers Stadium.

1971 — Willie Stargell hits his eleventh homer, setting a new major league record for the month of April. The Pirates lost to Los Angeles at Three Rivers Stadium.

## April 28

1875 — Walt Woods — B (P 1900)

1902 — Charles "Red" Lucas — B (P 1934–38)

1911 — Owen Wilson's bloop single scores two runs in the ninth and pulls the Pirates past Chicago 4–3 at Forbes Field.

1930 — Tom Sturdivant — B (P 1961–63)

1935 — Pedro Ramos — B (P 1969)

1947 — Pirates claim Bob Malloy from Cincinnati on waivers.

## April 29

1916 — Shortstop Honus Wagner nails the tying run at the plate after making a sensational stab of Greasy Neal's smash to preserve a 2–1 win over the Reds.

1934 — Pirates defeat Cincinnati 9–5 in the first game ever played in Pittsburgh on a Sunday.

## April 30

1887 — The Pittsburgh Alleghenies win their first game in the National League, defeating Chicago 6–2 at Recreation Park.

1892 — Anton Brottem — B (C 1921)

1943 — Pirates sell outfielder Jimmy Wasdell to the Phillies.

1948 — Phil Garner — B (3B, 2B 1977–present)

## MAY 1

1885 — George McQuillan — B (P 1913–15)

1896 — Heine Meine — B (P 1929–34)

1917 — John Berardino — B (INF 1950–52). (This is the same John Berardino who stars as Doctor Hardy in the soap opera "General Hospital.")

1957 — Pirates trade first baseman Dale Long and outfielder Lee Walls to the Cubs for second baseman Gene Baker and first baseman Dee Fondy. Fondy replaced Long at first base and Baker was used as a utility man. Long and Walls had initial success in Chicago but both were gone by 1960.

## May 2

1892 — Zip Collins — B (OF 1914–15)

1902 — Fred Sale — B (P 1924)

1941 — Clay Carroll — B (P 1978)

1954 — Frank Thomas collects seven hits in a doubleheader split with the Cubs.

## May 3

1867 — John O'Connor — B (C 1900–02)

1888 — Joe Kilhullen — B (C 1914)

1938 — Chris Cannizzaro — B (C 1968)

1940 — Infielder Debs Garms is purchased from the Boston Braves. (Garms is probably the least-known Pirate batting champion. He won the crown with a .355 average in 1940 while batting only 358 times. In '41 he hit .264 and was out of baseball in 1942.)

1947 — Pirates acquire pitchers Hank Behrman, Kirby Higbe, and Cal McLish; catcher Homer "Dixie" Howell; and infielder Gene Mauch from Brooklyn for outfielder Al Gionfriddo and cash. (The Dodgers wanted the money and Gionfriddo was basically a throw-in.)

## May 4

1875 — Lou Gertenrich — B (OF 1903)

1891 — Vic Saier — B (1B 1919)

1913 — Babe Adams hurls a two-hitter over the Reds and drives in the only run of the game with the Pirates only hit.

1952 — Pirates traded pitcher Bill Werle to the Cardinals for pitcher George Munger and cash.

1963 — Pitcher Tom Sturdivant is purchased by the Tigers. He won one game with Detroit before going to Kansas City.

## May 5

1859 — Bill Watkins — B (Manager 1898-99)

1929 — Burleigh Grimes defeats Boston, 7-2, with the help of a triple play — Grimes to Pie Traynor to Chuck Hargreaves, back to Traynor, to Dick Bartell, back to Hargreaves (1-5-2-5-4-2).

1935 — Jose Pagan — B (3B 1965-72, Coach 1974-78)

1941 — Tommy Helms — B (INF 1976-77)

1952 — Pirates send pitcher Jim Suchecki to the White Sox on waivers.

1956 — Catcher Jim Mangan is sent to the Giants on waivers.

## May 6

1883 — Ed Karger — B (P 1906)

1890 — Luke Boone — B (2B 1918)

1906 — Pirates become the first team in the National League to use a canvas to cover the infield during inclement weather.

1921 — Bob Chesnes — B (P 1948-50)

1923 — Earl Turner — B (C 1948, 50)

1926 — Dick Cole — B (INF 1951, 53-56)

1951 — Cliff Chambers pitches a no-hitter in the second game of a doubleheader at Boston. The 3-0 victory is Chambers' last in a Pirate uniform.

1956 — Alberto Lois — B (OF 1978-present)

1958 — Pirates send first baseman-outfielder Paul Smith to the Cubs on waivers.

## May 7

1877 — Gene Curtis — B (OF 1903)

1905 — Dave Barbee — B (OF 1932)

1925 — Glenn Wright turns an unassisted triple play, and the Pirates score six runs in the eighth inning for a 10–9 win against the Cardinals. With Jimmy Cooney on second and Rogers Hornsby on first in the ninth, Jim Bottomley hit a liner directly at Wright. The Bucs shortstop stepped on second to retire Cooney and tagged Hornsby, who had broken from first, to end the game.

1941 — Outfielder Lloyd Waner is traded to the Braves for pitcher Nick Strencevich.

1952 — Pirates send outfielder Bill Howerton to the Giants on waivers.

1956 — Bucs acquire pitcher Luis Arroyo and cash from St. Louis for pitcher Max Surkont. Arroyo later gained fame in New York as Whitey Ford's "personal" reliever in 1961.

1958 — Bob Skinner, Ted Kluszewski, and Frank Thomas all homer in the fifth inning against the Giants in San Francisco.

1962 — Pirates trade pitcher Wilmer "Vinegar Bend" Mizell to the Giants for first baseman Jim Marshall.

1974 — Houston's Tom Griffin pitches a one-hitter against the Bucs. Stargell's second inning single was the lone safety.

1977 — John Candelaria is used in relief to protect a 12–10 come-from-behind victory over the Reds.

## May 8

1874 — Eddie Boyle — B (C 1896)

1885 — Bill Powell — B (P 1909–10)

1929 — Carl Hubbell no hits the Bucs 11–0 in New York.

1940 — Pirates trade outfielder Johnny Rizzo to Cincinnati for outfielder Vince DiMaggio.

1958 — Bucs purchase pitcher Erwin Porterfield from the Red Sox.

1973 — Willie Stargell homers over the roof of the right field pavilion at Dodger Stadium for the second time in his career.

## May 9

1914 — Culley Rikard — B (OF 1941–42, 47)

1932 — Tony Bartirome — B (1B 1952). Tony has been the Pirates trainer since 1963.

1943 — Umpire Jocko Conlan calls Frankie Gustine out on an attempted steal of home against the Cardinals, precipitating a shower of cushions and bottles at Forbes Field.

1947 — Pirates sell pitcher Ken Heintzelman to the Phillies.

### May 10

1913 — Al Rubeling — B (INF 1943–44)

1914 — Russ Bauers — B (P 1936–41)

1972 — Pirates release pitcher Bob Veale.

1974 — Pirates release infielder Dal Maxvill. Maxvill is signed by Oakland and becomes one of Charlie Finley's rotating second basemen.

### May 11

1907 — Rip Sewell — B (P 1938–49)

1908 — Honus Wagner accounts for all five Pirate runs in a 5–2 win against the Giants.

1920 — Gene Hermanski — B (OF 1953)

1928 — Mel Wright — B (Coach 1973)

### May 12

1870 — Harry Truby — B (2B 1896)

1888 — Alex McCarthy — B (INF 1910–17)

1916 — Hank Borowy — B (P 1950)

1922 — Johnny Hetki — B (P 1953–54)

1941 — Pirates purchase catcher Bill Baker from Cincinnati.

1955 — Sam Jones pitches a no-hitter against the Pirates at Wrigley Field. Jones walked the first three batters in the ninth, then struckout the side to record the first no-hitter in Wrigley Field in 38 years.

1971 — Hall-of-Famer Heinie Manush dies at age 69.

### May 13

1883 — Jimmy Archer — B (C 1904, 18)

1932 — Jack Sheppard — B (C 1953–56)

1942 — Paul Waner, now with Boston, collects his 3,000th hit off Rip Sewell, but Bob Elliott's two home runs help the Pirates gain a 7–6 victory in 11 innings.

## May 13 (continued)

1953 — Pirates sell catcher Ed Fitzgerald to Washington.

1960 — Shortstop Dick Groat collects six hits at Milwaukee.

## May 14

1853 — Horace Phillips — B (Manager 1887–89)

1896 — Jake Stenzel equals the major league record with six hits.

1950 — Johnny Hopp has a six-hit game against the Cubs.

1957 — Pirates purchase pitcher Bob Smith from the Cardinals.

1969 — Pitcher Jim Shellenback is sent to Washington on waivers. The Pirates acquired pitcher Frank Krentzer and sent him to Columbus.

## May 15

1895 — James Smith — B (SS 1916)

1914 — Jimmy Wasdell — B (OF 1942–43)

1938 — Al McBean — B (P 1961–68, 70)

1948 — Pirates sell pitcher Nick Strincevich to the Phillies. He was 0–1 in six games with Philadelphia before leaving the majors.

1956 — Pirates trade first baseman-outfielder Preston Ward to Cleveland for catcher Hank Foiles. (Foiles caught 263 games in three years with Pittsburgh before moving on to Kansas City.)

1973 — Expos manager Gene Mauch uses a five-man infield against Dave Cash in the 11th inning, but Cash ruins the strategy with a single to give the Bucs a 9–8 win at Three Rivers.

## May 16

1867 — Frank Ward — B (OF 1891)

1914 — Giants' spit-baller Charley Tesreau loses a no-hitter with two out in the ninth on Joe Kelly's hit in Pirates 2–0 loss.

1953 — Rick Rhoden — B (P 1979–present)

1956 — Pirates trade outfielder Bobby Del Greco and pitcher Dick Littlefield to St. Louis for outfielder Bill Virdon. The 1955 Rookie of the Year regained his form with the Bucs. Del Greco and Littlefield flopped with the Cardinals.

## May 17

1868 — Fred Woodcock — B (P 1892)

1884 — Elmer Steele — B (P 1910–11)

1907 — Goat Anderson saves a 1–0 victory over Brooklyn for Lefty Leifield with a catch of Tim Jordan's drive toward the rightfield fence.

1933 — Ossie Virgil — B (INF 1965)

1950 — Pirates purchase catcher Ray Mueller from the Giants.

## May 18

1882 — Babe Adams — B (P 1907, 09–16, 18–26)

1892 — Bill Batsch — B (1916)

1935 — Ken Hamlin — B (SS 1957, 59)

1947 — Pirates trade first baseman-outfielder Johnny Hopp and cash to Brooklyn for outfielder Marv Rackley.

1968 — Bill Mazeroski plays in his 392nd consecutive game, a National League record for second basemen.

1970 — Pirates release pitcher Al McBean.

## May 19

1859 — Sam Barkley — B (2B 1887)

1896 — Bud Culloton — B (P 1925–26)

1916 — Second baseman Otto Knabe turns Fred Luderus' line drive into a double play and saves a 4–2 win over the Phillies.

1954 — Pirates send catcher Walker Cooper to the Cubs on waivers.

1955 — Eddie Whitson — B (P 1977–79)

1956 — Dale Long's home run streak begins in the ninth inning of the Bucs' victory against Chicago at Forbes Field.

## May 20

1891 — Joe Harris — B (1B 1927–28)

1900 — George Grantham — B (1B, 2B 1925–31)

1925 — Pirates trade first baseman Al Niehaus to Cincinnati for third baseman Tom Sheehan.

1936 — Woody Jensen's three-run homer caps a six-run ninth inning to defeat Philadelphia, 7–4.

## May 21

1859 — Fred Dunlap — B (2B 1888–90, Manager 1889)

1909 — Mace Brown — B (P 1935–41)

1924 — Ed Fitzgerald — B (C 1948–53)

1948 — Frankie Gustine goes five for five as the Pirates defeat the Dodgers 8–4.

1976 — Game between the Pirates and Cubs at Three Rivers Stadium is umpired by amateurs when the National League crew refuses to cross a vendor's picket line outside the stadium.

## May 22

1884 — Tom McCarthy — B (P 1908)

1894 — George "Hooks" Warner — B (3B 1916–17, 19)

1941 — George Spriggs — B (OF 1965–67)

1960 — The Pirates complete a three-game sweep of San Francisco with an 8–7 victory in 11 innings. Bob Skinner's two run homer tied the game in the ninth, and Hal Smith drove in the game winner with two out in the bottom of the eleventh.

1965 — Pirates trade infielder Dick Schofield to San Francisco for infielder Jose Pagan. (Schofield bounced around after the trade, but Pagan spent the next seven and a half seasons in Pittsburgh before ending his playing career in Philadelphia.)

1968 — Willie Stargell's three homers, double and single lead the Bucs to a 13–6 victory over the Cubs at Wrigley Field.

## May 23

1872 — Deacon Phillippe — B (P 1900–11)

1923 — Pirates trade second baseman Cotton Tierney and pitcher Whitey Glazner to the Phillies for second baseman Johnny Rawlings and pitcher Lee Meadows. (Meadows became one of the Bucs' top pitchers while Tierney and Glazner were little help to the Phillies.)

1925 — Clyde King — B (Coach 1965–67)

1942 — First baseman Elbie Fletcher's catch and tag of the Cubs Phil Cavaretta saves a 5–4 victory.

1951 — Pirates sell third baseman Bob Dillinger to the White Sox.

1955 — Catcher Sid Gordon is purchased by the Giants.

1963 — Pirates send outfielder Bob Skinner to Cincinnati for outfielder Jerry Lynch. Skinner did little for the Reds but helped St. Louis win the pennant in 1964. Lynch set the record for most pinch-hit homers before retiring after the 1966 season.

## May 24

1878 — John Pfiester — B (P 1903–04)

1918 — Jim Archer's seven assists equal the National League record for catchers.

1973 — Pirates sell second baseman Chuck Coggin to Atlanta.

## May 25

1932 — Jim Marshall — B (1B 1962)

1935 — Babe Ruth hits the final three home runs of his career in the Pirates 11–7 win over Boston. Number 714 off Guy Bush in the seventh was the first to clear the right field roof at Forbes Field.

1953 — Ralph Kiner becomes the twelfth player in major league history to hit 300 home runs with a blast at Forbes Field against the Giants.

## May 26

1874 — John Cronin — B (P 1898)

1942 — Chuck Hartenstein — B (P 1969–70)

1951 — Pirates trade shortstop Stan Rojek to the Cardinals for first baseman Rocky Nelson, outfielder Irv Dusak, and cash. Nelson left the Pirates late in '51 but returned to platoon with Dick Stuart at first base on the 1960 championship club.

1959 — In one of baseball's most remarkable pitching performances, Haddix retired 36 straight Milwaukee Braves and took a perfect game into the bottom of the 13th. Felix Mantilla led off with a grounder to third. Don Hoak's throw to first was low and skipped past Nelson for an error. Eddie Matthews then sacrificed Mantilla to second. With the perfect game gone, Haddix intentionally walked Hank Aaron and faced Joe Adcock with runners at first and second. Adcock hit the lefthander's second pitch over the fence in right center for what appeared to be a 3–0 Braves victory. When Aaron saw Mantilla score, he cut across the pitchers mound while Adcock completed his home run trot. Adcock was called out for passing Aaron and Hank was returned to second making the final score 1–0.

## May 27

1929 — George O'Donnell — B (P 1954)

1944 — Pirates purchase pitcher Ray Starr from Cincinnati.

## May 28

1919 — Steve Nagy — B (P 1947)

1923 — Bob Kuzava — B (P 1957)

1956 — Dale Long homers in his eighth consecutive game with a blast off Brooklyn's Carl Erskine at Forbes Field.

1960 — Pirates trade infielder Julian Javier to the Cardinals for Wilmer "Vinegar Bend" Mizell. (Mizell was the pitcher that put the Pirates over the top and on the way to the 1960 World Championship. Javier became the Cardinals starting second baseman and remained there until 1972.)

## May 29

1904 — Jim Stroner — B (3B 1929)

1925 — Bucs hit a record eight triples against the Cardinals.

Pirates sign free agent Stuffy McInnis.

1950 — Pittsburgh sells outfielder Marv Rickert to the White Sox.

## May 30

1878 — Mike Donlin — B (OF 1912)

1894 — Al Mamaux — B (P 1913–17)

1927 — Paul Waner lines into an unassisted triple play against the Cubs. Shortstop Jim Cooney took Waner's line drive, stepped on second to double Lloyd Waner and tagged Clyde Barnhart coming from first.

## May 31

1915 — Mamaux and Cooper throw back to back 1–0 shutouts against the Cubs in a doubleheader.

1973 — Willie Stargell hits an upper deck home run off the Braves Gary Gentry at Three Rivers Stadium. The Pirates beat Atlanta, 3–1.

## JUNE 1

1863 — Fred "Bones" Ely — B (SS 1896–1901

1869 — Bill Eagan — B (2B 1898)

1911 — Lou Tost — B (P 1947)

1931 — Hal R. Smith — B (C 1965)

1960 — Pirates sell catcher Danny Dravitz to Kansas City.

1965 — Bob Veale sets a Pirate record by fanning sixteen Phillies at Forbes Field as the Pirates win their 12th game in a row.

## June 2

1869 — Tom Leahy — B (OF 1897)

1938 — Gene Michael — B (SS 1966)

1948 — First baseman Ed Stevens and Shortstop Stan Rojek combine to turn a triple play against Boston, but the Pirates drop a 5–1 decision.

## June 3

1936 — Paul Waner makes an unbelievable one handed grab of Hal Lee's drive against the right field wall in the eighth inning to save a 7–5 win over the Boston Bees.

## June 4

1873 — George Yeager — B (C 1901)

1892 — Herb Kelly — B (P 1914–15)

1908 — Bob Klinger — B (P 1938–43)

1940 — Pirates crush the Boston Bees 14–2 in the first night game ever played at Forbes Field.

1953 — Larry Demery — B (P 1974–77)

1953 — Pirates trade outfielders Ralph Kiner and Catfish Metkovich, catcher Joe Garagiola, and pitcher Howie Pollet to the Cubs for catchers Bob Addis, Toby Atwell, first baseman-outfielder Preston Ward, pitcher Bob Schultz, and outfielder Gene Hermanski. (Of the five Pirate acquisitions, only Ward and Atwell were still around in 1954.)

## June 5

1874 — Jack Chesbro — B (P 1899–1902)

1890 — Eugene Madden — B (1916)

1895 — Ray Rohwer — B (OF 1921–22)

1951 — Rich Gossage — B (P 1977)

Pirates send first baseman Dale Long to the St. Louis Browns on waivers.

Outfielder Jack Maguire is acquired from the Giants on waivers.

1959 — Dick Stuart hits a homer off the Cubs' Glenn Hobbie over the centerfield wall for the longest homerun ever hit in Forbes Field.

1976 — Bill Robinson hits three home runs in a 15 inning, 11–9 loss against the Padres at Three Rivers Stadium.

1978 — Pirates sell infielder Fernando Gonzalez to San Diego.

## June 6

1870 — Jake Hewitt — B (P 1895)

1894 — Jake Stenzel, Denny Lyons, Lou Bierbauer, and Stenzel (again) homer in the third inning against Boston.

1902 — Fresco Thompson — B (2B 1925)

1917 — Honus Wagner ends his season long holdout, signing a contract with the understanding that he will play first base for the Pirates.

1941 — Rip Sewell sets a record for National League pitchers with eleven assists.

1949 — Pirates send pitcher Bob Muncrief to the Cubs on waivers.

Pitcher Kirby Higbe is traded to the Giants for pitcher Ray Poat and infielder Bobby Rhawn.

## June 7

1926 — Leroy Jarvis — B (C 1946–47)

1939 — Pirates sign free agent outfielder Chuck Klein. The former triple crown winner hit .300 in 85 games before returning to the Phillies for the 1940 season.

1949 — Pirates trade outfielder Marv Rackley to Brooklyn for first baseman-outfielder Johnny Hopp and cash.

1972 — Pirates outlast Padres, 1–0 in 18 innings, during a four hour and 27 minute marathon on a bases-loaded walk to Gene Alley.

1976 — Pirates and Reds combine for seven solo home runs at Three Rivers Stadium. Richie Zisk's pinch-hit shot in the eighth inning gives Pittsburgh a 5–4 win.

## June 8

1903 — Deacon Phillippe shuts out Boston, 4–0. This is the sixth straight shutout thrown by Pirate pitchers. Sam Leever blanked the Phillies, Phillippe and Leever stopped the Giants, and Kaiser Wilhelm and Ed Doheny also held the Phillies scoreless.

1910 — Bobby Bynne sets a record for National League third baseman with 12 assists.

1935 — George Brunet — B (P 1970)

1957 — Don Robinson — B (P 1978–present)

## June 9

1888 — Ray Miller — B (1B 1917)

1931 — Bill Virdon — B (OF 1956–65, 68, Coach 1968–71, Manager 72–73)

1939 — Julio Gotay — B (2B 1963–64)

1951 — Dave Parker — B (OF 1973–present)

1970 — Pirates sign pitcher Orlando Pena.

## June 10

1892 — Jap Barbeau — B (3B 1909)

1905 — Danny MacFayden — B (P 1940)

1912 — Howie Camnitz loses to the Dodgers and Nap Rucker, 1–0, in a game taking only one hour and 12 minutes.

1920 — Johnny Podgajny — B (P 1943)

1929 — Hank Foiles — B (C 1956–59)

1960 — Pirates send pitcher Ed Bauta to St. Louis, completing the Mizell deal.

1969 — Pitcher Joe Gibbon is obtained from San Francisco for pitcher Ron Kline. (Kline never won another game after leaving the Pirates.)

1977 — Pirates sign first baseman-outfielder Bobby Tolan, previously released by Philadelphia.

## June 11

1866 — Pop Schriver — B (C 1898–1900)

1894 — Pitcher Frank Killen is lost for 49 days when spiked while covering home in a game against Baltimore. Killen won 35 games in 1893 and due to his loss, the Alleghenie's dropped to sixth place.

1917 — Rightfielder Lee King makes an amazing bare-handed catch of Sherwood Magee's long drive, but the Bucs still lose a 2–0 decision to Boston.

1929 — Frank Thomas — B (OF, 3B 1951–58)

1948 — Dave Cash — B (2B 1969–73)

## June 12

1884 — Franz Otto Knabe — B (3B 1905, 16)

1889 — Ewell "Reb" Russell — B (OF 1922–23)

1919 — Pirates send third baseman Tony Boeckel to the Braves on waivers.

1926 — Walt Moryn — B (OF 1961)

1928 — Pirates set a major league record when seven Bucs get three or more hits against the Phillies.

1944 — Pitcher Johnny Gee is sold to the Giants. Gee never lived up to expectations, winning only five games in three and a half years with the Bucs. He was out of baseball in 1947.

1946 — Pirates trade outfielder Johnny Barrett to the Braves for outfielder Chuck Workman. Neither player was around after this season.

1950 — Pitcher Hank Borowy is purchased from the Phillies.

1953 — Tony Armas — B (OF 1976)

1970 — Dock Ellis pitches a no-hitter at San Diego Stadium. Mazeroski's diving catch of Ramon Webster's liner in the seventh kept the masterpiece intact and Ellis struckout Ed Speizio in the ninth to wrap it up.

## June 13

1883 — Mike Simon — B (C 1909–13)

1905 — John O'Connell — B (C 1928–29)

1931 — Pirates trade catcher Rollie Hemsley to the Cubs for catcher Earl Grace.

Adam Comorosky makes his second unassisted doubleplay of the season to set a National League record.

1959 — Pitcher Bob Smith is sent to Detroit on waivers.

Pirates claim pitcher Bob Porterfield from the Cubs on waivers.

1977 — Outfielder Jerry Hairston is purchased from the White Sox. Hairston had played under Chuck Tanner with the Sox and was obtained to strengthen the Pirate bench.

## June 14

1940 — Pirates obtain catcher Al Lopez from the Braves for catcher Ray Berres and cash. (Lopez became the Pirates starting receiver and caught 100 or more games the next four years.)

1947 — Pitcher Hank Behrman is sold to Brooklyn.

Bucs purchase pitcher Roger Wolff from the Indians. Wolff pitched in 13 games and did not return in 1948.

1953 — Third baseman Pete Castiglione is traded to the Cardinals for outfielder Hal Rice and cash.

1954 — Pirates send outfielder Hal Rice to the Cubs for outfielder Luis Marquez and cash.

1968 — Bob Moose bids to become the first Pirate to throw a no-hitter at Forbes Field. The dream ends with two out in the eighth on Julio Gotay's bloop single. Moose allowed one more hit in shutting out the Astros. When Forbes Field closed in 1970, no one had pitched a no-hitter there.

## June 15

1925 — Gene Baker — B (2B 1957–58, 60–61, Coach 1963)

1949 — Pirates purchase outfielder Ed Sauer from the Cardinals. Sauer was immediately traded to the Braves for catcher Phil Masi and cash. Masi was gone the next year.

The Bucs also sent infielder Bobby Rhawn to the White Sox on waivers.

1958 — Pirates obtain infielder Dick Schofield from St. Louis for third baseman Gene Freese, second baseman Johnny O'Brien and cash. Schofield sat behind Mazeroski and Groat until the latter was traded in 1962. After two years as the starting shortstop, he was traded to San Francisco for Jose Pagan.

1961 — Bucs acquire infielder Johnny Logan from Milwaukee for outfielder Gino Cimoli. Logan came to Pittsburgh after nine years as the Braves' starting shortstop. He became a utility infielder playing short and third with the Bucs.

Pittsburgh also purchased outfielder Walt Moryn from St. Louis.

1971 — Roberto Clemente makes the "greatest catch ever" in the Astrodome. He grabbed Bob Watson's liner running full speed and immediately crashed into the fence. He miraculously held the ball and saved the Bucs 3–0 victory.

1976 — Pirates and Astros are rained out in Houston! Actually, the playing field was the driest place in the city. Flash floods hit the area and Houston management called off the game with the fans unable to reach the Astrodome.

1977 — Pirates obtain infielder Jim Fregosi from Texas for catcher-first baseman Ed Kirkpatrick. (Fregosi became one of the Bucs most dependable pinchhitters before leaving in 1978 to become manager of the California Angels.)

### June 16

1875 — John Foreman — B (P 1895–96)

1890 — Fred Molowitz — B (1B 1917–19)

1913 — Pete Coscarart — B (2B 1942–46)

1916 — Boston's Tom Hughes pitches a no-hitter against the Pirates, winning 2–0.

1922 — Max Surkont — B (P 1954–56)

1943 — Pirates trade pitcher Dutch Dietz to the Phillies for pitcher Johnny Podgajny. (Podgajny lost his only four decisions with the Pirates.)

### June 17

1891 — Alexander "Zeb" Terry — B (SS 1919)

1910 — Joe Bowman — B (P 1937–41)

1932 — Bennie Daniels — B (P 1957–60)

### June 18

1893 — Ben Shaw — B (1B-C 1917–19)

1918 — Wilbur Cooper pitches a one-hitter against the Phillies but loses on an error and wild pitch, 1–0.

1932 — Ron Necciai — B (P 1952)

### June 19

1912 — Don Gutteridge — B (1948)

1949 — Jerry Reuss — B (P 1974–78)

## June 19 (continued)

1950 — Fernando Gonzalez — B (INF 1972–73, 77–78)

1961 — Catcher Don Leppert homers in the first game of a doubleheader with the Cardinals. It was Leppert's first major league at-bat.

1974 — Lee Lacy scores from the Dugout at Three Rivers! The unusual situation came about with the bases loaded, two out, and Dodger catcher Joe Ferguson batting with a 3–2 count. Everybody became confused on the next pitch which was ultimately ruled ball four, allowing Lacy to score. The Pirates took charge afterward and won, 7–2.

## June 20

1869 — Sam Nichol — B (OF 1888)

1889 — Ed Warner — B (P 1912)

1907 — Honus Wagner records the longest hit in Exhibition Park, a third inning triple to centerfield, in the Pirates 4–2 win against the Phillies.

1919 — Bill Clemensen — B (P 1939, 41, 46)

1926 — Clem Koshorek — B (INF 1952–53)

1941 — Pirates purchase pitcher Joe Sullivan from the Braves.

## June 21

1888 — George Van Haltren pitches a six hitter against the Pirates in Chicago, winning 1–0.

1897 — Spencer Adams — B (INF 1923)

1935 — Pirates released outfielder Babe Herman to Cincinnati. (Herman was off to a slow start with the Bucs but had two strong seasons with the Reds.)

1951 — Pirates trade outfielder Wally Westlake and pitcher Cliff Chambers to the Cardinals for pitchers Howie Pollett and Ted Wilks, infielder Dick Cole, outfielder Bill Howerton, and catcher Joe Garagiola.

1967 — Outfielder Al Luplow claimed from the Mets on waivers.

1971 — Bob Robertson's eight assists at first base set a major league record, and pitcher Dock Ellis sets a National League record with five putouts in the Bucs 6–0 win against the Mets in Pittsburgh.

## June 22

1877 — Gus Thompson — B (P 1903)

1890 — John Mercer — B (P 1910)

1925 — Max Carey gets two hits in the first and eighth innings to equal the major league record. George Grantham and Pie Traynor hit grand slams in the Pirates 24–6 demolition of the Cardinals.

1970 — Pirates sell pitcher Chuck Hartenstein to the Cardinals.

## June 23

1900 — Billy Harris — B (P 1931–34)

1908 — Don Osborn — B (Coach 1963–64, 70–72, 74–76)

1916 — Ken Jungles — B (P 1942)

1919 — Casey Stengel's home run defeats St. Louis, 3–2.

1945 — Pirates sell pitcher Ray Starr to the Cubs.

1956 — Pitcher Jack McMahon goes to Kansas City for second baseman Forrest "Spook" Jacobs in a waiver deal.

1971 — Clemente records his 2,000th hit in Pirates' victory over the Mets at Three Rivers.

## June 24

1867 — Jake Stenzel — B (OF 1892–96)

1869 — Kirtly Baker — B (P 1890)

1907 — Rollie Hemsley — B (C 1928–31)

1917 — Al Gerheauser — B (P 1945–46)

1952 — Pirates lose to Boston despite a triple play from shortstop Dick Groat to first baseman Catfish Metkovich.

1965 — Stargell hits three homers in 13–3 win at Dodger Stadium.

## June 25

1855 — Charlie Reilly — B (3B 1891)

1896 — William Webb — B (2B 1917)

1904 — Ralph Erickson — B (P 1929–30)

1912 — Pirates score 29 runs in 10–4, 19–3 doubleheader sweep against the Cardinals.

1924 — Relief pitcher Emil Yde ties game between Pirates and Cubs with a ninth inning double, then wins the game with a triple in the 14th.

1943 — John Gelnar — B (P 1964, 67)

## June 26

1893 — Elmer Ponder — B (P 1917, 19–21)

1903 — Babe Herman — B (OF 1935, Coach 1941)

1908 — Debs Garms — B (3B-OF 1940–41)

1918 — Elmer Singleton — B (P 1947–48)

1921 — Howie Pollett — B (P 1951–53, 56)

1935 — Lloyd Waner handles a doubleheader record 18 chances.

1943 — Bill Robinson — B (OF-INF 1975–present)

1975 — Pirates pitcher Sam McDowell is released. The Pittsburgh native won two games for the Bucs but was no longer the "Sudden Sam" of his American League days.

## June 27

1921 — Hank Behrman — B (P 1947)

1938 — Elmo Plaskett — B (C 1962–63)

1968 — Pirates purchase pitcher Bill Henry from San Francisco. Bucs also sell pitcher Juan Pizarro to Boston. Pizarro eventually returned to Pittsburgh in 1974.

## June 28

1880 — Mike Lynch — B (P 1904–05)

1938 — Orlando McFarlane — B (C 1962, 64)

1970 — Pirates sweep a doubleheader from the Cubs, 3–2 and 4–1 in the last games ever played at Forbes Field. Jim Nelson got the last win in front of 40,918 fans.

## June 29

1867 — Heinie Reitz — B (2B 1899)

1876 — Patsy Flaherty — B (P 1900, 04–05)

1907 — Leading 2–1, Deacon Phillippe survives a ninth-inning Cubs rally when Tommy Leach cuts down Harry Steinfeldt at the plate.

1910 — Burgess Whitehead — B (2B 1946)

## June 30

1895 — Johnny Miljus — B (P 1927–28)

1902 — Hal L. Smith — B (P 1932–35)

1909 — Pirates defeat the Cubs 3–2 in the first game ever played at Forbes Field.

1917 — After losing 40 of their first 60 games, Pirates' manager Jimmy Callahan is replaced by Honus Wagner. Hugo Bezdek is designated to handle business affairs while Wagner runs the team on the field. The Bucs defeat Cincinnati 5–4 in the Dutchman's debut.

1926 — Pirates sign free agent pitcher Joe Bush.

1931 — Don Gross — B (P 1958–60)

1933 — David L. Roberts — B (1B 1966)

## JULY 1

1891 — Fred Scheeren — B (OF 1914–15)

1913 — Frank Barrett — B (P 1950)

1918 — Al Tate — B (P 1946)

1921 — Outfielder Dave Robertson purchased from the Giants.

1939 — Pep Young, Arky Vaughan, and Ray Mueller combine to double up Pepper Martin at the plate and preserve a 4-3 win over St. Louis.

1965 — Coach Hal Smith is placed on the active roster. Smith caught four games and then returned to coaching status on July 14.

### July 2

1859 — Fred Carroll — B (C–OF 1887–89, 91)

Ed Beecher — B (OF 1887)

1888 — Grover Hartley — B (Coach 1932–33)

1897 — Chet Nichols — B (P 1926–27)

1955 — First Baseman Dale Long's diving catch of Pee Wee Reese's bunt and resulting double play in the bottom of the tenth inning saves a 7–6 Pirate victory over the Dodgers.

1976 — Bill Robinson's pinch hit homer in the tenth inning defeats Philadelphia on fireworks night at Three Rivers Stadium.

### July 3

1892 — Tony Brief — B (1B 1917)

1906 — Luke Hamlin — B (P 1942)

1917 — Honus Wagner resigns after five games as manager. Hugo Bezdek is named as his replacement.

## July 4

1884 — Lou Manske — B (P 1906)

1891 — Frank Edington — B (OF 1912)

1904 — Mel Ingram — B (1929)

1929 — Chuck Tanner — B (Manager 1977–present)

1947 — Jim Minshall — B (P 1974–75)

Jim Nelson — B (P 1970–71)

1969 — Willie Stargell hits a Tom Seaver pitch over the right field roof at Forbes Field in the fourth inning of an 11–6 loss to the Mets.

1977 — Dave Parker's shot over the right field fence in the bottom of the ninth caps a double header sweep of St. Louis.

## July 5

1877 — Harvey Cushman — B (P 1902)

1884 — Ward Miller — B (OF 1909)

1886 — Beals Becker — B (OF 1908)

1923 — Fire at Forbes Field damages the right field bleachers.

## July 6

1908 — Cy Blanton — B (P 1934–39)

1954 — Willie Randolph — B (2B 1975)

1955 — Jerry Lynch, Frank Thomas, and Dale Long hit home runs in the sixth inning of the first game of a double header with the Dodgers in Pittsburgh.

1956 — Second baseman Bill Mazeroski is called up from the Pirate's AAA farm club at Hollywood, California.

1970 — Pirate pitchers record four strikeouts in the ninth inning of a 7–5 victory against Philadelphia.

## July 7

1893 — Harry Wolfe — B (OF 1917)

1905 — Hal Finney — B (C 1931–34, 36)

1909 — Billy Herman — B (2B 1947, manager 1947)

1911 — Leo Nonnenkamp — B (1933)

1922 — Max Carey reaches base nine times in nine plate appearances with six hits and three walks in a 22 inning loss to the Giants.

1945 — Chuck Goggin — B (2B 1972–73)

1959 — National League defeats the American League 5–4 at Forbes Field in the first All-Star Game of the season. The first pitch is thrown out by Vice President Richard M. Nixon.

## July 8

1889 — Shortstop Jack Rowe and third baseman Deacon White end their season-long holdout. Rowe and White had been purchased from Detroit and demanded some of the purchase money in exchange for their services. They agreed to report when Ned Hanlon, also purchased from Detroit, became acting manager, relieving the ailing Horace Phillips.

1929 — Johnny Powers — B (OF 1955–58)

1950 — Jack Phillips' ninth inning grand slam off Harry Brecheen gives the Bucs a come from behind 7–5 victory at Forbes Field.

1971 — Bruce Kison gains his first Major League victory, defeating the Reds 7–1 in Pittsburgh.

1974 — Pirates trade infielder Kurt Bevacqua to Kansas City for cash and minor leaguer Cal Meier. Meier is assigned to the Pirates' AA farm club at Thetford Mines, Quebec.

1977 — Bench-clearing brawl erupts when Bruce Kison hits the Phillies' Mike Schmidt with a pitch in the first game of a four-game series at Pittsburgh. The ensuing brawl results in a dislocated finger for Schmidt. Willie Stargell attempts to break up the fight and suffers a pinched nerve in his left elbow rendering him ineffective for the rest of the season.

## July 9

1925 — Pie Traynor sets a record for third baseman by starting four double plays.

1932 — Orville "Coot"Veal — B (SS 1962)

1967 — Willie Stargell breaks a 1–1 tie in the bottom of the ninth with a game–winning homerun off the Reds' Jim Maloney. It is Stargell's first homer over the right field roof at Forbes Field.

1971 — Pirates turn the first triple play of the 1971 season. The Braves Leo Foster hits a grounder to third baseman Richie Hebner, who stepped on third for the first out, and then threw to Dave Cash at second. Cash's relay to Bob Robertson at first nipped Foster to complete the play. Pittsburgh rolled past Atlanta 11–2.

## July 10

1868 — Robert Lowe — B (2B 1904)

1873 — Harry Davis — B (1B 1896–98)

1886 — Blaine "Kid" Durbin — B (1909)

1894 — Clarence Berger — B (OF 1914)

1928 — Pirates come from behind to beat Philadelphia on back-to-back hits by Paul and Lloyd Waner.

1929 — Chuck Klein hits four homers at Forbes Field for the Phillies in their 9–6, ten inning victory.

1940 — Gene Alley — B (SS 1963–73)

1951 — Pirates send second baseman Hank Schenz to the Giants on waivers.

1956 — Bob Friend pitches three shutout innings in the All-Star Game as the National League's starting pitcher to win a 7–3 decision at Griffith Stadium in Washington, D.C.

1971 — Willie Stargell hits his 30th homer and 10th against the Braves, establishing a new record for most home runs against one club. The Pirates beat the Braves 5–4 in Pittsburgh.

## July 11

1884 — Harry Wolter — B (OF 1907)

1893 — Milt Stock — B (Coach 1951–52)

1908 — Vic Willis pitches a one–hitter against the Giants.

1921 — Hal Gregg — B (P 1948–50)

1944 — First All-Star Game played in Pittsburgh is won by the National League, 7–1, before 29,589 at Forbes Field.

1947 — Pirates purchase pitcher Mel Queen from the Yankees.

1960 — Bob Friend gains his second All-Star Game victory, pitching three shutout innings in the National Leagues 5–3 victory at Kansas City.

1961 — Roberto Clemente's tenth inning single brings home Willie Mays with the deciding run in the National League's 5–4 All-Star Game victory in San Francisco.

1973 — Willie Stargell hits his 302nd home run, passing Ralph Kiner and becoming the Pirates all-time home run leader during a 10–2 rout of the Padres in San Diego.

1974 — Pirates purchase catcher Chuck Brinkman from the White Sox. (Brinkman is better known for being Eddie's brother than for anything he did with the Pirates.)

## July 12

1894 — Lee Meadows — B (P 1923–29)

1919 — Johnny Wyrostek — B (OF 1942–43)

1935 — Dave Ricketts — B (C 1970, Coach 1970–73)

1946 — Leftfielder Maurice Van Robays' sparkling ninth inning catch of Johnny Wyrostek's pop fly, while stretched flat on the ground, preserves a 4–3 victory over the Phillies.

## July 13

1888 — Pirate pitchers complete the first doubleheader shutout in major league history with 4–0, 6–0 wins against Boston.

1940 — Frank Bork — B (P 1964)

1960 — Vern Law wins the second All-Star Game of the year, pitching two innings of the National League's 6–0 victory in Yankee Stadium.

## July 14

1870 — John O'Brien — B (2B 1899)

1874 — Jesse Tannehill — B (P 1897–1902)

1889 — Joe Conzelman — B (P 1913–15)

1892 — Floyd Farmer — B (INF-OF 1916)

1922 — Leo Mokan transferred to the Phillies.

1929 — Bob Purkey — B (P 1954–57, 66)

1936 — Earl Francis — B (P 1960–64)

## July 15

1929 — John "Red" Oldham — B (P 1925–26)

1935 — Donn Clendenon — B (1B 1961–68)

1942 — Don Bosch — B (OF 1966)

1947 — Enrique Romo — B (P 1979–present)

1968 — Coach Bill Virdon is signed to an active player's contract. Virdon played in six games before resuming his coach's status on August 13th.

1971 — Roberto Clemente's seventeenth inning homer ends the Pirates longest game of the season. Jim Nelson gets credit for the Pirates 4–3 win over the Padres.

## July 16

1896 — Jim Caton — B (SS 1917–20)

1920 — After pitching sixteen shutout innings against the Giants, Earl Hamilton falls apart and allows seven runs in the seventeenth. Rube Benton pitched the distance for New York.

1951 — Pirates sell outfielder Jack Maguire to the St. Louis Browns.

1970 — First game played in Three Rivers Stadium is won by the Reds 3–2 with 48,648 fans in attendance.

The Bucs become the first team to wear knit uniforms, now worn by all major league teams.

## July 17

1858 — Pete Browning — B (OF 1891)

1873 — George Gray — B (P 1899)

1914 — Pirates lose 21-inning contest to Brooklyn. Babe Adams went the distance and did not allow a single walk in taking the defeat.

1960 — Dick Groat reaches the 1,000 hit plateau with a single in the first game of two with the Reds. The Bucs split the twinbill with a 5–0 win in the nitecap.

1971 — Dock Ellis ties the club record for starters by winning his 13th straight decision, defeating San Diego, 9–2.

## July 18

1894 — Wilbur Fisher — B (1916 — no position listed, as he appeared only once as a Pirate)

Bill Haeffner — B (C 1920)

1916 — Johnny Hopp — B (1B-OF 1948–50)

1918 — Albert Lyons — B (P 1947)

1925 — John McCall — B (P 1950)

1971 — Joe Ferguson's ninth inning homer breaks up Luke Walker's no-hit bid but the Bucs hold on to win their eleventh straight game, defeating the Dodgers, 3–2. The win gave Pittsburgh an 11.5 game lead, their largest of the season.

## July 19

1865 — Bill Hart — B (P 1895, 98)

1888 — Ed Sweeney — B (P 1919)

1891 — Earl Hamilton — B (P 1918–23)

1923 — Pie Traynor, Spencer Adams, and Charlie Grimm team up on a triple play against Boston.

1935 — Nick Koback — B (C 1953–55)

1950 — Frank McKinney sells his share of the Pirates to John Galbreath and Tom Johnson. Galbreath takes over the club presidency from McKinney.

1955 — Vernon Law hurls 18 innings in a 4–3 win over the Braves.

### July 20

1880 — Harry Cassady — B (OF 1904)

1902 — Heinie Manush — B (OF 1938–39)

1926 — Second baseman Eddie Moore goes to the Braves on waivers.

1946 — John Lamb — B (P 1970–71, 73)

1950 — Pirates purchase third baseman Bob Dillinger from the Philadelphia Athletics.

1974 — Pitcher Juan Pizarro signs with the Pirates. The veteran pitched effectively in seven games but was not called back in '75.

### July 21

1877 — Irv Young — B (P 1908)

1911 — Barney Dreyfuss purchases pitcher Marty O'Toole from St. Paul for a "record" $22,500. Dreyfuss also purchases O'Toole's catcher Billy Kelly for an additional $5,000.

1927 — Dick Smith — B (INF 1951–55)

### July 22

1859 — John Glasscock — B (SS 1893–94)

1880 — George Gibson — B (C 1905–16, Manager 1920–22, 32–34)

1885 — Sheldon LeJeune — B (OF 1915)

1899 — Ginger Beaumont strokes six hits and scores six runs to set a major league record.

1910 — Deacon Phillippe hits a grand slam off Brooklyn pitcher Fred Miller.

1932 — Jack McMahan — B (P 1956)

1934 — R. C. Stevens — B (1B 1958–60)

## July 23

1876 — Ginger Beaumont — B (OF 1899–06)

1901 — Ed Holley — B (P 1934)

1930 — Pie Traynor's home runs in the ninth inning of the first game and 13th inning of the second game propel the Bucs to a sweep of the Phillies.

1965 — Bob Friend pitches a one-hitter and defeats Chicago, 6–0. Hobie Landrith had the Cubs only hit, a single in the fourth.

1974 — The First All-Star Game played at Three Rivers Stadium is won by the National League, 7–1. Pittsburgh representative Ken Brett was credited with the victory.

## July 24

1887 — First baseman Alex McKinnon dies of typhoid fever, McKinnon was the Alleghenie's starting first baseman in their first season.

1893 — Joe Schultz Sr. — B (INF 1916)

1927 — Preston Ward — B (1B-OF 1953–56)

1960 — The Pirates drop out of first place for the first time since May 28th when Billy O'Dell pitches the Giants to a 6–3 victory.

1970 — Roberto Clemente Night at Three Rivers Stadium. The honoree made a spectacular, sliding catch on Dennis Menke's foul near the bull pen to highlight the Pirates 11–0 defeat of the Astros.

## July 25

1908 — Honus Wagner goes five-for-five and the Pirates defeat the Giants in New York, 7–2, before a crowd of 25,000, the largest attendance for a game at that time.

1917 — Pirates acquire first baseman George Kelley from the Giants on waivers.

1921 — Marv Rackley — B (OF 1949)

1935 — Larry Sherry — B (Coach 1977–78)

1956 — Roberto Clemente's inside-the-park grand slam in the ninth inning brings the Bucs a 9–8 victory at Forbes Field.

## July 26

1917 — Jim Bloodworth — B (2B 1947)

1921 — Tom Saffell — B (OF 1949–51, 55)

1920 — Ed Bockman — B (3B 1948–49)

1942 — Jose Martinez — B (INF 1969-70)

1971 — Dave Ricketts is released as a coach and signed as an active player. He appeared in 14 games before returning to coach's status on August 15th.

## July 27

1880 — Henry McIlveen — B (P 1914)

1884 — Alan Storke — B (INF 1906–09)

1898 — James Zack Taylor — B (Coach 1947–48)

1907 — Pirates defeat Phillies with the help of a triple play from first baseman Jim Nealon to Wagner at short, and back to Nealon.

1944 — Pirates release pitcher Harry Shuman to the Phillies.

1949 — Pitcher Harry Gumbert claimed on waivers from Cincinnati.

1977 — Pirates acquire pitcher Dave Pagan from Seattle for a player to be named later. Pitcher Rick Honeycutt is assigned from the Pirates Shreveport club to Seattle on August 22nd, completing the deal.

## July 28

1867 — Bill Day — B (P 1890)

1868 — Charles "Duke" Esper — B (P 1890–92)

1932 — Tony Piet drives in seven runs in two innings, tying a major league record.

1939 — The Phillies send pitcher Max Butcher to Pittsburgh for first baseman Gus Suhr in a waiver deal. (Butcher won 10 or more games four times with the Bucs while Suhr retired after 10 games with the Phillies in 1940.)

1968 — Pirates pitcher Al McBean belts a grand slam off the Cardinals Larry Jaster in the fifth inning of a 7–1 Bucs win.

## July 29

1887 — George Cutshaw — B (2B 1918–21)

1915 — At age 41, Honus Wagner hits a grand slam off the Dodgers' Jeff Pfeffer in the eighth inning. He becomes the oldest player to hit a bases-loaded home run in major league history.

1916 — Pirates trade catcher Art Wilson to the Cubs for outfielder Frank Schulte and catcher Bill Fisher.

1933 — Fred Lindstrom tallies pinch singles in both games of a twinbill with the Reds, extending his hitting streak to 25 games.

1940 — Pirates lose a 7–6 decision to the Dodgers in a game highlighted by a fist fight between Arky Vaughan and Babe Phelps.

## July 30

1870 — William Merritt — B (C 1894–97)

1890 — Casey Stengel — B (OF 1918–19)

1896 — Pirates trade first baseman Jake Beckley to the Giants for first baseman Harry Davis. (Beckley moved on to the Reds in '97 and hit .300 in seven of the next eight seasons paving his way to a Hall of Fame election in 1971. Davis was not as successful but did lead the American League in RBI's with Philadelphia in 1905 and 1906.)

1912 — Johnny Rizzo — B (OF 1938-40)

1928 — Bill Hall — B (C 1954, 56, 58)

1948 — Pirates claim pitcher Paul Erickson from the Giants on waivers. (Erickson never pitched a big league game for the Buccos.)

1968 — Clemente makes "impossible" catch on a ball hit by the Braves' Mike Lum during a doubleheader sweep at Forbes Field.

1973 — Pirates sign catcher Jerry May, previously released by the Mets. (May never appeared in a game in his second stint with the Pirates.)

1975 — Infielder Paul Popovich is released, ending his major league career.

## July 31

1870 — Joe Sugden — B (C 1893-97)

1882 — Erv Kantlehner — B (P 1914-16)

1893 — Charles Ward — B (SS 1917)

1913 — Lee Handley — B (3B 1937-41, 44-46)

1939 — Vic Davalillo — B (OF 1971-73)

1944 — Frank Brosseau — B (P 1969-71)

1957 — Manager Bobby Bragan offers a drink of orange juice to the umpires following his ejection from a game in Milwaukee.

## AUGUST 1

1906 — Brooklyn pitcher Harry McIntire holds the Bucs hitless through 10 innings at Brooklyn. With two out in the 11th, Claude Ritchey singles and the Pirates win in the 13th on an unearned run. McIntire's 10 and 2/3rds hitless innings pitched are the most in a game until Harvey Haddix's masterpiece in 1959.

1917 — Elmer Rambert — B (P 1939-40)

1918 — Pirates beat the Braves, 2-0, in 21 innings at Boston.

1950 — Milt May — B (C 1970-73)

1970 — Willie Stargell's two homers and three doubles in Atlanta tie the major league record for most extra base hits in a game. Stargell, Bob Robertson, and Jose Pagan homer in the seventh inning as the Bucs outslug the Braves, 20-10.

1973 — Pirates sell outfielder Vic Davalillo to Oakland.

## August 2

1881 — Fred Veil — B (P 1903–04)

1894 — Pirates score in their 14th consecutive inning, setting a National League record.

1906 — Billy Posdel — B (Coach 1949–53)

## August 3

1889 — Gus Getz — B (OF–3B 1918)

1950 — Pirates sell pitcher Hank Borowy to Detroit.

1957 — Manager Bobby Bragan is fired and replaced by coach Danny Murtaugh. The Pirates are 36–67 under Bragan and the firing comes just two days after the infamous "orange juice incident." Murtaugh is given the job on an interim basis, after it had been turned down by coach Clyde Sukeforth. The Bucs finish 26–25 under Murtaugh and he remains the Pirates skipper until 1964 when he was forced from the job by poor health.

1966 — Pirates release pitcher Bob Purkey. (Purkey finished where he started in 1954, after spending his most productive seasons with the Reds. In his second tour with Pittsburgh, he recorded only one decision after being purchased from St. Louis in April.)

## August 4

1867 — Jake Beckley — B (1B 1888–89, 91–96)

1879 — Pat O'Connor — B (C 1908–10)

1883 — Lew Moren — B (P 1903–04)

1896 — Cliff Lee — B (C 1919–20)

1947 — Pirates purchase pitcher Al Lyons from the New York Yankees.

1967 — Pitcher Pete Mikkelsen goes to the Cubs on waivers. Pete went on to Los Angeles where he had some fine years.

## August 5

1921 — Harold Arlin broadcasts the game between the Pirates and Phillies. It is the first game ever broadcast on radio.

1936 — Bill Mazeroski — B (2B 1956–72, Coach 1973)

1943 — Nellie Briles — B (P 1971–73)

1970 — Second baseman Bill Mazeroski sets a National League Record for most putouts at his position with 4,781, in the Pirates win over the Phillies in Pittsburgh. Maz ended his career with 4,974 putouts.

1971 — Pirates defeat Montreal at Jarry Park, but lose third baseman Jose Pagan who suffered a fractured arm when hit by a pitch. Rennie Stennett, Dave Cash, and Bill Mazeroski filled in for Pagan, who returned in time to drive in the winning run in the seventh game of the World Series.

1977 — Frank Taveras hits his first major league home run, an inside the park grand slam off the Reds Doug Capilla, and the Bucs completed a doubleheader sweep in Cincinnati. The Pirates move to within one game of the division leading Phillies, after having been ten games out on July 3rd.

## August 6

1881 — Baylard "Bud" Sharpe — B (1B 1910)

1926 — Clem Labine — B (P 1960–61)

1928 — Burleigh Grimes wins number 20, with the help of a Paul Waner home run, defeating Brooklyn, 4–3.

1949 — Pirates purchase first baseman Jack Phillips from the Yankees.

1955 — Steve Nicosia — B (C 1978–present)

1969 — Willie Stargell becomes the first player to hit a home run over the bleachers at Dodger Stadium. The blast, measured at 512 feet, highlights an 11–3 victory.

1973 — Roberto Clemente is inducted into Baseball's Hall of Fame at Cooperstown, New York. The five-year waiting period had been waived for Clemente, who died in a plane crash on New Year's Eve, 1972. Clemente is the first Latin American player elected to the Hall.

## August 7

1864 — Adonis Terry — B (P 1892–94)

1886 — Bill McKechnie — B (INF 1907, 1910–12, 18–20, Coach 1922, Manager 1922–26)

1894 — Jake Daubert — B (1915)

1915 — Les Fleming — B (1B 1949)

Al Mamaux and Bob Harmon combine to shutout Philadelphia in a double-header sweep, 9–0 and 6–0.

1922 — Ten Pirates collect two or more hits in a game against the Phillies.

1936 — Jerry McNertney — B (C 1973)

1946 — Pirates are sold by the Dreyfuss family after owning the club for 46 years. The club is purchased by Indianapolis banker Frank McKinney, realtor John Galbreath of Columbus, Ohio, singer-actor Bing Crosby, and Pennsylvania native Tom Johnson. The purchase price did not exceed 2.5 million dollars.

1951 — Jim Sadowski — B (P 1974)

## August 8

1865 — Billy Gumbert — B (P 1890, 92)

1903 — Clise Dudley — B (P 1933)

1922 — Rabbitt Maranville's 13 at-bats in a doubleheader with the Phillies equals the Major League record.

## August 9

1924 — Kiki Cuyler collects six hits in a game against the Phillies.

1930 — Roman Mejias — B (OF 1955, 57–61)

1963 — Pirates and Colt 45's split the longest doubleheader in Forbes Field history, lasting until 2:30 A.M. Robert Clemente's bases-loaded single in the 11th inning of the second game saves the Pirates a 7–6 win after dropping the lidlifter in 15 innings.

1976 — John Candelaria pitches the first Pirate no–hitter in Pittsburgh, defeating the Dodgers 2–0.

## August 10

1877 — Charles "Truck" Egan — B (INF 1901)

1892 — Elmer Jacobs — B (P 1916–18)

1971 — Pitcher Mudcat Grant is sold to Oakland.

Pirates trade outfielder John Jeter and pitcher Ed Acosta to San Diego for pitcher Bob Miller. Pittsburgh becomes Miller's tenth major league team.

## August 11

1891 — Walt Barbare — B (INF 1919–20)

1907 — Forrest "Woody" Jensen — B (OF 1931–39)

1958 — Roberto Clemente's stellar catch of Joe Adcock's drive to right centerfield in the ninth inning at Forbes Field saves a 6–4 win over Milwaukee and moves the Pirates into a tie for second place.

## August 12

1867 — Bud Lally — B (OF 1891)

1879 — Wyatt Lee — B (P 1904)

1894 — Paul Carpenter — B (P 1916)

1912 — Bud Hafey — B (OF 1935–36)

## August 12 (continued)

1964 — Jerry Lynch hits a three run homer over the right field roof at Forbes Field off Mets pitcher Dennis Ribant in a 5–4 Pirate victory.

1966 — Reds and Pirates combine for 11 home runs but Manny Mota's two-run single was the deciding blow in the Bucs 14–11 win at Crosley Field. Art Shamsky hit three homers, Bob Bailey two, Deron Johnson, Pete Rose, Willie Stargell, Jesse Gonder, Roberto Clemente, and Jerry Lynch one each. The win gives the Pirates a two-game lead over the second place San Francisco Giants.

1978 — Pirates fall 11.5 games behind the first place Phillies following a 10–1 pasting in Philadelphia.

## August 13

1909 — George Susce — B (C 1939)

1917 — Sid Gordon — B (OF-3B 1954–55)

1930 — Wilmer "Vinegar Bend" Mizell — B (P 1960–62)

1935 — Jim "Mudcat" Grant — B (P 1970–71)

1969 — Roberto Clemente hits three homers in a 10–5 win over the Giants in San Francisco.

## August 14

1902 — Homer Blankenship — B (P 1928)

1914 — Pitcher Marty O'Toole conditionally sold to the Giants.

1925 — Pitcher Babe Adams and outfielder Carson Bigbee are released, and outfielder Max Carey is sold to Brooklyn. These moves came after the players questioned Fred Clarke's presence with the team. Clarke was advising manager Bill McKechnie and had insulted Carey by telling the manager to replace him with the bat boy. Clarke eventually resigned his post on October 26th.

1930 — Dale Coogan — B (1B 1950)

1938 — Pirates turn five double plays en route to a 2–0 win against the Cubs.

1960 — Pirates open up a six-game lead with a doubleheader sweep of the second place Cardinals. Don Hoak's single won the second game in the 11th inning at Forbes Field.

1971 — Bob Gibson no-hits the Pirates 11–0 at Three Rivers Stadium.

## August 15

1864 — George "Doggie" Miller — B (C 1887–93)

1906 — George "Red" Peery — B (P 1927)

1908 — James "Bernie" Walter — B (P 1930)

56

1915 — Pirates purchase pitcher Rube Benton from Cincinnati.

1945 — Duffy Dyer — B (C 1975–78)

1969 — Pitcher Jim Bunning traded to Los Angeles for infielder Chuck Goggin, minor leaguer Ron Mitchell, and cash. (Bunning was a tremendous flop with the Pirates and finished his career back in Philadelphia after pitching with the Pirates and Dodgers in '69.)

1971 — Cardinals defeat Pirates 6–4, sweeping the four-game series in Pittsburgh and cutting the Bucs' Eastern Division lead to four games.

### August 16

1872 — Willie Clark — B (1B 1898–99)

Fred Steere — B (SS 1894)

1889 — Hank Robinson — B (P 1911–13)

1909 — Andy Bednar — B (P 1930–31)

1913 — Ernie Bonham — B (P 1947–49)

1922 — Gene Woodling — B (OF 1947)

1929 — Curt Roberts — B (2B 1954–56)

1947 — Ralph Kiner becomes the first Pirate to hit three homers in a game, hitting his fourth consecutive homer over a two-game span. Hank Greenberg and Billy Cox hit two home runs each in the Pirates 12–7 defeat of St. Louis at Forbes Field.

### August 17

1891 — Arch Reilly — B (3B 1917)

1892 — Johnny Rawlings — B (2B 1923–26)

1907 — Tommy Leach steals home and makes three super catches in centerfield during a 5–1 victory over Boston.

1951 — Outfielder-third baseman Frank Thomas recalled from New Orleans (AAA).

1952 — Mike Edwards — B (2B 1977)

1968 — Chris Cannizzaro hits his first major league home run, a two-run shot off the Scoreboard, in the Pirates 3–0 win against the Dodgers at Forbes Field.

1971 — Bill Mazeroski records his 2,000th hit but the Bucs drop a 6–5 decision to Houston in Pittsburgh.

### August 18

1891 — Wally Gerber — B (INF 1914–15)

## August 18 (continued)

1893 — Burleigh Grimes — B (P 1916–17, 28–29, 34)

      Bernie Duffy — B (P 1913)

1927 — Roger Bowman — B (P 1953, 55)

1931 — Paul Waner collects five hits in a 14–5 decision over Philadelphia.

1934 — Roberto Clemente — B (OF 1955–72)

1940 — Paul Popovich — B (INF 1974–75)

1952 — Pirates sell shortstop George Strickland and pitcher Ted Wilks to Cleveland.

## August 19

1893 — James "Ike" McAuley — B (SS 1914–16)

1915 — Pirates lost pitcher Rube Benton to the Giants due to a prior claim between the Giants and Cincinnati.

1941 — Manager Frankie Frisch ejected by umpire Jocko Conlan in the second game of a doubleheader in Brooklyn. Frisch was thumbed out when he came on the field with an umbrella to protest the playing of the game under bad conditions. The Bucs dropped both games.

1968 — Pirates release pitcher Bill Henry.

1973 — Jim Rooker pitches a five hitter and goes three for three at the plate while shutting out San Francisco 5–0. The Pirates are two games out of first place in the East.

## August 20

1869 — Bob Gibson — B (P 1890)

1908 — Al Lopez — B (C 1940–46)

1913 — Pirates trade third baseman Bob Byrne and pitcher Howie Camnitz to the Phillies for outfielder Cozy Dolan. (Dolan hit poorly with the Bucs and was traded to St. Louis after the season.)

1974 — Pirates sign pitcher Juan Pizzaro.

1975 — Danny Murtaugh's 1,000th win comes with a 3–1 decision over the Giants in Pittsburgh.

1978 — Pirates sweep a doubleheader from Houston, 7–6 and 3–1, in Pittsburgh. Jerry Reuss won his first game of the season in the nitecap, the Bucs seventh straight win and ninth in their last ten games. The Pirates are now six games behind Philadelphia.

1905 — Jim Mosolf — B (OF 1929–31)

1907 — Cobe Jones — B (SS 1928–29)

1908 — Ray Berres — B (C 1937–40)

1916 — Murray Dickson — B (P 1949–53)

1920 — Wilbur Cooper starts his second triple play of the season, a major league record, in a 3–1 loss to Philadelphia.

1977 — Second baseman Rennie Stennett breaks his leg in a 5–4 loss to the Giants at Three Rivers Stadium. Stennett was challenging Dave Parker for the National League batting crown but the injury finished him for the season and he has not yet completely recovered.

**August 22**

1857 — Ned Hanlon — B (OF 1889, 91, Manager 1889, 91)

1881 — Howie Camnitz — B (P 1904, 06–13)

Harry Swacina — B (1B 1907–08)

1883 — Owen Wilson — B (OF 1908–13)

1893 — Lyle Bigbee — B (P 1921)

1917 — Carson Bigee's 11 at-bats in a 22-inning game equals the major league record. It was the third straight extra inning contest between the Pirates and Dodgers and the longest game in Pirates history, a 6–5 loss.

1938 — Jim Tobin defeats Chicago 4–2 in the finale of a three-game series in Wrigley Field. The Bucs leave town 5.5 games ahead of New York and eight in front of the Cubs.

1940 — Frankie Gustine starts four doubleplays setting a National League record for second baseman.

1949 — Doug Bair — B (P 1976)

1972 — Nellie Briles pitches a one-hitter and defeats San Francisco, 1–0 in Candlestick Park. Ken Henderson's seventh inning single was the only hit and Henderson was the only baserunner. Rennie Stennett saved the game with a leaping catch to rob Bobby Bonds of a homerun in the ninth inning.

1974 — Following a collision with teammate Pablo Cruz, Pirate farmhand Alfredo Edmead of Salem in the Carolina League dies of a fractured skull.

**August 23**

1901 — Guy Bush — B (P 1935–36)

1907 — Howie Camnitz pitches a five-inning no-hitter in the second game of a double-header at New York. The Pirates won 1–0.

1910 — Leftfielder Fred Clarke throws out four Phillies runners to equal the record in a 6–2 victory.

1965 — Third baseman Gene Freese is purchased by the White Sox.

1970 — Roberto Clemente's tenth hit over two consecutive games sets a National League record in the Pirates 11–0 win at Los Angeles. Clemente had eight singles, a double, and a homer in the two games with the Dodgers.

1977 — Al Oliver's homer off Rollie Fingers in the bottom of the ninth saves the game for the Pirates after Gene Tenace had homered off Rich Gossage in the top of the inning. Pittsburgh won, 7–6.

## August 24

1889 — Jewel Ens — B (INF 1922–25, Coach 1927–29, 35–39, Manager 1929–32)

1897 — Al Bool — B (C 1930)

1921 — Pirates lose a doubleheader to the Giants before 35,000 at the Polo Grounds. Babe Adams lost the first game, ending his nine-game winning streak. The Pirates lead was cut to 5.5 games over New York.

1936 — Bucs bang out 25 hits in a 17–5 trouncing of St. Louis.

1977 — Dave Parker is tagged out in a collision with the Dodgers, and two other runners are also thrown out at the plate in a 2–1 loss in Pittsburgh.

1978 — Pirates win their tenth straight, 5–4 against Atlanta. The Bucs scored all their runs in the seventh, three on Bert Blyleven's bases loaded double. The Pirates pull into a second-place tie with Chicago, 3.5 games behind the faltering Phillies.

## August 25

1894 — Norman "Tony" Boeckel — B (1B 1917, 19)

1910 — Bobby Byrne steals third and home, after doubling in the 12th inning, to defeat the Dodgers.

1913 — Sam Naron — B (Coach 1952–64)

1926 — Jim Suchecki — B (P 1952)

1959 — Pirates trade first baseman Ted Kluszewski to the White Sox for outfielder Harry Simpson. Klu had one last hurrah in the '59 World Series when he hit three home runs in Chicago's loss to Los Angeles.

1973 — Richie Hebner's leadoff home run in the 11th inning gives the Pirates a 6–5 win over the Braves, leaving the Bucs 1.5 games out of first place.

## August 26

1894 — Earl "Sparky" Adams — B (INF 1923)

1935 — Lloyd Waner's 18 put outs in a doubleheader are a major league record for a centerfielder.

1938 — Pirates lose their third straight game to the last place Phillies. The 6–4 defeat at Forbes Field cuts the Bucs lead over the Giants to 4.5 games.

1974 — Pittsburgh moves into first place by sweeping a doubleheader in San Diego. Pittsburgh won the first game in the 12th on a bases-loaded walk to Al Oliver, Gene Clines' sacrifice fly and two more walks to Richie Zisk and Bob Robertson.

The Pirates' 10–2 win in the second game coupled with the Cardinals' loss to Los Angeles puts the Pirates in first by .0002 percentage points.

## August 27

1875 — Dave Wright — B (P 1895)

1894 — Charlie Engle — B (INF 1930)

Eddie Mulligan — B (INF 1928)

1921 — Giants complete a five game sweep with a 3–1 win over the Bucs cutting Pittsburgh's lead to 2.5 games.

1965 — Clemente throws out Walt Bond at third base on a swinging bunt by Bob Lillis. The play ended an Astros' rally but Houston still led until the ninth when the Bucs scored six times, tying the game on Stargell's bases loaded bloop single. In the 11th inning Bob Bailey singled but was forced at second when Al McBean attempted to sacrifice. McBean moved to second on a wild pitch and Andy Rodgers singled down the third base line to win the game.

## August 28

1898 — Charlie Grimm — B (1B 1919–24)

1974 — Ed Kirkpatrick's two-out double in the 11th inning gives the Pirates their sixth straight win, a 3–1 victory over the Giants in San Francisco. The Bucs lead the Cardinals by 1.5 games.

## August 29

1888 — Ensign Cotrell — B (P 1911)

1892 — Roy Wood — B (OF 1913)

1907 — L. Floyd "Pep" Young — B (2B 1933–40)

1909 — Pirates trade third baseman Jap Barbeau, infielder Allen Storke, and cash to the Cardinals for third baseman Bob Byrne.

## August 29 (continued)

1918 — Joe Schultz, Jr. — B (C 1939–41)

1919 — Billy Cox — B (SS 1941, 46–57)

1929 — Manager Donie Bush resigns and is replaced by coach Jewel Ens.

## August 30

1870 — Will Thompson — B (P 1892)

1878 — Charlie Starr — B (INF 1908)

1899 — Kiki Cuyler — B (OF 1921–27)

1916 — Johnny Lindell — B (P 1953)

1938 — Jim Tobin defeats New York 7–1, giving the Pirates a 6.5 game lead in the National League pennant race.

The Bucs also buy outfielder Heinie Manush from Toronto of the International League for the pennant drive.

1959 — Elroy Face wins his 22nd consecutive game over two years, and 17th of the season with a triumph over the Phillies at Forbes Field. Face came in to pitch the tenth inning and Eddie Bouchee greeted the reliever with a home run to break a 5–5 tie. The Bucs rallied for two runs in the bottom of the inning making Face the winner.

## August 31

1866 — Charles "Duke" Farrell — B (3B 1892)

1868 — Phillip "Red" Ehret — B (P 1892–94)

1869 — Monte Cross — B (SS 1894–95)

1883 — Syd Smith — B (C 1914–15)

1888 — Wally Rehg — B (OF 1912)

1953 — Pirates sell pitcher Johnny Lindell to the Phillies. The former outfielder was in his second-to-last year and won only once for Philadelphia.

1968 — Pitcher Elroy Face purchased by Detroit. Face was in his 15th season with Pittsburgh. He retired after the 1969 campaign with Montreal.

1970 — Pirates trade pitcher Denny Riddleberger and cash to Washington for pitcher George Brunet. Riddleberger had been with the Bucs AAA team in Columbus, Ohio.

1971 — Pie Traynor Night at Three Rivers Stadium. Pittsburgh defeats Philadelphia, 7–5.

# SEPTEMBER 1

1890 — Sam Brenegan — B (C 1914)

Pirates drop a tripleheader to Brooklyn, 10–9, 3–2, and 8–4.

1894 — Fred Nicholson — B (OF 1919–20)

1919 — Jim Hopper — B (P 1946)

1922 — Vic Barnhart — B (SS 1944–46)

1964 — Bob Veale sets the club mark with his 184th strikeout in a 10–2 win over the Phillies.

1971 — Pirates defeat the Expos, 8–4, at Jerry Park, becoming the first team in major league history to use an all black line-up. Here is the starting defensive alignment: 1B — Al Oliver, 2B — Rennie Stennett, SS — Jackie Hernandez, 3B — Dave Cash, LF — Willie Stargell, CF — Gene Clines, RF — Roberto Clemente, C — Manny Sanguillen, and P — Dock Ellis.

## September 2

1890 — Pirates break longest losing streak at 23 games.

1907 — Ben Sankey — B (SS 1929–31)

1908 — Lefty Leifield pitches a complete game and the Pirates steal six bases, including Fred Clarke's steal of home in an 8–2 win against Cincinnati. The Pirates are in second place, percentage points behind New York.

1966 — Roberto Clemente records his 2,000th hit and the Pirates move into first place with a 2–1 win against the Cubs at Forbes Field. Clemente's homer gave him 101 RBIs, the first time he has reached the 100 mark.

1978 — Pirates defeat Atlanta, 4–3, in 12 innings at Three Rivers Stadium. Phil Garner led off the 12th with a base hit and moved to second on a passed ball. Steve Brye sacrificed Garner to third and Braves manager Bobby Cox ordered Rick Camp to intentionally walk both Frank Taveras and Omar Moreno bringing up Dave Parker, the league's leading hitter. The Cobra smashed a single to right, scoring Garner to end the game.

## September 3

1854 — Harry Decker — B (C 1890)

1885 — Ed Konetchy — B (1B 1914)

1894 — Connie Mack becomes manager, replacing A. C. Buckenberger.

1915 — Pirates sell outfielder Zip Collins to the Braves.

1922 — Pie Traynor's stop of Grover Cleveland Alexander's tenth inning smash and diving tag of Bob O'Farrell off third, saves a 2–0 win over the Cubs.

## September 3 (continued)

1973 — Pirates purchase catcher Carl Taylor from Kansas City.

1978 — Willie Stargell's 2,000th career hit keys a three-run rally and the Pirates defeat Atlanta on Dale Berra's homer in the ninth. Stargell's hit off Craig Skok in the seventh was followed by a walk to John Milner. Gene Garber came on to face Phil Garner who crushed a home run over the wagon gate in dead center field, giving Pittsburgh a 3–2 lead. The Braves tied the score in the eighth but Willie Stargell reached first when he was hit by Garber on an 0–2 pitch, leading off the ninth. Willie was replaced by Matt Alexander who promptly stole second, causing John Milner to be walked intentionally. Berra followed with his drive into the left-field pavilion, putting the Pirates 2.5 games behind Philadelphia.

## September 4

1869 — Elmer Horton — B (P 1896)

1907 — Tommy Leach throws out two runners at the plate in a 2–0 win over the Reds.

1908 — Pitcher's duel between Vic Willis and the Cubs Miner Brown ends in a 1–0 win for the Pirates. In the ninth, Fred Clarke singled, and Tommy Leach sacrificed him to second. Wagner's hit over Evers moved Clarke to third, and Honus took second on Evers' throw to the plate. Warren Gill was hit by a pitch and Owen Wilson ended the game with an RBI single. On the game-ending play, Gill did not run all the way to second, but stopped when he saw Clarke score. Frank Chance called for the ball, stepped on second and claimed Gill should be out on a force play, and the run should not count. Umpire Hank O'Day ruled in the Pirates' favor and the 1–0 verdict stood. That play was the prelude to the infamous Fred Merkle boner play which took place about a week later.

1978 — Pirates sweep a labor day twinbill from the Mets at Three Rivers to move within one game of first place. Jim Bibby pitched a shutout in the second game and Ed Ott had six hits in eight at-bats in the 7–4, 7–0 wins.

## September 5

1883 — Albert "Lefty" Leifield — B (P 1905–12)

1936 — Bill Mazeroski — B (2B 1956–72, Coach 1973)

1950 — Pirates sell first baseman-outfielder Johnny Hopp to the Yankees.

1969 — Roberto Clemente's fantastic back-handed, tumbling grab of Al Spangler's drive to right center helps down the Cubs, 9–2 at Wrigley Field. Steve Blass pitched a four-hitter giving up all four hits to Billy Williams. Blass also hit his first major league home run.

1978 — Pirates move to within a half game of the Phillies as Jerry Reuss shuts out New York, 8–0.

## September 6

1903 — Tom Thevenow — B (SS, 2B, 3B 1931–35, 38)

1910 — Johnny Lanning — B (P 1940–43, 45–46)

1912 — Vince DiMaggio — B (OF 1940–44)

1921 — Jack Phillips — B (1B 1949–52)

1948 — Pirates turn six doubleplays in a 2–1 win over St. Louis.

1962 — Pitcher Larry Foss goes to the Mets on waivers.

1964 — Pirates claim Dave Roberts from Philadelphia on waivers.

1973 — Danny Murtaugh replaces Bill Virdon as Pirates' manager. The Pirates are three games out of first with 16 games left to play.

### September 7

1877 — Ed Poole — B (P 1900–02)

1879 — Charles Case — B (P 1904–06)

1883 — John Flynn — B (1B 1910–11)

1895 — Fred Blackwell — B (C 1917–19)

1908 — Pirates sweep a morning-afternoon doubleheader against St. Louis. Honus Wagner was five for five in the first game.

1942 — Bucs score 11 runs in the sixth inning of the first game of a doubleheader with the Cardinals.

### September 8

1893 — Bill Gleason — B (2B 1916–17)

1896 — Val Picinich — B (C 1893)

1898 — Grover Lovelace — B (1922)

1912 — Frank Oceak — B (Coach 1958–64, 70–72)

1916 — Jim Bagby Jr. — B (P 1947)

1958 — Roberto Clemente socks three triples in a 4–1 victory over the Reds.

1976 — Pirates sell pitcher Ramon Hernandez to the Cubs.

### September 9

1857 — Abner Dalrymple — B (OF 1887–88)

1886 — John "Dots" Miller — B (2B, 1B 1909–13)

1895 — Dan Costello — B (OF 1914–16)

1898 — Frankie Frisch — B (Manager 1940–46)

1899 — Waite Hoyt — B (P 1933–37)

## September 9 (continued)

1913 — Hugh Mulcahy — B (P 1947)

1931 — Pete Naton — B (C 1953)

1970 — Dave Ricketts released as a player and signed as a coach.

## September 10

1878 — Brandy Davis — B (OF 1952–53)

1895 — George Kelly — B (1B 1917)

1924 — Ted Kluszewski — B (1B 1958–59)

1928 — Bob Garber — B (P 1956)

1958 — Dick Stuart's tenth inning home run gives Bob Friend his 20th win: 6–4 over the Giants.

1966 — Pirates lose to Cardinal rookie Dick Hughes on Tim McCarver's bases-loaded hit off the right field wall. The Bucs fall a game behind the Dodgers.

1978 — Pirates lose their third straight in New York and fall four games behind Philadelphia. Trailing 7–5 in the seventh, pinch hitter John Milner belted a three-run homer to put the Bucs in the lead. Stargell's pinch single off Dwight Bernard gave the Pirates a 9–7 lead but they lost the game in the eighth when Stargell's throw hit Gil Flores who had put down a bunt.

## September 11

1868 — Steve Brodie — B (OF 1897–18)

1905 — Glenn Spencer — B (P 1928, 30–32)

1940 — Jackie Hernandez — B (SS 1971–73)

1944 — David A. Roberts — B (P 1979–present)

1959 — Roy Face's 22-game winning streak stopped by the Dodgers 5–4.

1974 — Pitcher Dock Ellis is lost for the rest of the season when a line drive by Willie Montanez hits and fractures his right hand. The Phillies won, 5–3, cutting the Bucs lead to 2.5 games in the Eastern Division.

## September 12

1891 — Mark Baldwin hurls two complete games, winning 13–3 and 8–4.

1926 — George Freese — B (3B 1955)

1947 — Ralph Kiner sets a record with his eighth homer in his fourth consecutive game, while passing Johnny Mize in the home run derby. The Pirates defeated Boston, 4–3 at Forbes Field.

1964 — Pirates send catcher Smokey Burgess to the White Sox on waivers.

1966 — First baseman David L. Roberts is purchased by Baltimore.

1974 — Working on a three-hitter, Jerry Reuss falls apart, and the Phillies defeat the Pirates, cutting their lead to 1.5 games. In the eighth inning, pinch hitter Jerry Martin singled, Larry Bowa doubled, and Mike Schmidt hit a three-run homer. Willie Montanez doubled, knocking out Reuss. Bruce Kison then served up an RBI single to pinch hitter Jay Johnstone, tying the game, 4–4. Del Unser pinch hit and slammed a two-run homer to beat the Bucs.

1975 — Pirates traded a player to be named later (Art Howe) to Houston for infielder Tommy Helms.

1978 — Pirates break a five-game losing streak with a 5–1 win at Philadelphia, splitting the two-game series with the Phillies. Dave Parker hit two home runs as the Bucs left town four games out of first.

### September 13

1879 — John Donahue — B (C-1B 1900–01)

1908 — Charlie Starr's error accounts for all three Cincinnati runs in a 3–2 Pirate defeat, dropping the Bucs into third place.

1939 — Tom Parsons — B (P 1963)

1956 — Roy Face pitches in his ninth consecutive game to set a Major League record.

1970 — Matty Alou drops an easy fly ball as the Cubs beat the Pirates, 3–2, and stay alive in the Eastern division pennant race. The Bucs led 2–1 with two out in the ninth when Alou muffed Willie Smith's short fly to center. Don Kessinger and Glenn Beckert followed with singles, and Billy Williams' hit off reliever George Brunet won the game. The Pirates lead is cut to a half game over the Mets, and one over Chicago.

### September 14

1875 — John R. Gilbert — B (OF 1904)

1931 — Don Williams — B (P 1958–59)

1933 — Freddie Green — B (P 1959–61, 64)

1938 — Frank Carpin — B (P 1965)

1970 — Pirates purchase pitcher Mudcat Grant from Oakland.

### September 15

1872 — Lew Carr — B (SS 1901)

1907 — Fritz Ostermueller — B (P 1944–48)

1950 — Dave Pagan — B (P 1977)

1952 — Pirates begin wearing batting helmets.

1966 — Pirates fall 2.5 games back dropping the first game of a three-game series at Los Angeles, 5–3. The Dodgers led 5–1 in the ninth when Clemente and Stargell hit back-to-back homers off Don Drysdale with two out. Los Angeles scored all their runs in the first off Vern Law and Billy O'Dell, only two earned because of Alley's error with two out.

1974 — Pirates lose their fifth consecutive game, third straight in Montreal. The Bucs led 4–1 in the seventh, but Jose Morales hit a three-run homer, his first in the majors, to put the Expos in front. Pittsburgh is 1.5 games behind St. Louis.

### September 16

1870 — Sam Moran — B (P 1895)

1876 — Arthur "Otto" Kruger — B (INF 1903–04)

1903 — Barney Dreyfuss and Boston Americans' president Henry Killea agree to the first World Series.

1923 — Con Dempsey — B (P 1951)

1935 — Gus Suhr sets a National League record by playing in his 619th straight game at first base.

1941 — Lloyd Waner plays in his 77th straight game without striking out.

1944 — Chuck Brinkman — B (C 1974)

1974 — Pirates drop a 13 inning game in the opener of a three-game series in St. Louis, falling 2.5 games out of first. Al Oliver's first-inning homer off Bob Gibson put the Bucs in front, but Ted Simmons' single, a balk by Jerry Reuss, and Joe Torre's single tied the game. Lou Brock led off the 13th with a single and proceeded to steal second, his 109th theft of the season. Simmons' fly to Stargell in left scored Brock with the go-ahead run. With two out in the bottom of the inning, Gene Clines singled off Al Hrabosky. Rennie Stennett popped up, but Torre dropped the ball, leaving runners at first and second. Hrabosky then struck out Richie Hebner to end the game.

1975 — Rennie Stennett goes seven for seven against the Cubs at Wrigley Field. Stennett's hits are the most by any player in a nine-inning game. The Pirates 22–0 victory is also the largest margin of victory in any shutout game.

### September 17

1870 — Dick Padden — B (2B 1896–98)

1882 — Frank Schulte — B (OF 1916–17)

1893 — Charles "Whitey" Glazner — B (P 1920–23)

1899 — John "Sheriff" Blake — B (P 1920)

1918 — Bob Dillinger — B (3B 1950–51)

1930 — Jim Umbricht — B (P 1959–61)

1966 — Donn Clendenon's three-run homer salvages the final game of the Dodger series. The Pirates are 2.5 games out of first.

1973 — The Pirates defeat New York, 10–3, and take a 1.5 game lead in the Eastern Division. Willie Stargell banged out four extra base hits including his fortieth home run.

1977 — Frank Taveras swipes his 64th base, breaking Max Carey's record as the Pirates all-time base stealer in a 6–3 defeat of Montreal.

### September 18

1889 — Heinie Groh — B (3B 1927)

1908 — Pittsburgh falls five games off the pace, losing two at New York. Christy Matthewson pitched a shutout in the first game.

1925 — Harvey Haddix — B (P 1959–63, Coach 1979–present)

1930 — Remy Kremer cops his 20th victory, besting the Phillies, 6–5.

1938 — Russ Bauers, pitching with one day's rest, defeats Philadelphia, 1–0. Paul Waner's single drove in Al Todd with the only run. The Pirates hold a 3.5 game lead over the Cubs.

1948 — Ken Brett — B (P 1974–75)

1960 — Vern Law wins his 20th, defeating Cincinnati, 5–3 in the first game of a doubleheader. Vinegar Bend Mizell's three hitter gives the Bucs a 1–0 second game decision, cutting the magic number to seven.

1971 — Pirates clinch a tie for the Eastern Division title with a 4–0 win against the Mets in Pittsburgh. Richie Zisk hit his first major league home run and Steve Blass pitched a two-hitter.

### September 19

1865 — Jim Donely — B (3B 1897)

1890 — Stuffy McInnis — B (1B 1925–26)

1949 — Ralph Kiner becomes the first National League player to hit 50 home runs in two different seasons with a blast against the Giants.

1951 — Pirates send outfielder Dino Restelli to Washington on waivers.

1953 — Danny O'Connell hits safely in the 26th consecutive game.

1974 — Pittsburgh moves to within a half game of first with an 8–6 win. Trailing 4–2 in the seventh, Manny Sanguillen and Al Oliver singled off Rich Folkers. Al Hrabosky came in and was greeted by a Stargell double, putting the Bucs in the lead. Richie Zisk was walked intentionally, and Richie Hebner slammed a three-run homer to put the Bucs in front, 8–3. The Cardinals pulled to within two in the ninth but Dave Giusti came on to strikeout Reggie Smith, Ted Simmons, and Joe Torre with the tying runs on base.

1978 — The Pirates survive a nine-run Cubs' comeback and win in the 11th on Dave Parker's homer off Bruce Sutter. Pittsburgh led 11–2 in the seventh but a two-run single by pinch hitter Dave Johnson and an Ivan DeJesus' double tied the game in the ninth.

## September 20

1888 — Harry Gardner — B (P 1911–12)

1907 — Nick Maddox no-hits Brooklyn, 2–1, the first in Pirate history.

1916 — John "Red" Juelich — B (2B 1939)

1922 — Vic Lombardi — B (P 1948–50)

1941 — Denny Ribant — B (P 1967)

1951 — Pirates send first baseman Rocky Nelson to the White Sox on waivers.

1966 — Vern Law's pitching and homers by Jesse Gonder and Donn Clendenon give the Pirates a 6–0 win, leaving Pittsburgh 1.5 games out of first place. The Bucs turned four doubleplays in the game against the Giants, setting a National League record for a season with 215.

1969 — Bob Moose hurls a no-hitter at Shea Stadium, beating the Amazing Mets, 4–0.

1973 — The Pirates lead is cut to a half game with a 4–3 defeat in 13 innings at New York. With two out in the top of the 13th, Dave Augustine drove a pitch to the very top of the left field wall. The ball dropped into Cleon Jones' glove and the Mets left fielder threw a strike to Bud Harrelson. Harrelson's throw to the plate nailed Richie Zisk who tried to score from first. The Mets scored off Luke Walker in the bottom of the inning in the game that turned the pennant race in their favor.

## September 21

1860 — Tom Brown — B (OF 1887)

1891 — Gil Britton — B (SS 1913)

1896 — Connie Mack announces his resignation, effective at the end of the season.

1900 — Del Lundgren — B (P 1924)

1901 — Vic Willis pitches a two-hitter and defeats Christy Matthewson 2–1 to split the series at the Polo Grounds. Fred Clarke's two-out double down the right field foul line drove in both Pirate runs. Pittsburgh is three games out of first.

1915 — Max Butcher — B (P 1939–45)

1925 — Kiki Cuyler's tenth straight hit ties the National League record.

1940 — Debs Garms clinches the batting title with five hits against the Reds.

1942 — Sam McDowell — B (P 1975)

1978 — Pirates leave Chicago 1.5 games behind Philadelphia after a 14 inning win against the Cubs. Rennie Stennett led off the last inning with a walk, and pinch runner Matt Alexander stole second. On the play, Dave Rader's throw went into centerfield and Alexander headed for third. Bobby Murcer's throw toward third hit the runner in the back and he was able to come home with the winning run.

### September 22

1893 — Ira Flagstead — B (OF 1929–30)

1908 — The Bucs score a 3–2 victory at Brooklyn in 11 innings. In the 11th, Al Storke tripled home Honus Wagner, and Storke scored on an error by second baseman Whitey Alperman. A homer by Tom Catterson ended the scoring as the Bucs move to within 1.5 games of the Giants and Cubs.

1928 — Burleigh Grimes wins his 25th, 9–7 over the Phillies.

1929 — Harry Bright — B (INF 1958–60)

1971 — Luke Walker and Dave Giusti combine to defeat the Cardinals 3–2 in St. Louis, clinching the National League Eastern Division title.

### September 23

1880 — Cy Neighborn — B (OF 1908)

1889 — Joe Kelly — B (OF 1914)

1895 — John Mokan — B (OF 1921–22)

1901 — Mack Hillis — B (2B 1928)

1908 — Pirates move one game out of first with a 2–1 win in Brooklyn. Wagner and Storke drove in the Pittsburgh runs, and Lefty Leifield got the win — the Bucs seventh in their last 10 games.

1922 — Glenn Donoso — B (1955–56)

1924 — Dino Restelli — B (OF 1949, 51)

1942 — Jim Rooker — B (P 1973–present)

1951 — Murray Dickson wins his 20th, 3–0 over the Reds. Dickson accounted for almost a third of the Pirates 64 wins during the season.

1956 — The largest crowd to attend a game at Forbes Field, 44,932, watch the Pirates lose to the Dodgers, 8–3.

1974 — Pirates defeat St. Louis 1–0 in ten innings to move to within a half game of first place. Pinch hitter Paul Popovich led off the tenth with a bloop single and left the game in favor of pinch runner Miguel Dilone. Rennie Stennett sacrificed and Richie Hebner won the game with a single.

## September 24

1881 — Bob Vail — B (1908)

1891 — Wesley "Paddy" Siglin — B (2B 1914–16)

1910 — Dixie Walker — B (OF 1948–49)

1929 — James Mangan — B (C 1952, 54)

1973 — Willie Stargell robs Ken Singleton of a homer in the fifth, homers himself in the sixth, and throws out Tony Scott at home in the seventh inning of a 3–0 defeat of the Expos in the second game of a doubleheader in Jarry Park. The Pirates lost the first game, 5–4, and head home for the final week only one half game out of first place.

1974 — Pirates move into first place with a 7–3 win at St. Louis. Stargell's three-run homer in the seventh gave Bruce Kison the win.

1978 — Rookie Scott Sanderson pitches a three-hitter and beats Pittsburgh 4–0. The loss leaves the Pirates four games back with seven left, including the final four with the first place Phillies.

## September 25

1889 — Dave Robertson — B (OF 1921)

1947 — Billy Herman resigns as Pirate manager and is replaced by Billy Burwell.

1960 — The Pirates clinch their first National League pennant in 33 years despite a 10 inning, 4–2 loss in Milwaukee. In the seventh inning, it is announced that the Cubs have beaten St. Louis, eliminating the second-place Cardinals.

1961 — Pirates send pitcher Freddie Green to Washington on waivers.

1970 — Pittsburgh wins the first game of a three-game series with the Mets, 4–3 at Three Rivers Stadium. Matty Alou's two-out single put the Bucs in front in the seventh and Willie Stargell's RBI single gave the Pirates a two-run margin going to the ninth. The Mets scored in the ninth and Tommy Agee was at second with one out. Joe Gibbon fanned Art Shamsky and Agee was thrown out by Sanguillen as he tried to steal third.

1974 — The Cardinals regain first place with an 11-inning, 13–12 win in Busch Memorial Stadium. Pittsburgh scored five runs in the first inning off Bob Forsch, but Ken Reitz' two-run double in the third and two-run homer in the fifth off John Morlan gave St. Louis a 9–6 lead. RBI doubles by Rennie Stennett and Al

Oliver scored two runs in the sixth, and the Bucs tied the game in the ninth when Dave Parker was hit by a pitch, moved to second on Sanguillen's single and scored on Bake McBride's error. Singles by pinch hitter Art Howe, Stargell, and Sanguillen put the Pirates back in front, and Ed Kirkpatrick's double gave the Bucs a 12-9 lead. With Manny Jiminez pitching, Ted Sizemore led off for the Cardinals with a single, Reggie Smith walked, and Simmons doubled home both runners. Jim Minshall replaced Jiminez to face Joe Torre who hit a grounder to Stennett at second. Stennett's throw was wild, and Simmons scored to tie the game. Bake McBride's bunt single moved the pinch runner to third, and Jim Dwyer's sacrifice fly put the Cardinals back in first place.

## September 26

1910 — Joe Sullivan — B (P 1941)

1925 — Bobby Shantz — B (P 1961)

1926 — Lefty Leifield pitches a six inning no-hitter as the Pirates won the second game of a doubleheader with the Phillies, 8-0.

1961 — Joe Gibbon pitches a one-hitter in an 8-0 win against the Dodgers in the second game of a doubleheader. Bob Aspromonte had the only hit, a single in the sixth.

## September 27

1891 — Doug Baird — B (3B 1915-17)

1906 — Marty Lang — B (P 1930)

1913 — Dick Lanahan — B (P 1940-41)

1919 — Johnny Pesky — B (Coach 1965-67)

1922 — Ralph Kiner — B (OF 1946-53)

1930 — Dick Hall — B (OF-P 1952-57, 59)

1935 — Dave Wickersham — B (P 1968)

1938 — Pirates drop the first game of a three-game series for first place in Chicago, 2-1. The game ended when Al Todd struckout with the potential tying run at third.

1952 — Ralph Kiner hits his 37th home run and becomes the first player to lead the league for seven consecutive seasons.

1970 — Bucs clinch the National League Eastern Division title with a 2-1 victory over the Mets at Three Rivers Stadium. Dock Ellis got the win, and Dave Giusti notched the save as the Pirates swept the three-game series from New York.

## September 28

1865 — Lou Bierbauer — B (2B 1891-96)

1889 — Pete Compton — B (OF 1916)

1890 — Everette Booe — B (OF 1913)

73

1902 — Leon Chagnon — B (P 1929–30, 32–34)

1938 — Gabby Hartnett's "Homer in the Gloamin" with two out in the ninth at Wrigley Field gives Chicago a 6–5 victory and drops the Pirates out of first place. The Cubs took a lead in the second but Johnny Rizzo's 21st homer tied the score in the sixth. Arky Vaughan's infield hit, walks to Gus Suhr and Pep Young, and Lee Handley's two-run single put the Bucs on top. The Cubs came right back with doubles by Hartnett and Rip Collins, a bunt single by Billy Jurges, and Stan Hack's run scoring ground out to even the score after six innings. The Bucs regained the lead in the eighth when Vaughan walked Suhr singled, and pinch hitter Heinie Manush singled off reliever Larry French to drive in Vaughan with the Pirates fourth run. Handley followed with a run-scoring single, but the rally died when Manush was thrown out at the plate by Jurges on Al Todd's grounder, and Bob Klinger hit into a doubleplay.

When Collins led off the Chicago eighth, Pie Traynor brought on Bill Swift to replace Klinger. Swift passed Jurges and served up an RBI double to pinch hitter Tony Lazzeri. Billy Herman's single tied the game but pinch runner Joe Marty was nailed at the plate and Mace Brown came in to retire the side. The Pirates went down in the ninth and Brown retired the first two batters for the Cubs when Hartnett stepped up. In darkness that was beginning to make the game unplayable, Brown fired two strikes past the Cubs player-manager. The next pitch never got past the plate, as Hartnett drove it over the wall in left field. The Pirates still had five games left but never recovered from Hartnett's blow.

1942 — Grant Jackson — B (1977–present)

1966 — Pirates sweep Philadelphia, while the Dodgers lose to St. Louis leaving the Bucs 1.5 games behind Los Angeles with three games left. Manager Harry Walker gambled on starting veteran Billy O'Dell who combined with Steve Blass in holding the Phillies to five hits in the first game. Donn Clendenon's 28th homer gave the Pirates a 2–1 victory, and Bob Veale notched his 16th win in the nitecap, thanks to three great plays by third baseman Jose Pagan.

1974 — Home runs by Richie Zisk and Richie Hebner lead the Pirates to a 7–3 win at New York, putting the Bucs one game up on St. Louis. Jim Rooker recorded his 15th victory.

## September 29

1859 — Ed Morris — B (P 1887–89)

1884 — Royal Shaw — B (1908)

1908 — Pirates sweep St. Louis at Exhibition Park, 7–0 and 6–5. Howie Camnitz took a no-hitter into the ninth inning of the first game but lost it on a single by Champ Osteen. The second game win puts the Pirates a half-game behind New York, tied for second with Chicago.

1932 — Paul Giel — B (P 1959–60)

1938 — Bill Lee pitches in his fourth consecutive game and gains his 22nd win and the Cubs tenth in a row, pounding the demoralized Pirates, 10-1. The Pirates have dropped all three games in Chicago and head to Cincinnati 1.5 games behind the Cubs.

1950 — Ken Macha — B (INF 1974, 77–78)

1974 — Rookie Bob Apodaca pitches his first complete game and the Mets defeat the Pirates, 7–2, dropping the Bucs into a tie for first with the Cardinals.

1978 — Pirates sweep a twi-night doubleheader from the first place Phillies at Three Rivers Stadium to move within a half game of the lead. Trailing 2–0 in the fourth, Frank Taveras led off with a triple and scored on Omar Moreno's single. Dave Parker followed with a hit off Ted Sizemore's glove, and Willie Stargell put the Bucs ahead with a blast into the rightfield pavilion. The Phillies came back to tie and Ed Ott led off the Pirates' ninth with a fly ball to right center field. Garry Maddox and Bake McBride converged on the ball, then got confused and let it drop. As Ott dove into third, the relay throw from the outfield skipped past Mike Schmidt into the Phillies dugout, allowing Ott to score the winning run.

Greg Luzinski gave Philadelphia a 1–0 lead in the second game with a homer off Bruce Kison, but Kison tied the game himself with his second major league home run, off Steve Carlton. The tie stood until the ninth when Parker led off with a triple off Carlton, and Bill Robinson and Stargell were walked intentionally. Warren Brusstar came on to face Phil Garner and committed a balk, allowing Parker to score the winning run.

### September 30

1908 — Pirates win their last home game of the regular season, defeating St. Louis, 7-5. Sam Leever won in relief of Vic Willis, putting Pittsburgh all alone in second place, .004 points behind New York.

1946 — Boston Braves trade second baseman Billy Herman, pitcher Elmer Singleton, infielder Whitey Wietelman, and pitcher Stan Wentzel to Pittsburgh for third baseman Bob Elliott and catcher Hank Camelli. Herman became the Pirates' manager in 1947, Elliott the League's MVP in 1948 when he led the Braves into the World Series against Cleveland.

1949 — Ralph Kiner hits his 54th home run and 13th in September, over the scoreboard clock at Forbes Field, in a 3–2 win over the Reds.

1972 — Roberto Clemente collects his 3,000th hit as the Pirates defeat the Mets, 5–0 at Three Rivers Stadium. Clemente's last hit was a double to left-centerfield off lefthander Jon Matlack.

1978 — Pirates squander a four-run lead and lose to Philadelphia as the Phillies clinch the division title. With one out, singles by Omar Moreno, Dave Parker, and Bill Robinson loaded the bases against Randy Lerch. Willie Stargell followed with a drive that kept carrying until it cleared the fence in straight-away centerfield, giving the Bucs a 4–1 lead. Lerch cut the Pirate lead with a home run in the second off Don Robinson. The Phillies pitcher stunned the crowd with another homer in the fourth, cutting the Bucs lead to a run. Then with two on in the sixth, Greg Luzinski belted a home run into the left field seats to put Philadelphia ahead, 6–4. The Phillies scored four more times in the eighth but five hits scored five runs in the Pirate ninth and brought the potential tying run to the plate in Willie Stargell. The captain was shooting for home run all the way and fanned against Tug McGraw. Phil Garner's bouncer to Larry Bowa ended the Pirates' season in second place.

## OCTOBER 1

1892 — Roy Sanders — B (P 1918)

1895 — Carmen Hill — B (P 1915-16, 18-19, 26-29)

1903 — Pirates win the first World Series game ever played, 7–3 over the Americans in Boston, behind Deacon Phillippe's pitching and Jimmy Sebring's home run.

1908 — Jim Russell — B (OF 1942-47)

1927 — Johnny Miljus pitches the Pirates to a 9–6 win at Cincinnati, clinching the National League championship. Miljus came on in the sixth after Pie Traynor's bases-loaded single gave the Bucs their margin of victory.

1935 — Chuck Hiller — B (2B 1968)

1938 — Cincinnati defeats Pittsburgh, 9–6 and the Cubs split a doubleheader with St. Louis, eliminating the Pirates in the National League pennant race.

1966 — Pirate title hopes end with a double loss to the Giants at Forbes Field. Roberto Clemente's 29th home run put the Bucs in front and Pittsburgh led 4–3 in the eighth when Ollie Brown's double tied the game and Jim Davenport's pop fly fell in, scoring Brown with the tie breaking run. In the Pirates eighth, Donn Clendenon reached second with two out. Jesse Gonder hit a grounder off Juan Marichal's glove and Marichal threw low to first base. Clendenon headed for home but was cut down by Willie McCovey's perfect throw to the plate. Bobby Bolin pitched a one-hitter in the second game, allowing only a bloop single by Bill Mazeroski in the second inning. The loss mathematically eliminated the Pirates in the National League race.

1973 — San Diego defeats Pittsburgh in a makeup game on the last day of the season, ending any chance for the Pirates to win the Eastern Division title. The 4–3 loss at Three Rivers Stadium leaves the Pirates in third place, 2.5 games behind the champion Mets.

1974 — Bucs clinch a tie for first with a 6–5 win against Chicago. The Cubs led 5–4 in the eighth when pinch hitter Bob Robertson belted a two-run homer off Dave LaRoche to give Dave Giusti the victory.

### October 2

1869 — Scott Stratton — B (P 1891)

1874 — Ernie Diehl — B (OF-SS 1903-04)

1891 — Eddie Murphy — B (OF 1926)

1903 — Pirates lose game two of the World Series, 3–0, in Boston.

1908 — Pirates move into first by a half game, sweeping a doubleheader at St. Louis. Lefty Leifield won the first game, 7–4, and homers by Wagner and George Gibson gave Camnitz the second game, 2–1.

1920 — Pirates and Reds play a tripleheader at Forbes Field to determine the second and third place teams. Starting at noon, the Reds won 13–4 and 7–3 to clinch second place despite Johnny Morrison's 6–0 win in the third game which was shortened by darkness.

1932 — Maury Wills — B (3B 1967–68)

1946 — Bob Robertson — B (1B 1967, 69–76)

1947 — Billy Meyer is named to manage the Pirates, replacing Billy Burwell who became the interim skipper after Billy Herman left prior to the last game of the season.

First baseman Hank Greenberg is released in accordance with his wish to retire as an active player.

1971 — San Francisco defeats Pittsburgh in the first game of the National League Championship Series at San Francisco.

1974 — Pittsburgh wins the National League Eastern Division title. The Cubs scored first off Jim Rooker with four runs in the first inning and the Bucs trailed 4–2 entering the ninth. Rick Reuschel walked Richie Zisk and Manny Sanguillen to open the ninth. Ed Kirkpatrick sacrificed the runners ahead and pinch hitter Dave Parker drove in Zisk with a grounder to Rob Sperring off Reuschel's glove. Bob Robertson pinch hit and waved at the third strike but the pitch got past catcher Steve Swisher. Swisher recovered but his throw hit Robertson in the back and Sanguillen scored the tying run. With one out in the 10th, Al Oliver lined a triple into the leftfield corner off Ken Frailing. Stargell and Gene Clines were walked intentionally, and Oscar Zamora came in for Chicago. Sanguillen topped a roller up the third baseline, and when Bill Madlock could not make the play, the championship was wrapped up.

1977 — Kent Tekulve and Rich Gossage each appear in their 72nd games to break the existing club record in a 3–2 defeat of the Cubs. Dave Parker clinches his first batting title, ending the season with a .338 average.

### October 3

1872 — Fred Clarke — B (OF 1900–11, 13–15, Manager 1900–15, Coach 1925)

1903 — Pirates win game three of the World Series, 4–2.

1905 — John Riddle — B (C 1948, Coach 1948–50)

1917 — Frank Kalin — B (OF 1940)

1931 — Bob Skinner — B (OF 1954, 56–63, Coach 1974–75, 79–present)

1936 — Jack Lamabe — B (P 1962)

1970 — First game of the playoffs is picketed by the major league umpires and worked by minor leaguers in the Pirates 3–0, ten-inning loss to the Reds.

1971 — Pirates defeat San Francisco, 9–4 in the second game of the Championship Series.

## October 4

1874 — Jim Gardner — B (P 1895, 97–99)

1908 — The Cubs defeat Pittsburgh on the last day of the season to eliminate the Pirates in the National League Pennant race. Frank Schulte's single put Chicago ahead, and the Cubs took a two-run lead in the fifth when Schulte brought home Johnny Evers with a single to center. In the Pittsburgh sixth, Roy Thomas led off with a single and moved to second on an error. With two out, Honus Wagner doubled home Thomas, and Ed Abbaticchio's single scored the Dutchman with the tying run. The Cubs came back in their half of the sixth on a Joe Tinker double, an intentional walk to Johnny Kling by Vic Willis, and Three-Finger Brown's run scoring single. The Cubs scored in the seventh and eighth for a 5–2 win. The Pirates finish second behind the Cubs in the National League. The crowd of 30,347 was the largest ever at Wrigley Field.

1914 — Bill Schuster — B (SS 1937)

1918 — George Munger — B (P1952, 56)

1970 — Pirates lose game two of the Championship Series, 3–1 against the Reds in Pittsburgh.

1975 — Reds defeat Pittsburgh 8–3 in the first game of the NLCS at Riverfront Stadium.

## October 5

1873 — Claude Ritchey — B (2B 1900–06)

1887 — Jim Bagby Sr. — B (P 1923)

1927 — New York 5, Pittsburgh 4 in the first game of the World Series at Forbes Field.

1960 — Pirates defeat New York 6–4 in the first game of the World Series in Pittsburgh.

1970 — Pirates lose the third and final game of the series, 3–2 in Cincinnati.

1971 — Pittsburgh takes a 2–1 lead in the NLCS with a 2–1 victory over the Giants at Three Rivers Stadium.

1974 — Los Angeles defeats Pittsburgh, 3–0, in the first game of the Championship Series at Pittsburgh.

1975 — Pittsburgh loses 6–1 in the second game of the NLCS at Cincinnati.

## October 6

1866 — Eddie Burke — B (Of 1890)

1893 — Louis "Pat" Duncan — B (OF 1915)

1903 — Pittsburgh takes a 3–1 lead in the World Series with a 5–4 win against Boston at Exposition Park.

1908 — Tom Padden — B (C 1932–37)

1927 — New York wins game two of the World Series, defeating the Pirates, 6–2 at Pittsburgh.

1946 — Gene Clines — B (OF 1970–74)

1960 — New York evens the series with a 16–3 win over the Bucs in game two at Forbes Field.

1971 — Pittsburgh wins the National League Championship with a 9–5 win against the Giants at Three Rivers Stadium.

1974 — Pirates lose game two of the series, 5–2, to the Dodgers in Los Angeles.

## October 7

1868 — Brickyard Kennedy — B (P 1903)

1892 — Adam Debus — B (INF 1917)

1895 — Fred Fussell — B (P 1928–29)

1903 — Boston wins game five of the World Series, 11–2, in Pittsburgh.

1925 — Pirates lose the first game of the World Series, dropping a 4–1 decision to the Senators at Forbes Field.

1927 — Pirates lose an 8–1 decision to the Yankees in game three, played at Yankee Stadium.

1972 — Pirates open the Championship Series with a 5–1 win over Cincinnati in Pittsburgh.

1975 — Pittsburgh loses the third and final game of the NLCS to Cincinnati, 5–3, in ten innings, despite John Candelaria's record 14 strikeouts.

## October 8

1870 — Tom Colcolough — B (P 1893–95)

1887 — Doc Crandall — B (Coach 1931–33)

Donnie Buch — B (Manager 1927–29)

1903 — Boston evens the World Series with a 6–3 triumph over the Pirates in Pittsburgh.

1909 — Pirates defeat Detroit, 4–1, in the first game of the World Series at Forbes Field.

Catcher Mike Simon is acquired from the Boston Braves.

1917 — Danny Murtaugh — B (2B 1948–51, Coach 1956–57, Manager 1957–64, 70–71, 73–76)

1921 — George "Catfish" Metkovich — B (OF-1B 1951–53)

1925 — Pittsburgh's 3–2 win against Washington evens the World Series at one game apiece.

1927 — Yankees win the World's Championship with a 4–3 win, completing a four game sweep of the Pirates.

1940 — Pitcher Danny MacFayden released by the Pirates.

1944 — Ed Kirkpatrick — B (1B-OF 1974–77)

1960 — Whitey Ford blanks the Bucs, 10–0 in game three of the World Series, played in New York.

1972 — Pirates drop a 5–3 decision to the Reds in Pittsburgh in game two of the National League Championship series.

1974 — Pittsburgh stays alive by winning game three of the NLCS, 7–0 at Los Angeles. Bruce Kison's win leaves the Pirates trailing the Dodgers, two games to one.

1976 — Pitcher Bob Moose dies in an auto accident at age 29.

## October 9

1865 — Al Maul — B (P 1888–89, 91)

1903 — John Tising — B (P 1936)

1909 — Pittsburgh loses game two of the World Series, 7–2 to the Tigers at Forbes Field.

1944 — Freddie Patek — B (SS 1968–70)

1947 — Bob Moose — B (P 1967–76)

1960 — Pittsburgh wins game three of the Series, defeating the Yankees 3–2 in New York.

1971 — Pirates drop the first game of the World Series, 5–3 to the Orioles in Baltimore.

1972 — Pirates win game three of the NLCS, 3–2 in Cincinnati.

1974 — Los Angeles wins the National League Championship, pounding out a 12–1 victory over the Pirates.

### October 10

1868 — Dave Anderson — B (P 1890)

Ad Gumbert — B (P 1893–94)

1879 — Homer Hillerbrand — B (P 1905–06, 08)

1892 — Elmer Jacobs — B (P 1916–18)

1894 — Myrl Brown — B (P 1922)

1903 — Boston takes a four-games-to-three lead with a 7–3 win in Pittsburgh.

1925 — Washington wins game three of the World Series, defeating the Pirates, 4–3 in Washington.

1960 — Pittsburgh takes a three-games-to-two lead in the World Series with a 5–2 win in Yankee Stadium.

1961 — Pitcher Al Jackson and outfielder Joe Christopher are selected by the New York Mets in the National League expansion draft.

Catcher Hal Smith, outfielder Roman Mejias, and pitchers Bobby Shantz and Jim Umbricht are selected by the Houston Colt 45s.

1970 — Outfielder Angel Mangual is sold to Oakland.

1972 — The NLCS is tied 2–2 following the Reds 7–1 defeat of the Pirates at Cincinnati.

### October 11

1909 — Pirates defeat the Tigers, 8–6 in game three of the World Series.

1912 — Wayne Osborne — B (P 1935)

1925 — Washington wins game four of the Series, 4–0 in Washington. The Pirates and Senators are tied with two wins each.

1971 — Baltimore takes a 2–0 lead in the World Series with an 11–3 rout of the Pirates.

1972 — Pirates lose the fifth and final game of the National League Championship Series when Bob Moose wild pitches home George Foster with the winning run in the Reds 4–3 ninth inning win at Riverfront Stadium.

### October 13

1876 — Rube Waddell — B (P 1900–01)

1888 — Jack Onslow — B (Coach 1925–26)

1889 — Frank Smykal — B (SS 1916)

1903 — Steve Swetonic — B (P 1929–33, 35)

Boston wins the first World's Championship with a 3–0 defeat of the Pirates in the eighth game of the series.

1909 — Pittsburgh defeats Detroit, 8–4 at Forbes Field, in game five of the World Series.

1913 — Xavier Rescigno — B (P 1943–45)

1925 — Pittsburgh evens the series with a 3–2 win against the Senators at Pittsburgh in the sixth game of the series.

1932 — Dick Barone — B (SS 1960)

1942 — Bob Bailey — B (3B 1962–66)

1959 — Outfielder Harry Simpson is purchased by the White Sox.

1960 — Bill Mazeroski's lead-off homer in the ninth inning gives Pittsburgh the World's Championship with a 10–9 win at Forbes Field in the seventh game of the World Series.

1971 — Pirates defeat Baltimore 4–3 in the first night game in World Series history. The Bucs win at Three Rivers Stadium evens the series after four games.

**October 14**

1856 — Alexander McKinnon — B (1B 1887)

1886 — Ona Dodd — B (3B 1912)

1903 — Pitcher Ed Doheny is committed to an insane asylum. Doheny had shown signs of a breakdown and was committed after attacking his nurse and physician.

1909 — Detroit wins game six of the Series, defeating Pittsburgh 5–4 in Detroit.

1913 — Hugh Casey — B (P 1949)

1915 — Ken Heintzelman — B (P 1937–42, 46–47)

1934 — Tom Cheney — B (P 1960–61)

1946 — Al Oliver — B (OF-1B 1968–77)

1952 — Pirates trade outfielder Gus Bell to Cincinnati for outfielders Cal Abrams, Gail Henley, and catcher Joe Rossi.

1968 — Pirates lose first baseman Donn Clendenon, outfielder Manny Mota, and third baseman Maury Wills to Montreal in the expansion draft.

Pitchers Al McBean, Dave Roberts, and infielder Ron Slocum are selected by San Diego.

1971 — Pirates score a 3–2 victory in game five of the World Series against Baltimore, their third straight win at Three Rivers Stadium.

### October 15

1887 — Bob Harmon — B (P 1914–16, 18)

1896 — John "Mule" Watson — B (P 1920)

1903 — George Haas — B (OF 1925)

1925 — Pirates become World Champions with a 9–7 defeat of the Washington Senators at Forbes Field in the seventh game of the World Series.

1926 — Don Carlsen — B (P 1951–52)

1927 — Bill Henry — B (P 1968)

1928 — Gail Henley — B (OF 1954)

1936 — Arthur "Red" Swanson — B (P 1955–57)

1976 — Pirates sell pitcher Jim Minshall to Seattle.

### October 16

1866 — Fred Lake — B (1B 1898)

1895 — Bill Skiff — B (C 1921)

1889 — Jake Kafora — B (P 1913–14)

1904 — Walter "Boom-Boom" Beck — B (P 1945)

1909 — Pirates shutout Detroit 8–0 for the World's Championship in the seventh game.

1919 — Edison Bahr — B (P 1946–47)

1928 — Lenny Yochim — B (P 1951–54)

1971 — Baltimore defeats Pittsburgh, 3–2 in ten innings at Memorial Stadium, forcing a seventh game.

### October 17

1870 — George Nicol — B (OF-P 1894)

1873 — Frank "Pop" Dillon — B (1B 1894–1900)

1915 — Mike Sandlock — B (C 1953)

1929 — Harding "Pete" Peterson — B (C 1955, 57–59)

## October 17 (continued)

1971 — Pirates win the World's Championship with a 2–1 decision over Baltimore in game seven at Memorial Stadium. Roberto Clemente is named the series' most valuable player for his outstanding performance.

## October 18

1859 — Samuel "Cliff" Carroll — B (OF 1888)

1881 — John "Hans" Lobert — B (3B 1903)

1894 — Phil Morrison — B (P 1921)

1909 — Today is proclaimed a general holiday in Pittsburgh by mayor W. A. Magee to celebrate the Pirates World Series victory.

1973 — Pirates trade second baseman Dave Cash to the Phillies for pitcher Ken Brett. (The Pirates have Rennie Stennett to play second and Brett is needed to shore up a weak pitching staff.)

## October 19

1874 — Tom McCreery — B (OF 1898–1900)

1931 — Don Leppert — B (C 1961–62, Coach 1968–76)

1946 — Pirates purchase pitcher Art Herring from Brooklyn.

1948 — Lorenzo Lanier — B (1971, no position noted as he only appeared in six games)

1964 — Harry Walker is named Pirate manager, replacing Danny Murtaugh who stepped down for health reasons.

## October 20

1891 — Leo "Pat" Bohen — B (P 1914)

1864 — Jocko Fields — B (OF-C 1887–89, 91)

1955 — Branch Rickey retires from his post as Pirate General Manager.

1970 — Pirates assign outfielder Angel Mangual to Oakland, completing the Mudcat Grant deal.

## October 21

1917 — Frank Papish — B (P 1950)

1941 — Ron Davis — B (P 1969)

1946 — Pirates trade pitcher Cookie Cuccurullo to the Yankees for pitcher Ernie Bonham.

1965 — Pitcher Vern Law is named the National League Comeback Player of the Year. Law had placed himself on the voluntarily retired list in 1963 but returned in 1964 with a respectable season and completed his comeback with 17 wins in 1965, the most for Law since winning 20 games and the Cy Young award in 1960.

1969 — Pitcher Dave Giusti, catcher Dave Ricketts, and outfielder Frank Vanzin are obtained from the Cardinals for catcher Carl Taylor. Giusti became one of Baseball's top relief pitchers and helped the Bucs win five division titles in six years.

1970 — Danny Murtaugh is named the National League's Manager of the Year. Murtaugh returned to lead the Pirates after a five year absence and led Pittsburgh to its first pennant since 1960.

### October 22

1895 — Johnny Morrison — B (P 1920–27)

1918 — Harry Walker — B (Manager 1967–69)

1942 — Wilbur Wood — B (P 1964–65)

1974 — Pirates trade outfielder Gene Clines to the Mets for catcher Duffy Dyer.

### October 23

1910 — Billy Sullivan — B (C 1947)

1931 — Jim Bunning — B (P 1968–69)

### October 24

1870 — Phil Routcliffe — B (OF 1890)

1871 — George "Heinie" Smith — B (2B 1899)

1906 — Pete McClanahan — B (1931)

1927 — Cal Hogue — B (P 1952–54)

1944 — John Jeter — B (OF 1960–70)

1953 — Omar Moreno — B (OF 1975–present)

### October 25

1893 — Vic Aldridge — B (P 1925–27)

1918 — Nanny Fernandez — B (3B 1950)

1939 — Pete Mikkelsen — B (P 1966–67)

## October 25 (continued)

1972 — Pirates trade pitcher Gene Garber to Kansas City for pitcher Jim Rooker. Both players were in the minor leagues at the time, but Rooker has been a steady winner with the Bucs, and Garber was a top reliever with the Phillies and now the Braves.

## October 26

1867 — Bill Garfield — B (P 1889)

1884 — Harry Camnitz — B (P 1909)

1890 — Bob Coleman — B (C 1913–14)

1919 — Jack Cassini — B (1949)

1925 — Fred Clarke resigns as a Pirate coach in the aftermath of the Adams, Bigbee, Carey incident on August 14th.

1955 — Joe L. Brown is named Pirate's general manager, succeeding Branch Rickey.

## October 27

1918 — Ed Albosta — B (P 1946)

1919 — Pirates purchase catcher Spud Davis from the Phillies.

## October 28

1867 — Bill Wilson — B (C-OF 1890)

1890 — Percy Jones — B (P 1930)

1900 — Wally Roettger — B (OF 1934)

1917 — Joe Page — B (P 1954)

1925 — Luis Marquez — B (OF 1954)

1935 — Bob Veale — B (P 1962–72)

## October 29

1865 — Mark Baldwin — B (P 1891–93)

1866 — Gus Weyhing — B (P 1895)

1882 — Arthur "Solly" Hofman — B (OF 1903, 12–13)

1931 — Gair Allie — B (SS 1954)

1944 — Jim Bibby — B (P 1978–present)

1959 — Morris Eckhouse — B (author)

### October 30

1866 — Pete Conway — B (P 1889)

1914 — Aldon "Lefty" Wilke — B (P 1941-42, 46)

1917 — Bobby Bragan — B (Manager 1956-57)

1920 — Antonio Ordenana — B (SS 1943)

### October 31

1862 — James "Hardie" Henderson — B (P 1888)

1874 — Harry Smith — B (C 1902-07)

1892 — Ray O'Brien — B (OF 1916)

1924 — Dee Fondy — B (1B 1957)

1973 — Pirates trade catcher Milt May to Houston for pitcher Jerry Reuss. (May is considered the best number two catcher in baseball, but the Pirates are still looking for a top notch starter. After a great 1975 season, Reuss slipped and was traded just before the start of the 1979 season.)

### NOVEMBER 1

1892 — Earl Blackburn — B (C 1912)

1907 — Larry French — B (P 1929-34)

1934 — Howie Goss — B (OF 1962)

1954 — Miguel Dilone — B (OF 1974-77)

1976 — Joe O'Toole and Harding Peterson are named vice presidents following Joe L. Brown's retirement. Peterson is in charge of player personnel and O'Toole is the business administrator and treasurer.

### November 2

1866 — Frank Genins — B (OF-INF 1895)

1956 — Gary Hargis — B (INF 1979-present)

### November 3

1866 — Harry Staley — B (P 1888-89, 91)

1898 — Homer Summa — B (OF 1920)

1917 — Len Gilmore — B (P 1944)

1955 — Bobby Bragan is named Pirates manager, replacing Fred Haney.

# November 4

1877 — Tommy Leach — B (3B-OF 1900–12, 18)

1922 — Eddie Basinski — B (2B 1947)

1925 — Spook Jacobs — B (2B 1956)

1930 — Dick Groat — B (SS 1952, 55–62)

1957 — Carl Mastrocola — B (author)

1973 — Pirates trade pitcher Nellie Briles and infielder Fernando Gonzalez to Kansas City for outfielder-infielder Ed Kirkpatrick and infielder Kurt Bevacqua.

# November 5

1895 — Tom McNamara — B (1922)

1899 — John Wisner — B (P 1919–20)

1908 — Ralph Birkofer — B (P 1933–36)

1909 — Harry Gumbert — B (P 1949–50)

1976 — Manager Chuck Tanner acquired from Oakland for catcher Manny Sanguillen and cash. Tanner replaced the retiring Danny Murtaugh at the helm of the Bucs, and Sanguillen was reacquired a year later.

Pirates sell infielder Tommy Helms to Oakland. He was reacquired before the start of the season.

# November 6

1877 — Tom Sheehan — B (P 1925–26)

1889 — Ed Mensor — B (OF 1912–14)

1925 — Bob Addis — B (OF 1953)

1930 — Pirates trade shortstop Dick Bartell to the Phillies for infielder Tom Thevenow and pitcher Claude Willoughby.

1953 — John Candelaria — B (1975–present)

1974 — A letter written by former Senators' outfielder Sam Rice, opened upon his death, states that he did indeed catch Earl Smith's drive in Game Three of the 1925 World Series.

1976 — Pitcher Tom Carroll is obtained from Cincinnati for pitcher Jim Sadowski.

# November 7

1910 — Bill Brubaker — B (3B 1932–40)

1932 — Dick Stuart — B (1B 1958–62)

## November 8

1870 — Billy Hoffer — B (P 1898–99)

1920 — Wally Westlake — B (OF 1947–51)

1937 — Rex Johnson — B (OF 1964)

## November 9

1868 — Bill Phillips — B (P 1890)

1885 — Gene Moore — B (P 1909–10)

1886 — Nick Maddox — B (P 1907–10)

1897 — Johnny Gooch — B (C 1921–28, Coach 1937–38)

1906 — Fred Brickell — B (P 1926–30)

1933 — George Witt — B (P 1957–61)

## November 10

1867 — Billy Earle — B (C 1892–93)

1890 — Eddie Eayrs — B (P 1913)

1896 — Jimmy Dykes — B (Coach 1959)

## November 11

1891 — Walter "Rabbit" Maranville — B (SS 1921–24)

1899 — Pie Traynor — B (3B 1920–35, 37, Manager 1934–39)

1923 — Lee Howard — B (P 1946–47)

1949 — Dave Augustine — B (OF 1973–74)

## November 12

Nothing of importance happened on this date.

## November 13

1895 — Ray Steineder — B (P 1923–24)

1913 — Jack Hallett — B (P 1942–43, 46)

1915 — Ted Wilks — B (P 1951–52)

1947 — Gene Garber — B (P 1969–70, 72)

1960 — Greg Brown — B (CF 1979–present)

**November 14**

1881 — Fred Carisch — B (C 1903–06)

1881 — Jim Wallace — B (OF 1905)

1893 — Joe Leonard — B (3B 1914)

1898 — Claude Willoughby — B (P 1931)

1947 — Pirates purchase first baseman Eddie Stevens and shortstop Stan Rojek from Brooklyn.

**November 15**

1914 — Maurice Van Robays — B (OF 1939–43, 46)

1928 — Gus Bell — B (OF 1950–52)

**November 16**

1960 — Dick Groat named National League Most Valuable Player. Groat won the League batting title and led the Pirates to their first championship in 33 years.

1966 — Roberto Clemente named National League Most Valuable Player. Clemente passed the 100 RBI mark for the first time in his career and brought the Pirates to within three games of a National League title. He won the award in a close race with Dodger pitcher Sandy Koufax.

**November 17**

1892 — Don Flinn — B (OF 1917)

1913 — Stu Martin — B (2B 1941–42)

1933 — Orlando Pena — B (P 1970)

1947 — Tom Dettore — B (P 1973)

**November 18**

1896 — Bill Hughes — B (P 1921)

1924 — Rocky Nelson — B (1B 1951, 59–61)

Roy Wise — B (P 1944)

1925 — Gene Mauch — B (INF 1947)

1933 — Curt Raydon — B (P 1958)

1943 — Jim Shellenback — B (P 1966–67, 69)

1947 — Pirates trade outfielder Jim Russell, pitcher Al Lyons, and catcher Bill Salkeld to the Boston Braves for first baseman-outfielder Johnny Hopp and second-baseman Danny Murtaugh.

### November 19

1862 — Billy Sunday — B (OF 1888–90)

1905 — Elmer Tutweiler — B (P 1928)

1930 — Joe Morgan — B (Coach 1972)

1938 — Manny Jimenez — B (OF 1967–68)

1945 — Bobby Tolan — B (1B-OF 1977)

1962 — Pirates trade shortstop Dick Groat and pitcher Diomedes Olivo to St. Louis for pitcher Don Cardwell and second-baseman Julio Gotay. (Groat led St. Louis to a pennant in 1964 while Cardwell never lived up to expectations in Pittsburgh.)

### November 20

1880 — George McBride — B (SS 1905)

1887 — John Scheneberg — B (P 1913)

1948 — Pirates purchase pitcher Bob Muncrief from Cleveland.

### November 21

1869 — Billy Clingman — B (INF 1895)

1870 — Alex Beam — B (P 1889)

Freddie Lindstrom — B (OF 1933–34)

1935 — Pirates trade pitcher Claude Passeau and catcher Earl Grace to the Phillies for catcher Al Todd.

1962 — Pitcher John Lamabe and first baseman Dick Stuart are traded to Boston for catcher Jim Pagliaroni and pitcher Don Schwall.

### November 22

1901 — Walt Tauscher — B (P 1928)

1907 — Dick Bartell — B (SS 1927–30)

1934 — Pirates trade pitcher Larry French and outfielder Freddie Lindstrom to the Cubs for pitchers Donnie Bush, Jim Weaver, and outfielder Babe Herman.

1947 — John Morlan — B (P 1973–74)

1954 — Outfielder Roberto Clemente is purchased from the Dodgers AAA farm club in Montreal. (Scout Clyde Sukeforth gets the credit for discovering Clemente who was being hidden from big league scouts so he would not be drafted.)

## November 23

1860 — Chief Zimmer — B (C 1900–02)

1894 — Jesse Petty — B (P 1929–30)

1897 — Clarence Jonnard — B (C 1922)

1922 — Grady Wilson — B (SS 1948)

1971 — Pirate coach Bill Virdon is named manager of the Pirates. Danny Murtaugh retired following the Bucs triumph in the 1971 World Series.

## November 24

1874 — Ed Doheny — B (P 1901-03)

1890 — Ralph Comstock — B (P 1918)

1930 — Bob Friend — B (P 1951–65)

## November 25

1903 — Jim Weaver — B (P 1935–37)

1933 — Jim Waugh — B (P 1952–53)

1934 — Lazaro Naranjo — B (P 1956)

1941 — Mike Ryan — B (C 1974)

## November 26

1873 — James "Gussie" Gannon — B (P 1895)

1897 — Bill Warwick — B (C 1921)

1916 — Bob Elliott — B (OF-3B 1939–46)

1922 — Ben Wade — B (P 1955)

1922 — Joe Muir — B (P 1951–52)

1947 — Richie Hebner — B (3B 1968–76)

1963 — Pirates purchase third baseman Gene Freese from the Reds.

## November 27

1882 — Jim Kane — B (1B 1908)

1884 — Jack Kading — B (1B 1910)

1888 — Marty O'Toole — B (P 1911–14)

1892 — Joe Bush — B (P 1926–27)

1923 — Bob Schultz — B (P 1953)

1937 — Bill Short — B (P 1967)

1939 — Dave Giusti — B (P 1970–76)

## November 28

1870 — Leo Fohl — B (C 1902)

1916 — Max West — B (1B-OF 1948)

1927 — Pirates trade outfielder Kiki Cuyler to the Cubs for catcher Earl Adams and outfielder Floyd Scott.

1962 — Third baseman Don Hoak is traded to the Phillies for outfielder Ted Savage.

1966 — Pitcher Juan Pizarro is purchased from the White Sox.

1967 — Pirates trade pitcher Dennis Ribant to Detroit for pitcher Dave Wickersham.

## November 29

1864 — Billy Sowders — B (P 1889–90)

1884 — Marc Campbell — B (SS 1907)

1910 — Ed Leip — B (2B 1940–42)

1931 — Paul Pettit — B (P 1951, 53)

1950 — Mike Easler — B (OF 1977–present)

## November 30

1870 — Frank Killen — B (P 1893–98)

1901 — Clyde Sukeforth — B (Coach 1951–57)

1972 — Pirates trade outfielder Dick Sharon to Detroit for pitchers Jim Foor and Norm McRae.

# DECEMBER 1

1900 — Eppie Barnes — B (1B 1923–24)

1901 — Mike Cvengros — B (P 1927)

1912 — Cookie Lavagetto — B (2B 1934–36)

1925 — Cal McLish — B (P 1947–48)

1941 — Pirates purchase pitcher Hank Gornicki from the Cardinals.

1965 — Pitcher Joe Gibbon is traded to San Francisco for outfielder Matty Alou and cash. (Alou was a light hitter with the Giants but under the guidance of manager Harry Walker, Matty became the league batting champion in 1966.)

1966 — Pirates trade third baseman Bob Bailey and infielder Gene Michael to Los Angeles for shortstop Maury Wills. (Wills was moved to third base with Pittsburgh but did not lead the Bucs to a pennant as expected, and was drafted by the expansion franchise in Montreal in 1968.)

## December 2

1876 — Roscoe Miller — B (P 1904)

1896 — Sam "Mike" Wilson — B (C 1921)

1934 — Andre Rodgers — B (INF 1965–67)

1940 — Pirates purchase second baseman Stu Martin from the Cardinals.

1946 — Pirates purchase second baseman Eddie Basinski from Brooklyn.

1952 — Pitcher Elroy Face is purchased from the Dodgers AAA farm club in Montreal.

1970 — Pirates trade pitcher Bruce Dal Canton, catcher Jerry May, and shortstop Freddie Patek to Kansas City for pitcher Bob Johnson, shortstop Jackie Hernandez, and catcher Jim Campanis.

1976 — Danny Murtaugh dies of a heart attack at age 59.

## December 3

1925 — Harry Simpson — B (OF 1959)

1945 — Lou Marone — B (P 1969–70)

1952 — Catcher Clyde McCullough is traded to the Cubs for Dick Manville and cash.

1967 — Pirates purchase pitcher Ron Kline from the Twins.

## December 4

1892 — Johnny Meador — B (P 1920)

1936 — Pirates trade second baseman Cookie Lavagetto and pitcher Ralph Birkoffer to Brooklyn for pitcher Ed Brant.

1947 — First baseman Elbie Fletcher is sold to Cleveland.

### December 5

1868 — Frank Bowerman — B (C 1898–99)

1871 — Lew Wiltse — B (P 1901)

1872 — Emerson Hawley — B (P 1895–97)

1973 — Pitcher Luke Walker is purchased by Detroit.

### December 6

1882 — Cozy Dolan — B (OF-INF 1913)

1894 — Walt Mueller — B (OF 1922–24, 26)

1899 — Frank Luce — B (OF 1923)

1939 — Pitcher Bill Swift and cash are traded to the Braves for pitcher Danny Mac-Fayden.

1955 — Honus Wagner dies in Carnegie, Pennsylvania, at age 81.

1966 — Pirates trade pitcher Don Cardwell and outfielder Don Bosch to the Mets for pitcher Dennis Ribant and cash.

### December 7

1847 — James "Deacon" White — B (3B 1889)

1886 — Bobby Schang — B (C 1914–15)

1906 — Tony Piet — B (2B 1931–33)

1915 — Vinnie Smith — B (C 1941, 46)

Johnny Gee — B (P 1939, 41, 43–44)

1930 — Hal W. Smith — B (C 1960–61)

1935 — Don Cardwell — B (P 1963–66)

1936 — Bo Belinsky — B (P 1969)

1973 — Pitcher Bob Johnson is traded to Cleveland for outfielder Brunel Flowers. (Johnson had never lived up to the promise of his first year success with Kansas City. Flowers was highly regarded as a prospect but never played with the Pirates.)

1976 — Pitcher Grant Jackson is obtained from Seattle for shortstop Craig Reynolds and infielder Jimmy Sexton. (Pittsburgh gave up the two prospects for the veteran reliever who has been the Pirates number one lefthanded relief pitcher since joining the club.)

**December 8**

1857 — Jack Rowe — B (SS 1889)

1899 — Pirates purchase 14 Louisville Colonels for $25,000 and four Pittsburgh players. (The purchase was part of the deal which made Barney Dreyfuss owner of the Pirates. Barney's Colonels were about to be dropped from the league so he brought his best players to Pittsburgh before the Louisville team disbanded. Honus Wagner, Fred Clarke, Tommy Leach, and Deacon Phillippe were among the Pirate acquisitions.)

1937 — Jim Pagliaroni — B (C 1963–67)

1939 — Pirates acquire catcher Spud Davis from the Athletics.

1947 — Pittsburgh trades shortstop Billy Cox, infielder Gene Mauch, and pitcher Preacher Roe to Brooklyn for pitchers Hal Gregg, Vic Lombardi, and outfielder Dixie Walker.

1950 — Tim Foli — B (SS 1979–present)

**December 9**

1871 — Joe Kelly — B (OF 1891–92)

1904 — Adam Comorosky — B (OF 1926–33)

1914 — Hank Camelli — B (C 1943–46)

1940 — Pirates trade second baseman Pep Young to the Reds for Lou Riggs.

1948 — George "Doc" Medich — B (P 1976)

1957 — Pitcher Bob Purkey is traded to Cincinnati for pitcher Don Gross.

1964 — Pirates purchase infielder Andre Rogers from the Cubs.

**December 10**

1888 — Stan Gray — B (1B 1912)

1939 — Bob Priddy — B (P 1962, 64)

1940 — Outfielder Paul Waner is released.

1947 — Pitcher Elmer Riddle is purchased from the Reds.

1948 — Pirates trade second baseman Frankie Gustine and pitcher Cal McLish to the Cubs for pitcher Cliff Chambers and catcher Clyde McCullough.

1965 — Pitcher Bob Friend and cash are traded to the Yankees for pitcher Pete Mikkelsen.

1976 — Pirates trade outfielder Richie Zisk and pitcher Silvio Martinez to the White Sox for pitchers Rich Gossage and Terry Forster. (Zisk was planning to become a free agent so he was traded. The Bucs got one year out of Gossage and Forster before they both became free agents, signing with the Yankees and Dodgers respectively. Martinez was traded to St. Louis where he has become one of Baseball's outstanding young hurlers.)

### December 11

1885 — Art Wilson — B (C 1916)

1930 — Eddie O'Brien — B (SS, OF-P 1953, 55–58)

Johnny O'Brien — B (2B-P 1953, 55–58)

1952 — Fred Haney is named Pirate manager, succeeding Billy Meyer.

1975 — Pitcher Doc Medich is acquired from the Yankees for pitchers Dock Ellis, Ken Brett, and second baseman Willie Randolph. (Medich, a Pennsylvania native, was expected to become the ace of the staff after winning 35 games for the Yankees in two years. He has never equaled his early success with New York and spent only one year as a Pirate. Randolph became New York's second baseman and Ellis won 17 games in a comeback year as the Yankees won the American League title.)

### December 12

1864 — John Smith — B (P 1890)

1876 — Joe Rickert — B (OF 1898)

1879 — Mike Mitchell — B (OF 1913–14)

1913 — Pirates trade shortstop Art Butler, first baseman Dots Miller, outfielder-first baseman Cozy Dolan, outfielder Owen Wilson, and pitcher John Henry Johnson to the Cardinals for first baseman Ed Konetchy, third baseman Mike Mowrey, and pitcher Bob Harmon.

1932 — Pirates acquire outfielder Freddie Lindstrom from the Giants in a three team deal also involving the Phillies.

1941 — Shortstop Arky Vaughan is traded to Brooklyn for catcher Babe Phelps, infielder Pete Coscarart, and outfielder Jimmy Wasdell.

1946 — Pirates purchase second baseman Jimmy Bloodworth from the Tigers.

### December 13

1884 — Jim Nealon — B (1B 1906–07)

## December 13 (continued)

1899 — Bill May — B (P 1924)

1904 — Willis "Bill" Windle — B (1B 1928–29)

1935 — Joe Christopher — B (OF 1959–61)

1956 — Dale Berra — B (INF 1977–present)

## December 14

1896 — Charlie Hargreaves — B (C 1928–30)

1923 — Paul LaPalme — B (P 1951–54)

1943 — Jerry May — B (C 1964)

1947 — Dave Hamilton — B (P 1978)

1949 — Pirates purchase outfielder Marv Rickert from the Braves.

Pitcher Frank Papish is purchased from the Indians.

1962 — Pirates sell catcher Don Leppert to the Senators.

1963 — Pitcher Harvey Haddix is sold to Baltimore.

Pitcher Bob Allen is sold to Cleveland.

## December 15

1882 — Jay "Nig" Clarke — B (C 1920)

1905 — Infielder Dave Brain, Del Howard, and V. A. Lindaman are traded to Boston for pitcher Vic Willis.

1924 — Chappie McFarland — B (P 1905)

1946 — Art Howe — B (3B 1974–75)

1959 — Pirates sell catcher Hank Foiles to Kansas City.

## December 16

1876 — Fred Crolius — B (OF 1902)

1886 — Bill Otey — B (P 1907)

1938 — Pirates trade catcher Al Todd, outfielder Johnny Dickshot, and cash to the Braves for catcher Ray Mueller.

1960 — Pitcher Bobby Shantz is acquired from Washington for pitcher Bennie Daniels and first baseman R. C. Stevens.

1967 — Pitcher Jim Bunning is obtained from the Phillies for pitchers Woody Fryman, Bill Laxton, Harold Clem, and infielder Don Money. (Bunning was plagued by injuries as a Pirate and the veteran did not turn out to be the pitcher that would bring a championship to Pittsburgh. Fryman and Money are still going strong.)

### December 17

1880 — Cy Falkenberg — B (P 1903)

1896 — Jim Mattox — B (C 1922–23)

1947 — Charlie Sands — B (C 1971–72)

### December 18

1915 — Johnny Barrett — B (OF 1942–46)

1929 — Gino Cimoli — B (OF 1960–61)

### December 19

1887 — Art Butler — B (SS 1912–13)

1892 — Arnie Stone — B (P 1923–24)

1897 — Billy Zitzman — B (OF 1919)

1898 — Lou Koupal — B (P 1925–26)

1916 — Eddie Yount — B (1939)

1917 — Ray Poat — B (P 1949)

1918 — Tom O'Brien — B (OF 1943–45)

1953 — Pirates sell catcher Mike Sandlock to the Phillies.

### December 20

1876 — Jimmy Williams — B (3B 1899–1900)

1891 — Joe Wilhoit — B (OF 1917)

1904 — Spud Davis — B (C 1940–41, 44–45, Coach 1941–43, 46, Manager 1946)

1904 — Pirates trade first baseman Kitty Bransfield, infielder-outfielder Otto Kreuger, and outfielder Harry McCormick to the Phillies for first baseman Del Howard.

### December 21

1878 — Warren Gill — B (1B 1890)

1898 — Floyd "Pete" Scott — B (OF 1928)

## December 21 (continued)

1930 — Danny Kravitz — B (C 1956–60)

1959 — Pirates trade pitcher Ron Kline to the Cardinals for outfielder Gino Cimoli and pitcher Tom Cheney.

1961 — Shortstop Coot Veal is purchased from Washington.

## December 22

1919 — Al Munchak — B (Coach 1977–present)

1923 — Bob Hall — B (P 1953)

Pirates claim pitcher Jim Bagby, Sr., from the Indians on waivers.

1938 — Matty Alou — B (OF 1966–70)

## December 23

1871 — Sam Leever — B (P 1898–1910)

1883 — Sam Frock — B (P 1909–10)

1943 — Dave May — B (OF 1978)

1946 — Pirates purchase catcher Clyde Klutz from the Cardinals.

## December 24

1858 — Willie Kuehne — B (INF 1887–89)

1877 — George "Del" Howard — B (1B 1905)

1910 — Lloyd Johnson — B (P 1934)

1933 — Bill Bell — B (P 1952, 55)

1950 — Frank Taveras — B (SS 1971–72, 74–79)

## December 25

1855 — Pud Galvin — B (P 1887–89, 91–92)

1899 — Earl Kunz — B (P 1923)

1935 — Al Jackson — B (P 1959, 61)

## December 26

1892 — Lee King — B (OF 1916–18)

1895 — John Hollingsworth — B (P 1922)

1946 — Pirates trade catcher Al Lopez to Cleveland for outfielder Gene Woodling.

1950 — Mario Mendoza — B (SS 1974–78)

### December 27

1867 — William "Ducky" Hemp — B (OF 1890)

1869 — Bill Bishop — B (P 1887)

1912 — Jim Tobin — B (P 1937–39)

1952 — Craig Reynolds — B (SS 1975–76)

1958 — Joe L. Brown is named "Major League Executive of the Year" by *The Sporting News.*

### December 28

1870 — Heinie Peitz — B (C 1905–06)

1915 — Hank Sweeney — B (1B 1944)

1949 — John Milner — B (1B-OF 1978–present)

1953 — Pirates trade infielder Danny O'Connell and cash to Milwaukee for pitchers Max Surkont, Larry LaSalle, Fred Waters, outfielder Sam Jethroe, and outfielder-third baseman Sid Gordon.

1957 — Pittsburgh acquires first baseman Ted Kluszewski from Cincinnati for first baseman Dee Fondy.

### December 29

1895 — Clyde Barnhardt — B (OF 1920–28)

1937 — George Perez — B (P 1958)

1954 — Pirates sell pitcher Bob Schultz to the Tigers.

### December 30

1888 — Ovid Nicholson — B (OF 1912)

1890 — James Voix — B (2B 1912–16)

1943 — Pirates trade catcher Babe Phelps to the Phillies for first baseman Babe Dahlgren.

### December 31

1884 — Bobby Byrne — B (3B 1909–13)

1972 — Roberto Clemente dies in a plane crash en route to Nicaragua from Puerto Rico, with relief supplies for earthquake victims.

## 2. THE PIRATES ALL-TIME ROSTER

### Non-Pitchers

| Player | Pos | Years | Born | Died | Games |
|---|---|---|---|---|---|
| Abbaticchio, Edward J. (Ed) | INF | 1907–10 | 4/15/77 | 1/6/57 | 332 |
| Abrams, Calvin R. (Cal) | OF | 1953–54 | 3/2/24 | | 136 |
| Abstein, William H. (Bill) | 1B | 1906, 09 | 2/2/85 | 4/8/40 | 145 |
| Adams, Earl J. (Sparky) | INF | 1928–29 | 8/26/94 | | 209 |
| Adams, Spencer D. | INF | 1923 | 6/21/97 | 11/25/70 | 25 |
| Addis, Robert G. (Bob) | OF | 1953 | 11/6/25 | | 4 |
| Alexander, Matthew (Matt) | INF-OF | 1978– | 1/30/47 | | 51 |
| Alley, L. Eugene (Gene) | SS | 1963–73 | 7/10/40 | | 1,195 |
| Allie, Gair R. | SS | 1954 | 10/29/31 | | 121 |
| Alou, Mateo R. (Matty) | OF | 1966–70 | 12/22/38 | | 743 |
| Altenberg, Jesse H. | OF | 1916–17 | 1/2/95 | 3/12/73 | 19 |
| Anderson, Alfred W. (Alf) | SS | 1941–42, 46 | | | 126 |
| Anderson, Edward J. (Goat) | OF | 1907 | 1/13/80 | 3/15/23 | 127 |
| Archer, James P. (Jimmy) | C | 1904, 18 | 5/13/83 | 3/29/58 | 31 |
| Armas, Antonio R. (Tony) | OF | 1976 | 7/12/53 | | 4 |
| Atwell, Maurice D. (Toby) | C | 1953–56 | 3/8/24 | | 232 |
| Augustine, David R. (Dave) | OF | 1973–74 | 11/28/49 | | 20 |
| Bailey, Robert S. (Bob) | 3B | 1962–66 | 10/13/42 | | 596 |
| Baird, J. Douglass (Doug) | 3B | 1915–17 | 9/27/91 | 6/13/67 | 316 |
| Baker, Eugene W. (Gene) | 2B | 1957–58 60–61 | 6/15/25 | | 182 |
| Baker, William P. (Bill) | C | 1941–43, 46 | 2/22/11 | | 169 |
| Barbare, Walter L. (Jap) | INF | 1919–20 | 8/11/91 | 10/28/65 | 142 |
| Barbeau, William J. (Jap) | 3B | 1909 | 6/10/82 | 9/10/69 | 91 |
| Barbee, David M. (Dave) | OF | 1932 | 5/7/05 | 7/1/68 | 97 |
| Barkley, Samuel W. (Sam) | 2B | 1887 | 5/19/59 | 4/20/12 | 89 |
| Barnes, Everett D. (Eppie) | 1B | 1923–24 | 12/1/00 | | 2 |
| Barney, Edmund J. (Ed) | OF | 1915–16 | 1/23/90 | 10/4/67 | 77 |
| Barnhart, Clyde L. | OF | 1920–28 | 12/29/95 | | 814 |
| Barnhart, Victor D. (Vic) | SS | 1944–46 | 9/1/22 | | 74 |
| Barone, Richard A. (Dick) | SS | 1960 | 10/13/32 | | 2 |
| Barrett, John J. (Johnny) | OF | 1942–46 | 12/18/15 | 8/17/74 | 564 |
| Bartell, Richard W. (Dick) | SS | 1927–30 | 11/22/07 | | 355 |
| Bartirome, Anthony J. (Tony) | 1B | 1952 | 5/9/32 | | 118 |
| Basgall, Romanus (Monty) | 2B | 1948–49, 51 | 2/8/22 | | 200 |
| Basinski, Edwin F. (Eddie) | 2B | 1947 | 11/4/22 | | 56 |
| Batsch, William G. (Bill) | — | 1916 | 5/18/92 | 12/31/63 | 1 |
| Beard, C. Theodore (Ted) | OF | 1948–52 | 1/7/21 | | 137 |
| Beaumont, Clarence H. (Ginger) | OF | 1899–06 | 7/23/76 | 4/10/56 | 989 |
| Becker, Beals | OF | 1908 | 7/5/86 | 8/16/43 | 20 |
| Beckley, Jacob P. (Jake) | 1B | 1888–89 91–96 | 8/4/67 | 6/25/18 | 928 |
| Beecher, Edward H. (Ed) | OF | 1887 | 7/2/59 | 9/12/35 | 41 |
| Bell, David R. (Gus) | OF | 1950–52 | 11/15/28 | | 391 |
| Bell, Fern L. | OF | 1939–40 | 1/21/13 | | 89 |
| Bennett, J. Fred | OF | 1931 | 3/15/02 | 5/12/57 | 32 |
| Berardino, John | INF | 1950, 52 | 5/1/17 | | 59 |
| Berger, Clarence E. | OF | 1914 | 7/10/94 | 6/30/59 | 6 |
| Berger, John H. (Tun) | INF | 1890–91 | 1867 | 6/11/07 | 147 |

# Non-Pitchers (continued)

| Player | Pos | Years | Born | Died | Games |
|---|---|---|---|---|---|
| Bernier, Carlos R. | OF | 1953 | 1/28/29 | | 105 |
| Berra, Dale A. | INF | 1977– | 12/13/56 | | 117 |
| Berres, Raymond F. (Ray) | C | 1937–40 | 8/21/08 | | 144 |
| Bevacqua, Kurt A. | INF | 1974 | 1/23/47 | | 18 |
| Bierbauer, Louis W. (Lou) | 2B | 1891–96 | 9/28/65 | 2/1/26 | 707 |
| Bigbee, Carson L. | OF | 1916–26 | 3/31/95 | 10/17/64 | 1,147 |
| Bisland, Rivington M. | SS | 1912 | 2/17/90 | 1/11/73 | 1 |
| Blackburn, Earl S. | C | 1912 | 11/1/92 | 8/3/66 | 1 |
| Blackwell, Frederick W. (Fred) | C | 1917–19 | 9/7/95 | | 33 |
| Bloodworth, James H. (Jimmy) | 2B | 1947 | 7/26/17 | | 88 |
| Bockman, J. Edward (Eddie) | 3B | 1948–49 | 7/26/20 | | 149 |
| Boeckel, Norman D. (Tony) | 3B | 1917, 19 | 8/25/94 | 2/16/24 | 109 |
| Booe, Everett L. | OF | 1913 | 9/28/90 | 5/21/69 | 29 |
| Bool, Albert J. (Al) | C | 1930 | 8/24/97 | | 78 |
| Boone, Lute J. (Luke) | 2B | 1918 | 5/6/90 | | 27 |
| Bosch, Donald J. (Don) | OF | 1966 | 7/15/42 | | 3 |
| Bowerman, Frank E. | C | 1898–99 | 12/5/68 | 11/30/48 | 178 |
| Boyland, Dorian S. | 1B-OF | 1978 | 1/6/55 | | 5 |
| Boyle, Edward J. (Eddie) | C | 1896 | 5/8/74 | 2/9/41 | 2 |
| Brain, David L. (Dave) | INF | 1905 | 1/24/79 | 5/25/59 | 85 |
| Brand, Ronald G. (Ron) | C | 1963 | 1/13/40 | | 46 |
| Bransfield, William E. (Kitty) | 1B | 1901–04 | 1/7/75 | 5/1/47 | 507 |
| Brenegan, Olaf S. (Sam) | C | 1914 | 9/1/90 | 4/20/56 | 1 |
| Brenzel, William R. (Bill) | C | 1932 | 3/3/10 | | 9 |
| Brickell, G. Frederick (Fred) | OF | 1926–30 | 11/9/06 | 4/8/61 | 265 |
| Brief, Anthony V. (Bunny) | 1B | 1917 | 7/3/92 | 2/10/63 | 36 |
| Bright, Harry J. | INF | 1958–60 | 9/22/29 | | 59 |
| Brinkman, Charles E. (Chuck) | C | 1974 | 9/16/44 | | 4 |
| Britton, S. Gilbert (Gil) | SS | 1913 | 9/21/91 | | 3 |
| Brodie, Walter S. (Steve) | OF | 1897–98 | 9/11/68 | 10/30/35 | 142 |
| Brottem, Anton C. (Tony) | C | 1921 | 4/30/92 | 8/5/29 | 30 |
| Brown, James R. (Jimmy) | INF | 1946 | 4/25/10 | | 79 |
| Brown, Thomas T. (Tom) | OF | 1887 | 9/21/60 | 10/27/27 | 47 |
| Browne, Earl J. | 1B-OF | 1935–36 | 3/5/11 | | 17 |
| Browning, Louis R. (Pete) | OF | 1891 | 7/17/58 | 9/10/05 | 50 |
| Brubaker, Wilbur L. (Bill) | 3B | 1932–40 | 11/7/10 | | 466 |
| Brye, Stephen R. (Steve) | OF | 1978 | 2/4/49 | | 66 |
| Burgess, Forrest H. (Smokey) | C | 1959–64 | 2/6/27 | | 613 |
| Burke, Edward D. (Eddie) | OF | 1890 | 10/6/66 | 11/26/07 | 31 |
| Burke, James T. (Jimmy) | 3B | 1901–02 | 10/12/74 | 3/26/42 | 74 |
| Burns, Thomas E. (Tom) | 3B | 1892 | 3/30/57 | 3/19/02 | 12 |
| Butler, Arthur E. (Art) | SS | 1912–13 | 12/19/87 | | 125 |
| Byrne, Robert M. (Bobby) | 3B | 1909–13 | 12/31/84 | 12/31/64 | 590 |
| Camelli, Henry R. (Hank) | C | 1943–46 | 12/9/14 | | 107 |
| Campanis, James A. (Jim) | C | 1973 | 2/9/44 | | 6 |
| Campbell, A. Vincent (Vin) | OF | 1910–11 | 1/30/88 | | 139 |
| Campbell, Marc T. | SS | 1907 | 11/29/84 | 2/13/46 | 2 |
| Cannizzaro, Christopher J. (Chris) | C | 1968 | 5/3/38 | | 25 |

## Non-Pitchers (continued)

| Player | Pos | Years | Born | Died | Games |
|---|---|---|---|---|---|
| Capron, Ralph E. | OF | 1912 | 3/11/93 | | 1 |
| Carey, Max G. | OF | 1910–26 | 1/11/90 | 5/20/76 | 2,171 |
| Cargo, Robert J. (Chick) | SS | 1892 | 1871 | 2/21/70 | 2 |
| Carisch, Frederick B. (Fred) | C | 1903–06 | 11/14/81 | | 78 |
| Carr, Lewis S. (Lew) | SS | 1901 | 8/15/72 | 6/15/54 | 9 |
| Carroll, Frederick H. (Fred) | C-OF | 1887–89, 91 | 7/2/64 | 11/7/04 | 381 |
| Carroll, Samuel C. (Cliff) | OF | 1888 | 10/18/59 | 6/12/23 | 5 |
| Cash, David (Dave) | 2B | 1969–73 | 6/11/48 | | 420 |
| Cassady, Harry D. | OF | 1904 | 7/20/80 | | 12 |
| Cassini, Jack D. | — | 1949 | 10/26/19 | | 8 |
| Castiglione, Peter P. | 3B | 1947–53 | 2/13/21 | | 473 |
| Caton, James H. (Buster) | SS | 1917–20 | 7/16/96 | 1/8/48 | 231 |
| Christopher, Joseph O. | OF | 1959–61 | 12/13/35 | | 141 |
| Cimoli, Gino N. | OF | 1960–61 | 12/13/29 | | 122 |
| Clancey, William E. (Bill) | 1B | 1905 | 4/12/78 | 2/10/48 | 56 |
| Clark, William O. (Willie) | 1B | 1898–99 | 8/16/72 | 11/32 | 137 |
| Clark, Fred C. | OF | 1900–11, 13–15 | 10/3/72 | 8/14/60 | 1,442 |
| Clarke, Jay J. (Nig) | C | 1920 | 12/15/82 | 6/15/49 | 3 |
| Clarke, William S. | INF | 1929–30 | 1/24/07 | | 61 |
| Clemente, Roberto W. | OF | 1955–72 | 8/18/34 | 12/31/72 | 2,433 |
| Clements, Edward (Ed) | SS | 1890 | | Deceased | 1 |
| Clendenon, Donn A. | 1B | 1961–68 | 7/15/35 | | 982 |
| Cleveland, Elmer E. | 3B | 1888 | 1862 | 10/8/13 | 30 |
| Clines, Eugene A. | OF | 1970–74 | 10/6/46 | | 452 |
| Clingman, William F. (Billy) | INF | 1895 | 11/21/69 | 5/14/58 | 106 |
| Clymer, Otis E. | OF | 1905–07 | 1/20/80 | 2/27/26 | 129 |
| Cole, Richard R. (Dick) | INF | 1951, 53–56 | 5/6/26 | | 426 |
| Cole, Leonard L. | INF | 1912 | 4/15/86 | 1/6/16 | 12 |
| Coleman, John F. | OF-P | 1887–88, 90 | 3/6/63 | 5/31/22 | 234 |
| Coleman, Robert H. (Bob) | C | 1913–14 | 9/26/90 | 7/16/59 | 97 |
| Collins, James A. (Ripper) | 1B | 1941 | 3/30/04 | 4/16/70 | 49 |
| Collins, John E. (Zip) | OF | 1914–15 | 5/2/92 | | 155 |
| Colman, Frank L. | OF | 1942–46 | 3/2/18 | | 244 |
| Comorosky, Adam A. | OF | 1926–33 | 12/9/04 | 3/2/51 | 617 |
| Compton, Albert S. (Pete) | OF | 1916 | 9/28/89 | 3/15/78 | 5 |
| Conroy, William E. (Wid) | SS | 1889 | 10/30/66 | 12/6/59 | 99 |
| Coogan, Dale, R | 1B | 1950 | 8/14/30 | | 53 |
| Cooley, Duff C. | OF | 1900 | 3/29/73 | 8/9/37 | 66 |
| Cooper, W. Walker | C | 1954 | 1/8/15 | | 14 |
| Corcoran, John A. | INF | 1954 | 1873 | 11/1/01 | 6 |
| Corkhill, John S. | OF | 1891–92 | 4/11/58 | 4/4/21 | 109 |
| Coscarart, Peter J. (Pete) | 2B | 1942–46 | 6/16/13 | | 531 |
| Costello, Daniel F. (Dan) | OF | 1914–16 | 9/9/95 | 3/26/36 | 152 |
| Cox, William R. (Billy) | SS | 1941, 46–47 | 8/29/19 | | 163 |
| Crandall, Delmar W. (Del) | C | 1965 | 3/5/30 | | 60 |
| Crane, Samuel N. (Sam) | 2B | 1890 | 1/2/54 | 6/26/25 | 22 |
| Crolius, Fred J. | OF | 1902 | 12/16/76 | 8/25/60 | 9 |
| Cronin, Joseph E. (Joe) | 2B | 1926–27 | 10/12/06 | | 50 |
| Cross, Montford M. (Monte) | SS | 1894–95 | 8/31/69 | 6/21/34 | 121 |
| Curtis, Eugene (Gene) | OF | 1903 | 5/7/77 | 1/2/18 | 5 |
| Cutshaw, George W. | 2B | 1918–21 | 7/29/87 | 8/22/73 | 494 |

## Non-Pitchers (continued)

| Player | Pos | Years | Born | Died | Games |
|---|---|---|---|---|---|
| Cuyler, Hazen S. (Kiki) | OF | 1921–27 | 8/30/99 | 2/11/50 | 625 |
| Dahlgren, Ellsworth T. (Babe) | 1B | 1944–45 | 6/15/12 | | 302 |
| Dalrymple, Abner F. | OF | 1887–88 | 9/9/57 | 1/25/39 | 149 |
| Daubert, Harry J. (Jake) | — | 1915 | 8/7/94 | 10/9/24 | 1 |
| Davalillo, Victor J. (Vic) | OF | 1971–73 | 7/31/39 | | 275 |
| Davis, Alfonso D. (Lefty) | OF | 1901–02 | 2/4/75 | 2/7/19 | 146 |
| Davis, Harry H. | 1B | 1896–98 | 7/10/73 | 8/11/47 | 173 |
| Davis, R. Brandon (Brandy) | OF | 1952–53 | 9/10/28 | | 67 |
| Davis, Ronald E. (Ron) | OF | 1969 | 10/21/41 | | 62 |
| Davis, Virgil L. (Spud) | C | 1940–41 44–45 | 12/20/04 | | 233 |
| Debus, Adam J. | INF | 1917 | 10/7/92 | | 38 |
| Decker, E. Harry | C | 1890 | 9/3/54 | Deceased | 92 |
| Delahanty, Thomas J. (Tom) | 3B | 1896 | 3/9/72 | 1/10/51 | 1 |
| Del Greco, Robert G. | OF | 1952, 56 | 4/7/33 | | 113 |
| DeMontreville, Eugene N. | SS | 1894 | 3/26/74 | 2/18/35 | 2 |
| Dickshot, John O. | OF | 1936–38 | 1/24/10 | | 120 |
| Diehl, Ernest G. (Ernie) | OF-SS | 1903–04 | 10/2/74 | 11/6/58 | 13 |
| Dillinger, Robert B. (Bob) | 3B | 1950–51 | 9/17/18 | | 70 |
| Dillon, Frank E. (Pop) | 1B | 1899–00 | 10/17/73 | 9/12/31 | 35 |
| Dilone, Miquel A. | OF | 1974–77 | 11/1/54 | | 75 |
| DiMaggio, Vincent P. | OF | 1940–44 | 9/16/12 | | 670 |
| Dodd, Ona M. | 3B | 1912 | 10/14/86 | 3/31/29 | 5 |
| Dolan, Alvin J. | OF-INF | 1913 | 12/6/82 | 12/10/58 | 35 |
| Donahue, John A. | C-1B | 1900–01 | 7/13/79 | 7/19/13 | 5 |
| Donely, James B. (Jim) | 3B | 1897 | 7/19/65 | 3/5/15 | 44 |
| Donlin, Michael J. (Mike) | OF | 1912 | 5/30/78 | 9/24/33 | 77 |
| Donovan, Patrick J. (Patsy) | OF | 1892–99 | 3/16/65 | 12/25/53 | 1,029 |
| Dorsey, Jeremiah (Jerry) | OF | 1911 | 1885 | | 2 |
| Dugas, Augustin J. (Gus) | OF | 1930, 32 | 3/24/07 | | 64 |
| Duncan, Louis B. (Pat) | OF | 1915 | 10/6/93 | 7/17/60 | 3 |
| Dunlap, Frederick C. (Fred) | 2B | 1888–90 | 5/21/59 | 12/1/02 | 220 |
| Durbin, Blaine A. (Kid) | — | 1909 | 7/10/86 | | 1 |
| Dusak, Ervin F. (Erv) | OF | 1951–52 | 7/29/20 | | 41 |
| Dyer, Don R. (Duffy) | C | 1975–78 | 8/15/45 | | 269 |
| Eagan, Charles E. (Truck) | INF | 1901 | 8/10/77 | 3/19/49 | 4 |
| Eagan, William (Bad Bill) | 2B | 1898 | 6/1/69 | 2/14/05 | 19 |
| Earle, William M. (Billy) | C | 1892–93 | 11/10/67 | 5/30/46 | 32 |
| Easler, Michael A. (Mike) | OF | 1977– | 11/29/50 | | 64 |
| Edington, J. Frank (Stump) | OF | 1912 | 7/4/91 | 11/29/69 | 15 |
| Edwards, Michael L. (Mike) | 2B | 1977 | 8/17/52 | | 7 |
| Ellam, Roy B. | SS | 1918 | 2/8/86 | 10/28/48 | 26 |
| Elliot, Lawrence L. (Larry) | OF | 1962–63 | 3/5/38 | | 12 |
| Elliott, Robert I. (Bob) | OF, 3B | 1939–46 | 11/26/16 | 5/4/66 | 1,047 |
| Ely, Frederick W. (Bones) | SS | 1896–01 | 6/7/63 | 1/10/52 | 742 |
| Engle, Charles (Charlie) | INF | 1930 | 8/27/03 | | 67 |
| Ens, Jewel W. | INF | 1922–25 | 8/24/89 | 1/17/50 | 67 |
| Epps, Abrey L. | C | 1935 | 3/3/12 | | 1 |
| Falsey, Peter J. (Pete) | — | 1914 | 4/24/91 | | 3 |

| Player | Pos | Years | Born | Died | Games |
|---|---|---|---|---|---|
| Farmer, Floyd H. (Jack) | INF-OF | 1916 | 7/14/92 | 5/21/70 | 55 |
| Farmer, William (Bill) | C | 1888 | | Deceased | 2 |
| Farrell, Charles A. (Duke) | 3B | 1892 | 8/31/66 | 2/15/25 | 152 |
| Fernandes, Edward P. (Ed) | C | 1940 | 3/11/18 | 11/27/68 | 28 |
| Fernandez, Frolian (Nanny) | 3B | 1950 | 10/25/18 | | 65 |
| Fields, John J. (Jocko) | OF-C | 1887–89, 91 | 10/20/64 | 10/14/50 | 186 |
| Finney, Harold W. (Hal) | C | 1931–34, 36 | 7/7/05 | | 123 |
| Fischer, William C. (Bill) | C | 1916–17 | 3/2/91 | 9/4/45 | 137 |
| Fisher, Wilbur M. | — | 1916 | 7/18/94 | | 1 |
| Fitzgerald, Edward R. (Ed) | C | 1948–53 | 5/21/24 | | 295 |
| Flagstead, Ira J. | OF | 1929–30 | 9/22/93 | 3/13/40 | 70 |
| Flanagan, James P. (Steamer) | OF | 1905 | 4/20/81 | 4/21/47 | 7 |
| Fleming, Leslie H. (Les) | 1B | 1949 | 8/7/15 | | 24 |
| Fletcher, Elburt P. (Elbie) | 1B | 1939–43 46–47 | 3/18/16 | | 916 |
| Flinn, Don R. | OF | 1917 | 11/17/92 | 3/9/59 | 14 |
| Flynn, John A. | 1B | 1910–11 | 9/7/83 | 3/23/35 | 129 |
| Fohl, Leo A. (Lee) | C | 1902 | 11/28/70 | 10/30/65 | 1 |
| Foiles, Henry L. (Hank) | C | 1956–59 | 6/10/29 | | 345 |
| Foli, Timothy J. (Tim) | SS | 1979– | 12/8/50 | | 133 |
| Fondy, Dee V. | 1B | 1957 | 10/31/24 | | 95 |
| Fox, George (Paddy) | 1B | 1899 | | Deceased | 13 |
| Freese, Eugene L. (Gene) | 3B | 1955–58 64–65 | 1/8/34 | | 472 |
| Freese, George W. | 3B | 1955 | 9/12/26 | | 51 |
| Fregosi, James L. (Jim) | INF | 1977–78 | 4/4/42 | | 56 |
| Ganley, Robert S. (Bob) | OF | 1905–06 | 4/23/75 | 10/10/45 | 169 |
| Ganzel, John H. | 1B | 1898 | 4/7/75 | 1/14/59 | 15 |
| Garagiola, Joseph H. (Joe) | C | 1951–53 | 2/12/26 | | 217 |
| Garms, Debs G. | OF-3B | 1940–41 | | | 186 |
| Garner, Phillip M. (Phil) | INF | 1977– | 4/30/48 | | 457 |
| Gaston, Clarence E. | OF | 1978 | 3/17/44 | | 1 |
| Geary, Eugene F. J. (Huck) | SS | 1942–43 | 1/22/17 | | 55 |
| Genins, C. Frank | OF-INF | 1895 | 11/2/66 | 9/30/22 | 73 |
| Gerber, Walter H. (Wally) | INF | 1914–15 | 8/18/91 | 6/19/51 | 73 |
| Gertenrich, Louis W. | OF | 1903 | 5/4/75 | 10/23/33 | 1 |
| Getz, Gustave (Gus) | OF-3B | 1918 | 8/3/89 | 5/28/69 | 7 |
| Gibson, George C. | C | 1905–16 | 7/22/80 | 1/25/67 | 1,174 |
| Gilbert, Harry | 2B | 1890 | | | 2 |
| Gilbert, John G. | SS | 1890 | 1/8/64 | 11/12/03 | 2 |
| Gill, Warren D. | 1B | 1908 | 12/21/78 | 11/26/52 | 27 |
| Gillen, Samuel (Sam) | SS | 1893 | 1870 | 5/13/05 | 3 |
| Gionfriddo, Albert F. (Al) | OF | 1944–47 | 3/8/22 | | 191 |
| Glasscock, John W. | SS | 1893–94 | 7/22/59 | 2/24/47 | 152 |
| Gleason, William P. (Bill) | 2B | 1916–17 | 9/8/93 | 1/9/57 | 14 |
| Goggin, Charles F. (Chuck) | 2B | 1972–73 | 7/7/45 | | 6 |
| Gonder, Jesse L. | C | 1966–67 | 1/20/36 | | 81 |
| Gonzalez, J. Fernando | INF | 1972–73 77–78 | 6/19/50 | | 130 |
| Gooch, John B. | C | 1921–28 | 11/9/97 | 5/15/75 | 551 |

| Player | Pos | Years | Born | Died | Games |
|--------|-----|-------|------|------|-------|
| Gordon, Sidney (Sid) | OF-3B | 1954–55 | 8/13/17 | 6/17/75 | 147 |
| Goss, Howard W. (Howie) | OF | 1962 | 11/1/34 | | 89 |
| Gotay, Julio S. | 2B | 1963–64 | 6/9/39 | | 7 |
| Grace, R. Earl | C | 1931–35 | 2/24/07 | | 427 |
| Grantham, George F. | 1B-2B | 1925–31 | 5/20/00 | 3/16/54 | 913 |
| Gray, James D. (Reddy) | INF | 1890, 93 | | Deceased | 3 |
| Gray, Stanley O. (Stan) | 1B | 1912 | 12/10/88 | 10/11/64 | 6 |
| Gray, William (Bill) | OF | 1903 | 1/4/72 | 9/7/33 | 2 |
| Greenberg, Henry B. (Hank) | 1B | 1947 | 1/1/11 | | 125 |
| Grey, William T. (Bill) | 3B | 1898 | 4/15/71 | 12/8/32 | 137 |
| Grimm, Charles J. (Charlie) | 1B | 1919–24 | 8/28/98 | | 768 |
| Groat, Richard M. (Dick) | SS | 1952, 55–62 | 11/4/30 | | 1,258 |
| Groh, Henry K. (Heinie) | 3B | 1927 | 9/18/89 | 8/22/68 | 14 |
| Grosskloss, Howard H. | 2B | 1930–32 | 4/10/08 | | 72 |
| Guintini, Benjamin J. (Ben) | OF | 1946 | 1/13/20 | | 2 |
| Gustine, Frank W. (Frankie) | 2B-3B | 1939–48 | 2/20/20 | | 1,176 |
| Gutteridge, Donald J. | — | 1948 | 6/19/12 | | 4 |
| Haas, George W. | OF | 1925 | 10/15/03 | 6/30/74 | 4 |
| Haeffner, William B. (Bill) | C | 1920 | 7/18/94 | | 54 |
| Hafey, Daniel A. (Bud) | OF | 1935–36 | 8/6/12 | | 97 |
| Hairston, Jerry | OF | 1977 | 2/16/52 | | 51 |
| Hall, Richard W. (Dick) | OF-P | 1952–57, 59 | 9/27/30 | | 211 |
| Hall, William L. (Bill) | C | 1954, 56, 58 | 7/30/28 | | 57 |
| Halliday, Newton (Newt) | 1B | 1916 | 1897 | | 1 |
| Hallman, William H. (Bill) | OF | 1906–07 | 3/15/76 | 4/23/50 | 117 |
| Hamlin, Kenneth L. (Ken) | SS | 1957, 59 | 5/18/35 | | 5 |
| Hammond, Walter C. (Jack) | 2B | 1922 | 2/26/92 | 3/4/42 | 9 |
| Handley, Lee E. | 2B-3B | 1937–41, 44–46 | 7/31/13 | 4/8/70 | 843 |
| Hanlon, Edward H. (Ned) | OF | 1889, 91 | 8/22/57 | 4/14/37 | 235 |
| Hargis, Gary L. | INF | 1979– | 11/2/56 | | 1 |
| Hargreaves, Charles R. | C | 1928–30 | 12/14/96 | | 192 |
| Harris, Joseph (Joe) | 1B | 1927–28 | 5/20/91 | 12/10/59 | 145 |
| Hartman, Frederick O. | 3B | 1894 | 4/25/68 | 11/11/38 | 49 |
| Heard, Charles H. (Charlie) | OF-P | 1890 | 1/30/72 | 2/20/45 | 12 |
| Hebner, Richard J. (Richie) | 3B | 1968–76 | 11/26/47 | | |
| Hecker, Guy J. | 1B-P | 1890 | 4/3/56 | 12/4/38 | 86 |
| Helms, Thomas V. (Tommy) | | 1976–77 | 5/5/41 | | 77 |
| Hemp, William H. (Ducky) | OF | 1890 | 12/27/67 | 3/6/23 | 21 |
| Hemsley, Ralston B. (Rollie) | C | 1928–31 | 6/24/07 | 7/31/72 | 252 |
| Henley, Gail C. | OF | 1954 | 10/15/28 | | 14 |
| Herman, Floyd C. (Babe) | OF | 1935 | 6/26/03 | | 26 |
| Herman, William J. (Billy) | 2B | 1947 | 7/7/09 | | 15 |
| Hermanski, Eugene V. (Gene) | OF | 1953 | 5/11/20 | | 41 |
| Hernandez, Jacinto (Jackie) | SS | 1971–73 | 9/11/40 | | 214 |
| Hillebrand, Homer H. | 1B-P | 1905–06, 08 | 10/10/79 | 1/20/74 | 47 |
| Hiller, Charles J. (Chuck) | 2B | 1968 | 10/1/35 | | 11 |
| Hillis, Malcom D. (Mack) | 2B | 1928 | 7/23/01 | 6/16/61 | 11 |
| Hinchman, William W. (Bill) | OF | 1915–18, 20 | 4/4/83 | 2/21/63 | 445 |
| Hines, Paul A. | OF | 1890 | 3/1/52 | 7/10/35 | 31 |
| Hoak, Donald A. (Don) | 3B | 1959–62 | 2/5/28 | 10/9/69 | 576 |

## Non-Pitchers (continued)

| Player | Pos | Years | Born | Died | Games |
|---|---|---|---|---|---|
| Hoffmeister, Jesse H. | 3B | 1897 | | Deceased | 48 |
| Hofman, Arthur F. (Solly) | OF | 1903, 12–13 | 10/29/82 | 3/10/56 | 48 |
| Hood, Wallace J. (Wally) | OF | 1920 | 2/9/95 | 5/2/65 | 2 |
| Hopkins, Michael J. (Mike) | C | 1902 | | | 1 |
| Hopp, John L. (Johnny) | 1B-OF | 1948–50 | 7/18/16 | | 331 |
| Howard, George E. (Del) | 1B | 1905 | 12/24/77 | 12/24/56 | 123 |
| Howe, Arthur H. (Art) | 3B | 1974–75 | 12/15/46 | | 92 |
| Howell, Homer E. (Dixie) | C | 1947 | 4/24/19 | | 76 |
| Howerton, William R. (Bill) | OF | 1951–52 | 12/12/21 | | 93 |
| Hunter, Frederick C. (Newt) | 1B | 1911 | 1/5/80 | 10/26/63 | 65 |
| Hyatt, R. Hamilton (Ham) | OF-1B | 1909–10, 12-14 | 11/1/84 | 9/63 | 305 |
| Ingram, Melvin D. (Mel) | — | 1929 | 7/4/04 | | 3 |
| Jackson, Charles H. | OF | 1917 | 2/7/94 | 5/27/68 | 41 |
| Jacobs, Forrest V. (Spook) | 2B | 1956 | 11/4/25 | | 11 |
| Janowicz, Victor F. (Vic) | C-3B | 1953–54 | 2/26/30 | | 83 |
| Jarvis, Leroy G. (Roy) | C | 1946–47 | 6/7/26 | | 20 |
| Jensen, Forrest D. (Woody) | OF | 1931–39 | 8/11/07 | | 738 |
| Jeter, John | OF | 1969–70 | 10/24/44 | | 113 |
| Jethroe, Samuel (Sam) | OF | 1954 | 1/20/22 | | 2 |
| Jiminez, Manuel E. (Manny) | OF | 1967–68 | 11/19/38 | | 116 |
| Johnston, Rex D. | OF | 1964 | 11/8/37 | | 14 |
| Johnston, Wheeler R. (Doc) | 1B | 1915–16 | 9/9/87 | 2/17/61 | 161 |
| Jones, Coburn D. (Cobe) | SS | 1928–29 | 8/21/07 | 6/3/69 | 27 |
| Jonnard, Clarence J. | C | 1922 | 11/23/97 | | 10 |
| Jordan, Michael H. (Mike) | OF | 1890 | | Deceased | 37 |
| Judnich, Walter F. (Walt) | OF | 1949 | 1/24/17 | 7/12/71 | 10 |
| Juelich, John W. (Red) | 2B | 1939 | 9/20/16 | 12/25/70 | 17 |
| Kading, John F. (Jack) | 1B | 1910 | 11/27/84 | 6/2/64 | 8 |
| Kafora, Frank J. (Jake) | C | 1913–14 | 10/16/89 | 3/23/28 | 22 |
| Kalin, Frank B. | OF | 1940 | 10/3/17 | | 3 |
| Kane, James J. (Jim) | 1B | 1908 | 11/27/82 | 10/2/47 | 55 |
| Keene, William B. (Bill) | 1B | 1911 | 1891 | | 6 |
| Keliher, Maurice M. (Mickey) | 1B | 1911–12 | 1/11/90 | 9/5/30 | 4 |
| Kelly, Joseph J. (Joe) | OF | 1891–92 | 12/9/71 | 8/14/43 | 56 |
| Kelly, George L. | 1B | 1917 | 9/10/95 | | 8 |
| Kelly, James R. (Jim) | OF | 1914 | 2/1/90 | | 32 |
| Kelly, Joseph H. (Joe) | OF | 1914 | 9/23/89 | 8/16/77 | 141 |
| Kelly, William J. (Bill) | C | 1911–13 | 1889 | | 102 |
| Kelsey, George W. | C | 1907 | | | 2 |
| Kelty, John E. J. | OF | 1890 | 1867 | Deceased | 59 |
| Kilhullen, Joseph I. (Pat) | C | 1914 | 5/3/88 | 11/2/22 | 1 |
| Kiner, Ralph M. | OF | 1946–53 | 9/27/22 | | 1,095 |
| King, Edward Lee | OF | 1916–18 | 12/26/92 | 9/16/67 | 155 |
| Kinslow, Thomas F. (Tom) | C | 1895 | 1/12/66 | 2/22/01 | 19 |
| Kirkpatrick, Edward L. (Ed) | 1B-OF | 1974–77 | 10/8/44 | | 309 |
| Kluszewski, Theodore B. (Ted) | 1B | 1958–59 | 9/10/24 | | 160 |
| Kluttz, Clyde F. | C | 1947–48 | 12/12/17 | | 167 |

| Player | Pos | Years | Born | Died | Games |
|--------|-----|-------|------|------|-------|
| Knabe, Franz Otto | 3B | 1905, 16 | 6/12/84 | 5/17/61 | 3 |
| Knox, Clifford H. (Cliff) | C | 1924 | 1/7/02 | 9/24/65 | 6 |
| Koback, Nicholas N. (Nick) | C | 1953–55 | 7/19/35 | | 16 |
| Kolb, Gary A. | OF–C | 1968–69 | 3/13/40 | | 103 |
| Kommers, Frederick R. (Fred) | OF | 1913 | 3/31/86 | 6/14/43 | 40 |
| Konetchy, Edward J. (Ed) | 1B | 1914 | 9/3/85 | 5/27/47 | 154 |
| Kopacz, George F. | 1B | 1970 | 2/26/41 | | 10 |
| Koshorek, Clement J. (Clem) | INF | 1952–53 | 6/20/26 | | 99 |
| Kravitz, Daniel (Danny) | C | 1956–60 | 12/21/30 | | 156 |
| Krueger, Arthur W. (Otto) | INF-OF | 1903–04 | 9/17/76 | 2/20/61 | 166 |
| Kuehne, William J. (Willie) | INF | 1887–89 | 10/24/58 | 10/27/21 | 337 |
| Kuhns, Charles B. (Charlie) | 3B | 1897 | | 7/15/22 | 1 |
| | | | | | |
| Lacy, Leondaus (Lee) | OF | 1979- | 4/10/48 | | 84 |
| Ladd, A. C. Hiram (Hi) | OF | 1898 | 2/9/70 | 5/7/48 | 1 |
| Lake, Frederick L. (Fred) | 1B | 1898 | 10/16/66 | 11/24/31 | 5 |
| Lally, Daniel J. (Bud) | OF | 1891 | 8/12/67 | 4/14/36 | 41 |
| Lanier, Lorenzo (Rimp) | — | 1971 | 10/19/48 | | 6 |
| LaRoque, Samuel H. (Sam) | 2B | 1890-91 | 2/26/64 | Deceased | 1 |
| Latimer, Clifford W. (Tacks) | C | 1900 | 4/12/33 | 4/24/36 | 4 |
| Lavagetto, Harry A. (Cookie) | 2B | 1934-36 | 12/1/12 | | 225 |
| Layne, Herman | OF | 1927 | 2/13/01 | 8/27/73 | 11 |
| Leach, Thomas W. (Tommy) | 3B-OF | 1900-12, 18 | 11/4/77 | 9/29/69 | 157 |
| Leahy, Thomas J. (Tom) | OF | 1897 | 6/2/69 | 6/12/51 | 24 |
| Lee, Clifford W. (Cliff) | C | 1919-20 | 8/4/69 | | 79 |
| Leip, Edgar E. (Ed) | 2B | 1940-42 | 11/29/10 | | 21 |
| LeJeune, Sheldon A. (Larry) | OF | 1915 | 7/22/85 | 4/21/52 | 18 |
| Leonard, Joseph H. (Joe) | 3B | 1914 | 11/14/93 | 5/4/20 | 53 |
| Leppert, Donald G. (Don) | C | 1961-62 | 10/19/31 | | 67 |
| Lezotte, Abel | 1B | 1896 | 4/13/70 | Deceased | 7 |
| Lindstrom, Frederick C. | OF | 1933-34 | 11/21/05 | | 235 |
| Linton, Claud C. (Bob) | C | 1929 | 4/18/02 | | 17 |
| Lobert, John B. (Hans) | 3B | 1903 | 10/18/81 | 9/14/68 | 5 |
| Logan, John (Johnny) | INF | 1961-63 | 3/23/27 | | 152 |
| Lois, Alberto | OF | 1978- | 5/6/56 | | 14 |
| Long, R. Dale | 1B | 1951, 55-57 | 2/6/26 | | 296 |
| Lopez, Alfonso R. (Al) | C | 1940-46 | 8/20/08 | | 656 |
| Lovelace, Grover T. | — | 1922 | 9/8/98 | | 1 |
| Lowe, Robert L. (Bobby) | 2B | 1904 | 7/10/68 | 12/8/51 | 1 |
| Luce, Frank E. | OF | 1923 | 12/6/99 | 2/3/42 | 9 |
| Luplow, Alvin D. (Al) | OF | 1967 | 3/13/89 | | 55 |
| Lynch, Gerald T. (Jerry) | OF | 1954-56, 63-66 | 7/17/30 | | 544 |
| Lyons, Dennis P. A. | 3B | 1893-94 96-97 | 3/12/66 | 1/2/29 | 357 |
| Lytle, Edward B. (Pop) | OF | 1890 | 3/10/62 | 12/21/50 | 15 |
| | | | | | |
| Macha, Kenneth E. (Ken) | INF | 1974, 77-78 | 9/29/50 | | 69 |
| Mack, Cornelius A. (Connie) | C | 1891-96 | 2/22/62 | 2/8/56 | 325 |
| Madden, Eugene (Gene) | — | 1916 | 6/5/90 | 4/6/49 | 1 |
| Madison, Arthur M. (Art) | INF | 1899 | 1/14/71 | 1/27/33 | 42 |

# Non-Pitchers (continued)

| Player | Pos | Years | Born | Died | Games |
|---|---|---|---|---|---|
| Madlock, Bill Jr. | 3B | 1979 | 1/12/51 | | 85 |
| Maggert, Harl V. | OF | 1907 | 2/13/83 | 1/7/63 | 3 |
| Maguire, Jack | OF | 1951 | 2/5/25 | | 8 |
| Mangan, James D. | C | 1952, 54 | 9/24/29 | | 25 |
| Mangual, Angel L. | OF | 1969 | 3/19/47 | | 6 |
| Manush, Henry E. (Heinie) | OF | 1938-39 | 7/20/01 | 5/12/71 | 25 |
| Maranville, Walter J. V. | SS | 1921-24 | 11/11/91 | 1/5/54 | 601 |
| Marquez, Luis A. | OF | 1954 | 10/28/25 | | 14 |
| Marshall, Joseph H. (Joe) | INF-OF | 1903 | | 1932 | 10 |
| Marshall, R. James (Jim) | 1B | 1962 | 5/25/32 | | 55 |
| Martin, Stuart M. (Stu) | 2B | 1941-42 | 11/17/13 | | 130 |
| Martinez, Jose | INF | 1969-70 | 7/26/42 | | 96 |
| Masi, Phillip S. (Phil) | C | 1949 | 1/6/17 | | 48 |
| Mattox, James P. (Jim) | C | 1922-23 | 12/17/96 | | 51 |
| Mauch, Eugene W. (Gene) | INF | 1947 | 11/18/25 | | 16 |
| Maul, Albert J. (Al) | OF-1B | 1888-89, 91 | 10/9/65 | 5/3/58 | 189 |
| Maxvill, C. Dallas (Dal) | SS | 1973-74 | 2/18/39 | | 82 |
| May, David L. (Dave) | OF | 1978 | 12/23/43 | | |
| May, Jerry L. | C | 1964-70 | 12/14/43 | | 417 |
| May, Milton S. (Milt) | C | 1970-73 | 8/1/50 | | 212 |
| Mazeroski, William S. (Bill) | 2B | 1956-72 | 9/5/36 | | 2,163 |
| McAuley, James E. (Ike) | SS | 1914-16 | 8/19/93 | 4/6/28 | 24 |
| McBride, George F. | SS | 1905 | 11/20/80 | 7/2/73 | 27 |
| McCarthy, Alexander G. | INF | 1910-17 | 5/12/88 | | 372 |
| McCarthy, John A. (Jack) | OF | 1898-99 | 3/26/69 | 9/11/31 | 275 |
| McClanahan, Peter (Pete) | — | 1931 | 10/24/06 | | 7 |
| McCormick, Harry E. (Moose) | OF | 1904 | 2/28/81 | 7/9/62 | 66 |
| McCreery, Thomas L. (Tom) | OF | 1898-00 | 10/19/74 | 7/3/41 | 214 |
| McCullough, Clyde E. | C | 1949-52 | 3/4/17 | | 352 |
| McFarlane, Orlando J. | C | 1962, 64 | 6/28/38 | | 45 |
| McGinn, Frank J. | OF | 1890 | | 11/19/97 | 1 |
| McInnis, John P. (Stuffy) | 1B | 1925-26 | 9/19/90 | 2/16/60 | 106 |
| McKechnie, William B. (Bill) | INF | 1907, 10-12 18, 20 | 8/7/86 | 10/29/65 | 368 |
| McKinnon, Alexander J. | 1B | 1887 | 8/14/56 | 7/24/87 | 48 |
| McNamara, Thomas H. (Tom) | — | 1922 | 11/5/95 | 5/5/74 | 1 |
| McNertney, Gerald E. (Jerry) | C | 1973 | 8/7/36 | | 9 |
| McShannic, Peter R. (Pete) | 3B | 1888 | 3/20/64 | 11/30/46 | 26 |
| Meier, Arthur E. (Dutch) | OF | 1906 | 3/30/79 | | 82 |
| Mejias, Roman G. | OF | 1955, 57-61 | 8/9/30 | | 308 |
| Mendoza, Mario A. | SS | 1974-78 | 12/26/50 | | 324 |
| Mensor, Edward E. | OF | 1912-14 | 11/6/89 | | 127 |
| Merewether, Arthur F. (Art) | — | 1922 | 7/7/02 | | 1 |
| Merritt, George W. | OF-P | 1901-03 | 4/14/80 | 2/21/38 | 15 |
| Merritt, William H. (Bill) | C | 1894-97 | 7/30/70 | 11/17/37 | 242 |
| Merson, John W. (Jack) | 2B | 1951-52 | 1/17/22 | | 124 |
| Metkovich, George M. | OF-1B | 1951-53 | 10/8/21 | | 271 |
| Michael, Gene E. | SS | 1966 | 6/2/38 | | 30 |
| Miller, George F. (Doggie) | C | 1887-93 | 8/15/64 | 4/6/09 | 757 |
| Miller, Jacob G. (Jake) | OF | 1922 | 2/5/97 | | 3 |
| Miller, John B. (Dots) | 2B, 1B | 1909-13 | 9/9/86 | 9/5/23 | 710 |

## Non-Pitchers (continued)

| Player | Pos | Years | Born | Died | Games |
|--------|-----|-------|------|------|-------|
| Miller, Raymond P. (Ray) | 1B | 1917 | 6/9/88 | 4/7/27 | 6 |
| Miller, Ward T. | OF | 1909 | 7/5/84 | 9/4/58 | 15 |
| Miller, William | OF | 1902 | | | 1 |
| Milner, John D. | OF-1B | 1978- | 12/28/49 | | 236 |
| Mitchell, Michael F. (Mike) | OF | 1913-14 | 12/12/79 | 7/16/61 | 130 |
| Moeller, Daniel E. (Danny) | OF | 1907-08 | 3/23/85 | 4/14/51 | 47 |
| Mokan, John L. (Johnny) | OF | 1921-22 | 9/23/95 | | 50 |
| Mollwitz, Frederick A. | 1B | 1917-19 | 6/16/90 | 10/3/67 | 211 |
| Montemayor, Felipe A. | OF | 1953, 55 | 2/7/30 | | 64 |
| Moore, G. Edward (Eddie) | 2B | 1923-26 | 1/18/99 | | 263 |
| Moreno, Omar E. | OF | 1975- | 10/24/53 | | 521 |
| Moryn, Walter J. (Walt) | OF | 1961 | 6/12/26 | | 40 |
| Mosolf, James F. (Jim) | OF | 1929-31 | 8/21/05 | | 87 |
| Mota, Manuel R. (Manny) | OF | 1963-68 | 2/18/38 | | 642 |
| Mowrey, Harry H. (Mike) | 3B | 1914 | 3/24/84 | 3/20/47 | 79 |
| Mueller, Ray C. | C | 1939-40, 50 | 3/8/12 | | 157 |
| Mueller, Walter J. | OF | 1922-24, 26 | 12/6/94 | 8/16/71 | 121 |
| Mulligan, Edward J. (Eddie) | INF | 1928 | 8/27/94 | | 27 |
| Murphy, J. Edward (Eddie) | OF | 1926 | 10/2/91 | 2/20/69 | 16 |
| Murphy, Leo J. | C | 1915 | 1/7/89 | 8/12/60 | 34 |
| Murphy, Morgan E. | C | 1898 | 2/14/67 | 10/3/38 | 5 |
| Murtaugh, Daniel E. (Danny) | 2B | 1948-51 | 10/8/17 | 12/2/76 | 416 |
| | | | | | |
| Naton, Peter A. (Pete) | C | 1953 | 9/9/31 | | 6 |
| Nealon, James J. (Jim) | 1B | 1906-07 | 12/13/84 | 4/2/10 | 259 |
| Neeman, Calvin A. (Cal) | C | 1962 | 2/18/29 | | 24 |
| Neighbors, Cecil F. (Cy) | OF | 1908 | 9/23/80 | 5/20/64 | 1 |
| Nelson, Glenn R. (Rocky) | 1B | 1951, 59-61 | 11/18/24 | | 337 |
| Newell, John A. | 3B | 1891 | 1/14/68 | 1/28/19 | 5 |
| Nichol, Samuel A. (Sam) | OF | 1888 | 6/20/69 | 4/19/37 | 8 |
| Nicholson, Frederick (Fred) | OF | 1919-20 | 9/1/94 | | 129 |
| Nicholson, Ovid | OF | 1912 | 12/30/88 | 3/24/68 | 6 |
| Nicol, George E. | OF-P | 1894 | 10/17/70 | 8/10/24 | 8 |
| Nicosia, Steven R. (Steve) | C | 1978- | 8/6/55 | | 71 |
| Niehaus, Albert B. (Al) | 1B | 1925 | 6/1/01 | 10/14/31 | 17 |
| Nonnenkamp, Leo W. (Red) | — | 1933 | 7/7/11 | | 1 |
| | | | | | |
| O'Brien, Edward J. (Eddie) | SS-OF-P | 1953, 55-58 | 12/11/30 | | 231 |
| O'Brien, John J. | 2B | 1899 | 7/14/70 | 5/13/13 | 79 |
| O'Brien, John T. (Johnny) | 2B-P | 1953, 55-58 | 12/11/30 | | 283 |
| O'Brien, Raymond J. (Ray) | OF | 1916 | 10/31/92 | 3/31/42 | 16 |
| O'Brien, Thomas E. (Tommy) | OF | 1943-45 | 12/19/18 | | 232 |
| O'Brien, Thomas F. (Tom) | OF-1B | 1898, 1900 | 2/20/73 | 2/4/01 | 209 |
| O'Connell, Daniel F. | INF | 1950, 53 | 1/21/27 | 10/2/69 | 228 |
| O'Connell, John C. | C | 1928-29 | 6/13/05 | | 3 |
| O'Connor, Patrick F. | C | 1908-10 | 8/4/79 | 8/17-50 | 27 |
| Oldis, Robert C. (Bob) | C | 1960-61 | 1/5/28 | | 26 |
| Oliver, Albert (Al) | OF-1B | 1968-77 | 10/14/46 | | 1,302 |
| Ordenana, Antonio R. | SS | 1943 | 10/30/20 | | 1 |
| Osborne, Frederick W. | OF-P | 1890 | | Deceased | 41 |
| Ott, N. Edward (Ed) | C | 1974- | 7/11/51 | | 372 |

| Player | Pos | Years | Born | Died | Games |
|---|---|---|---|---|---|
| Padden, Richard J. (Dick) | 2B | 1896-98 | 9/17/70 | 10/31/22 | 323 |
| Padden, Thomas F. (Tom) | C | 1932-37 | 10/6/08 | 6/11/73 | 379 |
| Pagan, Jose | 3B | 1965-72 | 5/5/35 | | 625 |
| Pagliaroni, James V. (Jim) | C | 1963-67 | 12/8/37 | | 490 |
| Parker, David G. (Dave) | OF | 1973- | 6/9/51 | | 878 |
| Patek, Fred J. (Freddie) | SS | 1968-70 | 10/9/44 | | 292 |
| Peitz, Henry C. (Heinie) | C | 1905-06 | 12/28/70 | 10/23/43 | 123 |
| Pellagrini, Edward C. | INF | 1953-54 | 3/13/18 | | 151 |
| Pendleton, James L. (Jim) | OF | 1957-58 | 1/7/24 | | 49 |
| Peterson, Harding W. (Pete) | C | 1955, 57-59 | 10/17/29 | | 66 |
| Phelps, Edward J. (Babe) | C | 1902-04, 06-08 | 3/3/79 | 1/31/42 | 313 |
| Phelps, Ernest G. (Babe) | C | 1942 | 4/19/08 | | 95 |
| Phillips, Edward D. (Eddie) | C | 1931 | 2/17/01 | 1/26/68 | 106 |
| Phillips, Jack D. | 1B | 1949-52 | 9/6/21 | | 158 |
| Picinich, Valentine J. | C | 1933 | 9/8/96 | 12/5/42 | 16 |
| Piet, Anthony F. (Tony) | 2B | 1931-33 | 12/7/06 | | 411 |
| Pitler, Jacob A. (Jake) | 2B | 1917-18 | 4/22/94 | 2/3/68 | 111 |
| Plaskett, Elmo A. | C | 1962-63 | 6/27/38 | | 17 |
| Popovich, Paul E. | INF | 1974-75 | 8/18/40 | | 84 |
| Powers, John C. (Johnny) | OF | 1955-58 | 7/8/29 | | 90 |
| | | | | | |
| Rackley, Marvin E. (Marv) | OF | 1949 | 7/25/21 | | 11 |
| Rafter, John C. (Jack) | C | 1904 | 2/20/75 | 1/5/43 | 1 |
| Rand, Richard H. (Dick) | C | 1957 | 8/7/31 | | 60 |
| Randolph, Willie L. | 2B | 1975 | 7/6/54 | | 30 |
| Rawlings, John W. (Johnny) | 2B | 1923-26 | 8/17/92 | 10/16/72 | 219 |
| Raymond, Harry H. | 3B | 1892 | 2/20/66 | 3/21/25 | 12 |
| Regan, William W. (Bill) | 2B | 1931 | 1/23/99 | 6/11/68 | 28 |
| Rehg, Walter P. (Wally) | OF | 1912 | 8/31/88 | 4/5/46 | 8 |
| Reilly, Archer E. (Arch) | 3B | 1917 | 8/17/91 | 11/29/63 | 1 |
| Reilly, Charles T. (Charlie) | 3B | 1891 | 6/24/55 | 12/16/37 | 114 |
| Reiser, Harold P. (Pete) | OF | 1951 | 3/17/19 | | 74 |
| Reitz, Henry P. (Heinie) | 2B | 1899 | 6/29/67 | 11/10/14 | 34 |
| Restelli, Dino P. | OF | 1949, 51 | 9/23/24 | | 93 |
| Reynolds, G. Craig | SS | 1975-76 | 12/27/52 | | 38 |
| Rhawn, Robert J. (Bobby) | INF | 1949 | 2/13/19 | | 3 |
| Rhyne, Harold J. (Hal) | INF | 1926-27 | 3/30/99 | 1/7/71 | 171 |
| Rice, Harold H. (Hal) | OF | 1953-54 | 2/11/24 | | 106 |
| Rickert, Joseph P. (Joe) | OF | 1898 | 12/12/76 | 10/15/43 | 2 |
| Rickert, Marvin A. (Marv) | OF | 1950 | 1/8/21 | | 17 |
| Ricketts, David W. (Dave) | C | 1970 | 7/12/35 | | 14 |
| Riconda, Harry P. (Harry) | SS | 1929 | 3/17/97 | 11/15/58 | 8 |
| Riddle, John L. (Johnny) | C | 1948 | 10/3/05 | | 10 |
| Rikard, Culley | OF | 1941-42, 47 | 5/9/14 | | 153 |
| Ritchey, Claude C. | 2B | 1900-06 | 10/5/73 | 11/8/51 | 977 |
| Ritz, James L. (Jim) | 3B | 1894 | 1874 | 11/10/96 | 1 |
| Rizzo, John C. (Johnny) | OF | 1938-40 | 7/30/12 | | 246 |
| Roat, Frederick (Fred) | 3B | 1890 | 2/10/68 | Deceased | 57 |
| Roberts, Curtis B. (Curt) | 2B | 1954-56 | 8/16/29 | | 171 |
| Roberts, David L. (Dave) | 1B | 1966 | 6/30/33 | | 14 |

## Non-Pitchers (continued)

| Player | Pos | Years | Born | Died | Games |
|---|---|---|---|---|---|
| Robertson, Davis A. (Dave) | OF | 1921 | 9/25/89 | | 60 |
| Robertson, Robert E. (Bob) | 1B | 1967, 69-76 | 10/2/46 | | 750 |
| Robinson, William H. (Bill) | OF-INF | 1975- | 6/26/43 | | 634 |
| Rodgers, K. Andre | INF | 1965-67 | 12/2/34 | | 158 |
| Rodgers, William S. (Bill) | OF | 1944-45 | 12/5/22 | | 3 |
| Roettger, Walter H. (Wally) | OF | 1934 | 8/28/02 | 9/14/51 | 47 |
| Rohwer, Ray | OF | 1921-22 | 6/5/95 | | 83 |
| Rojek, Stanley A. (Stan) | SS | 1948-51 | 4/21/19 | | 384 |
| Rothfuss, John A. (Jack) | 1B | 1897 | 4/18/72 | 4/20/47 | 35 |
| Routcliffe, Phillip J. | OF | 1890 | 10/24/70 | 10/4/18 | 1 |
| Rowe, John C. (Jack) | SS | 1889 | 12/8/57 | 4/26/11 | 75 |
| Rubeling, Albert W. (Al) | INF | 1943-44 | 5/10/13 | | 139 |
| Russell, Ewell A. (Reb) | OF | 1922-23 | 6/12/89 | 9/30/73 | 154 |
| Russell, James W. (Jim) | OF | 1942-47 | 10/1/18 | | 721 |
| Ryan, Michael J. (Mike) | C | 1974 | 11/25/41 | | 15 |
| | | | | | |
| Saffell, Thomas J. (Tom) | OF | 1949-51, 55 | 7/26/21 | | 262 |
| Saier, Victor S. (Vic) | 1B | 1919 | 5/4/91 | 5/14/67 | 58 |
| Sales, Edward A. (Ed) | SS | 1890 | 1861 | 8/10/12 | 51 |
| Salkeld, William F. (Bill) | C | 1945-47 | 3/8/17 | 4/22/67 | 211 |
| Saltzgaver, Otto J. (Jack) | 2B | 1945 | 1/23/05 | | 52 |
| Sandlock, Michael J. (Mike) | C | 1953 | 10/17/15 | | 64 |
| Sands, Charles D. (Charlie) | C | 1971-72 | 12/17/47 | | 29 |
| Sanguillen, Manual D. (Manny) | C | 1967, 69-76 78- | 3/21/44 | | 1,253 |
| Sankey, Benjamin T. (Ben) | SS | 1929-31 | 9/2/07 | | 72 |
| Savage, Theodore E. (Ted) | OF | 1963 | 2/21/37 | | 85 |
| Schang, Robert M. (Bobby) | C | 1914-15 | 12/7/86 | 8/29/66 | 67 |
| Scheeren, Frederick (Fritz) | OF | 1914-15 | 7/1/91 | | 15 |
| Scheibeck, Frank | SS | 1894 | 6/28/65 | 10/22/56 | 28 |
| Schenz, Henry L. (Hank) | 2B | 1950-51 | 4/11/19 | | 83 |
| Schmidt, Walter, J. | C | 1916-24 | 3/20/87 | 7/4/73 | 732 |
| Schofield, J. Richard | SS | 1958-65 | 1/7/35 | | 576 |
| Schriver, William F. (Pop) | C | 1898-1900 | 6/11/66 | 12/27/32 | 223 |
| Schulte, Frank (Wildfire) | OF | 1916-17 | 9/17/82 | 10/2/49 | 85 |
| Schulte, Fred W. | OF | 1936-37 | 1/13/01 | | 103 |
| Schultz, Joseph C., Sr. | INF | 1916 | 7/24/93 | 4/13/41 | 77 |
| Schultz, Joseph C., Jr. | C | 1939-41 | 8/29/18 | | 22 |
| Schuster, William C. (Bill) | SS | 1937 | 8/4/14 | | 3 |
| Scott, Floyd J. (Pete) | OF | 1928 | 12/21/98 | 5/3/53 | 60 |
| Sebring, James D. (Jimmy) | OF | 1902-04 | 3/25/82 | 12/22/09 | 223 |
| Senerchia, Emanuel R. | 3B | 1952 | 4/6/31 | | 29 |
| Shafer, Ralph N. | — | 1914 | 3/17/94 | 2/5/50 | 1 |
| Shannon, William P. (Spike) | OF | 1908 | 2/7/78 | 5/16/40 | 32 |
| Sharpe, Bayard H. (Bud) | 1B | 1910 | 8/6/81 | 5/31/16 | 4 |
| Shaw, Benjamin N. (Ben) | 1B-C | 1917-18 | 6/18/93 | 3/16/59 | 23 |
| Shaw, Royal N. | — | 1908 | 9/29/84 | 7/3/69 | 1 |
| Sheehan, Thomas H. (Tommy) | 3B | 1906-07 | 11/6/77 | 5/22/59 | 170 |
| Sheely, Earl H. | 1B | 1929 | 2/12/93 | 9/16/52 | 139 |
| Shepard, Jack L. | C | 1953-56 | 5/13/32 | | 278 |

| Player | Pos | Years | Born | Died | Games |
|---|---|---|---|---|---|
| Shovlin, John J. | — | 1911 | 1/14/91 | | 2 |
| Shugart, W. Frank | SS | 1891-93 | 1867 | Deceased | 264 |
| Sicking, Edward J. (Eddie) | 2B | 1927 | 3/30/97 | | 6 |
| Siglin, Wesley P. (Paddy) | 2B | 1914-16 | 9/24/91 | 8/5/56 | 23 |
| Simon, Michael E. (Mike) | C | 1909-13 | 6/13/83 | 6/10/63 | 238 |
| Simpson, Harry L. | OF | 1959 | 12/3/25 | | 9 |
| Skiff, William F. (Bill) | C | 1921 | 10/16/95 | | 16 |
| Skinner, Robert R. (Bob) | OF | 1954, 56-63 | 10/3/31 | | 1,100 |
| Smith, Charles M. (Pop) | INF | 1887-89 | 10/12/56 | 4/18/27 | 325 |
| Smith, Earl C. | OF | 1955 | 3/14/28 | | 5 |
| Smith, Earl S. | C | 1924-28 | 2/14/97 | 6/9/63 | 344 |
| Smith, Elmer E. | OF-P | 1892-97, 01 | 3/28/68 | 11/5/45 | 760 |
| Smith, George H. (Heinie) | 2B | 1899 | 10/24/71 | 6/25/39 | 15 |
| Smith, Harold R. (Hal) | C | 1965 | 6/1/31 | | 4 |
| Smith, Harold W. (Hal) | C | 1960-61 | 12/7/30 | | 144 |
| Smith, Harry T. | C | 1902-07 | 10/31/74 | 2/17/33 | 178 |
| Smith, James L. (Jimmy) | SS | 1916 | 5/15/95 | 1/1/74 | 36 |
| Smith, Judson G. (Jud) | 3B | 1896, 01 | 1/13/69 | 12/7/47 | 16 |
| Smith, Louis O. (Bull) | OF | 1904 | | | 13 |
| Smith, Paul L. | 1B-OF | 1953, 57-58 | 3/19/31 | | 205 |
| Smith, Richard H. (Dick) | INF | 1951-55 | 7/21/27 | | 70 |
| Smith, Sydney (Syd) | C | 1914-15 | 8/31/83 | 6/5/61 | 6 |
| Smith, Vincent A. (Vinnie) | C | 1941, 46 | 12/7/15 | | 16 |
| Smith, Willard J. (Red) | C | 1917-18 | 4/11/92 | 10/10/66 | 26 |
| Smykal, Frank J. | SS | 1916 | 10/13/89 | 8/11/50 | 6 |
| Sothern, Dennis E. (Denny) | OF | 1930 | 1/20/94 | | 17 |
| Southworth, William H. | OF | 1918-20 | 3/9/93 | 11/15/69 | 331 |
| Spencer, Roy H. | C | 1925-27 | 2/22/00 | 2/8/73 | 80 |
| Spriggs, George H. | OF | 1965-67 | 5/22/41 | | 46 |
| Spurney, Edward F. (Ed) | SS | 1891 | 1/19/72 | 10/12/32 | 3 |
| Stankard, Thomas F. (Tom) | INF | 1904 | 3/20/82 | 6/13/58 | 2 |
| Stargell, Wilver D. (Willie) | OF-1B | 1962- | 3/6/40 | | 2,181 |
| Starr, Charles W. (Charlie) | INF | 1908 | 8/30/78 | 10/18/37 | 20 |
| Steere, Fred E. | SS | 1894 | 8/16/72 | 3/13/42 | 10 |
| Steinecke, William R. | C | 1931 | 2/7/07 | | 4 |
| Stengel, Charles D. (Casey) | OF | 1918-19 | 7/30/90 | 9/29/75 | 128 |
| Stennett, Renaldo A. (Rennie) | 2B | 1971-79 | 4/5/51 | | 1,079 |
| Stenzel, Jacob C. (Jake) | OF | 1892-96 | 6/24/67 | 1/6/19 | 437 |
| Steveñs, Edward L. (Ed) | 1B | 1948-50 | 1/12/25 | | 212 |
| Stevens, R. C. | 1B | 1958-60 | 7/22/34 | | 71 |
| Stewart, Edward P. (Bud) | OF | 1941-42 | 6/15/16 | | 155 |
| Stewart, John F. (Stuffy) | 2B | 1922 | 1/31/94 | | 3 |
| Storke, Alan M. | INF | 1906-09 | 9/27/84 | 3/18/10 | 37 |
| Strickland, George B. | SS | 1950-52 | 1/10/26 | | 237 |
| Stroner, James M. (Jim) | 3B | 1929 | 5/29/04 | 11/16/71 | 6 |
| Stuart, Richard L. (Dick) | 1B | 1958-62 | 11/7/32 | | 559 |
| Stuart, William A. (Bill) | SS | 1895 | | Deceased | 19 |
| Sugden, Joseph (Joe) | C | 1893-97 | 7/31/70 | 6/28/59 | 279 |
| Suhr, August R. (Gus) | 1B | 1930-39 | 1/3/06 | | 1,365 |
| Sullivan, John E. | C | 1908 | 2/16/73 | 6/5/24 | 1 |
| Sullivan, William J., Jr. | C | 1947 | 10/23/10 | 1/28/65 | 38 |

| Player | Pos | Years | Born | Died | Games |
|---|---|---|---|---|---|
| Summa, Homer W. | OF | 1920 | 11/3/98 | 1/29/66 | 10 |
| Sunday, William A. (Billy) | OF | 1888-90 | 11/19/62 | 11/6/35 | 287 |
| Susce, George C. | C | 1939 | 8/13/08 | | 31 |
| Swacina, Harry J. | 1B | 1907-08 | 8/22/81 | 6/21/44 | 79 |
| Swartwood, Cyrus E. (Ed) | OF | 1892 | 1/12/59 | 5/10/24 | 13 |
| Sweeney, Edward F. (Ed) | C | 1919 | 7/19/88 | 7/4/47 | 17 |
| Sweeney, Henry L. (Hank) | 1B | 1944 | 12/28/15 | | 1 |
| Tannehill, Jesse N. | OF-P | 1897-02 | 7/14/74 | 9/22/56 | 283 |
| Taveras, Franklin F. (Frank) | SS | 1971-72, 74-79 | 12/24/50 | | 724 |
| Taylor, Carl M. | C-OF | 1968-69, 71 | 1/20/44 | | 155 |
| Terry, Z. Alexander (Zeb) | SS | 1919 | 16/17/91 | | 129 |
| Thevenow, Thomas J. | SS-2B, 3B | 1931-35, 38 | 9/6/03 | 7/29/57 | 499 |
| Thomas, Frank J. | OF, 3B | 1951-58 | 6/11/29 | | 925 |
| Thomas, Roy A. | OF | 1908 | 3/24/74 | 11/20/59 | 102 |
| Thompson, L. Fresco | 2B | 1925 | 6/6/02 | 11/20/68 | 14 |
| Tierney, James A. (Cotton) | 2B | 1920-23 | 2/10/94 | 4/18/53 | 280 |
| Todd, Alfred C. (Al) | C | 1936-38 | 1/7/04 | | 342 |
| Tolan, Robert (Bobby) | 1B-OF | 1977 | 11/19/45 | | 49 |
| Traux, Frederick W. (Fred) | OF | 1890 | | Deceased | 1 |
| Traynor, Harold J. (Pie) | 3B | 1920-35, 37 | 11/11/99 | 3/16/72 | 1,941 |
| Truby, Harry G. | 2B | 1896 | 5/12/70 | 3/21/53 | 8 |
| Turner, Earl E. | C | 1948, 50 | 5/6/23 | | 42 |
| Turner, Terrence L. (Terry) | 3B | 1901 | 2/28/21 | 7/18/60 | 2 |
| Van Haltren, George E. | OF | 1892-93 | 3/30/66 | 9/29/45 | 137 |
| Van Robays, Maurice R. | OF | 1939-43, 46 | 11/15/14 | 3/1/65 | 529 |
| Vaughan, J. Floyd (Arky) | SS | 1932-41 | 3/9/12 | 8/30/52 | 1,411 |
| Veach, William W. | 1B | 1890 | 6/15/63 | 11/12/37 | 8 |
| Veal, Orville I. (Coot) | SS | 1962 | 7/9/32 | | 1 |
| Veltman, Arthur P. (Art) | C | 1934 | 3/24/06 | | 12 |
| Vernon, James B. (Mickey) | 1B | 1960 | 4/22/18 | | 9 |
| Viox, James H. (Jim) | 2B | 1912-16 | 12/30/90 | 1/6/69 | 506 |
| Virdon, William C. (Bill) | OF | 1956-65, 68 | 6/9/31 | | 1,415 |
| Virgil, Osvaldo J. (Ozzie) | INF | 1965 | 5/17/33 | | 39 |
| Wagner, John P. (Honus) | SS | 1900-17 | 2/24/74 | 12/6/55 | 2,432 |
| Wagner, William J. (Bill) | C | 1914-17 | 2/2/94 | 1/11/51 | 80 |
| Walker, Fred E. (Dixie) | OF | 1948-49 | 9/24/10 | | 217 |
| Wallace, James L. (Jim) | OF | 1905 | 11/14/81 | 5/16/53 | 7 |
| Walls, R. Lee | OF | 1952, 56-57 | 1/6/33 | | 183 |
| Waner, Lloyd J. | OF | 1927-41 44/45 | 3/16/06 | | 1,803 |
| Waner, Paul G. | OF | 1926-40 | 4/16/03 | 8/29/65 | 2,154 |
| Ward, Charles W. | SS | 1917 | 7/31/93 | 4/4/69 | 125 |
| Ward, Frank G. (Piggy) | OF | 1891 | 4/16/67 | 10/24/12 | 6 |
| Ward, Preston M. | 1B-OF | 1953-56 | 7/24/27 | | 305 |
| Warner, Hoke H. (Hooks) | 3B | 1916-17, 19 | 5/22/94 | 2/19/47 | 53 |
| Warwick, Firmin N. (Bill) | C | 1921 | 11/26/97 | | 22 |
| Wasdell, James C. (Jimmy) | OF | 1942-43 | 5/15/14 | | 126 |

## Non-Pitchers (continued)

| Player | Pos | Years | Born | Died | Games |
|---|---|---|---|---|---|
| Weaver, Arthur C. (Art) | C | 1903 | 4/7/79 | 3/23/17 | 16 |
| Weaver, William B. (Farmer) | OF | 1894 | 3/23/65 | 1/25/43 | 30 |
| Webb, William J. (Bill) | 2B | 1917 | 6/25/96 | 1/12/43 | 5 |
| West, Max E. | 1B-OF | 1948 | 11/28/16 | | 87 |
| Westlake, Waldon T. (Wally) | OF | 1947-51 | 11/8/20 | | 580 |
| White, James L. (Deacon) | 3B | 1889 | 12/7/47 | 7/7/39 | 55 |
| Whitehead, Burgess U. | 2B | 1946 | 6/29/10 | | 55 |
| Whitney, Arthur W. (Art) | 3B | 1887 | 1/16/58 | 8/17/43 | 119 |
| Whitted, George B. (Possum) | OF-3B | 1919-21 | 2/4/90 | 10/16/62 | 277 |
| Wietelmann, William F. | INF | 1947 | 3/15/19 | | 48 |
| Wilhoit, Joseph W. (Joe) | OF | 1917 | 12/20/91 | 9/25/30 | 9 |
| Williams, James T. W. | 3B | 1899-1900 | 12/20/76 | 1/16/65 | 158 |
| Wills, Maurice M. (Maury) | 3B | 1967-68 | 10/2/32 | | 202 |
| Wilson, Arthur E. (Art) | C | 1916 | 12/11/85 | 6/12/60 | 53 |
| Wilson, Grady H. | SS | 1948 | 11/23/22 | | 12 |
| Wilson, John Owen | OF | 1908-13 | 8/21/83 | 2/22/54 | 899 |
| Wilson, Samuel M. (Mike) | C | 1921 | 12/2/96 | | 5 |
| Wilson, William (Bill) | C-OF | 1890 | 10/23/67 | Deceased | 83 |
| Windle, Willis B. (Bill) | 1B | 1928-29 | 12/13/04 | | 3 |
| Wissman, David A. (Dave) | OF | 1964 | 2/17/41 | | 16 |
| Wolfe, Harry | OF | 1917 | 7/7/93 | | 3 |
| Wood, Roy W. | OF | 1913 | 8/29/92 | | 14 |
| Woodling, Eugene R. (Gene) | OF | 1947 | 8/16/22 | | 22 |
| Workman, Charles T. (Chuck) | OF | 1946 | 1/26/15 | 1/3/53 | 58 |
| Wright, F. Glenn | SS | 1924-28 | 2/6/01 | | 676 |
| Wright, Joseph (Joe) | OF | 1896 | | Deceased | 15 |
| Wyrostek, John B. (Johnny) | OF | 1942-43 | 7/12/19 | | 60 |
| | | | | | |
| Yaik, Henry | OF-C | 1888 | | Deceased | 2 |
| Yeager, George E. | C | 1901 | 6/4/73 | Deceased | 26 |
| Young, L. Floyd (Pep) | 2B | 1933-40 | 8/29/07 | 1/14/62 | 697 |
| Youngman, Henry | INF | 1890 | 1865 | 1/24/36 | 13 |
| Yount, F. Edwin (Eddie) | — | 1939 | 12/19/16 | | 2 |
| | | | | | |
| Zak, Frank T. (Frankie) • | SS | 1944-46 | 2/22/22 | 2/6/72 | 123 |
| Zimmer, Charles L. (Chief) | C | 1900-02 | 11/23/60 | 8/22/49 | 193 |
| Zisk, Richard W. (Richie) | OF | 1971-76 | 2/6/49 | | 578 |
| Zitzman, William A. (Billy) | OF | 1919 | 12/19/97 | | 11 |

## Pitchers

| Player | Years | Born | Died | W-L |
|---|---|---|---|---|
| Acosta, Eduardo E. (Ed) | 1970 | 3/9/44 | | 0-0 |
| Adams, Charles B. (Babe) | 1907, 09-16 18-26 | 5/18/82 | 7/27/68 | 194-139 |
| Albosta, Edward J. (Ed) | 1946 | 10/27/18 | | 0-6 |
| Aldridge, Victor E. (Vic) | 1925-27 | 10/25/93 | 4/17/43 | 40-30 |
| Anderson, David S. (Dave) | 1890 | 10/10/68 | 3/22/97 | 2-11 |
| Arroyo, Luis E. (Luis) | 1956-57 | 2/18/27 | | 6-14 |

116

## Pitchers (continued)

| Player | Years | Born | Died | W-L |
|---|---|---|---|---|
| Bagby, James C. J., Sr. (Jim) | 1923 | 10/5/87 | 7/28/54 | 3-2 |
| Bagby, James C. J., Jr. (Jim) | 1947 | 9/8/16 | | 5-4 |
| Bair, C. Douglas (Doug) | 1976 | 8/22/49 | | 0-0 |
| Bahr, Edson G. (Ed) | 1946–47 | 10/16/19 | | 11-11 |
| Baker, Kirtly | 1890 | 6/24/69 | 4/15/27 | 3-19 |
| Baldwin, Marcus E. (Mark) | 1891-93 | 10/29/65 | 11/10/29 | 48-55 |
| Barrett, Francis J. (Frank) | 1950 | 7/1/13 | | 1-2 |
| Bartholomew, Lester J. (Les) | 1928 | 4/4/03 | 9/19/72 | 0-0 |
| Bauers, Russell L. (Russ) | 1936-41 | 5/10/14 | | 29-30 |
| Beam, Alexander R. (Alex) | 1889 | 11/21/70 | 4/17/38 | 1-1 |
| Beck, Walter W. (Boom-Boom) | 1945 | 10/16/04 | | 6-1 |
| Bednar, Andrew F. (Andy) | 1930-31 | 8/16/09 | 11/25/57 | 0-0 |
| Behrman, Henry B. (Hank) | 1947 | 6/27/12 | | 0-2 |
| Belinsky, Robert (Bo) | 1969 | 12/7/36 | | 0-3 |
| Bell, William S. (Bill) | 1952, 55 | 10/24/33 | 10/11/62 | 0-1 |
| Benton, John C. | 1915 | 6/27/87 | 12/12/37 | 0-0 |
| Bibby, James B. (Jim) | 1978- | 10/29/44 | | 20-11 |
| Bigbee, Lyle R. | 1921 | 8/22/93 | 8/5/42 | 0-0 |
| Birkofer, Ralph J. | 1933-36 | 11/5/08 | 3/16/71 | 31-26 |
| Bishop, William R. (Bill) | 1887 | 12/27/69 | 12/15/32 | 0-3 |
| Blackburn, Ronald H. (Ron) | 1958-59 | 4/23/35 | | 3-2 |
| Blake, John F. (Sheriff) | 1920 | 9/17/99 | | 0-0 |
| Blankenship, Homer | 1928 | 8/4/02 | | 0-2 |
| Blanton, Darrell E. (Cy) | 1934-39 | 7/6/08 | 9/13/45 | 58-51 |
| Blass, Stephen R. (Steve) | 1964, 66-74 | 4/18/42 | | 103-76 |
| Blyleven, Rikalbert (Bert) | 1978- | 4/6/51 | | 26-15 |
| Boehler, George H. | 1923 | 1/2/92 | 6/23/58 | 1-3 |
| Bohen, Leo J. (Pat) | 1914 | 10/20/91 | 4/9/42 | 0-0 |
| Bonham, Ernest E. (Ernie) | 1947-49 | 8/16/13 | 9/15/49 | 24-22 |
| Bork, Frank B. | 1964 | 7/13/40 | | 2-2 |
| Borowy, Henry L. (Hank) | 1950 | 5/12/16 | | 1-3 |
| Bowman, Joseph E. (Joe) | 1937-41 | 6/17/10 | | 33-38 |
| Bowman, Roger C. | 1953, 55 | 8/18/27 | | 0-7 |
| Bowman, Sumner S. | 1890 | 2/9/67 | 1/11/54 | 2-5 |
| Brady, Charles (Charlie) | 1906-07 | | | 1-1 |
| Brame, Ervin B. (Erv) | 1928-32 | 10/12/01 | 11/22/49 | 52-37 |
| Brandom, Chester M. (Chick) | 1908-09 | 3/31/87 | 10/7/58 | 3-0 |
| Brandt, Edward A. (Ed) | 1937-38 | 2/17/05 | 11/1/44 | 16-14 |
| Brandt, William G. (Bill) | 1941-43 | 3/21/18 | 5/16/68 | 5-3 |
| Brett, Kenneth A. (Ken) | 1974-75 | 9/18/48 | | 22-14 |
| Briles, Nelson K. (Nellie) | 1971-73 | 8/5/43 | | 36-28 |
| Brosseau, Frank L. | 1969, 71 | 7/31/44 | | 0-0 |
| Brown, Mace S. | 1935-41 | 5/21/09 | | 55-45 |
| Brown, Myrl L. | 1922 | 10/10/94 | | 3-1 |
| Brunet, George S. | 1970 | 6/8/35 | | 1-1 |
| Bunning, James P. (Jim) | 1968-69 | 10/23/31 | | 14-23 |
| Burwell, William E. (Bill) | 1928 | 3/27/95 | 6/11/73 | 1-0 |
| Bush, Guy T. | 1935-36 | 8/23/01 | | 12-14 |
| Bush, Leslie A. (Joe) | 1926-27 | 11/27/92 | 11/1/74 | 7-8 |
| Butcher, A. Maxwell (Max) | 1939-45 | 9/21/10 | 9/15/57 | 67-60 |
| Butters, Thomas A. (Tom) | 1962-65 | 4/8/38 | | 2-3 |

## Pitchers (continued)

| Player | Years | Born | Died | W-L |
|--------|-------|------|------|-----|
| Cambria, Fred D. | 1970 | 1/22/48 | | 1-2 |
| Camnitz, Henry R. (Harry) | 1909 | 10/26/84 | 1/6/51 | 0-0 |
| Camnitz, S. Howard (Howie) | 1904, 06-13 | 8/22/81 | 3/2/60 | 116-83 |
| Camp, Winfield S. (Kid) | 1892 | 1870 | 3/2/95 | 0-1 |
| Candelaria, John R. | 1975- | 11/6/53 | | 70-38 |
| Cardwell, Donald E. (Don) | 1963-66 | 12/7/35 | | 33-33 |
| Carlsen, Donald H. (Don) | 1951-52 | 10/15/26 | | 2-4 |
| Carlson, Harold G. (Hal) | 1917-23 | 5/17/94 | 5/28/30 | 42-55 |
| Carpenter, Paul C. | 1916 | 8/12/94 | 3/14/68 | 0-0 |
| Carpin, Frank D. | 1965 | 9/14/38 | | 3-1 |
| Carroll, Clay P. | 1978 | 5/2/41 | | 0-0 |
| Case, Charles E. (Charlie) | 1904-06 | 9/7/79 | 4/16/54 | 23-17 |
| Casey, Hugh T. | 1949 | 10/14/13 | 7/3/51 | 4-1 |
| Chagnon, Leon W. | 1929-30, 32-34 | 9/28/02 | 7/30/53 | 19-14 |
| Chambers, Clifford D. (Cliff) | 1949-51 | 1/10/22 | | 28-28 |
| Cheney, Thomas E. (Tom) | 1960-61 | 10/14/34 | | 2-2 |
| Chesbro, John D. (Jack) | 1899-02 | 6/5/74 | 11/6/31 | 70-38 |
| Chesnes, Robert V. (Bob) | 1948-50 | 5/6/21 | | 24-22 |
| Churn, Clarence N. (Chuck) | 1957 | 2/1/30 | | 0-0 |
| Clemensen, William M. (Bill) | 1939, 41, 46 | 6/20/19 | | 1-1 |
| Colcolough, Thomas B. (Tom) | 1893-95 | 10/8/70 | 12/10/19 | 11-6 |
| Coleman, Joseph H. (Joe) | 1979- | 2/3/47 | | 0-0 |
| Coleman, John F. | 1890 | 3/6/63 | 5/31/22 | 0-2 |
| Colpaert, Richard C. (Dick) | 1970 | 1/3/44 | | 1-0 |
| Comstock, Ralph R. | 1918 | 11/24/90 | 9/13/66 | 8-9 |
| Conger, Richard (Dick) | 1941-42 | 4/3/21 | 2/16/70 | 0-0 |
| Conway, Peter J. (Pete) | 1889 | 10/30/66 | 1/14/03 | 2-1 |
| Conzelman, Joseph H. (Joe) | 1913-15 | 7/14/89 | | 7-8 |
| Cooper, A. Wilbur | 1912-24 | 2/24/92 | 8/7/73 | 202-159 |
| Cottrell, Ensign S. | 1911 | 8/29/88 | 2/27/47 | 0-0 |
| Cronin, John J. | 1898 | 5/26/74 | 7/13/29 | 2-2 |
| Cuccurullo, Arthur J. (Cookie) | 1943-45 | 2/8/18 | | 3-5 |
| Culloton, Bernard A. (Bud) | 1925-26 | 5/19/96 | 11/30/76 | 0-1 |
| Cushman, Harvey B. (Harv) | 1902 | 7/5/77 | 12/27/20 | 0-4 |
| Cvengros, Michael J. (Mike) | 1927 | 12/1/01 | 8/2/70 | 2-1 |
| | | | | |
| Dal Canton, J. Bruce | 1967-70 | 6/15/42 | | 20-8 |
| Daniels, Bennie | 1957-60 | 6/17/32 | | 8-16 |
| Daniels, Peter J. (Pete) | 1890 | 4/8/64 | 2/13/28 | 1-2 |
| Dawson, Ralph F. (Joe) | 1927-29 | 3/9/98 | | 10-15 |
| Day, William (Bill) | 1890 | 7/28/67 | 8/16/23 | 0-6 |
| Demery, Lawrence C. (Larry) | 1974-77 | 6/4/53 | | 29-23 |
| Dempsey, Cornelius F. (Con) | 1951 | 9/16/23 | | 0-2 |
| Dettore, Thomas A. (Tom) | 1973 | 11/17/47 | | 0-1 |
| Dickson, Murry M. | 1949-53 | 8/21/16 | | 66-85 |
| Dietz, Lloyd, A. (Dutch) | 1940-43 | 2/12/12 | 10/29/72 | 13-15 |
| Doheny, Edward R. (Ed) | 1901-03 | 11/24/74 | 12/29/16 | 39-14 |
| Donoso, Lino G. | 1955-56 | 9/23/22 | | 4-6 |
| Douglas, Charles W. (Whammy) | 1957 | 2/17/35 | | 3-3 |
| Dowd, James J. (Skip) | 1910 | 2/16/89 | 12/20/60 | 0-0 |
| Dudley, E. Clise | 1933 | 8/8/03 | | 0-0 |
| Duffy, Bernard A. (Bernie) | 1913 | 8/18/93 | 2/9/62 | 1-0 |

| Player | Years | Born | Died | W-L |
|---|---|---|---|---|
| Duggleby, William J. (Bill) | 1907 | 3/17/74 | 8/31/44 | 2-2 |
| Dunn, James W. (Jim) | 1952 | 2/25/31 | | 0-0 |
| Dunning, Andrew J. (Andy) | 1899 | | Deceased | 0-2 |
| Dusak, Ervin F. (Erv) | 1951 | 7/29/20 | | 0-1 |
| | | | | |
| Easton, John E. (Jack) | 1894 | 1867 | 11/ /03 | 0-1 |
| Eayrs, Edwin (Eddie) | 1913 | 11/10/90 | 11/30/69 | 0-0 |
| Ehret, Philip S. (Red) | 1892-94 | 8/31/68 | 7/28/40 | 53-59 |
| Ellis, Dock P. | 1968-75, 79 | 3/11/45 | | 96-80 |
| Erickson, Ralph L. | 1929-30 | 6/25/04 | | 1-0 |
| Esper, Charles H. (Duke) | 1890, 92 | 7/28/68 | 8/31/10 | 2-2 |
| Evans, William J. (Bill) | 1916-17, 19 | 2/10/93 | 12/21/46 | 2-13 |
| | | | | |
| Face, Elroy L. (Roy) | 1953, 55-68 | 2/2/28 | | 100-93 |
| Falkenberg, Frederick P. (Cy) | 1903 | 12/17/80 | 4/14/61 | 2-4 |
| Ferry, John F. (Jack) | 1910-13 | 4/7/87 | 8/29/54 | 10-8 |
| Fields, John J. (Jocko) | 1887 | 10/20/64 | 10/14/50 | 0-0 |
| Fisher, Harry D. | 1952 | 1/3/26 | | 1-2 |
| Flaherty, Patrick J. (Patsy) | 1900, 04-05 | 6/29/76 | 1/23/68 | 28-18 |
| Foor, James E. (Jim) | 1973 | 1/13/49 | | 0-0 |
| Foreman, John D. (Brownie) | 1895-96 | 8/6/75 | 12/10/26 | 11-9 |
| Forster, Terry J. | 1977 | 1/14/52 | | 6-4 |
| Foss, Larry C. | 1961 | 4/18/36 | | 1-1 |
| Francis, Earl C. | 1960-64 | 7/14/36 | | 16-23 |
| French, Lawrence H. (Larry) | 1929-34 | 11/1/07 | | 87-83 |
| Friend, Robert B. (Bob) | 1951-65 | 11/24/30 | | 191-218 |
| Frock, Samuel W. | 1909-10 | 12/23/83 | 11/3/25 | 3-2 |
| Fryman, Woodrow T. (Woody) | 1966-67 | 4/12/40 | | 15-17 |
| Fussell, Frederick M. (Fred) | 1928-29 | 10/7/95 | 10/23/66 | 10-11 |
| | | | | |
| Gables, Kenneth H. (Ken) | 1945-47 | 1/21/18 | 1/2/60 | 13-11 |
| Galvin, James F. (Pud) | 1887-89, 91-92 | 12/25/55 | 3/7/02 | 93-81 |
| Gannon, James E. (Gussie) | 1895 | 11/26/73 | 4/12/66 | 0-0 |
| Ganzel, John J. | 1898 | 4/7/75 | 1/14/59 | 0-0 |
| Garber, Robert M. (Bob) | 1956 | 9/10/28 | | 0-0 |
| Garber, H. Eugene (Gene) | 1969-70, 72 | 11/13/47 | | 0-3 |
| Gardner, Harry | 1911-12 | 9/20/88 | 8/2/61 | 1-1 |
| Gardner, James A. (Jim) | 1895, 97-99 | 10/4/74 | 4/24/05 | 24-20 |
| Garfield, William M. (Bill) | 1889 | 10/26/67 | 12/16/41 | 0-2 |
| Gastright, Henry C. (Hank) | 1893 | 3/29/65 | 10/9/37 | 3-1 |
| Gee, John A. (Johnny) | 1939, 41, 43-44 | 12/7/15 | | 5-8 |
| Gelnar, John R. | 1964, 67 | 6/25/43 | | 0-1 |
| Gerheauser, Albert (Al) | 1945-46 | 6/24/17 | 5/28/72 | 7-12 |
| Gibbon, Joseph C. (Joe) | 1960-65, 69-70 | 4/10/36 | | 44-46 |
| Gibson, Robert M. (Bob) | 1890 | 8/20/69 | 12/19/49 | 0-3 |
| Giel, Paul R. | 1959-60 | 9/29/32 | | 2-0 |
| Gilmore, Leonard P. (Len) | 1944 | 11/3/17 | | 0-1 |
| Giusti, David J. (Dave) | 1970-76 | 11/27/39 | | 47-28 |
| Glazner, Charles F. (Whitey) | 1920-23 | 9/17/93 | | 27-18 |
| Goar, Joshua M. (Jot) | 1896 | 1/31/70 | 4/4/47 | 0-1 |
| Gornicki, Frank T. (Hank) | 1942-43, 46 | 1/14/11 | | 14-19 |

## Pitchers (continued)

| Player | Years | Born | Died | W-L |
|---|---|---|---|---|
| Gossage, Richard M. (Rich) | 1977 | 6/5/51 | | 11-9 |
| Grant, George A. | 1931 | 1/6/03 | | 0-0 |
| Grant, James T. (Mudcat) | 1970-71 | 8/13/35 | | 7-4 |
| Gray, Charles | 1890 | 1867 | Deceased | 1-4 |
| Gray, George E. (Chummy) | 1899 | 7/17/73 | 8/14/13 | 3-3 |
| Green, Fred A. (Freddie) | 1959-61, 64 | 9/14/33 | | 9-6 |
| Gregg, Harold D. (Hal) | 1948-50 | 7/11/21 | | 3-5 |
| Grimes, Burleigh A. | 1916-17, 28-29, 34 | 8/18/93 | | 48-42 |
| Gross, Donald J. (Don) | 1958-60 | 6/30/31 | | 6-8 |
| Grunwald, Alfred H. (Al) | 1955 | 2/13/30 | | 0-0 |
| Gumbert, Addison C. (Ad) | 1893-94 | 10/10/68 | 4/23/25 | 26-21 |
| Gumbert, Harry E. | 1949-50 | 11/5/09 | | 1-4 |
| Gumbert, William S. | 1890, 92 | 8/8/65 | 4/13/46 | 7-9 |
| | | | | |
| Haddix, Harvey | 1959-63 | 9/18/25 | | 45-38 |
| Hall, Richard W. (Dick) | 1952-57, 59 | 9/27/30 | | 6-13 |
| Hall, Robert L. (Bob) | 1953 | 12/22/23 | | 3-12 |
| Hallett, Jack P. | 1942-43, 46 | 11/13/13 | | 6-10 |
| Hamilton, David E. (Dave) | 1978 | 12/14/47 | | 0-2 |
| Hamilton, Earl A. | 1918-23 | 7/19/91 | 11/17/68 | 55-55 |
| Hamlin, Luke D. | 1942 | 7/3/06 | | 4-4 |
| Harmon, Robert G. (Bob) | 1914-16, 18 | 10/15/87 | 11/27/61 | 37-52 |
| Harrell, Raymond J. (Ray) | 1940 | 2/16/12 | | 0-0 |
| Harris, William M. (Bill) | 1931-34 | 6/23/00 | 8/21/65 | 16-15 |
| Hart, William F. (Bill) | 1895, 98 | 7/19/65 | 9/19/36 | 19-26 |
| Hartenstein, Charles O. (Chuck) | 1969-70 | 5/26/42 | | 6-5 |
| Hastings, Charles M. (Charlie) | 1896-98 | 1871 | 8/3/34 | 14-24 |
| Hawley, Emerson P. (Pink) | 1895-97 | 12/5/72 | 9/19/38 | 72-60 |
| Heard, Charles H. (Charlie) | 1890 | 1/30/72 | 2/20/45 | 0-6 |
| Herbert, Wallace A. (Wally) | 1943 | 8/21/07 | | 10-11 |
| Hecker, Guy J. | 1890 | 4/3/56 | 12/4/38 | 18-8 |
| Heintzelman, Kenneth A. (Ken) | 1937-42, 46-47 | 10/14/15 | | 37-43 |
| Henderson, James H. (Hardie) | 1888 | 10/31/62 | 2/6/03 | 1-3 |
| Hendrix, Claude R. | 1911-13 | 4/13/89 | 3/22/44 | 41-29 |
| Henry, William R. (Bill) | 1968 | 10/15/27 | | 0-0 |
| Hernandez, Ramon G. | 1971-76 | 8/31/40 | | 23-12 |
| Herring, Arthur L. (Art) | 1947 | 3/10/07 | | 1-3 |
| Hetki, John E. (Johnny) | 1953-54 | 5/12/22 | | 7-10 |
| Hewitt, C. Jacob (Jake) | 1895 | 6/6/70 | 5/15/59 | 1-0 |
| Heyner, John | 1890 | | Deceased | 0-0 |
| Higbe, W. Kirby | 1947-49 | 4/8/15 | | 19-26 |
| Hill, Carmen P. | 1915-16, 18-19, 26-29 | 10/1/95 | | 47-31 |
| Hillebrand, Homer H. | 1905-06, 08 | 10/10/79 | 1/23/74 | 8-4 |
| Hoffer, William L. (Bill) | 1898-99 | 11/8/70 | 7/21/59 | 11-10 |
| Hogue, Calvin G. (Cal) | 1952-54 | 10/24/27 | | 2-10 |
| Holland, Alfred W. (Al) | 1977 | 8/16/52 | | 0-0 |
| Holley, Edward E. (Ed) | 1934 | 7/23/01 | Deceased | 0-3 |
| Hollingsworth, John B. (Bonnie) | 1922 | 12/26/95 | | 0-0 |
| Hopper, James M. (Jim) | 1946 | 9/1/19 | | 0-1 |

## Pitchers (continued)

| Player | Years | Born | Died | W-L |
|---|---|---|---|---|
| Horton, Elmer E. | 1896 | 9/4/69 | Deceased | 0-2 |
| Howard, George E. (Del) | 1905 | 12/24/77 | 12/24/56 | 0-0 |
| Howard, Lee V. | 1946-47 | 11/11/23 | | 0-1 |
| Hoyt, Waite C. | 1933-37 | 9/9/99 | | 35-31 |
| Hughes, William N. (Bill) | 1921 | 11/18/96 | 2/25/63 | 0-0 |
| Hughey, James U. (Jim) | 1896-97 | 3/8/69 | 3/29/45 | 12-18 |
| Husting, Berthold J. (Bert) | 1900 | 3/6/78 | 9/3/48 | 0-0 |
| Jackson, Alvin N. (Al) | 1959, 61 | 12/25/35 | | 1-0 |
| Jackson, Grant D. | 1977- | 9/28/42 | | |
| Jacobs, W. Elmer | 1916-18 | 8/10/92 | 2/10/58 | 12-30 |
| Jimenez, Juan A. | 1974 | 3/8/49 | | 0-0 |
| Johnson, Lloyd W. | 1934 | 12/24/10 | | 0-0 |
| Johnson, Robert D. (Bob) | 1971-73 | 4/25/43 | | 17-16 |
| Jones, Alexander H. (Alex) | 1889 | 1867 | Deceased | 1-0 |
| Jones, Henry M. | 1890 | | Deceased | 2-1 |
| Jones, Odell | 1975, 77-78 | 1/13/53 | | 5-7 |
| Jones, Percy L. | 1930 | 10/28/99 | | 0-1 |
| Jones, Timothy B. (Tim) | 1977 | 1/24/54 | | 1-0 |
| Jordan, Harry J. | 1894-95 | | Deceased | 1-2 |
| Jungles, Kenneth P. (Ken) | 1942 | 6/23/16 | 9/9/75 | 0-0 |
| Kantlehner, Ervine L. (Erv) | 1914-16 | 7/31/92 | | 14-29 |
| Karger, Edwin (Ed) | 1906 | 5/6/83 | 9/9/57 | 2-3 |
| Kelly, Herbert B. (Herb) | 1914-15 | 6/4/92 | 5/18/73 | 1-3 |
| Kennedy, William V. (Brickyard) | 1903 | 10/7/68 | 9/23/15 | 9-6 |
| Killen, Frank B. | 1893-98 | 11/30/70 | 12/4/39 | 109-75 |
| King, Charles F. (Silver) | 1891 | 1/11/68 | 5/19/38 | 14-29 |
| King, Nelson J. (Nellie) | 1954-57 | 3/15/28 | | 0-1 |
| Kinsella, Edward W. (Ed) | 1905 | 1/15/82 | | 81-63 |
| Kison, Bruce E. | 1971-79 | 2/18/50 | | |
| Kline, Ronald L. (Ron) | 1952, 55-59, 68-69 | 3/9/32 | | 66-84 |
| Klinger, Robert H. (Bob) | 1938-43 | 6/4/08 | 8/19/77 | 62-58 |
| Knell, Philip H. (Phil) | 1888, 94 | 1865 | Deceased | 1-2 |
| Koski, William J. (Bill) | 1951 | 2/6/32 | | 0-1 |
| Koupal, Louis L. (Lou) | 1925-26 | 12/19/98 | 12/8/61 | 0-2 |
| Kremer, Remy P. (Ray) | 1924-33 | 3/23/93 | 2/8/65 | 143-85 |
| Krumm, Albert (Al) | 1889 | | Deceased | 0-1 |
| Kunz, Earl D. | 1923 | 12/25/99 | 4/14/63 | 1-2 |
| Kuzava, Robert L. (Bob) | 1957 | 5/28/23 | | 0-0 |
| Labine, Clement W. (Clem) | 1960-61 | 8/6/26 | | 7-1 |
| Lamabe, John A. (Jack) | 1962 | 10/3/36 | | 3-1 |
| Lamb, John A. | 1970-71, 73 | 7/20/46 | | 0-2 |
| Lanahan, Richard A. (Dick) | 1940-41 | 9/27/13 | | 6-9 |
| Lang, Martin J. (Marty) | 1930 | 9/27/06 | 1/13/68 | 0-0 |
| Langford, J. Rick | 1976 | 3/20/52 | | 0-1 |
| Lanning, John Y. (Johnny) | 1940-43, 45-46 | 9/6/10 | | 33-29 |
| LaPalme, Paul E. | 1951-54 | 12/14/23 | | 14-33 |
| Law, Vernon S. (Vern) | 1950-51, 54-67 | 3/12/30 | | 162-147 |
| Lawson, Albert W. (Al) | 1890 | 3/23/76 | 10/28/52 | 0-2 |

## Pitchers (continued)

| Player | Years | Born | Died | W-L |
|---|---|---|---|---|
| Lee, Wyatt A. (Watty) | 1904 | 8/12/79 | 3/6/36 | 1-2 |
| Leever, Samuel (Sam) | 1898-10 | 12/23/71 | 5/19/53 | 194-100 |
| Leifield, Albert P. (Lefty) | 1905-12 | 9/5/83 | 10/10/70 | 108-83 |
| Lindell, John H. (Johnny) | 1953 | 8/30/16 | | 5-16 |
| Littlefield, Richard B. (Dick) | 1954-56 | 3/18/26 | | 15-23 |
| Lombardi, Victor A. (Vic) | 1948-50 | 9/20/22 | | 15-19 |
| Lucas, Charles F. (Red) | 1934-38 | 4/28/02 | | 47-32 |
| Luhrsen, William F. (Bill) | 1913 | 4/14/84 | 8/16/73 | 3-1 |
| Lundgren, E. Delmar (Del) | 1924 | 9/21/00 | | 0-1 |
| Lynch, Michael J. (Mike) | 1904-07 | 6/28/80 | 4/2/27 | 40-26 |
| Lyons, Albert H. (Al) | 1947 | 5/18/18 | 12/20/65 | 1-2 |
| | | | | |
| MacDonald, William P. (Bill) | 1950, 53 | 3/28/29 | | 8-11 |
| MacFayden, Daniel K. (Danny) | 1940 | 6/10/05 | 8/26/72 | 5-4 |
| Maddox, Nicholas (Nick) | 1907-10 | 11/9/86 | 11/27/54 | 44-20 |
| Mahaffey, LeeRoy (Roy) | 1926-27 | 2/9/03 | 7/23/69 | 1-0 |
| Main, Forrest H. (Woody) | 1948, 50, 52-53 | 2/12/22 | | 4-13 |
| Mamaux, Albert L. (Al) | 1913-17 | 5/30/94 | 1/2/63 | 49-36 |
| Manske, Louis (Lou) | 1906 | 7/4/84 | 4/27/63 | 1-0 |
| Marone, Louis S. (Lou) | 1969-70 | 12/3/45 | | 1-1 |
| Martin, Paul C. | 1955 | 3/10/32 | | 0-1 |
| Maul, Albert J. (Al) | 1888-89, 91 | 10/9/65 | 5/3/58 | 2-8 |
| Maxwell, J. Albert (Bert) | 1906 | 10/17/86 | 2/10/67 | 0-1 |
| May, William H. (Buckshot) | 1924 | 12/13/99 | | 0-0 |
| Mayer, J. Erskine | 1918-19 | 1/16/91 | 3/10/57 | 14-6 |
| McArthur, Oland A. (Dixie) | 1914 | 2/1/92 | | 0-0 |
| McBean, Alvin O. (Al) | 1961-68, 70 | 5/15/38 | | 65-43 |
| McCall, John W. (Windy) | 1950 | 7/18/25 | | 0-0 |
| McCarthy, Thomas P. (Tom) | 1908 | 5/22/84 | 3/28/33 | 0-0 |
| McCormick, James (Jim) | 1887 | 1856 | 3/10/18 | 13-23 |
| McCreery, Thomas L. (Tom) | 1900 | 10/19/74 | 7/3/41 | 0-0 |
| McDowell, Samuel E. (Sam) | 1975 | 9/21/42 | | 2-1 |
| McFarland, Charles E. (Chappie) | 1905 | 12/15/24 | | 1-3 |
| McIlveen, Henry C. (Irish) | 1906 | 7/27/80 | 7/18/60 | 0-1 |
| McKee, James M. (Jim) | 1972-73 | 2/1/47 | | 1-1 |
| McLaughlin, Warren A. | 1902 | 1/22/76 | 10/22/23 | 3-0 |
| McLish, Calvin C. (Cal) | 1947-48 | 12/1/25 | | 0-0 |
| McMahan, Jack W. | 1956 | 7/22/32 | | 0-0 |
| McQuillan, George W. | 1913-15 | 5/1/85 | 3/30/40 | 28-33 |
| Meador, John D. (Johnny) | 1920 | 12/4/92 | 4/11/70 | 0-2 |
| Meadows, H. Lee | 1923-29 | 7/12/94 | 1/29/63 | 88-52 |
| Medich, George F. (Doc) | 1976 | 12/9/48 | | 8-11 |
| Meekin, Jouett | 1900 | 2/21/67 | 12/14/44 | 0-2 |
| Meine, Henry W. (Heinie) | 1929-34 | 5/1/96 | 3/18/68 | 66-50 |
| Menefee, John (Jocko) | 1892, 94-95 | 1/21/68 | 3/11/53 | 5-9 |
| Mercer, John L. | 1910 | 6/22/90 | | 0-0 |
| Merritt, George W. | 1901, 03 | 4/14/80 | 2/21/38 | 3-0 |
| Mikkelsen, Peter J. (Pete) | 1966-67 | 10/25/39 | | 10-10 |
| Miljus, John K. (Johnny) | 1927-28 | 6/30/95 | 2/11/76 | 13-10 |
| Miller, Frank L. | 1916-19 | 3/13/86 | 2/19/74 | 41-49 |
| Miller, Robert L. (Bob) | 1971-72 | 2/18/39 | | 6-4 |

# Pitchers (continued)

| Player | Years | Born | Died | W-L |
|--------|-------|------|------|-----|
| Miller, Roscoe C. | 1904 | 12/2/76 | 4/18/13 | 7-8 |
| Minshall, James E. (Jim) | 1974-75 | 7/4/47 | | 0-1 |
| Mizell, Wilmer D. (Vinegar Bend) | 1960-62 | 8/13/30 | | 21-16 |
| Moore, Eugene (Gene) | 1909-10 | 11/9/85 | 8/31/38 | 2-1 |
| Moore, George R. | 1905 | 11/25/72 | 11/7/48 | 0-0 |
| Moose, Robert R. (Bob) | 1967-76 | 10/9/47 | 10/9/76 | 76-71 |
| Moran, Samuel (Sam) | 1895 | 9/16/70 | 8/29/97 | 2-4 |
| Moren, Lewis H. (Lew) | 1903-04 | 8/4/83 | 11/2/66 | 0-1 |
| Morlan, John G. | 1973-74 | 11/22/47 | | 2-5 |
| Morris, Edward (Ed) | 1887-89 | 9/29/59 | 4/12/37 | 49-59 |
| Morrison, John D. (Johnny) | 1920-27 | 10/22/95 | 3/20/66 | 89-71 |
| Morrison, Phillip M. (Phil) | 1921 | 10/18/94 | 1/18/55 | 0-0 |
| Muir, Joseph A. (Joe) | 1951-52 | 11/26/22 | | 2-5 |
| Mulcahy, Hugh N. | 1947 | 9/9/13 | | 0-0 |
| Muncrief, Robert C. (Bob) | 1949 | 1/28/16 | | 1-5 |
| Munger, George D. | 1952, 56 | 10/4/18 | | 3-7 |
| | | | | |
| Nagle, Walter H. (Judge) | 1911 | 3/10/80 | 5/27/71 | 3-2 |
| Nagy, Stephen (Steve) | 1947 | 5/28/19 | | 1-3 |
| Naranjo, Lazaro R. G. (Cholly) | 1956 | 11/25/34 | | 1-2 |
| Necciai, Ronald A. (Ron) | 1952 | 6/18/32 | | 1-6 |
| Nelson, James L. (Jim) | 1970-71 | 7/4/47 | | 6-4 |
| Nichols, Chester R. (Chet) | 1926-27 | 7/2/97 | | 0-3 |
| Nicol, George E. | 1894 | 10/17/70 | 8/10/24 | 3-4 |
| | | | | |
| O'Dell, William O. (Billy) | 1966-67 | 2/10/33 | | 8-8 |
| O'Donnell, George D. | 1954 | 5/27/29 | | 3-9 |
| Oldham, John C. (Red) | 1925-26 | 7/15/93 | 1/28/61 | 5-4 |
| Olivo, Diomedes A. | 1960, 62 | 1/22/19 | 2/15/77 | 5-1 |
| Osborn, F. Robert (Bob) | 1931 | 4/17/03 | 4/19/60 | 6-1 |
| Osborne, Frederick W. (Fred) | 1890 | | Deceased | 0-5 |
| Osborne, Wayne H. | 1935 | 10/11/12 | | 0-0 |
| Ostermuller, Frederick R. (Fritz) | 1944-48 | 9/15/07 | 12/17/57 | 49-42 |
| Otey, William T. (Bill) | 1907 | 12/16/86 | 4/23/31 | 0-1 |
| O'Toole, Martin J. (Marty) | 1911-14 | 11/27/88 | 2/18/49 | 25-35 |
| | | | | |
| Pagan, David P. (Dave) | 1977 | 9/15/50 | | 0-0 |
| Page, Joseph F. (Joe) | 1954 | 10/28/17 | | 0-0 |
| Papish, Frank R. | 1950 | 10/21/17 | 8/30/65 | 0-0 |
| Parker, Jay | 1899 | | Deceased | 0-0 |
| Parsons, Thomas A. (Tom) | 1963 | 9/13/39 | | 0-1 |
| Passeau, Claude W. | 1935 | 4/9/09 | | 0-1 |
| Patterson, Daryl A. | 1974 | 11/21/43 | | 2-1 |
| Payne, Harley F. | 1899 | 1/9/66 | 12/29/35 | 1-3 |
| Peery, George A. (Red) | 1927 | 8/15/06 | | 0-0 |
| Pena, Orlando G. | 1970 | 11/17/33 | | 2-1 |
| Pepper, H. McLaurin (Laurin) | 1954-57 | 1/18/31 | | 2-8 |
| Perez, George T. | 1958 | 12/29/37 | | 0-1 |
| Pettit, G. W. Paul | 1951, 53 | 11/29/31 | | 1-2 |
| Petty, Jesse L. | 1929-30 | 11/23/94 | 10/23/71 | 12-16 |
| Pfeffer, Edward J. (Jeff) | 1924 | 3/4/88 | 8/15/72 | 5-3 |

## Pitchers (continued)

| Player | Years | Born | Died | W-L |
|---|---|---|---|---|
| Pfiester, John T. J. (Jack) | 1903-04 | 5/24/78 | 9/3/53 | 1-4 |
| Phillippe, Charles L. (Deacon) | 1900-11 | 5/23/72 | 3/30/52 | 166-93 |
| Phillips, William C. (Bill) | 1890 | 11/9/68 | 10/25/41 | 1-9 |
| Pierro, William L. (Bill) | 1950 | 4/15/26 | | 0-2 |
| Pizzaro, Juan C. | 1967-68, 74 | 2/7/38 | | 10-12 |
| Poat, Raymond W. (Ray) | 1949 | 12/19/17 | | 0-1 |
| Podgajny, John S. (Johnny) | 1943 | 6/10/20 | 3/2/71 | 0-4 |
| Pollet, Howard J. (Howie) | 1951-53, 56 | 6/26/21 | 8/8/74 | 14-31 |
| Ponder, C. Elmer | 1917, 19-21 | 6/26/93 | 4/20/74 | 14-21 |
| Poole, Edward I. (Ed) | 1900-02 | 9/7/77 | 3/23/20 | 6-4 |
| Porterfield, Erwin C. (Bob) | 1958-59 | 8/10/23 | | 5-8 |
| Powell, William B. (Bill) | 1909-10 | 5/8/85 | 9/28/67 | 4-7 |
| Priddy, Robert S. (Bob) | 1962, 64 | 12/10/39 | | 2-2 |
| Purkey, Robert T. (Bob) | 1954-57, 66 | 7/14/29 | | 16-30 |
| | | | | |
| Queen, Melvin J. (Mel) | 1947-48, 50-52 | 3/4/18 | | 19-36 |
| | | | | |
| Rader, Drew L. | 1921 | 5/14/01 | | 0-0 |
| Rambert, Elmer D. (Pep) | 1939-40 | 8/1/17 | | 0-1 |
| Ramos, Pedro G. | 1969 | 4/28/35 | | 0-1 |
| Raydon, Curtis L. (Curt) | 1958 | 11/18/33 | | 8-4 |
| Rescigno, Xavier F. | 1943-45 | 10/13/13 | | 19-22 |
| Reuss, Jerry | 1974-78 | 6/19/49 | | 61-46 |
| Rhines, William P. (Billy) | 1898-99 | 3/14/69 | 1/30/22 | 16-20 |
| Rhoden, Richard A. (Rick) | 1979- | 5/16/53 | | |
| Ribant, Dennis J. | 1967 | 9/20/41 | | 9-8 |
| Riddle, Elmer R. | 1948-49 | 7/31/14 | | 13-18 |
| Robertaille, Anthony F. (Chick) | 1904-05 | 3/2/79 | 7/30/47 | 12-8 |
| Roberts, David A. (Dave) | 1979- | 9/11/44 | | |
| Robinson, Don A. | 1978- | 6/8/57 | | |
| Robinson, John H. (Hank) | 1911-13 | 8/16/89 | 7/2/65 | 26-17 |
| Roe, Elwin C. (Preacher) | 1944-47 | 2/26/15 | | 34-47 |
| Romo, Enrique | 1979- | 7/15/47 | | |
| Rooker, James P. (Jim) | 1973- | 9/23/42 | | |
| Rosebrough, Eli E. (Zeke) | 1898-99 | | Deceased | 0-3 |
| | | | | |
| Sadowski, James M. (Jim) | 1974 | 8/7/51 | | 0-1 |
| Sale, Frederick L. (Fred) | 1924 | 5/2/02 | 5/27/56 | 0-0 |
| Salveson, John T. (Jack) | 1935 | 1/5/14 | 12/28/74 | 0-1 |
| Sanders, Roy G. | 1918 | 8/1/92 | 1/17/50 | 7-9 |
| Scanlan. William D. (Doc) | 1903-04 | 3/7/81 | 5/29/49 | 1-4 |
| Scheneberg, John B. | 1913 | 11/20/87 | 9/9/50 | 0-1 |
| Schmidt, Frederick (Crazy) | 1890 | 2/13/66 | 10/5/40 | 1-9 |
| Schultz, Robert D. (Bob) | 1953 | 11/27/23 | | 0-2 |
| Schwall, Donald B. (Don) | 1963-66 | 3/2/36 | | 22-23 |
| Scott, John W. (Jack) | 1916 | 4/18/92 | 11/30/59 | 0-0 |
| Sewell, Truett B. (Rip) | 1938-49 | 5/11/07 | | 143-97 |
| Shantz, Robert C. (Bobby) | 1961 | 9/26/25 | | 6-3 |
| Sheehan, Thomas C. (Tom) | 1925-26 | 3/31/94 | | 1-3 |
| Shellenback, James P. (Jim) | 1966-67, 69 | 11/18/43 | | 1-1 |
| Short, William R. (Bill) | 1967 | 11/27/37 | | 0-0 |

## Pitchers (continued)

| Player | Years | Born | Died | W-L |
|---|---|---|---|---|
| Shuman, Harry | 1942-43 | 3/5/16 | | 0-0 |
| Singleton, B. Elmer | 1947-48 | 6/26/18 | | 6-8 |
| Sisk, Thomas W. (Tommie) | 1962-68 | 4/12/42 | | 37-35 |
| Slapnicka, Cyril C. (Cy) | 1918 | 3/23/86 | | 1-4 |
| Slattery, Phillip R. (Phil) | 1915 | 2/25/93 | 3/10/68 | 0-0 |
| Smith, Elmer E. | 1892, 94 | 3/28/68 | 11/5/45 | 6-7 |
| Smith, Harold L. (Hal) | 1932-35 | 6/30/02 | | 12-11 |
| Smith, John F. (Phenomenal) | 1890 | 12/12/64 | 4/3/52 | 1-3 |
| Smith, Robert G. (Bob) | 1957-79 | 2/1/31 | | 4-6 |
| Smith, Sherrod M. (Sherry) | 1911-12 | 2/18/91 | 9/12/49 | 1-0 |
| Songer, Donald C. (Don) | 1924-27 | 1/31/99 | 10/3/62 | 7-9 |
| Sowders, William J. (Bill) | 1889-90 | 11/29/64 | 2/2/51 | 9-13 |
| Sparks, Tully F. | 1899 | 4/18/77 | 7/15/37 | 8-6 |
| Spencer, Glenn E. | 1928, 30-32 | 9/11/05 | 12/30/58 | 23-29 |
| Staley, Henry E. (Harry) | 1888-89, 91 | 11/3/66 | 1/12/10 | 37-43 |
| Starr, Raymond F. (Ray) | 1944-45 | 4/23/06 | 2/9/63 | 6-7 |
| Steele, Elmer R. | 1910-11 | 5/17/84 | 3/9/66 | 9-11 |
| Steele, Robert W. (Bob) | 1917-18 | 3/29/94 | 1/27/62 | 7-14 |
| Steineder, Raymond J. (Ray) | 1923-24 | 11/13/95 | | 2-1 |
| Stone, E. Arnold (Arnie) | 1923-24 | 12/19/92 | 7/29/48 | 4-3 |
| Stoner, Ulysses S. G. (Lil) | 1930 | 2/28/99 | 6/26/66 | 0-0 |
| Stratton, C. Scott | 1891 | 10/2/69 | 3/8/39 | 0-2 |
| Strincevich, Nicholas M. (Nick) | 1941-42, 44-48 | 3/1/15 | | 42-40 |
| Struss, Clarence H. (Steamboat) | 1934 | 2/24/09 | | 0-1 |
| Sturdivant, Thomas V. (Tom) | 1961-63 | 4/28/30 | | 14-7 |
| Suchecki, James J. (Jim) | 1952 | 8/25/26 | | 0-0 |
| Sullivan, Joe | 1941 | 9/26/10 | | 4-1 |
| Surkont, Matthew C. (Max) | 1954-56 | 6/16/22 | | 16-32 |
| Swanson, Arthur L. (Red) | 1955-57 | 10/15/36 | | 3-3 |
| Swetonic, Stephen A. (Steve) | 1929-33, 35 | 8/13/03 | 4/22/74 | 37-36 |
| Swift, William V. (Bill) | 1932-39 | 1/10/08 | 2/23/69 | 91-79 |
| Swigart, Oadis V. (Oad) | 1939-40 | 2/13/15 | | 1-3 |
| Tannehill, Jesse N. | 1897-02 | 7/14/74 | 9/22/56 | 116-58 |
| Tate, Alvin W. (Al) | 1946 | 7/1/18 | | 0-1 |
| Tauscher, Walter E. (Walt) | 1928 | 11/22/01 | | 0-0 |
| Tekulve, Kenton C. (Kent) | 1974- | 3/5/47 | | |
| Terry, William H. (Adonis) | 1892-94 | 8/7/64 | 2/24/15 | 29-16 |
| Thies, Vernon A. (Jake) | 1954-55 | 4/1/26 | | 3-10 |
| Thompson, J. Gustav (Gus) | 1903 | 6/22/77 | 3/28/58 | 2-3 |
| Thompson, Will M. (Bill) | 1892 | 8/30/70 | 7/9/62 | 0-1 |
| Tising, John J. (Jack) | 1936 | 10/9/03 | 9/5/67 | 1-3 |
| Tobin, James A. (Jim) | 1937-39 | 12/27/12 | 5/19/69 | 29-24 |
| Tost, Louis E. (Lou) | 1947 | 6/1/11 | 2/22/67 | 0-0 |
| Trimble, Joseph G. (Joe) | 1957 | 10/12/30 | | 0-2 |
| Tutwiler, Elmer S. | 1928 | 11/19/05 | | 0-0 |
| Umbricht, James (Jim) | 1959-61 | 9/17/30 | 4/8/64 | 1-2 |
| Vail, Robert G. (Bob) | 1908 | 9/24/81 | 1953 | 1-1 |
| Vance, Clarence A. (Dazzy) | 1915 | 3/4/91 | 2/16/61 | 0-1 |

## Pitchers (continued)

| Player | Years | Born | Died | W-L |
|---|---|---|---|---|
| Veale, Robert A. (Bob) | 1962-72 | 10/28/35 | | 116-91 |
| Veil, Frederick W. (Bucky) | 1903-04 | 8/2/81 | 4/16/31 | 5-4 |
| Vitelli, A. Joseph (Joe) | 1944-45 | 4/12/08 | 2/7/67 | 0-0 |
| Wacker, Charles (Charlie) | 1909 | | | 0-0 |
| Waddell, George E. (Rube) | 1900-01 | 10/13/76 | 4/1/14 | 8-15 |
| Walker, J. Luke | 1965-66, 68-73 | 9/2/43 | | 40-42 |
| Walsh, Cornelius (Connie) | 1907 | 4/23/85 | 4/5/53 | 0-0 |
| Walsh, James G. (Junior) | 1946, 48-51 | 3/7/19 | | 4-10 |
| Walter, James B. (Bernie) | 1930 | 8/15/08 | | 0-0 |
| Warner, Edward E. (Ed) | 1912 | 6/20/89 | 2/2/54 | 1-1 |
| Waters, Fred W. | 1955-56 | 2/2/27 | | 2-2 |
| Watson, John R. (Mule) | 1920 | 10/15/96 | 8/25/49 | 0-0 |
| Waugh, James E. (Jim) | 1952-53 | 11/25/33 | | 5-11 |
| Weaver, James D. | 1935-37 | 11/25/03 | | 36-21 |
| Webb, Cleon E. (Lefty) | 1910 | 3/1/85 | 1/12/58 | 2-1 |
| Welch, John V. (Johnny) | 1936 | 12/2/06 | 9/2/40 | 0-0 |
| Werle, William G. (Bill) | 1949-52 | 12/21/20 | | 28-35 |
| Weyhing, August P. (Gus) | 1895 | 9/29/66 | 9/3/55 | 1-0 |
| Wheeler, Floyd C. (Rip) | 1921-22 | 3/2/98 | 9/18/68 | 0-0 |
| White, O. Kirby | 1910-11 | 1/3/84 | 4/22/43 | 9-10 |
| Whitson, Eddie L. | 1977-79 | 5/19/55 | | 8-9 |
| Wickersham, David C. (Dave) | 1968 | 9/27/35 | | 1-0 |
| Wilhelm, Irving K. (Kaiser) | 1903 | 1/26/74 | 5/21/36 | 5-4 |
| Wilkie, Aldon J. (Lefty) | 1941-42, 46 | 10/30/14 | | 8-11 |
| Wilks, Theodore (Ted) | 1951-52 | 11/13/15 | | 8-10 |
| Williams, Donald F. (Don) | 1958-59 | 9/14/31 | | 0-0 |
| Willis, Victor G. (Vic) | 1906-09 | 4/12/76 | 8/3/47 | 90-47 |
| Willoughby, Claude W. | 1931 | 11/14/98 | 8/14/73 | 0-2 |
| Wiltse, Lewis D. (Snake) | 1901 | 12/5/71 | 8/25/28 | 1-4 |
| Winham, Lafayette S. (Lave) | 1903 | 1881 | 9/11/51 | 3-1 |
| Wise, Roy O. | 1944 | 11/18/24 | | 0-0 |
| Wisner, John H. | 1919-20 | 11/5/99 | | 2-3 |
| Witt, George A. | 1957-61 | 11/9/33 | | 10-13 |
| Wolfe, Edward A. (Ed) | 1952 | 1/2/29 | | 0-0 |
| Wolff, Roger F. | 1947 | 4/10/11 | | 1-4 |
| Wood, Charles A. (Spades) | 1930-31 | 1/13/09 | | 6-9 |
| Wood, Wilbur F. | 1964-65 | 10/22/41 | | 1-3 |
| Woodcock, Fred W. | 1892 | 5/17/68 | 8/11/43 | 1-2 |
| Woods, Walter S. (Walt) | 1900 | 4/28/75 | 10/30/51 | 0-0 |
| Wright, David W. (Dave) | 1895 | 8/27/75 | 1/18/46 | 0-0 |
| Yde, Emil O. | 1924-27 | 1/28/00 | 12/5/68 | 42-22 |
| Yellowhorse, Moses J. (Chief) | 1921-22 | 1/28/98 | 4/10/64 | 8-4 |
| Yochim, Leonard (Len) | 1951, 54 | 10/16/28 | | 1-2 |
| Young, Harley E. | 1908 | | | 0-2 |
| Young, Irving M. (Irv) | 1908 | 7/21/77 | 1/14/35 | 3-3 |
| Zachary, W. Chris | 1973 | 2/19/44 | | 0-1 |
| Ziegler, George J. | 1890 | 1872 | 7/22/16 | 0-1 |
| Zinn, James E. (Jimmy) | 1920-22 | 1/31/95 | | 8-7 |

## 3. TRADES SECTION

Even when the season is over, there is interest in baseball because of trades. Every team makes trades. The bad team makes a trade in hopes of turning the club around. The contender makes a trade to put the team "over the top." The championship team makes a trade because they cannot afford to stand pat.

The Pirates have been in each position throughout their history. Trades for such players as Don Hoak, Bill Virdon, Dave Giusti, Nellie Briles, Bill Madlock, and Tim Foli have resulted in championships for the Pirates. Other trades for pitchers Jim Bunning and Doc Medich, which held hope to turn the contending Pirates into champions, backfired completely. Trading Bob Elliott, Burleigh Grimes, and Dick Groat turned other teams into champions while hardly helping the Pirates. Batting champions Debs Garms and Matty Alou were acquired through trades.

Prior to 1915, outgoing and newcoming players are listed because the dates of the transactions are virtually impossible to ascertain. The rest of the trades are listed chronologically from 1915 through the end of the 1979 season.

Before a team can make a trade, there must be an original team to start with. In Pittsburgh, that team was the 1887 Alleghenies. The Alleghenies had played in the American Association from 1862-86 and most of the first National League players came from that team. Here is the first roster and where the player came from (if not originally with Pittsburgh).

| | | |
|---|---|---|
| Sam Barkley | 1B | |
| Ed Beecher | OF | |
| Bill Bishop | P | |
| Tom Brown | OF | |
| Fred Carroll | OF-C | |
| John Coleman | OF | |
| Abner Dalrymple | OF | (from Chicago) |
| Jocko Fields | OF-INF | |
| Pud Galvin | P | |
| Willie Kuehne | 3B | |
| Jim McCormick | P | (from Chicago) |
| Alex McKinnon | 1B | (from St. Louis) |
| Doggie Miller | C | |
| Ed Morris | P | |
| Pop Smith | INF | |
| Art Whitney | 3B | |

### 1888

NEWCOMERS:

| | | |
|---|---|---|
| Cliff Carroll | OF | Washington |
| Elmer Cleveland | 3B | New York (for Art Whitney) |
| Fred Dunlap | 2B | Detroit (purchase) |
| Hardie Henderson | P | Brooklyn AA |
| Al Maul | OF-1B | Philadelphia (purchase) |
| Harry Staley | P | St. Louis Whites (team disbanded) |
| Billy Sunday | OF | Chicago (purchase) |

OUTGOING:

| | | |
|---|---|---|
| Bill Farmer | C | Philadelphia AA |
| Art Whitney | 3B | New York (for Elmer Cleveland) |

127

## 1889

NEWCOMERS:

| | | |
|---|---|---|
| Pete Conway | P | Detroit (purchase) |
| Ned Hanlon | OF | Detroit (purchase) |
| Paul Hines | OF | Indianapolis |
| Jack Rowe | SS | Detroit (purchase) |
| Billy Sowders | P | Boston (for Pop Smith) |
| Deacon White | 3B | Detroit (purchase) |

OUTGOING:

| | | |
|---|---|---|
| John Coleman | OF-P | Philadelphia AA |
| Pop Smith | INF | Boston (for Billy Sowders) |

## 1890

(NOTE: In 1890 many National League players, including virtually all Pittsburgh players, jumped to the newly formed Players League.)

NEWCOMERS:

| | | |
|---|---|---|
| Dave Anderson | P | Philadelphia |
| Sumner Bowman | P | Philadelphia |
| Eddie Burke | OF | Philadelphia |
| John Coleman | OF-P | Philadelphia AA |
| Sam Crane | 2B | New York |
| Bill Day | P | Philadelphia |
| Harry Decker | C | Philadelphia |
| Duke Esper | P | Philadelphia AA |
| Reddy Gray | INF | Pittsburgh P |
| Guy Hecker | IB-P | Louisville AA |
| Ducky Hemp | OF | Louisville AA (1887)* |
| Sam LaRoque | 2B | Detroit (1888)* |
| Al Lawson | P | Boston (for Paul Hines) |
| Pop Lytle | OF | Chicago |
| Pop Smith | INF | Philadelphia |
| William Veach | 1B | Cleveland (for Bill Garfield) |

OUTGOING:

| | | |
|---|---|---|
| Jake Beckley | 1B | Pittsburgh P |
| Fred Carroll | C-OF | Pittsburgh P |
| Sam Crane | 2B | New York |
| Fred Dunlap | 2B | New York P |
| Duke Esper | P | Philadelphia (for Eddie Burke) |
| Jocko Fields | OF-C | Pittsburgh P |
| Pud Galvin | P | Pittsburgh P |
| Bill Garfield | P | Cleveland (for William Veach) |
| Ned Hanlon | OF | Pittsburgh P |
| Ducky Hemp | OF | Syracuse AA |
| Paul Hines | OF | Boston (for Al Lawson) |
| Willie Kuehne | INF | Pittsburgh P |
| Al Maul | OF-1B | Pittsburgh P |
| Ed Morris | P | Pittsburgh P |
| Jack Rowe | SS | Buffalo P |

*denotes players last year in the Major Leagues before joining Pittsburgh.

| | | |
|---|---|---|
| Harry Staley | P | Pittsburgh P |
| Billy Sunday | OF | Philadelphia (purchase) |
| Deacon White | 3B | Buffalo P |

## 1891

(NOTE: The Players League disbanded and most of the former Alleghenies returned to Pittsburgh.)

NEWCOMERS:

| | | |
|---|---|---|
| Mark Baldwin | P | Chicago P |
| Jake Beckley | 1B | Pittsburgh P |
| Lou Bierbauer | 2B | Brooklyn P |
| Pete Browning | OF | Cleveland P |
| Fred Carroll | C-OF | Pittsburgh P |
| Pop Corkhill | OF | Cincinnati (for Pete Browning) |
| Jocko Fields | OF-C | Pittsburgh P |
| Pud Galvin | P | Pittsburgh P |
| Ned Hanlon | OF | Pittsburgh P |
| Silver King | P | Chicago P |
| Connie Mack | C | Buffalo P |
| Al Maul | OF-1B | Pittsburgh P |
| Charlie Reilly | 3B | Columbus AA |
| Frank Shugart | SS | Chicago P |
| Harry Staley | P | Pittsburgh P |
| Scott Stratton | P | Louisville AA (for Sam LaRoque) |
| Piggy Ward | OF | Philadelphia (1889)* |

OUTGOING:

| | | |
|---|---|---|
| Sumner Bowman | P | Philadelphia AA |
| Eddie Burke | OF | Philadelphia AA |
| Sam LaRoque | 2B | Louisville AA (for Scott Stratton) |
| Phenomenal Smith | P | Philadelphia |
| Pete Browning | OF | Cincinnati (for Pop Corkhill) |
| Scott Stratton | P | Louisville AA |
| Harry Staley | P | Boston |

## 1892

NEWCOMER:

| | | |
|---|---|---|
| Tom Burns | 3B | Chicago |
| Patsy Donovan | OF | Washington |
| Billy Earle | C | St. Louis AA (1890)* |
| Red Ehret | P | Louisville AA |
| Duke Esper | P | Philadelphia |
| Duke Farrell | 3B | Boston AA |
| Joe Kelley | OF | Boston |
| Elmer Smith | OF-P | Cincinnati AA |
| Jake Stenzel | OF | Chicago (1890)* |
| Ed Swartwood | OF | Toledo AA (1890)* |
| George Van Haltren | OF | Baltimore (for Joe Kelly) |
| Adonis Terry | P | Baltimore |

OUTGOING:

| | | |
|---|---|---|
| Tun Berger | P | Washington |
| Ned Hanlon | OF | Baltimore |
| Silver King | P | New York |
| Sam LaRoque | 2B | Louisville AA |
| Charlie Reilly | 3B | Philadelphia |
| Piggy Ward | OF | Baltimore |
| Harry Raymond | 3B | Washington |
| Joe Kelly | OF | Baltimore (for George Van Haltren) |
| Pud Galvin | P | St. Louis (released) |

**1893**

NEWCOMERS:

| | | |
|---|---|---|
| Hank Gastright | P | Washington |
| Jack Glasscock | SS | St. Louis (for Frank Shugart) |
| Ad Gumbert | P | Chicago (purchase) |
| Frank Killen | P | Washington |
| Denny Lyons | 3B | New York (purchase) |

OUTGOING:

| | | |
|---|---|---|
| Duke Esper | P | Washington |
| Duke Farrell | 3B | Washington |
| Billy Gumbert | P | Louisville (purchase) |
| Jocko Menefee | P | Louisville (purchase) |
| Hank Gastright | P | Boston (purchase) |
| Frank Shugart | SS | St. Louis (for Jack Glasscock) |

**1894**

NEWCOMERS:

| | | |
|---|---|---|
| Monte Cross | SS | Baltimore (1892)* |
| Jack Easton | P | St. Louis (1892)* |
| Phil Knell | P | Louisville |
| Jocko Menefee | P | Louisville |
| Bill Merritt | C | Boston (purchase) |
| George Nicol | OF-P | Chicago (1891)* |
| Frank Scheibeck | SS | Toledo AA (1890)* |
| Farmer Weaver | OF | Louisville |

OUTGOING:

| | | |
|---|---|---|
| Billy Earle | C | Louisville |
| Doggie Miller | C | St. Louis (purchase) |
| George Van Haltren | OF | New York (purchase) |
| Bill Merritt | C | Cincinnati (purchase) |
| George Nicol | OF-P | Louisville |
| Frank Scheibeck | SS | Washington (purchase) |
| Phil Knell | P | Louisville |
| Adonis Terry | P | Chicago |

**1895**

NEWCOMERS:

| | | |
|---|---|---|
| Billy Clingman | INF | Cincinnati-Milwaukee AA (1895) |
| Frank Genins | OF-INF | St. Louis (1892)* |

| Bill Hart | P | Brooklyn (1892)* |
|---|---|---|
| Pink Hawley | P | St. Louis (for Ehret and Lyons) |
| Tom Kinslow | C | Brooklyn (for Ad Gumbert) |
| Gus Weyhing | P | Philadelphia (purchase) |
| Bill Merritt | C | Cincinnati (purchase) |

OUTGOING:

| Gene DeMontreville | SS | Washington (purchase) |
|---|---|---|
| Red Ehret | P | St. Louis (for Pink Hawley) |
| Jack Glasscock | SS | Louisville (purchase) |
| Ad Gumbert | P | Brooklyn (for Tom Kinslow) |
| Denny Lyons | 3B | St. Louis (for Pink Hawley) |
| Gus Weyhing | P | Louisville (purchase) |

## 1896

NEWCOMERS:

| Eddie Boyle | C | Louisville (purchase) |
|---|---|---|
| Harry Davis | 1B | New York (for Jake Beckley) |
| Tom Delahanty | 3B | Cleveland (purchase) |
| Bones Ely | SS | St. Louis (for Bill Hart) |
| Charlie Hastings | P | Cleveland (1893)* |
| Jim Hughey | P | Chicago (1893)* |
| Denny Lyons | 3B | St. Louis (for Monte Cross) |
| Jud Smith | 3B | St. Louis (1893)* |
| Harry Truby | 2B | Chicago (purchase) |
| Joe Wright | OF | Louisville (purchase) |

OUTGOING:

| Billy Clingman | INF | Louisville (purchase) |
|---|---|---|
| Monte Cross | SS | St. Louis (for Denny Lyons) |
| Bill Hart | P | St. Louis (for Bones Ely) |
| Tom Kinslow | C | Louisville (purchase) |
| Jake Beckley | 1B | New York (for Harry Davis) |

## 1897

NEWCOMERS:

| Steve Brodie | OF | Baltimore (for Jake Stenzel and cash) |
|---|---|---|
| Jim Donely | 3B | Baltimore (purchase) |
| Jesse Tannehill | P | Cincinnati (1894)* |

OUTGOING:

| Lou Bierbauer | 2B | St. Louis (purchase) |
|---|---|---|
| Tom Delahanty | 3B | Louisville (purchase) |
| Jake Stenzel | OF | Baltimore (for Steve Brodie) |
| Jim Donely | 3B | New York (purchase) |
| Tom Leahy | OF | Washington (purchase) |

## 1898

NEWCOMERS:

| Frank Bowerman | C | Baltimore (for Steve Brodie) |
|---|---|---|
| Willie Clark | 1B | New York (purchase) |
| John Cronin | P | Brooklyn (1895)* |
| Bill Eagan | 2B | Chicago (1892)* |

| Bill Grey | 3B | Cincinnati (1896)* |
|---|---|---|
| Bill Hart | P | St. Louis (trade)** |
| Bill Hoffer | P | Baltimore (purchase) |
| Fred Lake | 1B | Boston (purchase) |
| Jack McCarthy | OF | Cincinnati (1894)* |
| Tom McCreery | OF | New York (purchase) |
| Morgan Murphy | C | St. Louis (trade)** |
| Tom O'Brien | OF-1B | Baltimore (purchase) |
| Billy Rhines | P | Cincinnati (for Pink Hawley) |
| Pop Schriver | C | Cincinnati (for Pink Hawley) |

OUTGOING:

| Pink Hawley | P | Cincinnati (for Rhines and Schriver) |
|---|---|---|
| Jim Hughey | P | St. Louis (trade)** |
| Elmer Smith | OF-P | Cincinnati (purchase) |
| Joe Sugden | C | St. Louis (trade)** |
| Hi Ladd | OF | Boston (purchase) |
| Morgan Murphy | C | Philadelphia (purchase) |
| Steve Brodie | OF | Baltimore (for Frank Bowerman) |
| Frank Killen | P | Washington (purchase) |

## 1899

NEWCOMERS:

| Art Madison | INF | Philadelphia (1895)* |
|---|---|---|
| John O'Brien | 2B | Baltimore (purchase) |
| Harley Payne | P | Brooklyn (purchase) |
| Heinie Reitz | 2B | Washington (for Dick Padden) |
| Heinie Smith | 2B | Louisville (purchase) |
| Tully Sparks | P | Philadelphia (1897)* |

OUTGOING:

| John Cronin | P | Cincinnati (purchase) |
|---|---|---|
| Harry Davis | 1B | Louisville (purchase) |
| Tom O'Brien | OF-1B | New York (purchase) |
| Dick Padden | 2B | Washington (for Heinie Reitz) |

## 1900

(NOTE: Prior to the 1900 season, Louisville owner Barney Dreyfuss purchased controlling stock in the Pirates. As part of the deal, Dreyfuss traded 14 of his Colonels to Pittsburgh for four Pirates and $25,000. The Louisville franchise was subsequently dropped from the league.)

NEWCOMERS:

| Fred Clarke | OF | Louisville (trade)** |
|---|---|---|
| Duff Cooley | OF | Philadelphia (purchase) |
| Patsy Flaherty | P | Louisville (trade)** |
| Tacks Latimer | C | Louisville (trade)** |
| Tommy Leach | 3B-OF | Louisville (trade)** |
| Jouette Meekin | P | Boston (purchase) |
| Tom O'Brien | OF-1B | New York (purchase) |
| John O'Connor | C-1B | St. Louis (purchase) |
| Deacon Phillippe | P | Louisville (trade)** |

| Claude Ritchey | 2B | Louisville (trade)** |
| Rube Waddell | P | Louisville (trade)** |
| Honus Wagner | SS | Louisville (trade)** |
| Walt Woods | P | Louisville (trade)** |
| Chief Zimmer | C | Louisville (trade)** |

OUTGOING:

| Frank Bowerman | C | New York (purchase) |
| Jack Chesbro | P | Louisville*** (trade)** |
| Patsy Donovan | OF | St. Louis (purchase) |
| Paddy Fox | 1B | Louisville (trade)** |
| Art Madison | INF | Louisville (trade)** |
| Jack McCarthy | OF | Chicago (purchase) |
| Johnny O'Brien | 2B | Louisville (trade)** |
| Heinie Smith | 2B | New York (purchase) |

(***Chesbro returned to the Pirates when Louisville was disbanded)

## 1901

NEWCOMERS:

| Kitty Bransfield | 1B | Boston (1898) |
| Jimmy Burke | 3B | Chicago AL |
| Lefty Davis | 1B | Brooklyn (purchase) |
| Ed Dohney | P | New York (purchase) |
| Elmer Smith | OF-P | Cincinnati (purchase) |
| Jud Smith | 3B | Washington (1898) |
| George Yeager | C | Cleveland Al |

OUTGOING:

| Duff Cooley | OF | Boston (purchase) |
| Pop Dillon | OF | Detroit AL |
| Jiggs Donahue | C-1B | Milwaukee AL |
| Truck Eagan | INF | Cleveland AL |
| Bones Ely | SS | Philadelphia AL |
| Bert Husting | P | Milwaukee AL |
| Tacks Latimer | C | Baltimore AL |
| Tom McCreery | OF | Brooklyn (purchase) |
| Pop Schriver | C | St. Louis (purchase) |
| Rube Waddell | P | Chicago (purchase) |
| Jimmy Williams | 3B | Baltimore AL |
| Snake Wiltse | P | Philadelphia AL |

(NOTE: with the operation of the American League beginning in 1901, many players jumped to or from one league to the other. Any players going to or coming from American League teams simply jumped unless otherwise noted.)

## 1902

NEWCOMERS:

| Wid Conroy | SS | Milwaukee AL |
| Fred Crolius | OF | Boston (purchase) |
| Warren McLaughlin | P | Philadelphia (1900)* |
| Harry Smith | C | Philadelphia AL |

## 1902 (continued)

OUTGOING:

| | | |
|---|---|---|
| Ed Poole | P | Cincinnati (purchase) |

## 1903

NEWCOMERS:

| | | |
|---|---|---|
| Lou Gertenrich | OF | Milwaukee AL (1901)* |
| Brickyard Kennedy | P | New York (purchase) |
| Otto Krueger | INF | St. Louis (for Burke) |
| Art Weaver | C | St. Louis (purchase) |
| Lafe Winham | P | Brooklyn (waivers) |

OUTGOING:

| | | |
|---|---|---|
| Jimmy Burke | 3B | St. Louis (for Krueger) |
| Jack Chesbro | P | New York AL |
| Wid Conroy | INF | New York AL |
| Lefty Davis | OF | New York AL |
| Lee Fohl | C | Cincinnati (waivers) |
| Warren McLaughlin | P | Philadelphia (waivers) |
| Jack O'Connor | C | New York AL |
| Jesse Tannehill | P | New York AL |
| Chief Zimmer | C | Philadelphia (purchase) |

## 1904

NEWCOMERS:

| | | |
|---|---|---|
| Charlie Case | P | Cincinnati (1901)* |
| Patsy Flaherty | P | Chicago AL |
| Jack Gilbert | — | New York (purchase) |
| Wyatt Lee | P | Washington AL |
| Bobby Lowe | 2B | Chicago (purchase) |
| Moose McCormick | OF | New York (purchase) |
| Roscoe Miller | P | New York (purchase) |

OUTGOING:

| | | |
|---|---|---|
| Solly Hofman | OF | Chicago (purchase) |
| Bobby Lowe | 2B | Detroit AL (waivers) |
| Doc Scanlan | P | Brooklyn (waivers) |
| Kaiser Wilhelm | P | Boston (waivers) |

## 1905

NEWCOMERS:

| | | |
|---|---|---|
| Dave Brain | INF | St. Louis (for George McBride) |
| Del Howard | 1B | Philadelphia (trade)** |
| George McBride | SS | Milwaukee AL (1901)* |
| Heinie Peitz | C | Cincinnati (purchase) |

OUTGOING:

| | | |
|---|---|---|
| Kitty Bransfield | 1B | Philadelphia (trade)** |
| Harry Cassidy | OF | Washington AL (waivers) |
| Otto Krueger | INF-OF | Philadelphia (trade)** |
| Moose McCormick | OF | Philadelphia (trade)** |
| Ed Phelps | C | Cincinnati (purchase) |

## 1906

NEWCOMERS:

| | | |
|---|---|---|
| Charles Brady | P | Philadelphia (purchase) |
| Bill Hallman | OF | Chicago AL (1903)* |
| Chappie McFarland | C | St. Louis (purchase) |
| Ed Phelps | C | Cincinnati (purchase) |
| Vic Willis | P | Boston (for Brain and Howard) |

OUTGOING:

| | | |
|---|---|---|
| Dave Brain | INF | Boston (for Willis) |
| Del Howard | OF | Boston (for Willis) |
| Ed Karger | P | St. Louis (purchase) |
| Chappie McFarland | C | Brooklyn (waivers) |

## 1907

NEWCOMERS:

| | | |
|---|---|---|
| Ed Abbaticchio | 2B | Boston (for Beaumont and Ritchey) |
| Babe Adams | P | St. Louis (purchase) |
| Bill Duggleby | P | Philadelphia (purchase) |
| Harry Wolter | P | Cincinnati (purchase) |

OUTGOING:

| | | |
|---|---|---|
| Ginger Beaumont | OF | Boston (for Abbaticchio) |
| Otis Clymer | OF | Washington AL (waivers) |
| Bob Ganley | OF | Washington AL (waivers) |
| Claude Ritchey | 2B | Boston (for Abbaticchio) |

## 1908

NEWCOMERS:

| | | |
|---|---|---|
| Tom McCarthy | P | Cincinnati (purchase) |
| Spike Shannon | OF | New York (purchase) |
| Charlie Starr | INF | St. Louis (AL 1905)* |
| John Sullivan | C | Detroit AL (1905)* |
| Roy Thomas | OF | Philadelphia (purchase) |
| Irv Young | P | Boston (for McCarthy and H. Young) |

OUTGOING:

| | | |
|---|---|---|
| Beals Becker | OF | Boston (waivers) |
| Tom McCarthy | P | Boston (for Irv Young) |
| Tom Sheehan | P | Brooklyn (waivers) |
| Harry Smith | C | Boston (purchase) |
| Harley Young | P | Boston (for Irv Young) |

## 1909

NEWCOMERS:

| | | |
|---|---|---|
| Jap Barbeau | 3B | Cleveland AL (1906)* |
| Bobby Byrne | 3B | St. Louis (trade)** |
| Kid Durbin | — | Cincinnati (for Miller and cash) |
| Sam Frock | P | Boston (1907)* |

OUTGOING:

| | | |
|---|---|---|
| Jap Barbeau | 3B | St. Louis (for Bobby Byrne) |
| Ward Miller | OF | Cincinnati (for Durbin) |

| Charlie Starr | 2B | Boston (purchase) |
| Alan Storke | INF | St. Louis (for Bobby Byrne) |
| Roy Thomas | OF | Boston (purchase) |

## 1910

NEWCOMERS:

| Vin Campbell | OF | Chicago (1908)* |
| Bud Sharpe | 1B | Boston (purchase) |
| Elmer Steele | P | Boston AL (waivers) |
| Kirby "Red" White | P | Boston (waivers) |

OUTGOING:

| Ed Abbaticchio | INF | Boston (waivers) |
| Bill Abstein | 1B | St. Louis AL (waivers) |
| Sam Frock | P | Boston (purchase) |
| Vic Willis | P | St. Louis (purchase) |

## 1911

NEWCOMERS:

| Bill Kelly | C | St. Louis (purchase) |
| Marty O'Toole | P | Cincinnati (1908)* |

OUTGOING:

| Judge Nagle | P | Boston AL (purchase) |
| Elmer Steele | P | Brooklyn (purchase) |

## 1912

NEWCOMERS:

| Art Butler | SS | Boston (purchase) |
| King Cole | P | Chicago (for Leach and Leifield) |
| Mike Donlin | OF | Boston (purchase) |
| Solly Hofman | OF | Chicago (for Leach and Leifield) |

OUTGOING:

| Earl Blackburn | C | Cincinnati (purchase) |
| Vin Campbell | OF | Boston (for Donlin) |
| Ensign Cottrell | P | Chicago (waivers) |
| John Flynn | 1B | Washington AL (waivers) |
| Tommy Leach | OF-3B | Chicago (for Hofman and Cole) |
| Lefty Leifield | P | Chicago (for Hofman and Cole) |

## 1913

NEWCOMERS:

| Cozy Dolan | OF-INF | Philadelphia (purchase) |
| George McQuillan | P | Cincinnati (1911)* |
| Mike Mitchell | OF | Chicago (purchase) |

OUTGOING:

| Rivington Bisland | SS | St. Louis AL (waivers) |
| Bobby Byrne | 3B | Philadelphia (for Cozy Dolan) |
| Howie Camnitz | P | Philadelphia (for Cozy Dolan) |

# Photo
# Section

## 1909 WORLD CHAMPION PIRATES 1909

1-PRES. BARNEY DREYFUSS, 2-FRED CLARKE, PLAYING-MANAGER; 3-SECY. WM. H. LOCKE, 4-SS. HONUS WAGNER, 5-CF. TOMMY LEACH, 6-JOHN "DOTS" MILLER, 2B; 7-3B-ROBERT BYRNE, 8-CATCHER GEORGE GIBSON, 9- P. VIC WILLIS, 10- P. HOWARD CAMNITZ, 11- P. CHAS. "BABE" ADAMS, 12- P. ALBERT "LEFTY" LEIFIELD, 14 - P. SAM LEEVER, 15-NICK MADDOX, P.; 16- P. CHARLES "DEACON" PHILLIPPE, 17- P. CHESTER BRANDOM, 18- P. SAMUEL FROCK, 19- CATCHER PATRICK O'CONNOR, 20- CATCHER MICHAEL SIMON, 21- 1B BILL ABSTEIN, 22 -2B EDWARD ABBATICCHIO, 24- RF J. OWEN "CHIEF" WILSON, 25- OF R. HAMILTON HYATT.

*Front row, left to right:* Gooch, Spencer, Culloton, mascot Bill McKechnie, Jr., Ens, Cuyler, Kremer, Sheehan. *Middle:* Smith, Haas, Oldham, Thompson, McInnis, Carey, McKechnie, Clarke, Wright, Grantham, Bigbee, Traynor. *Rear:* Fraser, Hinchman, Onslow, Barnhart, Moore, Yde, Watters, B. Dreyfus, S. Dreyfus, Rawlings, Aldridge, Adams, Morrison, Meadows. *(Photo-Craft Studios)*

The Pirates, 1925. Frazer, Hinchman, Onslow, Barnhart, Aldridge, Watters, Barney and Sam Dreyfus, Rawlings, Yde, Adams, Morrison, Meadows, Oldham, Smith, Traynor, McInnis, Carey, McKechnie, Clark, Bigbee, Thompson, Spencer, Grantham, Austin, Haas, Moore, Culloton, Sheehan, Ens, Wright, Cuyler, Hemsley, Gooch.

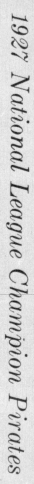

# 1927 National League Champion Pirates

FRONT ROW, *left to right:* OF. Paul Waner, INF. George Grantham, INF. Harold Rhyne, Manager Donie Bush, Club Pres. Barney Dreyfuss, Treasurer Sam Dreyfuss, Secy. Sam Watters, Catcher Johnny Gooch, OF. Clyde Barnhart, OF. Lloyd Waner, 1B. Joe Harris.

MIDDLE ROW, *left to right:* P. Johnny Miljus, P. Remy Kremer, P. Vic Aldridge, INF. Heinie Groh, P. Carmen Hill, P. Michael Cvengros, 3B. Pie Traynor, SS. Glenn Wright, P. Lee Meadows, Catcher Earl Smith, P. Emil Yde, Catcher Roy Spencer.

BACK ROW, *left to right:* P. Otis "Doc" Crandall, Scout Chick Fraser, Scout Bill Hinchman, Coach Jewel Ens, OF. Adam Comorosky, OF. Fred Brickell, P. Walt Tauscher, OF. Kiki Cuyler, INF. Joe Cronin, P. Joe Dawson, INF. Dick Bartell.

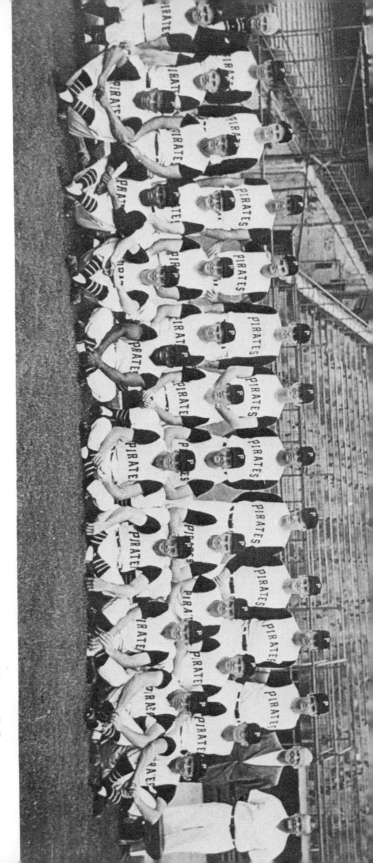

Pittsburgh Pirates—1960 National League Champions. *Front row:* G. Baker, bat boy Recker, J. Christopher, T. Cheney, E. Face, Rocky Nelson, W. Mazeroski, R. Oldis. *Middle:* manager D. Murtaugh, coach S. Narron, coach B. Burwell, coach L. Levy, Smokey Burgess, R. Schofield, G. Cimoli, R. Skinner, H.W. Smith, W. Virdon, D. Hoak. *Back:* travel manager B. Rice, H. Haddix, R. Friend, M. Vernon, R. Groat, J. Gibbon, R. Stuart, E. Francis, G. Witt, V. Law, F. Green, W. Mizell, coach D. Sissler, trainer D. Whealan.

## PITTSBURGH PIRATES
## 1971 WORLD CHAMPIONS

**FRONT ROW, seated, left to right:** Nelson Briles, Jose Pagan, Vic Davalillo, Ramon Hernandez, Coach Bill Virdon, Coach Don Osborn, Manager Danny Murtaugh, Coach Don Leppert, Coach Frank Oceak, Coach Dave Ricketts, Dock Ellis, Manny Sanguillen and Charlie Sands.

**MIDDLE ROW, standing, left to right:** Equipment Manager John Hallahan, Gene Alley, Bob Miller, Jack Hernandez, Dave Cash, Bill Mazeroski, Rennie Stennett, Roberto Clemente, Willie Stargell, Al Oliver, Milt May, Trainer Tony Bartirome, Team Physician Dr. Joseph Finegold, Traveling Secretary John Fitzpatrick.

**TOP ROW, standing, left to right:** Luke Walker, Carl Taylor, Dave Giusti, Bob Veale, Bob Moose, Bob Johnson, Bruce Kison, Steve Blass, Bob Robertson, Gene Clines and Rich Hebner.

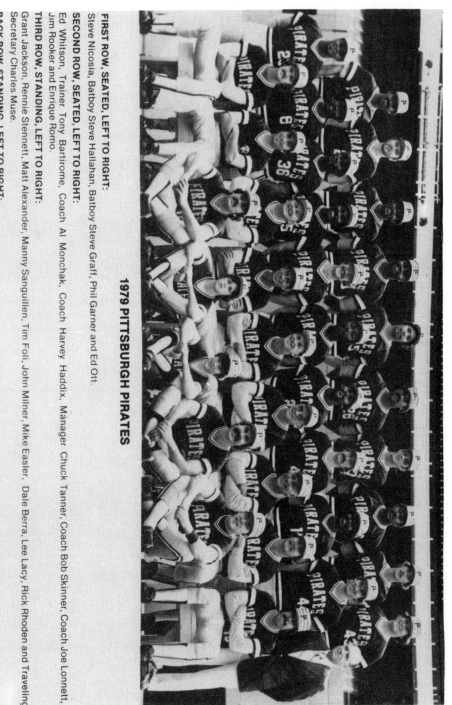

## 1979 PITTSBURGH PIRATES

**FIRST ROW, SEATED, LEFT TO RIGHT:**
Steve Nicosia, Batboy Steve Hallahan, Batboy Steve Graff, Phil Garner and Ed Ott.

**SECOND ROW, SEATED, LEFT TO RIGHT:**
Ed Whitson, Trainer Tony Bartirome, Coach Al Monchak, Coach Harvey Haddix, Manager Chuck Tanner, Coach Bob Skinner, Coach Joe Lonnett, Jim Rooker and Enrique Romo.

**THIRD ROW, STANDING, LEFT TO RIGHT:**
Grant Jackson, Rennie Stennett, Matt Alexander, Manny Sanguillen, Tim Foli, John Milner, Mike Easler, Dale Berra, Lee Lacy, Rick Rhoden and Traveling Secretary Charles Muse.

**BACK ROW, STANDING, LEFT TO RIGHT:**
Bill Robinson, Bert Blyleven, Omar Moreno, Dave Parker, John Candelaria, Jim Bibby, Kent Tekulve, Willie Stargell, Bruce Kison and Don Robinson.

Exposition Park, home of the Pirates from 1891 to 1909. The field was located across the Allegheny River from the Golden Triangle, close to where Three Rivers Stadium is now located, and the outfield was often flooded with water from the river. The park seated approximately two thousand.

John W. Galbreath, chairman of the board

Daniel M. Galbreath, president

Harding Peterson, present general manager

Bob Prince, one of the premiere broadcasters in baseball, who was known for years as the voice of the Pirates. He was 100 percent Pirate.

Forbes Field (named after the Pre-Revolutionary War general John Forbes) where the Pirates played for 60 years. Construction of the structure, which started March 1, 1909, took four months—ironically it also took four months to install the light standards in 1940. The structure required 650 carloads of sand and gravel, 110 carloads of cement, 90 carloads of brick, 130 carloads of structural steel, and 70 carloads of chairs. The field was located in the Oakland section of the city near Schenley Park. The first game was played on June 30, 1909, and the Pirates lost 3-2 to the Cubs. The first Pirate hit in the new field was by George Bigson. The last game played there was June 28, 1970 and the Pirates won a double header against the Cubs. There was never a no-hitter thrown in spacious Forbes Field. The seating capacity was 33,000 when first opened. After additions in right field and field box seats, the capacity increased to 35,000.

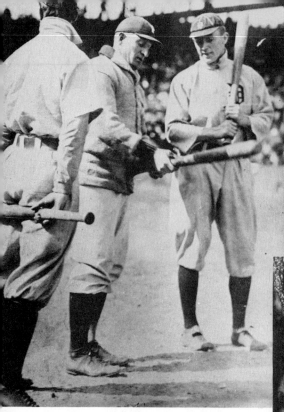

Honus Wagner and Ty Cobb, Pirate and Detroit leading hitters, discussing bats. *(Carnegie Library, Pittsburgh)*

Memorial to Honus Wagner who played from 1900 to 1917. He was considered the greatest shortstop in baseball history.

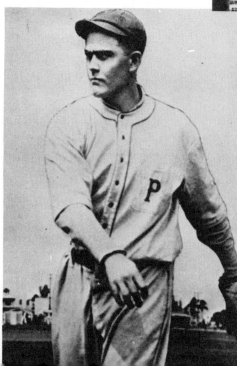

Charles "Babe" Adams, 1907-26

Paul Waner, known as Big Poison, played rightfield for the Pirates from 1926 to 1940. He was one of the Hall of Fame members that made 3,000 or more hits, and got 200 or more hits in eight seasons. He hit better than .300 fourteen times in National League, with a lifetime average of .333.

The front page of the *Pittsburgh Chronicle Telegraph,* October 15, 1925. *(Carnegie Library, Pittsburgh)*

Hall of Famer Lloyd Waner, Little Poison, was the other half of one of the greatest brother acts in baseball. He played center field in Pittsburgh from 1927 to 1941. As a rookie in 1927 he made 223 hits. He held a modern day record of 198 singles, and a lifetime average of .316.

Murry Dickson pitched for the Pirates from 1949 to 1953. He won 66 and lost 85.

Debs Garms, with Pittsburgh in 1940 and 1941, won the batting titles in 1940 with a .355 average. He played third base and outfield.

Dick Stuart—good hit, no field —split first base duties with Rocky Nelson in 1960. He led the Bucs with 23 home runs in 1960 and hit 117 in five years with Pittsburgh.

Ralph Kiner, the Pirates' leading righthanded slugger, is a member of the Hall of Fame. His prowess with the home run ball brought the fans to the stadium in the 1950s when the Pirates had little other talent.

Matty Alou played for Pittsburgh from 1966 to 1970. He won the batting championship in 1966 with a .342 average, and finished his career with a .309 average. *(Malcolm W. Emmons)*

Bob Friend pitching in the 1960 Series against the New York Yankees. Although he had a good year, from his point of view his performance in the Series was poor.

Joe L. Brown, general manager.

Pittsburgh Pirates' Rennie Stennett holds up seven fingers indicating his modern day record of seven straight hits during the game with the Chicago Cubs, 9/16/75. Stennett set another record by getting two hits in an inning, twice, as the Pirates crushed the Cubs 22-0. *(UPI Photo)*

Willie Stargell takes a bow after hitting a homerun in the 1979 N.L.C.S. vs. Cincinnati. *(Rich Wilson)*

John Candelaria facing the last batter in his no-hitter, August 9, 1976. He defeated the Dodgers 2–0. He was the first Pirate pitcher to pitch a no-hitter in Pittsburgh. *(UPI Photo)*

Pie Traynor, Pittsburgh's greatest third baseman and member of the Hall of Fame, played from 1922 through 1957. Traynor ended his career with a .320 average. He managed the Bucs from June 1934 to September 1939.

Maury Wills (center) is caught in a rundown while trying to score from third base during the third inning at Pittsburgh, September 6, 1967. Making the play for the Atlanta Braves are catcher Bob Uecker and pitcher Phil Niekro. Wills tried to score when Roberto Clemente bounced a ball to Niekro. Uecker got the put out. *(Associated Press)*

· The 3,000 hit of Roberto Clemente.

Dale Long, slugging Pittsburgh Pirates' first baseman, crosses the plate and receives congratulations by Frank Thomas after he set a new major league record by blasting his eighth homer in eight straight games, May 28, 1956. Long connected off Carl Erskine of Brooklyn. *(Wide World Photos)*

Pirates' Cliff Chambers (left) being congratulated by his teammates after hurling a no-hitter blanking the Braves 3-0, in the second game of a double-header at Braves Field, May 6, 1951. The 29-year old left-hander, whose record has never been outstanding, walked eight batters (only one of them reached third base), and he struck out four in the first no-hitter since the Braves' Vern Bickford performed the rare deed in 1950.

The scoreboard tells the story as Bob Moose of the Pirates pitches to Art Shamsky of the Mets in the ninth inning of a game at Shea Stadium, September 20, 1969. Moose got Shamsky on a grounder to second to end the game. The Pirates won, 4-0. *(UPI Photo).*

Yankee Gil McDougal (#12) is forced at second on Roger Maris' grounder to Pirate Rocky Nelson. Pirate Dick Groat, covering, throws to Fred Green, covering first, too late to get Maris for the double play. *(UPI Photo)*

Elroy Face pitching in the 1960 World Series.

Roberto Clemente and Dick Groat (partly hidden) grab Hal Smith as he crosses home plate on his 2-out homer in the seventh game of the 1960 Series off Jim Coates. He scored Clemente and Groat ahead of him to give the Bucs a 9-7 lead in the eighth inning. Forbes Field, October 13, 1960.

Pirates' Bob Robertson connects for a home run in the seventh inning of the October 11, 1971, World Series game in Pittsburgh. Willie Stargell and Roberto Clemente were on base at the time. *(AP Wirephoto)*

Murtaugh and Stengel before the first game of the 1960 World Series between the Pirates and the Yankees. *(Bob Olen Studios)*

Pittsburgh Pirates' Bill Virdon takes the first pitch thrown by New York Yankee Whitey Ford to open the third game of the 1960 World Series, at Yankee Stadium. *(UPI Photo)*

Roy Face (whom the Pirates' relief specialist pilot Danny Murtaugh refers to as the man with the "low fork ball") follows through after serving up a ninth inning pitch against the Yankees in the fifth 1960 World Series game at Yankee Stadium. Face came on in the seventh inning in relief of starter Harvey Haddix. Pirates won. 5–2. *(AP Wirephoto)*

Pittsburgh Pirates manager Danny Murtaugh follows his fourth game starting pitcher Vern Law from the mound in the seventh inning of the World Series game at Yankee Stadium on October 9, 1960. In the background, relief hurler Roy Face rubs up ball as he chats with catcher Smokey Burgess. Face held the Yankees in check and the Bucs went on to win 3–2 to even up the series. *(AP Wirephoto)*

Mazeroski, chased by a fan, gets ready to cross home plate and be greeted by fans and fellow players after his homer. *(UPI Telephoto)*

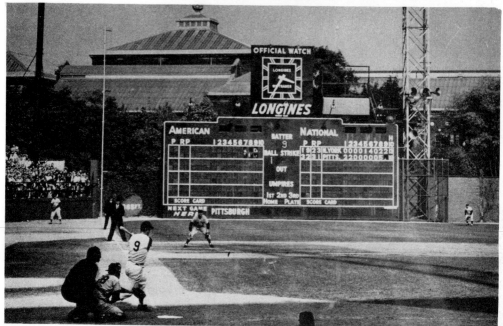

Pirate Bill Mazeroski hitting his Series-winning home run in the ninth game of the 1960 Series.

Yankee Bobby Richardson takes a ball on the first pitch of the seventh game of the 1960 World Series. Tossing the ball is Pirate Vernon Law, catching is Smokey Burgess, and the umpire is Bill Jackowski. *(UPI Telephoto)*

In the same game, Berra hits a grounder to Nelson at first base, and Mantle slides back into first as the tying run scores for the Yankees.

Dick Groat, Most Valuable Player in 1960, making pivot in a double play against the Giants.

Bill Mazeroski, considered the best second baseman of all time for the Pittsburgh Pirates, made spectacular plays as shown. He is best remembered for his home run in the 1960 World Series that made world champions of the Pirates. *(Post-Gazette photo by Morris Berman)*

Bill Mazeroski making a putout at second base. He was known for his quick hands in receiving and getting rid of a ball in a double play.

Dave Giusti, relief pitcher of the Pirates, caught in a pose as he delivers his famous palm ball in May 1970.

San Francisco Giants pitcher Gaylord Perry throws the resin bag onto the mound in obvious disgust after Pirates Richie Hebner belted him for a three-run homer in a 1971 National League playoff game at Pittsburgh. Hebner rounds second base at right. Umpire is Satch Davidson. Hebner's homer tied up the game at 5–5. *(AP Wirephoto)*

In the same series, Andy Etchebarren is hit by a Bruce Kison pitch. Kison set a Series record by hitting three men.

Pirates show their elation after winning the playoff. *(UPI Photo)*

Clemente hits a homer off Cueller in the seventh game.

Orioles' Frank Robinson strikes out in the fourth inning as pitcher Nelson Briles falls down. The ball is in catcher Ellie Hendricks' mitt. Ump is Jim Odom. *(AP Wirephoto)*

Milt May's game-winning single in the fourth game of the 1971 World Series between the Orioles and the Pirates.

José Pagan's double in the eighth inning scores Stargell with the winning run in the 1971 World Series against the Orioles.

Briles two-hits the Orioles in game five of the 1971 World Series.

Pirates first base coach Don Leppert (#43) argues with umpire John Rice about a long fly hit by Roberto Clemente in the third inning of a 1971 Series game in Pittsburgh. Leppert and the Pirates claimed the ball was fair when it went into the stand. The umpire ruled it was foul. His decision stood. Clemente singled on the next pitch. *(AP Wirephoto)*

Stargell reaching for the ball in left field, in the 1971 World Series.

Stargell greeted by Parker—the two key players in the Pirate Victory. *(Post-Gazette photo by Albert French)*

Clemente on the way to the 1971 Series Most Valuable Player.

Pirate exuberance after defeating the Orioles in 1971.

Sign on the Three Rivers Stadium in Pittsburgh proclaims that the Pirates "had 'em all the way" in their three-game series against the New York Mets, as the happy Bucs leave the field Sunday after winning the 1970 Eastern Division National League title by beating the Mets, 2-1. In center, coach Don Leppert (#43) congratulates pitcher Dave Giusti, who entered the game in the eighth and held the Mets. Others include: *(from left)* pitcher Bob Veale, Steve Blass, starting pitcher Dock Ellis (partially hidden), Dave Cash, and catcher Manny Sanguillen. *(AP Wirephoto)*

A pitched ball by Pirates pitcher Bob Moose bounces over the head of his catcher Manny Sanguillen, allowing George Foster of the Cincinnati Reds to score from third base in the ninth inning with the winning run. Reds pinch hitter Hal McRae watches the ball. The Reds won this 1972 championship, 4 – 3. Umpire is Augie Donatelli. *(AP Wirephoto)*

Pirates' Willie Stargell (left) is congratulated by teammates Matt Alexander and Dave Parker after blasting a three-run homer in the top of the eleventh inning to defeat the Cincinnati Reds, 5–2, in the first game of the 1979 National League Playoffs. Pirates next batter, John Milner (#34) reaches out also to congratulate Stargell. *(UPI Photo)*

Stargell jumps for joy as the Pirates defeated the Orioles in the 1979 World Series. *(Sunpapers photo by Irving H. Phillips, Jr.)*

| Ralph Capron | OF | Philadelphia (purchase) |
|---|---|---|
| Bill McKechnie | INF | Boston (purchase) |
| Wally Rehg | OF | Boston AL (waivers) |

## 1914

NEWCOMERS:

| Pat Bohen | P | Philadelphia AL (waivers) |
|---|---|---|
| Dan Costello | OF | New York AL (waivers) |
| Bob Harmon | P | St. Louis (trade)** |
| Ed Konetchy | 1B | St. Louis (trade)** |
| Mike Mowrey | 3B | St. Louis (trade)** |
| Marty O'Toole | P | New York (purchase) |
| Syd Smith | C | Cleveland AL (1911)* |

OUTGOING:

| Art Butler | SS | St. Louis (trade)** |
|---|---|---|
| Cozy Dolan | OF-INF | St. Louis (trade)** |
| Claude Hendrix | P | Chicago F |
| Solly Hofman | OF | Brooklyn F |
| Fred Kommers | OF | St. Louis F |
| Dots Miller | OF | St. Louis (trade)** |
| Mike Mitchell | OF | Washington AL |
| Marty O'Toole | P | New York (purchase) |
| Hank Robinson | P | St. Louis (purchase) |
| Mike Simon | C | St. Louis F |
| Owen Wilson | OF | St. Louis (trade)** |
| Roy Wood | OF | Cleveland Al (waivers) |

## 1915

| February | Pirates obtain first baseman Doc Johnston from the Cleveland Indians on waivers. Johnston was the Pirates starting first baseman in 1915 and 1916, replacing the traded Ed Konetchy. |
|---|---|
| February 24 | Pitcher George McQuillan is waived to the Phillies. He won only five games with Philadelphia and Cleveland in his last three seasons. |
| February 28 | Pirates send outfielder-first baseman Ham Hyatt to the Cardinals on waivers. Hyatt had led the league in pinchhitting in 1914 but played only one year in St. Louis. |
| August | Pirates release catcher Bobby Schang to the Giants. Schang only played one more year in the majors and was never a good hitter. |
| August | Outfielder Ed Barney is obtained from the Yankees on waivers. He hit well when he first came to Pittsburgh but was dropped after a bad year in 1916. |
| August 15 | Bucs purchase pitcher Rube Benton from Cincinnati. The Reds had already agreed to send Benton to the Giants, and the agreement between the Pirates and Reds was nullified. Benton was a consistent winner with New York until 1921. |
| September | Pirates sell infielder Alex McCarthy to the Cardinals. McCarthy was the starting second baseman in 1912 but never hit well in a reserve roll. He returned in '16 to end his career. |
| December | Pirates obtain pitcher Elmer Jacobs from Philadelphia Phillies on waivers. Jacobs lost 30 games in just over two years with the Bucs before he returned to the Phillies. |

137

## 1916

| | |
|---|---|
| July 29 | Pirates trade catcher Art Wilson to the Cubs for catcher Bill Fisher and outfielder Frank Schulte. Wilson had hit well in two years with Chicago's Federal League club but not in the majors. Fisher was a platoon player with Pittsburgh in 1916 and 1917. Schulte was once a league-leading home run hitter, but near the end of his career. |
| August | Pittsburgh sends catcher George Gibson to the Giants on waivers. Gibson was at the end of his playing career, but returned to manage the Bucs in 1920-22 and 1932-34. |
| September | Pitcher Erv Kantlehner goes to the Phillies on waivers. A big loser in two years with Pittsburgh, he only pitched three games in Philadelphia. |

## 1917

| | |
|---|---|
| May 24 | Pirates send shortstop Ike McAuley to the Cardinals on waivers. Seldom used with Pittsburgh, he only played three games with the Cardinals. |
| June | Pittsburgh purchases outfielder Pete Compton from the Boston Braves. Compton played five games with the Bucs and was returned to Boston. |
| June 14 | Pittsburgh trades third baseman Doug Baird to the Cardinals for pitcher Bob Steele. Baird was the starting third baseman in St. Louis for two years, then bounced from one team to another for the rest of his career. Steele was 7-14 in his only year with the Bucs. |
| | Pirates send outfielder Frank Schulte to the Phillies. He played only one more year and retired. |
| July | Outfielder Joe Wilhoit is acquired from the Braves on waivers. He played only nine games for the Pirates and was waived to the Giants. |
| July 25 | Pirates obtain first baseman George Kelly from the Giants on waivers. The Giants loaned Kelly to Pittsburgh for eight games. He returned to New York in September and blossomed into a superstar. He was elected to the Hall of Fame in 1973. |

## 1918

| | |
|---|---|
| January 9 | Pittsburgh traded shortstop Chuck Ward, pitchers Al Mamaux, and Burleigh Grimes to Brooklyn for outfielder Casey Stengel and second baseman George Cutshaw. Cutshaw became the Pirates starting second baseman. Stengel was a starter with the Dodgers but a sub with the Bucs. Grimes won 20 games four times in Brooklyn, Mamaux faded after a couple good seasons, and Ward was used as a back-up. |
| May | Pirates purchase third baseman Bill McKechnie from the Reds. He was the starting third baseman in 1918, did not play at all the next year, and had just 40 games in 1920. He became manager of the Pirates in 1922. |
| July | Pittsburgh trades pitcher Elmer Jacobs to the Phillies for pitcher Erskine Mayer. Jacobs had his only winning season in 1918. Mayer was twice a 20-game winner with Philadelphia and pitched well in limited duty before leaving in 1919. |
| August | Third baseman Gus Getz is acquired after being released by Cleveland. Getz played only seven games in Pittsburgh and was released. |

## 1919

| | |
|---|---|
| February | Pirates acquire shortstop Zeb Terry, after he was released by the Braves. |

|  | Terry was a light hitter, but became the starting shortstop in his only season with Pittsburgh. |
| March | Pirates release outfielder Lee King to the Giants. King was seldom used (with the exception of 1917 when he played 111 games) Had one good year with New York. |
| June 12 | Pittsburgh waives third baseman Tony Boeckel to the Braves. Boeckel was a starter from the time he went to Boston until 1924. |
| July | Pirates obtain outfielder Fred Nicholson from Detroit on waivers. Nicholson became the league's leading pinch hitter in 1920. He was then traded to Boston in the Rabbit Maranville deal. |
| August | Outfielder Casey Stengel goes to the Phillies for outfielder Possum Whitted. Whitted was moved to third base where he started in 1920. Stengel continued to be used in a utility role with Philadelphia. |
| November | Pirates acquire catcher Nig Clarke on waivers from the Phillies. Clarke was in his final season and played just three games. |
| August | Pitcher Erskine Mayer is sent to the White Sox on waivers. He won just once with his last major league club. |

## 1920

| April | Pittsburgh releases shortstop Zeb Terry to the Cubs. Terry's hitting improved with Chicago and he was the starter in '21 and '22. |
| May | Bucs release pitcher Frank Miller to the Braves. Miller won 11 games in 1922 after being out of the Majors in '20 and '21. He was out of the majors for good after the next season. |

## 1921

| April | Pirates send outfielder Cliff Lee to the Phillies on waivers. Lee had three good years with Philadelphia, hitting over .300 in each. He faded quickly afterward. |
| May | Pittsburgh obtains shortstop Rabbit Maranville from the Braves for outfielders Billy Southworth and Fred Nicholson, shortstop Walt Barbare, and cash. Maranville became the Bucs first quality shortstop since an aged Honus Wagner moved to first base in 1917. Barbare replaced the Rabbit in Boston, Southworth hit .300 each year in beantown, but Nicholson left after two seasons. |
| June 8 | Pirates release pitcher Charles Ponder to the Cubs. He was in his last year. |
| July | Catcher Tony Brottem is acquired after being released by Washington. Brottem played just 30 games in a Pirate uniform. |

## 1922

| April | Third baseman-outfielder Possum Whitted is waived to Brooklyn. A starter in his last two years with the Bucs, Whitted was out of the majors after just one game with the Dodgers. |

## 1923

| May 23 | Pirates trade second baseman Cotton Tierney and pitcher Whitey Glazner to the Phillies for second baseman John Rawlings and pitcher |

|              | Lee Meadows. Meadows replaced Glazner in the Bucs rotation and won 85 games over the next five years. Rawlings replaced Tierney for the season but was used little afterward. Glazner had little success in Philadelphia, and Tierney was traded to Brooklyn after the season. |
|---|---|
| December 22 | Pirates obtain pitcher Jim Bagby from Cleveland. Bagby won 31 games for the 1920 Indians but never pitched as well afterward. He won only three games with Pittsburgh in his final major league season. |

## 1924

| May | Pitcher Jeff Pfeffer is acquired from the Cardinals on waivers. Pfeffer was once a standout with Brooklyn in the middle teens and won five games with the Pirates, his last major league club. |
|---|---|
| November | Pirates trade pitcher Wilbur Cooper, first baseman Charlie Grimm, and shortstop Rabbit Maranville to the Cubs for pitcher Vic Aldridge, first basemen Al Niehaus, and George Grantham. Cooper was near the end of a great career and had just one fair season in Chicago. Maranville was expendable with the arrival of Glenn Wright and had an off year with the Cubs. Grimm continued to star with the Cubs and eventually became their player manager. Grantham hit .300 in each of his six years with Pittsburgh—moving to second base in 1927, back to first, and then back to second in '29. Aldridge had three fair seasons with the Pirates and Niehaus was traded before the end of the season. |

## 1925

| May 20 | Pittsburgh trades first baseman Al Niehaus to the Reds for pitcher Tom Sheehan. Niehaus left after 17 games and did not play another season in the majors after hitting well in 51 games with the Reds. Sheehan won only once in two years with Pittsburgh. |
|---|---|
| May 29 | Pirates sign first baseman Stuffy McInnis as a free agent. McInnis was near the end of a long career in which he was an all star with the Athletics and Red Sox. He was still a great hitter and shared first with George Grantham. |

## 1926

| June 30 | Pittsburgh signs pitcher Joe Bush as a free agent. Bush was at the end of a great career and won seven games as a Pirate. |
|---|---|
| July | Second baseman Eddie Moore is waived to the Braves. Moore was the Bucs starter in 1925 but got off to a slow start and was sent packing. He had a couple more good years in a sporadic career. |

## 1927

| February | First baseman Joe Harris comes to Pittsburgh from Washington on waivers. Harris became the starter as George Grantham moved to second base. A perennial .300 hitter, '27 was his last big year and he went to Brooklyn in 1928, his last season. |
|---|---|
| June 15 | Pirates release pitcher Joe Bush. He caught on with the Giants but was no longer an effective pitcher. |
| July 1 | Free agent Heinie Groh signs with the Pirates. Heinie brought his "bottle bat" to Pittsburgh and played 14 games in his last big league season. |

| July 10 | Pitcher Johnny Miljus is purchased from Cleveland. The only Serbian in baseball, Miljus pitched well and won the pennant clincher on October first. |
|---|---|
| November 28 | Pirates trade outfielder Kiki Cuyler to the Cubs for second baseman Earl Adams and outfielder Floyd Scott. Cuyler was in large part responsible for Cub pennants in '29 and '32 but was expendable with the addition of rookie Lloyd Waner. Adams was the starting second baseman in his first year with the Bucs, and Scott was a utility player. |
| December | Pitcher Fred Fussell comes from the Cubs for pitcher Mike Cvengros. Fussell spent two less-than-spectacular years in Pittsburgh, while Cvengros did not pitch at all in '28 and retired after the 1929 campaign. |

## 1928

| February | Pirates reacquire pitcher Burleigh Grimes from the Giants for pitcher Vic Aldridge. Aldridge fell apart in New York but Grimes produced an outstanding season, winning 25 games. He was injured after a strong start in '29 and went to Boston after the season. |
|---|---|
| June | First baseman Joe Harris is released to Brooklyn. His hitting fell off sharply and this was his last major league season. |
| June | Pirates release catcher Johnny Gooch to Brooklyn. Gooch finished well with the Dodgers and was then traded after the season. |
| December | Shortstop Glenn Wright is traded to Brooklyn for pitcher Jesse Petty. Wright had some outstanding seasons with the Dodgers, while Petty had a fair season in Pittsburgh and did nothing afterward. |

## 1929

| June | Outfielder Ira Flagstead was acquired on waivers from Washington. He spent one year with the Bucs as a backup for Paul Waner. |
|---|---|
| August | Pitcher Carmen Hill is waived to the Cardinals. He was off to a bad start and never recovered. |

## 1930

| April | Third baseman Sparky Adams is purchased by the Cardinals. Adams had been playing second with the Pirates and was coming off a poor season. He started at third for St. Louis and had two excellent years with the champion Cardinals. |
|---|---|
| April | Pitcher Percy Jones is purchased from the Braves. Jones did not win in nine games with the Pirates in his last season. |
| September | Outfielder Denny Southern is purchased from the Phillies. He had no success in limited play with the Pirates. |
| November 6 | Pirates trade shortstop Dick Bartell to the Phillies for shortstop Tom Thevenow and pitcher Claude Willoughby. Phillies got the better of the trade as Bartell had four outstanding years in Philadelphia. Thevenow replaced Bartell but was not nearly as good, and Willoughby never won a game with the Pirates. |
| | Pitcher Jesse Petty is waived to the Cubs. He was finished. |

## 1931

| January | Pirates obtain catcher Ed Phillips from the Phillies. 1931 was his only season as a regular, and he was dropped after a poor year. |
|---|---|
| May | Second baseman Bill Regan is acquired after being released by the Red |

141

|  |  |
|---|---|
| | Sox. A starter with the Red Sox in 1930, he was a sub in '31, his last season in the majors. |
| June 13 | Catcher Earl Grace is acquired from the Cubs for catcher Rollie Hemsley. Grace was a platoon player and hit well in five years with Pittsburgh. Hemsley hit well when he first went to Chicago but fell off and was traded. |

## 1932

|  |  |
|---|---|
| | Pirates sell second baseman George Grantham to the Reds. He had one good year in Cincinnati and then faded out. |
| May | Pittsburgh acquires catcher Tom Padden after he had been released by the Yankees. Padden spent six years with the Bucs as a number two catcher, with varying degrees of success. |
| December | Pirates obtain outfielder Fred Lindstrom in a three-way deal involving the Phillies and Giants. This ended with Lindstrom coming to Pittsburgh from New York, outfielder Gus Dugas going from the Pirates to the Phillies, and pitcher Glenn Spencer leaving the Bucs for New York. Outfielder Chick Fullis went to the Phillies from the Giants for outfielder George Davis. Lindstrom played well alongside the Waner brothers but was traded to the Cubs after the 1934 season. Spencer never won a game for the Giants, and Dugas was no help to the Phillies. |

## 1933

|  |  |
|---|---|
| December | Pirates acquire outfielder Wally Roettger and pitcher Red Lucas from the Reds for second baseman Tony Piet and outfielder-infielder Adam Comorosky. Roettger played little in his last season, but Lucas was a Pirate for five years and won 15 of 19 decisions in 1936. Piet's average dropped in Cincinnati and he was traded after one year plus. Comorosky had two average seasons with the Reds. |

## 1934

|  |  |
|---|---|
| July | Pittsburgh obtains pitcher Ed Holley, released by the Cubs. He never won for the Bucs in his last big league season. |
| November | Pirates send pitcher Leon Chagnon to the Giants. He was in his last season and lost his only two decisions with New York. |
| November 22 | Pittsburgh trades pitcher Larry French and outfielder Fred Lindstrom to the Cubs for pitchers Guy Bush and Jim Weaver, and outfielder Babe Herman. Weaver pitched well, but Bush did not pitch nearly as well as he had in Chicago. Herman was gone before the end of the season. French rebounded from a bad 1934 season and resumed his place as one of the league's top pitchers. Lindstrom had not lived up to expectations in Pittsburgh and played only two more years. |
| December | Pitcher John Salveson is acquired following his release from the Giants. Salveson went to the White Sox without ever winning for the Bucs. |

## 1935

|  |  |
|---|---|
| June | Pirates release pitcher John Salveson to the White Sox. No loss at all. |
| June 21 | Pittsburgh releases outfielder Babe Herman to the Reds. Herman recovered from his bad start with the Pirates and had two good years in Cincinnati. |

| December 21 | Pirates trade pitcher Claude Passeau and catcher Earl Grace to the Phillies for catcher Al Todd. Passeau had three fair seasons in Philadelphia, then went to the Cubs where he became one of their all-time great pitchers. Todd became the starting catcher in 1937 and had two good years before he was traded to Boston. Grace spent two subpar years with the Phillies. |

Pirates release infielder Tom Thevenow to Cincinnati. He had one good year as a utility man with the Reds.

## 1936

| January 30 | Pirates obtain outfielder Fred Schulte, released by Washington. Schulte was near the end of an excellent career. He played well as a reserve in '36 and retired after 29 games in '37. |
| December 4 | Pittsburgh trades pitcher Ralph Birkofer and infielder Cookie Lavagetto to Brooklyn for pitcher Ed Brandt. Brandt spent two average years with the Bucs. Birkofer never won a game with the Dodgers, but Lavagetto became their starting third baseman and gained fame with his pinch hit to break-up Bill Bevens' no-hitter and win the fourth game of the 1947 World Series against New York. |

## 1937

| April 16 | Pirates obtain pitcher Joe Bowman from the Phillies for outfielder-first baseman Earl Browne. Browne spent two unspectacular years in Philadelphia and had five fair seasons with the Bucs. |
| June | Pittsburgh sends pitcher Waite Hoyt to Brooklyn on waivers. Hoyt won seven games in his last full season. He was elected to the Hall of Fame in 1969. |
| October | Pirates waive catcher Tom Padden to the Cardinals. He never played with St. Louis, returning to the majors in 1943 for 20 games with the Phillies and Senators. |

## 1938

| January | Pitcher Jim Weaver is purchased by the St. Louis Browns. He only pitched one game in St. Louis. |
| December 6 | Pirates acquire catcher Ray Mueller from the Braves for catcher Al Todd, outfielder Johnny Dickshot, and cash. Mueller had a lousy year and left after the next season. Todd and Dickshot never played a game for Boston. |

## 1939

| June 7 | Pirates sign outfielder Chuck Klein as a free agent. A brilliant hitter in his prime with the Phillies, Klein hit .300 with the Bucs before returning to the Phillies where he finished his career. |
| June 15 | Pittsburgh acquires first baseman Elbie Fletcher from the Braves for infielder Bill Schuster and cash. Fletcher became the Bucs starting first baseman and remained there for four more seasons. Schuster did nothing for Boston. |

In a separate transaction, the Pirates swapped pitcher Jim Tobin to Boston for pitcher Johnny Lanning. Tobin became one of the Braves top pitchers although he led the league in losses in 1942. Lanning was

| | |
|---|---|
| | used primarily in relief and had two good seasons when he was first acquired. |
| July 28 | Pirates obtain pitcher Max Butcher from the Phillies for first baseman Gus Suhr in a waiver deal. Suhr was expendable with the addition of Fletcher and had a strong finish with the Phillies but only played ten games in 1940. Butcher pitched well with the Pirates but his terrible start with the Phillies resulted in his leading the league in losses. He was a steady starter for the Bucs until 1945. |
| October 27 | Catcher Spud Davis is purchased from the Phillies. A top receiver in his prime, he was platooned with Al Lopez before his career was interrupted by the war. |
| December 6 | Pitcher Bill Swift is traded with cash to the Braves for pitcher Danny MacFayden. The trade helped neither team. |

### 1940

| | |
|---|---|
| January 22 | Pirates acquire pitcher Ray Harrell from the Phillies on waivers. He pitched only three games as a Pirate. |
| March 20 | Pittsburgh releases catcher George Susce. He had been the third string catcher and never played much. |
| April | Pirates purchase infielder Ed Leip from the Senators. He was hardly used in three seasons. |
| May 3 | Outfielder-third baseman Debs Garms is purchased from the Braves. Basically a utility man, Garms squeezed out enough at-bats to win the National League batting crown while playing primarily third base. He only played one more season with the Pirates. |
| May 8 | Pirates trade outfielder Johnny Rizzo to Cincinnati for outfielder Vince DiMaggio. Rizzo set a Pirate record with 23 homers as a rookie, then slipped in '39 and was off to a bad start when the trade was made. He played only 31 games with Cincinnati and went to the Phillies where he regained his first year form. The eldest DiMaggio was a strikeout king but also a good hitter and starter until he was traded in 1945. |
| June 14 | Pittsburgh acquires catcher Al Lopez from the Braves for catcher Paul Burris and cash. Lopez was an outstanding defensive catcher and spent seven years with the Bucs. Burris saw little action with the Braves. |
| October 8 | Danny MacFayden is released. No loss. |
| December 2 | Pirates purchase second baseman Stu Martin from the Cardinals. Martin was a back-up for Frankie Gustine at second in '41 and '42. |
| December 9 | Pittsburgh trades second baseman Pep Young to Cincinnati for third baseman Lew Riggs. Both players were near the end and the trade helped neither team. |
| December 10 | Pirates release outfielder Paul Waner. He had a few more good years but nothing like the ones that resulted in his election to the Hall of Fame in 1952. |

### 1941

| | |
|---|---|
| April 22 | Pitcher Mace Brown is sold to the Dodgers. The great reliever did little with the Dodgers but had three good seasons with the Red Sox to finish his career. |
| May 7 | Pirates trade outfielder Lloyd Waner to the Braves for pitcher Nick Strincevich. Waner played just 19 games in Boston, returning to the Pirates in '44 to finish his career. Strincevich was in the starting rotation from '44-'46. |

| May 12 | Bucs purchase catcher Bill Baker from Cincinnati. He was used as a third stringer. |
|---|---|
| June 20 | Pitcher Joe Sullivan is purchased from the Braves. He pitched primarily in relief in his only season with the team. |
| August | Pirates purchase pitcher Dutch Dietz from the Reds. He won seven games as a relief pitcher in 1941 but was never as effective afterward. |
| December 1 | Bucs purchase pitcher Hank Gornicki from the Cardinals. He was little help, used mostly in relief. |
| December 12 | Pirates trade shortstop Arky Vaughan to Brooklyn for pitcher Luke Hamlin, catcher Babe Phelps, outfielder Jimmy Wasdell, and second baseman Pete Coscarart. Vaughan had two big years before going to the war, coming back for two seasons as a utility player in '47 and '48. Coscarart moved to short and played well for four years as the starter. Phelps was platooned with Lopez in his last big league season. Wasdell spent an average season with the Pirates and was traded in early 1943. Hamlin was once a 20 game winner, but won only four games with the Pirates. |

## 1942

No deals made

## 1943

| April 30 | Pirates sell outfielder Jimmy Wasdell to the Phillies. He had his best years in Philadelphia, a starter in each of his three years there. |
|---|---|
| June 16 | Pirates trade pitcher Dutch Dietz to the Phillies for pitcher Johnny Podgajny. Podgajny lost all four decisions in his only year with the team. Dietz was 1-1 with the Phils in his last big league season. |
| December 30 | Pittsburgh trades catcher Babe Phelps to the Phillies for first baseman Babe Dahlgren. Dahlgren had two great seasons as the Bucs starting first baseman. Dietz never played for the Phillies. |

## 1944

| May 27 | Pirates purchase pitcher Ray Starr from the Reds. He won six games and was traded at the beginning of the 1945 season. |
|---|---|
| June 12 | Pitcher Johnny Gee is purchased by the Giants. Gee was a tremendous disappointment with the Pirates and little help to the Giants. |
| July 27 | Pittsburgh released pitcher Harry Shuman to the Phillies. Shuman never won a game in three seasons in the majors. |

## 1945

| March 31 | Pirates trade outfielder Vince DiMaggio to the Phillies for pitcher Al Gerheauser. Gerheauser had lost 35 games in two years in Philadelphia and was no better in Pittsburgh. DiMaggio continued to fan, and after one fine year, dropped sharply in 1946 and retired. |
|---|---|
| June 27 | Pitcher Ray Starr is sold to the Cubs. He did little with Chicago in his last season. |

## 1946

| January 5 | Pirates purchase infielder Jimmy Brown from the Cardinals. Brown was at the end of his career and used strictly as a utility player. |

April 23    Pittsburgh sells first baseman Babe Dahlgren to the St. Louis Browns. Dahlgren had his last success with Pittsburgh and retired after 28 games with the Browns.

June 12     Pirates trade outfielder Johnny Barrett to the Braves for outfielder-third baseman Chuck Workman. Both players were off to bad starts and neither lasted past the 1946 season.

September 30 Pirates trade third baseman-outfielder Bob Elliott and catcher Hank Camelli to the Braves for second baseman Billy Herman, outfielder Stan Wentzel, infielder Whitey Wietelmann and pitcher Elmer Singleton. The Pirates basically gave up Elliott to get Herman who would manage the team in 1947. Herman did not last through the season. Elliott became the Braves starting third baseman, won the Most Valuable Player award in 1947, and led the Braves into the 1948 World Series which they lost to Cleveland. The rest of the players obtained by the Pirates were no help to the club and Camelli was a reserve with Boston.

October 19  Pirates purchase pitcher Art Herring from Brooklyn. He had an ERA over eight in his last major league season.

October 21  Pitcher Ernie Bonham is acquired from the Yankees for pitcher Cookie Cuccurullo. Bonham was past his peak but had a couple good seasons for the Bucs. Cuccurullo never pitched for the Yankees.

December 2  Pirates purchase second baseman Ed Basinski from Brooklyn. Basinski batted under .200 and was gone after one season.

December 12 Second baseman Jimmy Bloodworth is purchased from Detroit. He was platooned with Basinski in his only season with the Pirates.

December 23 Pittsburgh obtains catcher Clyde Klutz from the Cardinals for cash. Klutz had his best season in '47 but slipped sharply the next year and went to the Browns in 1951.

December 26 Outfielder Gene Woodling is acquired from the Indians for catcher Al Lopez. The Bucs gave up on Woodling after a trial in '47 and he went on to have a great career in the American League, mostly with the Yankees. Lopez played one year with Cleveland and went on to become an outstanding manager with the Indians and White Sox.

## 1947

January 18  Pittsburgh purchases first baseman Hank Greenberg from the Tigers. Greenberg left Detroit after leading the American League in homers. His home run production dropped with the Bucs but he led the league in walks, and while the team's win-loss record did not improve, the power tandem of Greenberg and Ralph Kiner caused an attendance increase of a half million.

January 25  Pirates obtain pitcher Hi Bithorn from the Cubs on a waiver claim. Bithorn never pitched for the Bucs, going to the White Sox on March 22nd.

February 10 Pitcher Jim Bagby, Jr. is purchased from the Red Sox. Bagby was at the end of his career after nine successful seasons with Boston and Cleveland. He won five games for the Bucs in '47.

March 22    Pitcher Hi Bithorn is claimed on waivers by the White Sox. He had won 18 games with the Cubs in 1943 but could not repeat his success with Chicago's other team.

March 25    Pirates buy pitcher Lou Tost from the Braves. He pitched just one game as a Pirate.

| | |
|---|---|
| April 28 | Pirates claim pitcher Bob Malloy from Cincinnati on waivers. Malloy never pitched for the Pirates. |
| May 3 | Pirates purchase pitchers Kirby Higbe and Cal McLish, catcher Dixie Howell, and infielder Gene Mauch from the Dodgers. Higbe was over the hill, Howell was platooned with Klutz, and McLish and Mauch saw almost no action. |
| | In a separate deal, the Pirates traded outfielder Al Gionfriddo to the Dodgers for pitcher Hank Behrman. Gionfriddo was a starter with the 1945 Pirates, but never played as well again. He is best remembered for his catch robbing Joe DiMaggio of a home run in the sixth game of the 1947 World Series. Behrman never pitched very well after a sensational rookie campaign. He never won a game for the Pirates. |
| May 9 | Pirates send pitcher Ken Heintzelman to the Phillies for cash. Ken did not do much until 1949 when he won 17 games with Philadelphia. He did nothing after that. |
| June 14 | Pirates purchase pitcher Roger Wolff from Cleveland. A 20-game winner in 1943, he was finished by '47 and the Pirates were his last club. |
| | Pitcher Hank Behrman is sold to the Dodgers. He did little after returning to Brooklyn. |
| July 11 | Pitcher Mel Queen, Sr. is purchased from the Yankees. Queen spent four plus years with the Pirates as a reliever and spot starter. |
| August 4 | Pitcher Al Lyons is purchased from the Yankees. Lyons lost two of three decisions in Pittsburgh and was part of the November 18th trade with the Braves. |
| November 14 | Pirates purchase shortstop Stan Rojek and first baseman Ed Stevens from the Dodgers. Stevens had his best major league season as the Bucs starter at first in 1948 but was replaced by Johnny Hopp in '49 and gone after the 1950 season. Rojek became the starting shortstop for two years, being traded to the Cardinals in 1951. |
| November 18 | Pirates obtain first baseman Johnny Hopp and second baseman Danny Murtaugh from the Braves for catcher Bill Salkeld, pitcher Al Lyons and outfielder Jim Russell. Murtaugh became the Bucs starting second baseman and had an outstanding season, leading National League second basemen in putouts, doubleplays, and assists while driving in a career high 71 runs. He remained with the Pirates until 1952 when he became a minor league manager, returning as a coach in 1956, and becoming manager in 1957. Hopp was used primarily as an outfielder in 1948, then at first in '49 and '50. Salkeld spent two years in Boston as a second-string catcher, and Lyons won only one game with the Braves. Russell got off to a great start and was the Braves centerfielder until an illness finished him for the season. He never played as well afterward. |
| December 4 | First baseman Elbie Fletcher is purchased by Cleveland. Fletcher was sold to open first base for Ed Stevens. Fletcher could not make Cleveland's championship team in '48 and played his final season with the Braves in 1949. |
| December 8 | Pirates trade shortstop Billy Cox, pitcher Preacher Roe and infielder Gene Mauch to Brooklyn for pitchers Vic Lombardi, Hal Gregg and outfielder Dixie Walker. Walker was a former batting champion but could only play part time at age 37 and was gone in two years. Lombardi and Gregg were supposed to improve with Pittsburgh but did just about nothing for the Bucs. Roe was considered erratic with the Pirates but won 90 games in six years as a starter with the Dodgers. Cox was moved to third base and became a great fielder as one of the "Boys of Summer." |

December 10   Pitcher Elmer Riddle is purchased from Cincinnati. Riddle was felled by a leg injury after a good start in 1948 and optioned to the minors in '49 after losing eight of nine decisions.

## 1948

January 15   Pittsburgh purchases third baseman Eddie Bockman from Cleveland. He spent two years sharing third base with Frankie Gustine and then Pete Castiglione.

March 26   Bucs purchase third baseman Don Gutteridge from the Red Sox. Gutteridge had been a starter with the Browns and Cardinals, but was at the end of his career and no help to the Pirates.

April 5   Pirates obtain shortstop Grady Wilson from the Phillies on a waiver claim. Wilson was hardly used in his only big league season.

May 15   Phillies purchase pitcher Nick Strincevich from the Pirates. He was finished.

July 30   Pirates obtain pitcher Paul Erickson from the Giants. Pittsburgh was Erickson's fourth team of the season, but he never pitched a game for the Bucs.

November 20   Pirates purchase pitcher Bob Muncrief from Cleveland. Muncrief had been a steady winner for the Browns but was ineffective with the Pirates and put on waivers.

December 10   Pirates trade second baseman Frankie Gustine and pitcher Cal McLish to the Cubs for pitcher Cliff Chambers and catcher Clyde McCullough. Gustine had reached the end of his career and McLish was not impressive in Chicago but had good years with Cleveland later in his career. Chambers pitched a no-hitter in 1951 and was traded almost immediately. McCullough was platooned with three different catchers in three years.

## 1949

January 29   Pitcher Murray Dickson is purchased from the Cardinals. Dickson won 20 games with a terrible team in 1951, then led the league in losses in '52 and '53 before going to the Phillies.

February 8   Pirates claim outfielder Walt Judnich from the Indians on waivers. Judnich was at the end after some good years with the St. Louis Browns.

May 18   Pittsburgh trades first baseman Johnny Hopp and cash to Brooklyn for outfielder Marv Rackley. The deal was cancelled and the players returned to their original teams in June.

June 6   Pittsburgh trades pitcher Kirby Higbe to the Giants for pitcher Ray Poat and infielder Bobby Rhawn. The trade helped neither club.
         Pitcher Bob Muncrief is claimed by the Cubs on waivers. No loss.

June 7   Outfielder Marv Rackley is returned to Brooklyn for first baseman Johnny Hopp and cash.

June 15   Infielder Bobby Rhawn is claimed by the Chicago White Sox on waivers.

         Pirates purchase catcher Ed Sauer from the Cardinals. Pittsburgh immediately traded Sauer to the Braves for catcher Phil Masi and cash. Both players had good years with their new clubs. Sauer retired after the season, and Masi was traded.

| | |
|---|---|
| July 27 | Pirates obtain pitcher Harry Gumbert from the Reds on waivers. Gumbert had his best years with New York in the late '30s but was near the end of his career and did not help the Pirates. |
| August 6 | Pirates purchase first baseman John Phillips from the Yankees. Phillips was platooned with Hopp and then Ralph Kiner. |
| November 4 | Second baseman Hank Schenz is purchased from the Dodgers. A light hitter, he played little with Pittsburgh. |
| December 14 | Bucs acquire pitcher Frank Papish from Cleveland in a cash deal. Papish pitched only four games for Pittsburgh and was released. |

## 1950

| | |
|---|---|
| February 9 | White Sox purchase catcher Phil Masi from the Pirates. Masi finished his career with three strong seasons as a White Sox. |
| May 17 | Catcher Ray Mueller is purchased from the Giants. Mueller platooned with Clyde McCullough in his second stint as a Pirate and released at the end of the season. |
| May 29 | Pirates sell outfielder Marv Rickert to the White Sox. He was off to a bad start in Pittsburgh and finished his career with the Sox. |
| June 12 | Pirates purchase pitcher Hank Borowy from the Phillies. Borowy was well past his prime and sold to the Tigers in August. |
| July 20 | Third baseman Bob Dillinger is purchased from the Athletics. Dillinger slipped after coming to the National League after outstanding years with St. Louis and a good start in Philadelphia. He was sold to the White Sox in 1951. |
| August 3 | Pirates sell pitcher Hank Borowy to the Tigers. |
| September 5 | Pittsburgh sells first baseman Johnny Hopp to the Yankees. Hopp was used sparingly in three years with New York. |

## 1951

| | |
|---|---|
| May 15 | Third baseman Bob Dillinger is sold to the White Sox. |
| May 26 | Pirates obtain first baseman Rocky Nelson and outfielder Erv Dusak from the Cardinals for shortstop Stan Rojek. Dusak was seldom used. Nelson was claimed on waivers by the White Sox in September. Rojek was about finished and only spent one season with St. Louis. |
| June 5 | Pirates obtain outfielder Jack Maguire from the Giants on waivers. After eight games he was sold to the Browns. |
| | First baseman Dale Long is obtained by the St. Louis Browns on a waiver claim. Long went to the minors and then returned to Pittsburgh in 1955. |
| June 21 | Pirates trade pitcher Cliff Chambers and outfielder Wally Westlake to the Cardinals for catcher Joe Garagiola, pitchers Ted Wilks and Howie Pollet, infielder Dick Cole, and outfielder Bill Howerton. Chambers won 11 games in '51 at St. Louis but never equaled the brilliance of his no-hit performance. Westlake did not have much success with the Cardinals and was gone in '52. Pollet and Wilks were well past their primes and neither was much help to the Pirates. Cole had one good year in '54 playing short and third. Garagiola shared the catching duties with Clyde McCullough until he was traded in 1953. |
| July 10 | Hank Schenz is claimed by the Giants on waivers. The second baseman finished his career by playing eight games with the Giants. |
| July 16 | Pirates sell outfielder Jack Maguire to the St. Louis Browns. |

149

September 19   Outfielder Dino Restelli is claimed on waivers by the Senators. He never played for Washington, and the 1951 season was his last.

September 20   White Sox claim first baseman Rocky Nelson from the Pirates on waivers.

## 1952

March 4        Pirates purchase pitcher Jim Suchecki from the Browns.

April 9        Pittsburgh purchases pitcher Hooks Iott from the Reds.

May 4          Pitcher Bill Werle is traded to the Cardinals for pitcher George Munger and cash. Neither pitcher was a factor with their new teams.

May 5          Pitcher Jim Suchecki is claimed by the White Sox on waivers.

May 7          Outfielder Bill Howerton is claimed by the Giants on waivers.

August 18      Pirates sell shortstop George Strickland and pitcher Ted Wilks to the Indians. Strickland did not hit much but played a solid shortstop for the Indians for seven years.

October 14     Pirates trade outfielder Gus Bell to the Reds for outfielder Cal Abrams and Gail Henley and catcher Joe Rossi. Bell went on to have an outstanding career with Cincinnati, while the three Pittsburgh acquisitions had limited success with the Pirates.

December 3     Catcher Clyde McCullough is traded to the Cubs for pitcher Dick Manville and cash. McCullough was strictly a reserve catcher with Chicago. Manville did nothing with the Bucs.

## 1953

April 17       Pirates purchase infielder Ed Pellagrini from Cincinnati. He was used as a sub at second in '53 and third in '54.

May 13         Catcher Ed Fitzgerald is sold to Washington. Fitzgerald was off to a terrible start with Pittsburgh but went on to have a good year with the Senators.

June 4         Pittsburgh trades outfielders Ralph Kiner and Catfish Metkovich, catcher Joe Garagiola, and pitcher Howie Pollet to the Cubs for first baseman-outfielder Preston Ward, catcher Toby Atwell, outfielders Gene Hermanski and Bob Addis, and pitcher Bob Schultz. Kiner missed the home run title for the first time in his career and retired after the 1955 season. The rest of the players are hardly worth talking about.

June 14        Pirates trade third baseman Pete Castiglione to the Cardinals for catcher Hal Rice and cash. Rice was traded after a good year in '53 but had a bad start in '54. Castiglione was at the end of his career and little help to the Cardinals.

August 31      Pirates sell pitcher Johnny Lindell to the Phillies. Lindell was once an outstanding outfielder with the Yankees but had converted to pitching and was off to an awful start with Pittsburgh. He was seldom used by the Phillies and played only one more season.

December 19    Catcher Mike Sandlock is sold to the Phillies. He did not make the team.

December 28    Pittsburgh trades infielder Danny O'Connell and cash to Milwaukee for pitchers Max Surkont, Fred Waters, and Larry LaSalle, outfielder-third baseman Sid Gordon, and outfielder Sam Jethroe. O'Connell became the Braves starting second baseman while the only Pirate acquisitions to make a contribution were Gordon who led the team in hitting as a part-time player and Surkont who moved into the starting rotation and lost 32 games in two years before being traded.

| | |
|---|---|
| January 13 | Pirates traded pitcher Murray Dickson to the Phillies for pitcher Andy Hansen and infielder Jack Lohrke. Dickson still managed to lead the league in losses for a third year in a row at Philadelphia but went on to have some good years with the Phillies and a number of other clubs. Hansen and Lohrke never played a game for the Pirates. |
| May 14 | Catcher Walker Cooper is waived to the Cubs. Cooper was off to a bad start in one of his last seasons. He finished respectably at Chicago and then returned to the Cardinals where he had been a star in the '40s. |
| June 14 | Pirates trade catcher Hal Rice to the Cubs for outfielder Luis Marquez. Neither player hit much and both were gone by the end of the season. |
| December 29 | Pirates sell pitcher Bob Schultz to Detroit. He was finished. |

## 1955

| | |
|---|---|
| January 11 | Pitcher Paul LaPalme is traded to the Cardinals for pitcher Ben Wade and cash. LaPalme spent just one season in St. Louis. Wade never won a game for Pittsburgh. |
| May 23 | Pirates sell third baseman-outfielder Sid Gordon to the Giants. Gordon finished his career in New York where he had his best playing days. |

## 1956

| | |
|---|---|
| May 5 | Pittsburgh sends catcher Jim Mangan to the Giants on waivers. Mangan was hardly used by the Giants in his last major league season. |
| May 7 | Pirates trade pitcher Max Surkont to St. Louis for pitcher Luis Arroyo and cash. Surkont was about finished and retired after the 1957 season. Arroyo had little success with the Pirates but moved on to the Yankees, where he had two great years as a relief pitcher, especially in 1961 when he won 15 games and saved 19. |
| May 15 | Pittsburgh obtains catcher Hank Foiles from the Indians for first baseman-outfielder Preston Ward. Foiles either held or shared the catcher's spot until he was sold in 1959. Ward was a successful player in Cleveland and later Kansas City. |
| May 16 | Pirates acquire outfielder Bill Virdon from the Cardinals for outfielder Bobby Del Greco and pitcher Dick Littlefield. The Virdon trade was the first of several that built the 1960 World Champions. He was off to a bad start after being named Rookie of the Year in 1955. He righted himself with the Bucs and remained the Pirates centerfielder until 1965. Del Greco and Littlefield were out of St. Louis by 1957. |
| June 23 | Pirates and Athletics exchange pitcher Jack McMahan and second baseman Spook Jacobs. Neither player was around in 1957. |

## 1957

| | |
|---|---|
| April 10 | Pirates trade infielder Dick Cole to the Braves for outfielder Jim Pendleton. Pendleton hit well in limited duty before he was traded to Cincinnati in 1959. Cole was a solid utility man in Pittsburgh but lasted only one year in Milwaukee. |
| May 1 | Outfielder Lee Walls and first baseman Dale Long are traded to the Cubs for first baseman Dee Fondy and infielder Gene Baker. Long had some good years but never lived up to the eight-game home run streak of 1956 and Walls had a surprising year in 1958 with 24 homers, but did little after that. Fondy hit .300 with the Bucs but was traded after the |

| | |
|---|---|
| | season. Baker was strictly a utility player and stayed in the organization first as a coach and now a scout. |
| May 14 | Pirates purchase pitcher Bob Smith from the Cardinals. Smith was a fair relief pitcher with Pittsburgh until he was waived in 1959. |
| December 28 | Pirates trade first baseman Dee Fondy to Cincinnati for first baseman Ted Kluszewski. Kluszewski was platooned at first with Dick Stuart but his home run production had fallen drastically from his glory days with the Reds. He was traded to the White Sox where he had one last hurrah with three homers in their World Series loss to the Dodgers in 1959. Fondy's hitting fell way off with Cincinnati and '58 was his last season. |

## 1958

| | |
|---|---|
| May 6 | Pittsburgh waives outfielder-first baseman Paul Smith to the Cubs on waivers. He saw almost no action in his one year with Chicago. |
| May 8 | Pirates purchase pitcher Bob Porterfield from the Red Sox. Bob was the Senators ace starter in the early '50s but used strictly in relief with Pittsburgh for two seasons. |
| June 15 | Pirates obtain infielder Dick Schofield from the Cardinals for third baseman Gene Freese and infielder Johnny O'Brien. Schofield had the misfortune to join the Pirates when Mazeroski and Groat had the keystone positions tied down. He probably spent the best years of his career on the bench until he replaced Groat in 1963. Freese had good years with three teams in three years and returned to the Bucs in 1964. O'Brien had no success with the Cardinals. |

## 1959

| | |
|---|---|
| January 31 | Pirates trade pitcher Ron Blackburn, outfielders Johnny Powers and Jim Pendleton, and outfielder-third baseman Frank Thomas to Cincinnati for catcher Smokey Burgess, pitcher Harvey Haddix, and third baseman Don Hoak. The trade put the Bucs on top. Burgess was a brilliant hitter and dangerous off the bench when he was not catching. Hoak was a firebrand who gave the club some much-needed leadership, and Haddix pitched effectively (with the exception of one night in Milwaukee when he threw his magnificent 12 innings of perfect baseball). Thomas dropped from 35 homers to 12 and the Reds dumped him, after which he returned to form. The other players had limited success with the Reds. |
| April 13 | Pittsburgh claims pitcher Paul Giel from the Giants. Giel saw little action in his two years with the Bucs. |
| June 13 | Pittsburgh sent pitcher Bob Smith to the Tigers on waivers. The Pirates also sent pitcher Bob Porterfield to the Cubs on waivers. The Bucs missed neither pitcher. |
| August 25 | Pirates trade first baseman Ted Kluszewski to the White Sox for outfielder Harry Simpson. Simpson played only nine games in his last major league season. |
| October 13 | Pittsburgh sells outfielder Harry Simpson to the White Sox. He was finished. |
| December 15 | Pirates sell catcher Hank Foiles to the Athletics. With the addition of Burgess, Foiles was expendable but continued to play well as a part-timer with several teams. |

| December 21 | Pirates trade pitcher Ron Kline to the Cardinals for pitcher Tom Cheney and outfielder Gino Cimoli. Kline left St. Louis after one season but later became a great relief pitcher in the American League and returned to Pittsburgh in 1969. Cimoli saw a good deal of action in two years with the Bucs, mostly in leftfield. Cheney was used as a spot starter. |

## 1960

| May 28 | Pittsburgh trades second baseman Julian Javier to the Cardinals for pitcher Wilmer "Vinegar Bend" Mizell. Mizell won 13 games for the Pirates in 1960 and his addition gave Pittsburgh the added mound strength needed to win the World's Championship. Javier became the Cardinals starting second baseman and helped them to titles in 1964, '67, and '68. |
| June 1 | Pirates sell catcher Danny Kravitz to the Athletics. He was the third string catcher behind Burgess and Hal Smith, and Kravitz' season with Kansas City was his last. |
| June 10 | Pittsburgh sends pitcher Ed Bauta to the St. Louis Cardinals as part of the May 28 deal. He never pitched for the Pirates and was used in relief by the Cardinals. |
| December 16 | Pirates trade pitcher Bernie Daniels and first baseman R. C. Stevens to Washington for pitcher Bobby Shantz. Shantz had one good year in Pittsburgh as a relief pitcher before he was lost to Houston in the expansion draft of 1961. Stevens saw little action with the expansion Senators but Daniels was one of their top starters. |

## 1961

| June 15 | Second baseman Johnny Logan is acquired from the Braves for outfielder Gino Cimoli. Logan had been the Braves starting second baseman for years but was used strictly as a utility man in his three years with Pittsburgh. Cimoli's average dropped 100 points after joining the Braves and he was gone before the 1962 season. |
| | Pirates purchase outfielder Walt Moryn from the Cardinals. He was at the end of his career and retired after the season. |
| September 25 | Pitcher Freddie Green is waived to the Senators. He had an outstanding season, teaming with Roy Face in 1960 but did nothing afterward. |
| December 21 | Pittsburgh purchases shortstop Coot Veal from the Senators. He played only one game for the Bucs. |

## 1962

| May 7 | Pirates trade pitcher Vinegar Bend Mizell to the Mets for first baseman Jim Marshall. Mizell had never equaled his success of 1960 and he never won a game for the Mets. Marshall was at the end of his career and saw little action behind Dick Stuart and Donn Clendenon. |
| September 6 | Pittsburgh sends pitcher Larry Foss to the Mets on waivers. Foss was no help to the Mets in limited action. |
| November 21 | Pirates trade shortstop Dick Groat and pitcher Diomedes Olivo to the Cardinals for pitcher Don Cardwell and infielder Julio Gotay. Olivo fell apart after a great year as a relief pitcher in 1962, but Groat filled a hole at shortstop and helped the Cardinals to the World's Championship in 1964. Cardwell had a fair year in '63, then hurt his arm and won only |

|  | once in '64. He was never the outstanding starter the Pirates had hoped for and was traded to the Mets after the 1966 season. Gotay was a throw in and never played much. |
|---|---|
| November 21 | Pirates obtain pitcher Don Schwall and catcher Jim Pagliaroni from the Red Sox for first baseman Dick Stuart and pitcher John Lamabe. Schwall had slumped after a sensational rookie year in Boston. He had little success as a starter but became a reliever and pitched well until he was traded in 1966. Pagliaroni platooned with Burgess for two years and then became the full time starter in '65 and '66. Stuart led the American League in RBIs in '63 and had two more good years with the Red Sox and Phillies. Lamabe was a successful relief pitcher but slumped when forced into a starting role in 1964. |
| November 28 | Third baseman Don Hoak is traded to the Phillies for outfielder Ted Savage. Hoak was going downhill and retired in 1964, becoming a member of the Pirates' radio broadcast team in 1965. He died suddenly in 1969 after managing the Bucs AAA farm club at Columbus, Ohio. Savage was a highly touted prospect but never lived up to the billing and batted less than .200 in his only season with the Pirates. |
| December 14 | Pirates sell catcher Don Leppert to Washington. He played two seasons in the Capitol and later returned to the Bucs as a coach. |

## 1963

| April 2 | Howie Goss is traded to Houston for outfielder Manny Mota and cash. Goss struck out over 100 times in his only season with the Colt .45's while Mota began building a reputation as one of the top reserve players in baseball. He spelled Willie Stargell in leftfield and was the Bucs top pinchhitter until he was drafted by Montreal in 1968. |
|---|---|
| May 4 | Pirates sell pitcher Tom Sturdivant to the Tigers. Once a big winner with the Yankees in the late fifties, he was just about finished. |
| May 23 | Outfielder Bob Skinner is traded to Cincinnati for outfielder Jerry Lynch. Skinner had little success at Cincinnati but played well as a part-time outfielder and pinch hitter with the Cardinals before retiring to become a coach and manager. Lynch joined Mota to give Pittsburgh two of the best pinch hitters in baseball. |
| November 26 | Pirates purchase third baseman Gene Freese from Cincinnati. Freese teamed with young Bob Bailey in his second stay with the Pirates before he was sold in 1965. |
| December 14 | Pitcher Harvey Haddix is sold to Baltimore. Haddix was now strictly a relief pitcher and had two good years with the Orioles before becoming a coach. |
|  | Pirates sell pitcher Bob Allen to Cleveland. Allen never pitched for Pittsburgh but spent five seasons as a reliever with the Indians. |

## 1964

| September 6 | Pirates claim first baseman-outfielder Dave Roberts from the Phillies. Roberts never played for Philadelphia and did little in one year with the Pirates. |
|---|---|
| September 12 | Pirates send catcher Smokey Burgess to the White Sox on waivers. Burgess was used almost exclusively as a pinch hitter in leading the league in '65 and '66 before retiring after the 1967 campaign. |

| February 11 | Pirates trade pitcher Bob Priddy and cash to San Francisco for catcher Del Crandall. Priddy pitched in relief until 1971 with a variety of teams and was never extremely effective. Crandall was obtained to help Jim Pagliaroni with the catching. He was in his second to last season after having been the Braves top catcher for many years. |
|---|---|
| March 24 | Pittsburgh purchases outfielder Johnny Jeter from Baltimore. Jeter did not reach the majors until 1969 and was traded away after the 1970 season. |
| May 22 | Pirates trade infielder Dick Schofield to San Francisco for infielder Jose Pagan. Schofield stopped hitting with the Giants and bounced around until 1971. Pagan could play just about anywhere but was used primarily at third. He was platooned with Richie Hebner from '69 until '72. |
| August 23 | Third baseman Gene Freese is sold to the White Sox. With Pagan, Freese was expendable and he retired after the 1966 season. |
| December 1 | Pitcher Joe Gibbon is traded to the Giants for outfielder Matty Alou and cash. Alou was not much of a hitter with San Francisco but he replaced Bill Virdon in centerfield, and, under the tutelage of manager Harry Walker, Matty raised his average 100 points and won the batting crown in 1966. Gibbon was fair as a swing man with the Giants and returned to Pittsburgh in a 1969 trade. |
| December 10 | Pitcher Bob Friend is traded to the Yankees with cash for pitcher Pete Mikkelsen. Friend was all but finished after a long and often brilliant career in Pittsburgh. The '66 season was Friend's last. Mikkelsen did not do much for the Pirates but went on to have some exceptional years with the Dodgers. |

## 1966

| April 7 | Pitcher Bob Purkey is purchased from St. Louis. Purkey made 10 relief appearances for the Bucs and retired after the season. |
|---|---|
| June 15 | Pitcher Don Schwall is traded to Atlanta for pitcher Billy O'Dell. Schwall never lived up to expectations after being acquired from Boston in 1962. O'Dell won a couple big games down the stretch in '66 and retired after starting and relieving in 1967. |
| September 12 | Pirates sell first baseman-outfielder Dave Roberts to Baltimore. He never played for the Orioles. |
| November 28 | Pitcher Juan Pizarro is purchased from the White Sox. Pizarro had been a top starter for Chicago in the sixties but was used primarily in relief until he was sold to Boston in 1968. |
| December 1 | Pittsburgh obtains shortstop Maury Wills from Los Angeles for third baseman Bob Bailey and infielder Gene Michael. Wills had fallen into disfavor with the Dodgers. He was moved to third base, creating the "million dollar infield" with Mazeroski, Alley, and Clendenon. Maury was expected to lead the Bucs to a title in '67 and, after failing, was left unprotected and drafted by Montreal in 1968. Bailey was a high priced bonus baby but did not achieve his potential with the Pirates or Dodgers, finally coming into his own with the Expos in the middle seventies. Michael spent one poor year in Los Angeles and then went to the Yankees where he had several good years as their starting shortstop and has since become their general manager. |
| December 6 | Pitcher Don Cardwell and outfielder Don Bosch are traded to the Mets for pitcher Dennis Ribant and cash. Ribant had become the Mets first |

winning pitcher and great things were expected with a team like the Pirates to support him. He had a mediocre season in 1967 and was traded before the '68 campaign. Cardwell pitched well in New York and helped the Mets win it all in 1969. Bosch was a throw in.

## 1967

| | |
|---|---|
| April 7 | Catcher Jimmy Price is sold to Detroit. He spent the rest of his career behind Bill Freehan. |
| June 21 | Outfielder Al Luplow is obtained from the Mets on waivers. He was strictly a bench player. |
| August 4 | Pitcher Pete Mikkelsen is waived to the Cubs. |
| November 28 | Pirates trade pitcher Dennis Ribant to Detroit for pitcher Dave Wickersham. Ribant never equalled his brief success with the Mets and played for four teams in his final two seasons. Wickersham had been one of the Tiger's top starters but saw little action his one year with Pittsburgh in a relief role. |
| December 3 | Pirates purchase pitcher Ron Kline from the Twins. Kline had an amazing year in '68, leading all relief pitchers with 12 wins. It was his last effective season. He was traded to San Francisco in 1969. |
| December 16 | Pittsburgh acquires pitcher Jim Bunning from Philadelphia for pitchers Harold Clem, Woodie Fryman, Bill Laxton, and infielder Don Money. Injuries and lack of offensive support resulted in a disastrous season for the 36-year-old Bunning. He was traded to Los Angeles in 1969. Money has had an excellent career with the Phillies and now with Milwaukee. Fryman had some successful seasons with Philadelphia, helped Detroit to a division title in 1972, and is still haunting the Bucs as a reliever with Montreal. |

## 1968

| | |
|---|---|
| June 27 | Pirates purchase pitcher Bill Henry from the Giants. The veteran was used in short relief and never won a game for Pittsburgh. |
| | Pitcher Juan Pizarro is sold to the Red Sox. Well past his prime, Pizarro hung on until 1974 when he returned to Pittsburgh for his final season in the majors. |
| August 31 | Pitcher Elroy Face is sold to Detroit. For 15 years Face was a mainstay in the Pirate bullpen but, at age 40, did not fit into the Bucs youth movement. He pitched only two games with the Tigers, then went to Montreal where he spent his final season with the expansion Expos. |

## 1969

| | |
|---|---|
| March 28 | Pirates trade catcher Chris Cannizzaro and pitcher Tommy Sisk to San Diego for outfielder Ron Davis. Davis spent one below average year with the Pirates and never returned to the majors. Sisk lost 13 of 15 decisions with the expansion team but Cannizzaro was the starting catcher and the Padres representative on the All-Star team. |
| June 10 | Pirates trade pitcher Ron Kline to San Francisco for pitcher Joe Gibbon. Kline was finished but Gibbon finished well with the Pirates winning five of six decisions, all in relief. He was released after an off year in 1970. |

| August 15 | Pitcher Jim Bunning is traded to Los Angeles for infielder Chuck Goggin, outfielder Ron Mitchell, and cash. This trade finished the Bunning fiasco. He won three games at the end of the season for the Dodgers and was returned to Philadelphia where he ended his career two years later. Goggin and Mitchell were both minor leaguers, Mitchell never reached Pittsburgh, and Goggin was traded in 1973. |
|---|---|
| October 21 | Pirates trade outfielder-infielder Carl Taylor to St. Louis for pitcher Dave Giusti and catcher Dave Ricketts. Taylor had hit .348 as a utility man in 1969 but did not come close to that during the rest of his career. Giusti had been a good starter with Houston but had an off year as a swingman in St. Louis. With Pittsburgh, he was used exclusively in relief and led all relief pitchers with nine wins in 1970. In 1971 he became "Fireman of the Year" and the Pirates went all the way. He remained one of the outstanding relief pitchers in baseball until he was traded to Oakland in 1977. Ricketts was a good bullpen catcher and became a coach in 1970. |

## 1970

| June 22 | Pirates sell pitcher Chuck Hartenstein to the Cardinals. He had done little for the Bucs and lasted only six games in St. Louis. |
|---|---|
| August 31 | Pirates trade pitcher Denny Riddleberger and cash to Washington for pitcher George Brunet. Brunet was used in short relief but did not pitch much and was traded to St. Louis after the season. Riddleberger was a minor leaguer who had a couple of good years in relief with the Senators and Indians. |
| September 14 | Pitcher Jim "Mudcat" Grant is purchased from Oakland. Grant led Minnesota to the World Series as a starter in 1965 and as a reliever had been off to a great start with the Athletics. With the Pirates he won two big games against the Mets in 1970 and was doing well in '71 when he was sold back to Oakland. |
| December 2 | Pirates trade shortstop Freddie Patek, pitcher Bruce Dal Canton, and catcher Jerry May to Kansas City for Pitcher Bob Johnson, shortstop Jackie Hernandez, and catcher Jim Campanis. Johnson was the key to the deal for Pittsburgh. He led American League righthanders in strikeouts and paced the Royals in complete games in 1970. He had three good years with the Bucs but was not nearly as good as expected. Hernandez was a light hitter who shared shortstop with Gene Alley and played brilliantly in the 1971 World Series. Patek became the Royals starting shortstop and was a standout until becoming a free agent after the 1979 season. Dal Canton was used first as a starter and then a reliever and had four successful seasons in Kansas City. |

## 1971

| January 29 | Pirates trade outfielder Matty Alou and pitcher George Brunet to the Cardinals for pitcher Nellie Briles and outfielder Vic Davalillo. Alou was replaced in center by Al Oliver and Briles became one of the Pirates most dependable pitchers as a reliever and spot starter. Davalillo was an excellent pinch hitter and reserve outfielder. |
|---|---|
| August 10 | Pirates sell pitcher Jim Grant to Oakland. Grant had been an outstanding pitcher out of the Bucs bullpen and helped the Athletics capture the Western Division title after returning to Oakland. |

Outfielder Johnny Jeter and pitcher Ed Acosta are traded to San Diego for pitcher Bob Miller. Jeter and Acosta were both in the minor leagues. Both were gone by 1973. The Pirates were Miller's tenth big league team and the journeyman reliever pitched well in two seasons with Pittsburgh.

September 3    Pirates purchase outfielder-first baseman Carl Taylor from the Royals. He played seven games in '71 and was not back in '72.

## 1972

October 25    Pirates trade pitcher Gene Garber to Kansas City for pitcher Jim Rooker. Both players were in the minors at the time but Rooker was one of the Pirates top starters with five straight seasons of ten or more wins. Garber had a good year with the Royals but was traded to Philadelphia in 1974 and has become one of the leagues' top relief pitchers, first with the Phillies and then the Braves.

November 30    Outfielder Dick Sharon is traded to Detroit for pitchers Jim Foor and Norm McRae. Sharon was a highly regarded prospect but faded quickly after two years with Detroit and one with San Diego. McRae never pitched for the Bucs, and Foor only made three appearances in 1973.

## 1973

April 2    Pirates trade catcher Charlie Sands to Detroit for pitcher Chris Zachery. Zachery lost one game in his last major league season. Sands never played for the Tigers.

May 4    Catcher Jerry McNertney is purchased from the Athletics. He was a starter with Seattle and Milwaukee but played only nine games in his last major league season.

May 24    Second baseman Chuck Goggin is sold to the Braves. Goggin played well in Atlanta in '73, the only time he got a chance to play consistently.

August 1    Pirates sell first baseman-outfielder Vic Davalillo to Oakland. Davalillo had an off year with the Pirates and Athletics but returned to the majors with Los Angeles after spending two years in the Mexican League and is once again a dangerous pinch hitter.

October 18    Second baseman Dave Cash is traded to Philadelphia for pitcher Ken Brett. With Rennie Stennett, Willie Randolph, and Mike Edwards in the system, the Bucs could afford to part with Cash. He had two great years with the Phillies, then played out his option and went to Montreal. Brett had two good years with the Bucs before he was traded to the Yankees in the Doc Medich deal.

October 31    Catcher Milt May is traded to Houston for pitcher Jerry Reuss. May became the Astros' catcher but did not live up to his billing as the best number two catcher in Baseball while playing behind Manny Sanguillen. He was traded to Detroit after two seasons. Reuss was the ace of the Pirate staff for three years, slipped in '77 and fell way off in '78. He was traded to Los Angeles in 1979.

December 4    Pirates trade pitcher Nellie Briles and infielder Fernando Gonzalez to the Royals for catcher-outfielder Ed Kirkpatrick and infielder Kurt Bevacqua. Bevacqua appeared in just 18 games and was traded back to Kansas City in '74. Kirkpatrick proved to be a valuable utility man and pinch hitter until he was traded in 1977. Briles moved into the Royals starting rotation but did not pitch as well as he had in Pittsburgh. Gonzalez played in only nine games with the Royals and eventually returned to Pittsburgh in 1977.

December 5 Pirates sell pitcher Luke Walker to Detroit. He pitched one year in Detroit and retired.

December 7 Outfielder Brunel Flowers is obtained from Cleveland for pitcher Bob Johnson. Flowers never reached the majors. Johnson spent one year in Cleveland, winning three of seven decisions.

## 1974

January 31 Shortstop Jackie Hernandez is traded to Philadelphia for catcher Mike Ryan. Hernandez never played for the Phillies and Ryan was in just 15 games playing behind Manny Sanguillen.

March 8 Pirates trade pitcher Jim Foor to Kansas City for pitcher Wayne Simpson. Both players were in the minor leagues, Foor never pitched for Kansas City, nor did Simpson who was traded in 1975.

April 1 Pitcher Tom Dettore and cash are traded to the Cubs for infielder Paul Popovich. Dettore had two good years as a reliever and spot starter with Chicago. Popovich was a key pinch hitter and reserve infielder down the stretch in 1974. He retired after the 1975 season.

July 8 Infielder Kurt Bevacqua is traded to Kansas City for infielder Cal Meier and cash. Bevacqua did not do well in Kansas City and was sent packing at the end of the season. Meier never played for the Bucs.

July 11 Pirates purchase catcher Chuck Brinkman from the White Sox. He played only four games as the Bucs third-string catcher.

October 22 Catcher Duffy Dyer is obtained from the Mets for outfielder Gene Clines. Dyer was Manny Sanguillen's back-up in '75 and '76, then was platooned with Ed Ott in '77 and '78 before playing out his option and signing with Montreal. An excellent defensive catcher, Dyer caught John Candelaria's no-hitter in 1976. Clines did not hit well with the Mets and was traded after one season.

## 1975

April 5 Pirates trade pitcher Wayne Simpson to the Phillies for outfielder Bill Robinson. After an outstanding rookie season with Cincinnati, Simpson had arm trouble. He never pitched for the Pirates and won his only decision with the Phillies. Robinson was at one time acquired by the Yankees and expected to become their next superstar. He never fulfilled that expectation but became a "super-sub" with the Pirates in 1975 and '76. In 1977 he got the chance to play full time and responded with a 100 RBI season. In '78 and '79 he was platooned with John Milner in leftfield.

December 11 Pitcher George "Doc" Medich is obtained from the Yankees for second baseman Willie Randolph and pitchers Ken Brett and Dock Ellis. Medich was expected to become the Pirates ace starter after three above-average years with New York. Unfortunately, the Pennsylvania native flopped and was traded to Oakland before the 1977 season. Randolph became the Yankees starting second baseman, Ellis rebounded from a bad year in 1975 to win 17 games and their addition helped New York win the American League championship. Brett was traded to the White Sox after just two games.

December 12 Pirates trade infielder Art Howe to the Astros for infielder Tommy Helms. Helms came back after a bad season with the Astros and played well at third base and second. He was sold to Oakland after the season. Howe had been unimpressive as a third baseman with the Bucs but came around with Houston and became their starting second baseman.

## 1976

September 8
Pitcher Ramon Hernandez is sold to the Cubs. The 36 year old reliever was at the end of the road and did not win another game in the majors.

October 15
Pirates sell pitcher Jim Minshall to the Mariners. Minshall did not make the Seattle ball club and has not returned to the majors.

November 5
Pirates acquire manager Chuck Tanner from Oakland for catcher Manny Sanguillen and cash. The New Castle, Pennsylvania, native was acquired to replace the retiring Danny Murtaugh. Sanguillen was slipping fast but reacquired after one year in Oakland to pinch hit and fill in at first and behind the plate. In a separate deal, infielder Tommy Helms was purchased by the Athletics. He was reacquired before the start of the '77 season.

November 6
Pitcher Jim Sadowski is traded to the Reds for pitcher Tom Carroll. Both pitchers were in the minor leagues and have not returned to the majors.

December 7
Pirates trade infielders Craig Reynolds and Jim Sexton to Seattle for pitcher Grant Jackson. Jackson became the Bucs lefthanded short man out of the bull pen and has been consistently effective since his acquisition. Reynolds was traded to Houston after an excellent second year with the Mariners. He made the All-Star team as an Astro in 1979. Sexton was also traded to Houston.

December 10
Pitchers Rich Gossage and Terry Forster are obtained from the White Sox for outfielder Richie Zisk and pitcher Silvio Martinez. Zisk was prepared to play out his option, so the Pirates traded him to Chicago where he drove in 100 runs, then played out his option and signed with Texas. Martinez was traded to St. Louis where he has become one of their top starters. Gossage had an outstanding season, pitching in relief. He also played out his option and signed with the Yankees. Forster had a subpar season, due in part to arm trouble, then he also played out his option and signed with the Dodgers.

## 1977

March 15
Pirates trade pitchers Dave Giusti, Doc Medich, Doug Bair, Rick Langford, and outfielders Tony Armas and Mitchell Page to Oakland for second baseman Phil Garner, infielder Tommy Helms, and pitcher Chris Batton. Veteran third baseman Richie Hebner had played out his option and the Pirates wanted Garner, a hard-nosed player who began his career at third, switched to second, and became an All-Star. Helms was finished and released in June while Batton has never pitched for the Pirates. Bair was traded to Cincinnati in place of Vida Blue and has become the Reds ace in the bullpen. Medich pitched for three teams in '77, played out his option and signed with Texas where he has pitched well but not as well as he did with the Yankees. Langford began to pitch well at the end of the '79 season. Giusti was effective in '77 before going to the Cubs and retiring after the season. Page got off to a great start but slipped in '79. Armas has not done much in a part-time role.

160

| April 4 | Pirates acquire outfielder Mike Easler from California for pitcher Randy Sealy. Easler had great minor league credentials but was never able to stick with the Bucs until 1979, after he had been sold to Boston and reacquired. Sealy has not pitched for California. |
| June 13 | Outfielder Jerry Hairston is purchased from the White Sox. Hairston had been a player under Chuck Tanner at Chicago. With Pittsburgh he hit under .200 and did not return in '78. |
| June 15 | Pirates trade catcher-first baseman Ed Kirkpatrick to Texas for first baseman Jim Fregosi. Fregosi was once an All-Star shortstop with California but was used mostly as a pinch hitter and third baseman in limited duty with the Pirates. He left the team in 1978 to become the Angels manager. Kirkpatrick played only 20 games with Texas and was traded to Milwaukee. |
| July 27 | Pitcher Dave Pagan is acquired from the Mariners for a player to be named later. |

Pitcher Rick Honeycutt was assigned to Seattle on August 22nd to complete the deal. Honeycutt, a highly touted prospect, moved into the Mariners starting rotation in 1978 and could be a star of the future. Pagan pitched in one game for the Bucs in 1977 and has not yet returned.

| December 8 | Pirates are involved in a four team deal with the Mets, Braves, and Rangers. Texas traded pitchers Adrian Devine and Tommy Boggs and outfielder Eddie Miller to the Braves for first baseman Willie Montanez. Montanez is then traded to New York for pitcher Jon Matlack and first baseman-outfielder John Milner. Finally, Milner and pitcher Bert Blyleven come to the Pirates for outfielder-first baseman Al Oliver and shortstop Nelson Norman. Oliver has always been one of the games' top hitters and was in the top ten in each of his first two years in the American League. Norman is the Rangers starting shortstop but has not proven himself as a hitter. Blyleven has been known as a pitcher with an abundance of talent but an inability to win the "big" game. After two good seasons and a great job in 1979 post-season action, Blyleven may now be ready to come into his own. Milner could not live up to the Mets hopes that he would be a superstar, but as platoon outfielder and pinchhitter Milner has accounted for more than his share of victories in two years with Pittsburgh. |

## 1978

| January 31 | Pirates purchase pitcher Elias Sosa from the Dodgers. He was traded to Oakland in the April 4th deal. |
| March 27 | Pirates sell pitcher Larry Demery to Toronto. Demery failed to pass a physical and was returned to the Pirates. |
| March 29 | Pitcher Tim Jones is traded to Montreal for pitcher Will McEnaney. McEnaney was a star with the Reds in his first full season but did not pitch well with Montreal or Pittsburgh. He has since moved on to St. Louis. Jones, a top prospect with Pittsburgh, has yet to see any action with the Expos. |
| April 4 | Pirates trade outfielder Miguel Dilone, pitcher Elias Sosa, and second baseman Mike Edwards to Oakland for catcher Manny Sanguillen. Manny is no longer an All-Star catcher but can fill in at first or behind the plate and is one of the Bucs top right handed pinch hitters. Sosa played out his option, had a great year in Oakland and signed with Montreal where he has become their number one reliever. Edwards is |

|  | the Athletics starter at second, he had a good rookie year but was not as successful in '79. Dilone is now with the Cubs. |
|---|---|
| May 28 | Pitcher Dave Hamilton is purchased from the Cardinals. Hamilton was up and down in 16 games with the Pirates and did not return in 1979. |
| June 5 | Infielder Fernando Gonzalez is purchased by the Padres. Gonzalez played well with San Diego and became the starting second baseman in 1979 but did not hit as well as in past years. |
| September 13 | Outfielder Dave May is purchased from Milwaukee. May was acquired for bench strength down the stretch but he appeared in only five games as a pinch hitter. |
| September 22 | Outfielder Clarence Gaston is purchased from the Braves. Gaston was also obtained just in case of an emergency and played in just one game. |
| October 27 | Pirates sell outfielder Mike Easler to Boston. Easler won the International League batting title with the Bucs AAA farm team at Columbus, Ohio. He never played for the Red Sox, being reacquired by Pittsburgh just before the start of the 1979 season. |
| December 5 | Pirates trade pitchers Odell Jones, Rafael Vasquez, and shortstop Mario Mendoza to Seattle for pitchers Enrique Romo, Rick Jones, and shortstop Tom McMillan. Romo came after two years as Seattle's ace reliever and took much of the pressure off Kent Tekulve who was the Pirates only right handed reliever in 1978. Jones and McMillan spent most of the year with the Pirates AAA team in Portland. Jones got off to a terrible start and lost 11 of 14 decisions in '79. Mendoza was the Mariners starting shortstop but batted under .200 and Vasquez was traded to Cleveland in December of 1979. |

## 1979

| April 5 | Outfielder Mike Easler is reacquired from the Red Sox for minor leaguers George Hill, Martin Rivas, and cash. Easler finally stuck with the Bucs after trials in '77 and '78. He was used almost exclusively as a pinch hitter. |
|---|---|
| April 8 | Pirates trade pitcher Jerry Reuss to Los Angeles for pitcher Rick Rhoden. Rhoden started the season on the disabled list, pitched in one game and then underwent surgery and missed the rest of the season. Reuss suffered another off season with the Dodgers, posting a 7-14 record. |
| April 19 | Shortstop Tim Foli and pitcher Greg Field are acquired from the Mets for shortstop Frank Taveras. Foli changed the entire look of the Pirates. Once known as a hothead, Tim solidified the inner defense and proved to be an outstanding number-two hitter behind Omar Moreno. The Pirates could no longer tolerate Taveras' erratic defense and Frank's offense was little help to the lowly Mets. |
| June 28 | Pirates acquire infielder Bill Madlock and pitcher Dave Roberts from San Francisco for pitchers Eddie Whitson, Al Holland, and Fred Breining. The Pirates needed another righthanded hitter and the two-time batting champion with the Cubs gave the Bucs one of the best offensive lineups in the league. He moved from second with the Giants to third with Pittsburgh and was surprisingly adequate defensively. Roberts was used as a long reliever and spot starter winning five of seven decisions. The Giants seemed to make the trade with an eye to the future. Holland is the oldest of the pitchers at age 27 and all have promising futures in the majors. |

# 4. 1979 SEASON IN REVIEW

The Pittsburgh Pirates 1979 season really began on August 12, 1978 when Chuck Tanner uttered the now famous quote, "This may not be the end, it may be just the beginning." The Pirates had just been humiliated in consecutive defeats at Philadelphia. They were in fourth place, eleven and a half games out of first place in the Eastern Division. The following day the Bucs launched a comeback that brought them within three and a half games of the Phillies prior to a four game final series with the Division leaders at Three Rivers Stadium.

The Pirates needed a sweep to stay alive. They fell one win short. The Pirates had not lost the title, they just ran out of time. More importantly, they had gained a winning attitude that would carry over to the start of the 1979 season.

The Pirates still figured to be chasing Philadelphia when the 1979 season opened. The Phillies had strengthened themselves with the addition of free agent Pete Rose and second baseman Manny Trillo. They were the logical favorite to win the division. Montreal, St. Louis, and Chicago might challenge but the race would be between the Pirates and Phillies. Many so called experts were already conceeding the title to Philadelphia.

The Bucs were less generous. The Pirates had also improved their club in the off season. Relief pitcher Enrique Romo had been acquired from Seattle after two outstanding seasons with the expansion Mariners and Dodger super sub Lee Lacy was purchased in the free agent market to add right-handed punch to the Pirate attack. Mike Easler had been purchased by the Red Sox, then reacquired by the Bucs and was coming east for the first time with the Pirates after winning the International League batting championship with Columbus in 1978. At catcher rookie Steve Nicosia would spend the entire season with Pittsburgh, replacing Duffy Dyer who opted for free agency and signed with the Expos.

Over the last three years, the Pirates inability to catch Philadelphia was due to poor defense and slow starts. Coming from Florida, the Pirates knew they could outplay the Phillies in September and would win the division if they could stay close at the beginning of the season.

Thoughts of a fast start were quickly dashed as the Bucs dropped two of three to the young and aggressive Expos to open the campaign, then went into Philadelphia and got beaten twice more. Poor pitching and sloppy defense were the problems against the Expos. The Pirates committed five errors in the opener and gave Montreal the game in the tenth on an unearned run. The Expos returned the favor the next day as Elias Sosa took Stargell's game-ending ground ball and fired it down the right field line, allowing the tying and winning runs to score. On Sunday, April 8, Enrique Romo came into the game in the seventh and failed to hold a one-run lead. He was touched for a two-run home run by Andre Dawson and gave up an unearned run when Omar Moreno misplayed Warren Cromartie's single to center as the Bucs went on to lose 5-4. In Philadelphia, the Pirates were simply out-played for two nights and limped home three games behind the Phils.

Don Robinson got the Pirates back on the track by stopping the Cardinals on April 12 by scattering seven hits and striking out a career high nine. The Bucs won two more against St. Louis to even their record at 4-4 on the strength of John Milner's big stick. Milner was named N. L. Player of the Week on April 16, after hitting .571 with two homers and eight RBIs. The Bucs also got strong pitching efforts out of Eddie Whitson and Jim Bibby.

On a bitterly cold and gray Easter Sunday, the Pirates reverted to their early season form and let a 4-1 lead slip through their hands, losing 9-4 in 10 innings.

The Phillies came to town for three games that didn't mean much in the standings but were very important for the Pirates' confidence. The Phillies were tied with St. Louis in second place, a game behind the surprising Expos. The Pirates trailed the Expos by just two games, but after the two losses in Veterans Stadium, the Bucs had something to prove. They wanted to reestablish what they had proven the last weekend of the 1978 season, that they were as good as if not better than the Phils. After a Monday night postponement, it was the Phillies who proved to be superior. They humiliated the Pirates, hammering Bert Blyleven for seven runs in two and two-third innings, and pounding Jim Bibby, for five more in an inning and two-thirds. Bake McBride delivered the crushing blow by hitting a three-run homer in the third, and Gary Maddox added insult to injury by smashing a grandslam in the fifth. The next night, McBride struck again putting the Phils in front with a two-out solo-homer in the third inning off Don Robinson. In the sixth, Pete Rose led-off with a single. Then Luzinski hit a ball that landed just this side of Mars and ended up in the fifth level. No opponent had ever accomplished that before. On the verge of losing their fourth straight to the Phillies, Stargell put the Pirates back in the game with a two-run homer in the eighth. The Bucs looked as though they were ready to make another comeback in the ninth when Steve Nicosia hit what appeared to be a game-tying home run. The ball died over the outfield, allowing leftfielder Greg Gross to make the catch at the wall. The roar of the over-anxious crowd prompted the fireworks man to mistakenly shoot the fireworks lending a morbid end to the disappointing series.

With the fast start fizzling the Pirates had to make a move. Skipper Chuck Tanner and G. M. Pete Peterson decided that the Bucs still needed help defensively. They traded shortstop Frank Taveras to the Mets for shortstop Tim Foli and pitcher Greg Fields on April 19. Taveras had the offensive punch and was one of the leagues' top base stealers. Defensively, he was erratic. At times he would make plays that few other shortstops could, but at other times he would have trouble with routine plays. Foli, on the other hand, was not considered an offensive threat, nor did he have the speed or range of Taveras. But Foli would consistently make the play on any ball that he could reach.

The Foli deal did not pay immediate dividends. The Bucs dropped three games in Houston to run their losing streak to six. Every game was decided by one run and Pirate errors were responsible for each of the Astros' winning runs.

Everything went wrong in that series. Foli went hitless in ten trips and committed a costly error in the game on April 22. Kison sprained his ankle sliding into second after Howe errantly threw his bunt away. Romo looked like he was going to have his first really good outing but after striking out the first two men he faced, he slipped off the mound and injured his groin. The Pirates left Houston with a 4-10 record five games behind the division leading Phillies.

The Bucs finally got a break when Reds starting pitcher, Tom Seaver, was unable to pitch due to a back injury. In his place, the Pirates faced rookie Frank Pastore and jumped on the youngster for six runs on ten hits in the first four innings. The Bucs added runs on homers by Milner and Parker to coast to a 9-2 win. The following day, the Pirates won an 11-inning contest when Lee Lacy scored Parker from third with a sacrifice fly. The real plus of this game was the pitching of Kent Tekulve. After struggling in the first part of the season, Teke pitched the final three and one-third innings without allowing a baserunner.

After coming out of Cincinnati, the Bucs would win one day and lose the next. They just could not put anything together. This inconsistency motivated the Pirate front office to put together a promotion called Win Streak Night. The plan worked like this: if the Pirates defeated the Mets on May 16, everyone would be invited back the next night as guests of the club to help cheer on a winning streak. Amazingly enough, it worked.

Leading 3-2 in the top of the ninth, Bert Blyleven ran into trouble when Steve Henderson led-off with a single and Stearns reached on an error by Dale Berra. Joel Youngblood sacrificed off Tekulve and Ed Kranepool, pinch-hitting for Doug Flynn, was intentionally passed. With Ron Hodges the announced pinch hitter, Tanner went to Grant Jackson. Manager Joe Torre countered by replacing Hodges with Gil Flores, who lifted a flyball to rightcenter. Omar Moreno took charge, but his throw to the plate was not in time to get Henderson with the tying run. The game was still tied in the 13th when Tanner sent Mike Easler in to pinch-hit for Enrique Romo. Easler responded by blasting Skip Lockwood's first pitch over the right field fence.

In the finale with the Mets, the Pirates trailed 5-4 going into the bottom of the eighth. After Garner and Parker struck out, Bill Robinson worked Jesse Orosco for a walk. Stargell followed with a drive into the right field seats for his second homer of the night to give the Bucs a 6-5 lead. Tekulve put away the Mets in the ninth by getting Hodges to fly out to Moreno and striking out Henderson and Taveras.

Pittsburgh then traveled to Chicago and kept the streak alive, over-powering the Cubs by a 9-5 margin. Stargell tied the game with a two-run homer in the third. It was his fourth home run and sixth RBI in three games.

May 19th was a day to renew old acquaintances. Jim Rooker came off the disabled list and the Major League umpires came off the picket line. Before the game started, Rooker yelled to home plate umpire John Kibler, "Don't worry, this is my first game too." Rooker had nothing to worry about. Through the first eight innings, he had allowed only two singles and a walk but with the help of two doubleplays and one man caught stealing, had faced the minimum number of batters. In the ninth, Rooker got Barry Foote to ground out to short, But Ted Sizemore laid down a perfect bunt single and pinch hitter Sam Mejias drew a walk. Tanner didn't want to let this game get away so he called in Romo. Bobby Mercer was the pinch-hitter for Ivan DeJesus and worked Romo for a walk to load the bases. After Mike Vail popped to short, Jackson was called in to face Bill Buckner. Buckner took the count to 3-2 and then fouled a ball deep down the right field line. Jackson finally won the confrontation as he got Buckner to ground out to second.

The Bucs completed the sweep of the Cubs the following afternoon when home runs by John Milner and Dale Berra gave the Bucs a 3-0 lead. The Cubs scored a pair in the fifth on doubles by Foote and DeJesus and a single by Scot Thompson. Both clubs got single tallies in the sixth. With two-out and a runner on third in the top of the seventh, Omar Moreno homered into the rightfield bleachers to give Pittsburgh another three-run lead. The Cubs came back in the bottom of the seventh on singles by DeJesus and Dave Kingman and a double by Buckner. Tekulve managed to get out of that jam with another one in the eighth as the Cubs put runners on second and third with two out. In the bottom of the ninth, Buckner led off with a drive to center that had extra bases written all over it until Moreno jumped into the ivy to make an unbelievable leaping grab.

On May 21, Pittsburgh traveled to Montreal and ran their winning streak to six. Moreno, Stargell and Ed Ott homered, and Blyleven pitched eight and one-third innings to record his first win. The Pirates lost the next two games in Canada and moved on to New York for a four game series with last place Mets.

Craig Swan had the Bucs shutout for the second time in ten days and the Mets clung to a 1-0 lead after seven innings. Lee Lacy opened the Pirate eighth with a single but Swan retired Ott and Dale Berra, forcing Tanner to pinch hit for starter Jim Rooker. Tanner picked Mike Easler and the hit-man delivered against the Mets again with a blast into the New York bullpen. Omar Moreno followed with a shot to the right field wall. As Moreno dove into third, the relay throw from Willie Montanez sailed past Richie Hebner and allowed Omar to score an insurance run. The Mets refused to quit and John Stearns' two-out single off reliever Bruce Kison scored Lee Mazzilli with the tying run after Maz had doubled home Joel Youngblood and moved to third on Moreno's error. As the game moved into extra innings, a thick fog slowly began to cover Shea Stadium. By the 11th inning it was virtually impossible to see. Leftfielder Bill Robinson pointed this out to third base umpire Jerry Dale as he took his position. Dale ignored Robby until Youngblood led off with a fly ball that Robinson never saw until it landed some 15 feet to his left. Tim Foli hustled out to leftfield and returned the ball to the infield, holding the runner at third. At that point both Robinson and Foli charged Dale and protested the unplayable conditions. After a conference with the other umpires, it was decided that the game could not be continued and the game was declared a 3-3 tie and would have to be replayed in its entirety.

After losing the second game of the series, Grant Jackson came out of the bullpen to halt a New York rally by fanning Elliott Maddox and Lee Mazzilli with the bases loaded in the eighth, preserving a 1-1 tie. Bill Robinson led off the ninth with a homer to give Jackson the win, and the following night Buck stopped New York again with the bases loaded in the eighth, gaining his sixth save in Pittsburgh's 6-1 triumph.

The Pirates returned to Pittsburgh on May 29th to face the Cubs. The Bucs picked up where they left off in Chicago, as Robinson and Jackson combined on an 8-0 pasting of the Cubs on Friday, followed by Jim Rooker's route-going two hitter and a ten inning 4-3 win on Tim Foli's two-out single with the bases loaded.

While the Bucs were sweeping the Cubs, the Phillies were suffering the humiliation of three straight shutout defeats in Montreal moving the Expos past Philadelphia into first place with the Pirates just 5.5 games back in fourth place.

The Pirates took their first look at the West Coast teams, which have traditionally proven troublesome for them in a three-game series with San Diego. The first game was no exception as Dave Winfield blasted two mammoth home runs, giving the Padres a 6-5 lead. The Pirates were still down by a run going into the top of the ninth. Kent Tekulve was trying to keep the Bucs close when Ozzie Smith singled, Jerry Turner doubled, and Kurt Bevacqua singled to give the Padres a three-run cushion. Hits by Moreno and Foli brought Dave Parker to the plate as the potential tying run. Suddenly the game was tied when the Cobra ripped a John D'Acquisto pitch over the wagon gate in center field. D'Acquisto retired Bill Robinson and was replaced by Bob Shirley who was greeted by a Stargell single to center. Padres' manager Roger Craig went to his ace, Rollie Fingers, but Phil Garner touched his former teammate for a double, sending Stargell to third. Fingers issued an intentional walk to Ed Ott, loading the bases with Dale Berra due up. Tanner called back Berra and sent Lee Lacy to the plate. Fingers jumped in front with two quick strikes, then missed with four consecutive pitches to force in the winning run.

Greybeard Gaylord Perry defeated the Bucs on Saturday night and on Sunday, June 3, when Don Robinson was unable to take his turn, Bruce Kison filled the void. The outcome was never in doubt—Bill Robinson smashed a three-run homer in the opening inning, and Omar Moreno, Parker, and Robinson again tagged solo shots in the third. When Lee Lacy connected for a circuit blast in the sixth, Pittsburgh had a comfortable 7-0 lead. But something much more important was happening. Kison had allowed only two base runners, both on walks, in the first six innings. Buster set the Padres down one-two-three in the seventh and recorded the first two outs in the eighth when rookie Barry Evans hit a grounder just inside the third-base line past Phil Garner. Official scorer Dan Donovan immediately ruled the ball a hit, and Kison was forced to settle for a one-hit shutout.

The Dodgers and Giants followed San Diego to Pittsburgh. The Pirates split six games, winning two of three from Los Angeles, including a 5-4 decision over former Buc Jerry Reuss, who had been traded for Rick Rhoden on April 8 from Los Angeles. They dropped two of three to San Francisco before heading to San Diego for the first West Coast swing of the season. The West Coast has always been a trouble area for the Bucs. Pittsburgh had not recorded a winning coast trip since 1974 and had an 18-36 record there over the last three years. Of those 18 wins, 10 came in San Diego.

In '79, the Pirates had requested and received a travel day before opening in San Diego on June 12. The Pirates had done this in an all-out effort to reverse their losing trend. And this year the Bucs knew that if they had any hope of winning the division, they must win in the West.

Opening the trip in San Diego, the Bucs had to face the crafty veteran Gaylord Perry. Pittsburgh was no match for Perry but did make the score respectable with Parker's three-run homer in the ninth. The next night, a former Pirate, Fernando Gonzalez got some revenge over his old team with a game-winning two-run homer over the left field wall. On June 14, the Pirates and Padres battled with a 1-1 tie into the 14th inning. In the 14th, Tanner called on Candelaria, who had been knocked out of the box in the second inning of the first game of the series. After getting two outs, Candy got Smith to ground to short, but Foli bobbled the ball for an error, Winfield drew a walk, and Barry Evans rapped a single to center to complete the sweep.

Heading north to Los Angeles, the Pirates were in trouble. Dodger Stadium had been the scene of some of the Bucs most discouraging defeats in the past three years. No lead seemed safe, every game at Chavez Ravine was a cliff hanger, regardless of the score. With over a third of the season gone, the Bucs had shown no signs of being any better than the second place teams of the past three years. The Pirates could be thankful that none of their Eastern Division rivals had taken advantage of their troubles in San Diego but a prolonged losing streak would probably put the Pirates well behind the leaders, exactly where they had been the last three seasons, unable to recover.

It was Bert Blyleven's job to stop the skid when he opposed Don Sutton on Friday, June 15th. The Bucs scored on a wild pitch in the first and held onto the 1-0 lead into the eighth. With two out and Dodgers at first and second, Tanner lifted Blyleven in favor of Kent Tekulve, who retired Ron Cey on a liner to Foli. The Pirates broke the game open in the ninth against one time Pirate, Ken Brett, with three straight hits, followed by three more off Dave Patterson, good for five runs and a 6-1 victory. On Saturday, Omar Moreno's three-run homer highlighted a four-run third and Don Robinson scattered five hits for a 6-3 win. The next afternoon, Jerry Reuss, made his second appearance against his former teammates but could not match the two-hit pitching of Eddie Whitson and Kent Tekulve as the Bucs took a 5-1 decision, sweeping the Dodgers in Los Angeles for the first time since 1971.

The Bucs pounded Giant pitchers John Montefusco and Vida Blue in a two-game series at San Francisco, winning 9-4 and 8-5, completing their most successful West Coast trip since 1974.

The Pirates had turned the corner in California. They survived three tough losses in San Diego and played their best ball of the season in the next five games. The Bucs were now a solid defensive team. With the addition of Tim Foli, they were no longer giving games away. Foli's defense was expected but his offensive contribution was an added dividend. A new batting stance, inspired by hitting instructor Bob Skinner, produced an average some 20 points higher than his lifetime mark. Tim also proved to be an ideal number-two hitter, protecting Omar Moreno and rarely striking out. Moreno was quickly gaining a reputation as an all around player with a surprising .310 average, 24 stolen bases and 25 RBIs. Phil Garner's five for five performance in the first game at San Francisco raised his average to .269, surprisingly high for the perennially slow starter.

After returning from San Francisco, the Bucs made it six straight and seven in a row over the Cubs. Blyleven was the benefactor of a 13 hit attack as the Pirates won 7-2. Then Pittsburgh stopped hitting. On June 23, Mike Krukow and Bruce Sutter limited the Bucs to three runs on seven hits and stopped the winning streak by taking a 4-3 decision. The next afternoon, Rick Reuschel whitewashed the Pirates and with home runs by Bill Buckner and Jerry Martin, breezed to a 5-0 win.

Pittsburgh then began a home-and-home series with a doubleheader against the Mets in New York. After winning an 8-1 laugher in the first game, the Bucs dropped three of the next four to the Eastern Division cellar-dwellers.

Rumors had been circulating since the June 15 trading deadline that the Pirates were working on a deal with the Giants involving two-time batting champion Bill Madlock and several other players. The rumor proved to be more fact than fiction when, on June 28, the clubs announced that Madlock was coming to Pittsburgh along with pitcher Dave Roberts for right-handed pitcher Ed Whitson and minor league pitchers Al Holland and Fred Breining.

Madlock had been in manager Joe Altobelli's doghouse since he ridiculed the Giants at Candlestick Park after Altobelli's team meeting on June 14. Madlock was returning to his lifetime .325 average after a miserable start, until that incident which led the Giant manager to bench his second baseman. Giants' general manager Spec Richardson said the dispute between Madlock and Altobelli had nothing to do with the trade but no one could understand why San Francisco would give up one of baseball's best pure hitters and a solid spot starter and reliever in Roberts for three unproven pitchers. Regardless of the Giants' motivation, the swap was considered a first-class heist by Pete Peterson.

The addition of Madlock also presented a problem for manager Chuck Tanner. He now had three infielders for two positions. Bill could replace second baseman Rennie Stennett or third baseman Phil Garner. Third was supposed to be Madlock's best defensive position, and the logical move seemed to be to move Garner to second where he had been an All-Star in Oakland. Stennett still had not recovered from the broken ankle of 1977 and was batting below .240. The addition of Madlock to the batting order would give the Bucs their most potent offense since the Pirates led the N. L. in batting with Richie Zisk, Al Oliver, Parker, Stargell, Stennett, Richie Hebner, and Sanguillen in 1974.

Before the newest Pirates would report, the Bucs prepared to face the surprise team of 1979 on June 29. The Expos were running a strong first in the Eastern Division, 6.5 games ahead of the second-place Pirates. Bill Lee was Montreal's starter in the first game when the Bucs took a lead on Moreno's single, a stolen base and Tim Foli's single. After Parker bounced into a double play, Bill Robinson drove a poorly thrown change-up over the left field fence, and Lee Lacy followed with a blast to the same spot for a 3-0 lead. It was 6-2 in the sixth when Tommy Hutton came off the Expos bench and slammed a three-run homer off starter Bruce Kison, but that was as close as Montreal got. The next day, Pittsburgh took an early lead but homers by Andre Dawson, Larry Parrish, and Rod Scott had the Expos in front 5-2 going to the last of the ninth. With two out, hits by Moreno and Foli scored Garner and brought Dave Parker to the plate representing the tying run. Dick Williams went to his bullpen and produced veteran Woody Fryman. Parker swung at the first pitch and hit a weak bouncer to second. The rally was finished.

The Pirates were probably fortunate to have Sunday's doubleheader rained out. After returning from the coast, the Bucs had fallen in six of the last 10 games, losing five of seven in Three Rivers Stadium. Pittsburgh arrived in St. Louis, still in second place and looking forward to the arrival of Madlock for the four-game series with the Cardinals. Tanner inserted Madlock into the sixth slot in the batting order, replacing Rennie Stennett who had been batting eighth. Ed Ott and Phil Garner moved down a notch and the new offense produced a four-run lead over the Cards after four innings. Don Robinson was cruising along until Jerry Mumphrey, Garry Templeton, and Lou Brock singled and Tony Scott doubled, cutting the Pittsburgh lead to a run. The Kid recovered to fan Keith Hernandez but George Hendrick delivered a two-out single, scoring Scott with the tying run. Moreno led off the Pirates' seventh with a double and Tim Foli's single broke the tie. Dave Roberts and Grant Jackson kept the Cardinals in check and the Bucs held on for a 5-4 win. John Candelaria and Enrique Romo teamed up for a four-hitter the next night and Dave Parker pounded Bob Forsch for three hits. The Cobra homered and later doubled to score Tim Foli from first with what proved to be the winning run in a 4-1 victory. On the Fourth of July, Willie Stargell provided the fireworks with two home runs and Bill Madlock drove in three runs with a pair of doubles. The Bucs withstood a St. Louis rally for their third straight win, 6-4. Jim Rooker went after his 100th win on Thursday but could not match rookie John Fulgham who spaced out nine hits in a 2-0 win, only after the Bucs nearly pulled the game out in the ninth. With one down, Madlock singled and Ott doubled Bill to third, bringing Phil Garner to the plate. Garner fanned, but John Milner drove a ball deep toward the right field wall. George Hendrick made a leaping catch to end the winning streak and the Pirates moved on to Cincinnati.

Bruce Kison and Mike LaCoss squared off in a classic pitchers' duel on July 6 but both were gone when Joe Morgan worked Grant Jackson for a walk in the ninth. Johnny Bench laid down a rare sacrifice bunt against Kent Tekulve, who then intentionally walked Dan Driessen. Ray Knight hit a grounder to Foli, who turned the play on Morgan and got the force out at third. With two out, George Foster, hampered by a leg injury, limped off the bench and delivered a single to score Driessen with the winning run. The Bucs were soundly defeated by Paul Moskau on Saturday, and Fred Norman followed with another complete game victory in the first game of a Sunday doubleheader. Now struggling offensively, the Pirates manufactured a run in the first inning of the nitecap on Moreno's double, a sacrifice bunt by Foli and Parker's grounder to Morgan. The Reds came back in much the same manner when Ken Griffey doubled and came around on flys by Junior Kennedy and Joe Morgan in the sixth. The game was still tied 1-1 in the ninth when Dave Tomlin replaced Tom Hume to face lefthanded hitters, Parker, Stargell, and Milner. Parker fanned, but Captain Willie followed with a dramatic home run to salvage the final game of the series.

The three losses in Cincinnati had dropped the Bucs into fourth place, seven games behind Montreal as they revisited the Astrodome where they had had so much trouble back in April. Things were different this time when Jim Bibby pitched eight strong innings and Moreno, Milner, and Madlock chipped in two hits apiece in a 4-3 win. Bruce Kison held the Astros to five hits on July 11 and back-to-back homers by Parker and Stargell gave the Bucs a 5-1 decision. Houston held a 2-1 lead in the seventh inning of the final game of the series, when John Milner walked and Bill Madlock put the Bucs ahead with a home run into the leftfield seats off Joe Niekro. Bert Blyleven faltered, but Kent Tekulve put out the fire and the Pirates completed their first sweep in the Dome since 1976 with a 5-3 win.

The Pirates reached the All-Star break by taking two of three at Atlanta, ending the first half of the season in fourth place with 46 wins and 39 defeats, four games behind the Montreal Expos.

As the teams broke for the All-Star Game, here's a look at the standings:

|  | W | L | GB |
|---|---|---|---|
| Montreal | 50 | 35 | — |
| Chicago | 47 | 38 | 3 |
| Philadelphia | 50 | 41 | 3 |
| Pittsburgh | 46 | 39 | 4 |
| St. Louis | 44 | 42 | 6½ |
| New York | 37 | 49 | 13½ |

After knocking off the Phillies in consecutive series, the Expos were proving to be true contenders. They were getting outstanding pitching from starters Bill Lee and Steve Rogers and relievers Elias Sosa and Woody Fryman. Lee and Rogers each had nine wins. Sosa had 10 saves and a 2.07 ERA, while Fryman had six saves and a 2.06 ERA. The offense was led by outfielders Ellis Valentine and Andre Dawson, and All-Star catcher Gary Carter. All three had over ten home runs and over 45 RBIs.

The Cubs were somewhat of a surprise. They were led by the slugging of Dave Kingman and the relief pitching of Bruce Sutter and newly-acquired Dick Tidrow.

The Phillies at this point were spending more time in the emergency room than in the locker room. The pitching staff was plagued by injuries to Dick Ruthven, Larry Christenson and Randy Lerch, but the real blow came with the loss of the keystone combination of Larry Bowa and Manny Trillo. The Phils were hanging close on the strength of Mike Schmidt's home runs and the pitching of Steve Carlton and Nino Espinosa.

The Pirates were still in the race despite playing rather inconsistent ball. At times the Pirates were unbeatable but at other times they played lacklustre baseball. This didn't overshadow the remarkable seasons that some of the Bucs were having. "Pops" Stargell was turning in another great year following his comeback in 1978. He was leading the team with a .307 average and had 18 home runs and 41 RBIs in 61 games. Stargell always seemed to be a factor in a game whether he started or not. Bill Robinson was rebounding from a disappointing year in '78. His 19 homers led the club. Bill Madlock had raised his average 20 points since coming to Pittsburgh.

169

The performances of Stargell, Robinson, and Madlock were expected but there were some surprises. Omar Moreno, who had never been much of a hitter, received special instruction from former manager Harry "The Hat" Walker in the off-season. The time spent with Walker paid off as Moreno was batting .305 at the All-Star break. Moreno's success was due in part to the continued good hitting of Tim Foli. Phil Garner's .294 average in the first half was another surprise.

There were some disappointments too. John Milner, after getting off to a great start, slumped in June and carried a .248 average into the second half. Lee Lacy, batting .295 in limited play, had only nine RBIs.

As always, Dave Parker was something special. The Pirates representative in the All-Star Game was batting .297 with 16 home runs and 54 RBIs. This is a full season for some, but for the greatest player in the game, it was not nearly enough. Parker's magnificent defensive display in the National League's victory was enough to win the game's MVP award and seemed to portend a return to form in the second half.

The Pirates had no standouts on the mound. John Candelaria and Don Robinson were pitching inconsistently and both suffered from minor injuries. Blyleven recovered from a poor start to reel off six wins in seven starts and Candy led the staff with eight victories, but two part-time members of the starting rotation proved to be the Pirates' most effective hurlers. Bruce Kison was spectacular at times as a spot starter and long reliever, while Jim Bibby finally began living up to his potential, winning five of seven decisions and moved into the rotation on July 10th for the rest of the season.

Relievers Kent Tekulve and Enrique Romo struggled early but regained their effectiveness by mid-season while veteran Grant Jackson proved to be the Bucs most consistent pitcher in the bull pen with five wins and ten saves.

Entering the second half of the season, the Pirates had reason to be optimistic as the Astros came to Pittsburgh for a four-game series. Facing a stretch of 24 games in 18 days, the Pirates recent success would be tested. In preparation for this grueling schedule, the Bucs acquired pitcher Joe Coleman from Portland prior to facing Houston in a four-game series at Three Rivers Stadium.

Bill Virdon's club had squandered away just about all of their big lead over Cincinnati. The Pirates had no mercy for their former manager. The Bucs pounded Houston's league leading pitching staff for 9-4 and 4-2 wins in a doubleheader on July 19 and leapfrogged over Chicago and Philadelphia—back into second place. In the first inning the Astros jumped on Bert Blyleven for four hits and three runs. The Bucs came back in the second when Stargell doubled and Robinson singled him to third. Madlock followed with a run-producing single and Robinson moved to third when Jose Cruz fumbled the ball. Ed Ott's sacrifice fly scored Robinson and after Mad Dog moved into scoring position by stealing second, Phil Garner singled to tie the game. The Bucs jumped in front in the third on Stargell's two-run homer but the Astros finished Blyleven in tne fourth on Art Howe's leadoff homer, a walk to Bruce Bochy, and singles by pitcher Ken Forsch and Rafael Landestoy. Forsch held the Bucs in check until the sixth when with two out, Garner struck again, slamming a two-run homer over the left field wall to give Pittsburgh a 7-5 lead. The Pirates added two more runs for a 9-5 win and took a 2-0 lead in the first inning of the second game on John Milner's first inning round tripper. Kison was impressive again, allowing only two hits through the first eight innings and helping his own cause with an RBI single in the Pirates' two-run fifth. Buster tired in the ninth but Grant Jackson came on and saved a 4-2 win completing the sweep and moving the Bucs into second place (the Phillies were losing in San Francisco and Cubs had already lost to the Braves at Wrigley Field).

The Pirates scored early and often on July 20, pounding J. R. Richard for ten hits in 5.1 innings as John Candelaria went the distance for a 9-3 win. In Los Angeles, the Expos battled 11 innings before losing to the Dodgers, cutting their lead to one and a half games over the Pirates. On July 21, Houston held a 5-4 lead after seven innings and called on reliever Joe Sambito to protect the advantage. Sambito had not allowed an earned run in 40.2 innings before Bill Robinson led off the inning with a game-tying homer to right center field. Sambito retired Madlock and Ott, but red-hot Phil Garner connected with a Sambito pitch and drove it to the opposite field, for his third homer in three games, giving the Bucs their seventh straight win, the longest winning streak of the season.

The Braves invaded Pittsburgh on Sunday, July 22, for the first of back-to-back doubleheaders under threatening skies. The two teams seesawed back and forth in the first game until the sixth inning when Mike Easler came off the bench and delivered a two-run single to produce a 5-4 win. The Braves took a two-run lead in the nightcap on Dale Murphy's homer off Bibby. Singles by Moreno and Foli, followed by Parker's double cut the Atlanta lead in half, and Bibby put himself in the lead, following Steve Nicosia's fourth inning double with his second major league home run. Big Jim went on to hold the Braves hitless over the next four innings until he was replaced by Tekulve, who wrapped up his second save of the long afternoon and 16th of the season.

The sweep of the doubleheader put the Bucs just a half game behind Montreal after the Expos split a twinbill in San Francisco. The Bucs made it ten in a row as Blyleven limited the Braves to four hits and Foli equalled his career high with four RBIs in a 7-1 rout. Jim Rooker took another stab at win number 100 but dug a hole for himself in the second when Pepe Frias doubled and Bruce Benedict walked with nobody out. With Phil Niekro at the plate, the Bucs were looking for a bunt but the pitcher swung away and hit a grounder right at Bill Madlock who was moving to cover third. Madlock stepped on the base and threw to Garner at second. Garner's throw nipped Niekro at first to complete the Pirates first triple play since 1971. From there it was all downhill as Niekro limited the Pirates to two hits and ended the Pirates win streak with an 8-0 triumph.

The Bucs tried to get back in the win column and sent Bruce Kison to the mound against the Reds on July 24, but he did not get out of the first inning. The Pirates battled back to within a run in the fourth on Stargell's RBI single and a two-run homer by Madlock. Garner and Nicosia followed with singles, then Lee Lacy pinch hit for Joe Coleman and forced Nicosia at second for out number two. Omar Moreno came up and worked the count to 3-1 against Fred Norman. As the little lefty delivered, the runners took off. The pitch was ball four, but Johnny Bench threw to second anyway and umpire Dick Stello called Lacy out. Lee saw the call and began to leave the field when he saw Moreno heading to first. By the time he moved back toward second, Reds' shortstop Dave Conception had come over and tagged him out. The Reds proceeded to leave the field but Lacy charged Stello and was quickly joined by Chuck Tanner and just about every other Pirate that saw the play. The Pirates argued that since Moreno walked, Lacy was entitled to second and was misled by Stello's out call. The umpires then went into a conference and 34 minutes later decided that Stello had been wrong but Lacy was responsible for himself and was declared out. Tanner could only play the game under protest as the action resumed. Ken Griffey's two-run homer in the seventh gave the Reds a 6-4 lead and another Pirate rally fell short when Easler was called out on strikes with the tying run at third in the eighth. Cincinnati took an early lead on Wednesday but John Milner's two-run homer in the fifth, Dave Parker's single, and Willie Stargell's double pulled the Bucs even and the game went into extra innings. Dave Collins opened the tenth with a double off Kent Tekulve and Heity Cruz, followed with another two-base hit to score Collins with the deciding run. Dave Roberts only lasted two innings as the Reds scored eight runs in the first four innings and held on for a 9-7 win and a sweep of the series.

After dropping four in a row and losing most of the momentum gathered from the long winning streak, the Pirates found themselves still in second place, just two and a half games out. The Expos hadn't been able to forge a big lead but were gaining confidence with every day they spent in first place. The Expos had been in first place for over 50 days and with Philadelphia having all sorts of problems, and being unable to mount any type of challenge, the four game Pirate-Expo series in Montreal took on added importance.

171

Nearly 60,000 people turned out for the July 27 twi-night doubleheader in Olympic Stadium. The Expos were feeling the play-off type pressure in the first inning as Moreno led-off with a walk. He scored moments later when Ross Grimsley threw Foli's sacrifice bunt down into the right field corner. Tony Bernazard then booted Parker's ground ball, putting runners on the corners. Robinson brought in Foli with a sacrifice fly to give the Bucs a 2-0 lead. Stargell followed with a single, but Madlock ended the inning by grounding into a doubleplay.

The Expos settled down and by the second inning had tied the game on a Larry Parrish two-run home run to left. Garner homered to put the Bucs back in front in the fourth but Parrish rallied Montreal again, scoring Andre Dawson with a double down the left field line. In the seventh, the Pirates took the lead again when Madlock, Garner, and Nicosia singled to chase Grimsley. Warren Cromartie led off the seventh with a single to right and Rod Scott sacrificed him to second. With Tekulve pitching, Dawson flied out to Moreno and Tony Perez hit a dribbler down the third base side that Garner charged and made a good play, then threw the ball away allowing the Expos to tie the game. Garner exchanged the goat horns for a halo when he singled home Parker with the fifth and winning run.

The second game was all Blyleven. The Dutchman turned in one of his best outings of the season. Leading 5-0, thanks to John Milner's home run and four RBIs, Blyleven gave up a run on two hits in the third but from there on the Expos might as well have gone home. They did not get another hit until the eighth but by then it was 7-1. They got another hit in the ninth and lost 9-1.

On Saturday, the Pirates moved into first place by defeating the Expos 5-3. The Bucs had not been on the top rung of the Eastern Division ladder this late in the season since 1975. Jim Bibby picked up where Blyleven had left off the night before. He had a no-hitter for four innings. By that time the Bucs had built a four-run lead on the strength of a two-run homer by Parker and RBIs by Foli and Madlock. Pittsburgh made it 5-0 in the sixth when Nicosia singled, went to second on Bibby's sacrifice and scored on Moreno's single. Big Jim was touched for a run in the sixth when Dawson singled home Cromartie who had doubled, then gave up a two-run homer to Parrish before giving way to Jackson in the seventh. Tekulve came on in the eighth to wrap up the game and his 17th save.

Montreal would not fold yet. They rebounded behind the strong pitching of Steve Rogers who went the distance, scattering eight hits. Bruce Kison, who was coming off a terrible outing against the Reds, was the Pirate starter. He ran into trouble right away as Cromartie opened the home half of the first with a double. Scott sacrificed him to third. Kison then dug a hole for himself by allowing consecutive singles to Rusty Staub, Valentine, and Carter. With the bases loaded and one run in, Kison came in on Andre Dawson. Dawson ducked away from the pitch but somehow made contact with the ball and blooped it down the right field line for a three-run triple. The Pirates chipped away at the lead, getting a run in the third and one in the fourth but were never able to cluster hits off Rogers. The Expos added a run in the sixth to make it 5-2 going into the ninth. Willie Stargell led off the ninth and made it 5-3 with his 450th career home run, but the Bucs were back in second.

The Pirates came home for a week-long home stand with a two-game series against the Mets and the Cards, and a five-game weekend series with the Phillies.

Again the Mets proved to be troublesome. They jumped ahead by a 5-2 margin on July 30 only to see another comeback by the Battlin' Bucs. In the fifth, Moreno singled, stole second, and scored on Foli's double to make the score 5-3. Parker then drove in Foli with a single. Dave then stole second and dashed home with the tying run when Willie Montanez bobbled Milner's base hit. After three excellent innings of relief from Romo and Jackson, the Pirates won the game in the eighth on a double by Milner, singles by Madlock and Ott, a sacrifice fly from Moreno and another single by Foli, his fourth in the game. This win combined with a doubleheader split by Montreal in St. Louis put the Pirates percentage points out of first place. The next night the Pirates were not as fortunate. They could only collect one run on four hits off of Tom Hausman, Wayne Twitchell, and Ed Glynn, while the Mets got RBIs from Mazzilli and Montanez to post a 2-1 win.

Against the Cardinals on August 1, the Bucs had to battle again. Trailing 3-0 in the sixth, the Bucs bounced back for two runs on back-to-back triples by pinch hitter Manny Sanguillen and Omar Moreno and a sacrifice fly from Parker. The Pirates tied the game in the seventh when Ott singled and scored on what some thought to be an inside the park homer by pinch hitter Mike Easler. Unfortunately, Easler was thrown out at home. However, the Bucs won in the eighth on a single by Moreno and a double by Parker. The next night the Pirates were the ones who had to watch a lead slip through their fingers. The Cardinals began the winning rally in the eighth with Pittsburgh leading 4-1. Ken Reitz doubled and Jerry Mumphrey reached on Stennett's error. Jackson came in to face Mike Tyson who promptly singled home Reitz. Pinch hitter Dane Iorg followed with another single to score Mumphrey and put runners on the corners. Tyson scored the tying run on Templeton's ground ball and Iorg scored the winning run on Keith Hernandez's single to left.

With the Pirates trailing the Expos by a game and the Phillies tied with the Cubs in third, five games out, the five-game weekend series between the Bucs and Phils was as important for both clubs as the series in Montreal had been the week before. By winning the series, the Bucs would keep the pressure on the Expos and put Philadelphia even further out of the race. By losing the series, they could give Montreal added confidence and put the Phillies back in contention.

For the next five games, the Pirates played remarkable baseball. In the first game of the Friday night doubleheader, Schmidt put the Phils ahead with his 38th home run in the first inning. Willie Stargell answered with a two-run blast of his own in the home half of the first. The Phillies tied the game in the second when Bowa singled home Trillo from second. The Bucs regained the lead in the third when Moreno tripled and scored on Parker's single. Philadelphia came back again in the fourth. With one out, Garry Maddox singled, stole second, and scored on Trillo's single to left. Both starters, Kison and Ruthven, stopped any further scoring and were removed for pinch hitters. Romo came in to pitch the seventh and put the Phils down in order. However, Tug McGraw, who also came on in the seventh, did not fare as well. He was greeted by singles from Moreno and Foli and a thunderous blast by Parker into the right field seats to set the final margin at 6-3. In the nightcap, Jim Bibby picked up his fifth straight win by pitching a five hitter. The Pirates scored in the second when Madlock tripled home Robinson who had singled. The Bucs scored again in the third when Moreno singled, went to third on Foli's single, and scored on Parker's groundout. They added three in the fifth as Foli was hit by a pitch, and Parker and Milner followed with singles to load the bases. Robinson delivered a two-run double to left center and Madlock scored Milner with a sacrifice fly. All five runs came off starter Larry Christenson.

The largest Saturday afternoon crowd in Three Rivers Stadium history, 34,754, turned out for the game on August 4, and saw the Pirates continue to get excellent pitching. Candelaria, making his first start since suffering an injury to his already ailing back in a car accident on July 31, combined with Tekulve to blank the Phils on six hits. After Stargell drove in Parker in the third, the Pirates added to their lead in the fifth as Moreno led-off with a bunt single. After Foli and Parker failed, Moreno stole second. Stargell was intentionally walked and Milner followed with a single to score Moreno. Both Stargell and Milner advanced a base when Mike Anderson misplayed the ball. Madlock was intentionally passed and Ott drilled a hit to center, scoring Stargell and Milner with the third and fourth runs.

In this series, when the Pirate pitching faltered, the Pirate bats did not. In the first game of the Sunday doubleheader that is exactly what happened. The Phils scored twice in the second when Luzinski led-off with a walk and after Del Unser flied out, Maddox and Tim McCarver both singled. Trillo then hit a slow chopper to Foli who charged the ball and tried to throw out Luzinski at the plate. His throw was wide, allowing everyone to be safe. Steve Carlton then followed with a sacrifice fly. The Pirates took the lead in the third. Nicosia led-off with a single, Blyleven bunted but Carlton threw the ball away, allowing Nicosia to go to third and Blyleven to go to second. Moreno singled them both home with a shot to center. Omar went to second on an error by McCarver and stole third to later score on Robinson's single. The Phils jumped on Blyleven with both feet in the fifth. Carlton led-off with a single, McBride and Bowa walked, and Rose drove home Carlton with a single that kept the bases loaded for Luzinski. The Bull put a quick end to Blyleven's day as he hammered Bert's pitch over the center field wall for a grand slam. Coleman was called on and was greeted with a Del Unser homer to right, for the eighth Phillie's run. The Bucs chipped away in the bottom of the fifth with a three-run home run by Lee Lacy to make the game 8-6. Nicosia homered in the sixth to make it a one-run game. Sanguillen, pinch-hitting for Coleman, struck out but reached on a wild pitch. Carlton was replaced by Kevin Saucier. Saucier put down a mild Pirate rally and was able to keep the Bucs in check until the eighth, when Nicosia banged out his fourth hit of the day, a double to right. He went to third when pinch hitter Willie Stargell grounded out to Trillo and scored the tying run on Foli's single. After trailing by five runs, the Pirates had fought back and went into the bottom of the ninth tied at 8-8. Saucier got Parker to ground out to second. Danny Ozark then went to his bullpen for righthanded reliever Rawley Eastwick to face the bottom six Buc batters who were all righthanded. Robinson popped out to center, and Lacy singled and stole second. Madlock was intentionally walked and Garner drew a walk to load the bases. Tanner then went to his bench and called upon lefty John Milner to pinch-hit for Nicosia, who had already homered, singled, and doubled twice. Ozark countered by bringing in lefty Tug McGraw. All Milner had to do was get the runner in from third. All Milner did was jump on McGraw's first pitch and drill it into the right field seats for a 12-8 win—and first place since Montreal had lost their first game in New York. After trading runs in the first inning of the series finale, the Phils took the lead in the fourth when Trillo scored Luzinski from third with a sacrifice fly. This minor success was too much for young Dickie Noles. Madlock led-off the fourth with a shot to third that Schmidt could not handle, and Noles walked Ott. After Stennett flied out to center, Noles walked Don Robinson and gave up a two-run double to Moreno and an RBI single to Foli to put the Bucs ahead 5-2. Romo and Tekulve closed out the game to complete the sweep and put the Phils eight and a half games off the pace of the first place Pirates.

As good as the Pirates were against the Phils, that's how bad they were in Chicago, losing two of three by the ridiculous scores of 15-2 and 11-3. The Pirates were able to salvage the middle game of the set only after Bill Robinson cut down the winning run at the plate in the ninth, and Garner smacked a three-run homer off Dick Tidrow in the tenth. Luckily, while the Pirates were struggling in Chicago, the Phillies went home and took out their frustrations on the Expos, sweeping the three-game set and allowing the Pirates to pick up a full game in the standings.

The defending champions had rebounded from their beating at Three Rivers and were within six games as the Bucs entered Vet Stadium for a twi-night doubleheader on August 10 and prepared to finish the Phillies. The Pirates scored first when Phil Garner tagged Phillies ace Steve Carlton for a solo home run in the second. Manny Trillo's double scored Del Unser with the tying run in their half of the second, and Pete Rose ripped a triple over Omar Moreno's head in center to bring in Tim McCarver with the go-ahead run. After Luzinski walked, Unser drove in Rose with a single and the Phils led 3-1. Carlton seemed to be in command with two out in the eighth when Dave Parker connected and sent a game-tying homer over the right field barrier. The contest went into extra innings and became a battle of the bullpens as Kevin Saucier matched Kent Tekulve pitch for pitch. Rawley Eastwick came on for Philadelphia in the 12th and was touched for a one out single by Manny Sanguillen. Tanner decided to go for the win and sent Willie Stargell up to bat for Tekulve. This time Stargell could only deliver an inning ending fly to center and Grant Jackson was called on to pitch. Bake McBride greeted the lefthander with a single, but pinch hitter Bob Boone forced McBride at second, and

Rose lined to Parker for the second out. Greg Luzinski was up next with Bud Harrelson on deck. Jackson pitched carefully to the Bull with the light-hitting infielder due up next, and ended up walking the Phillies left fielder. Harrelson slapped a hit through the left side and Boone came home with the winning run.

Philadelphia was gaining momentum and the Bucs knew that the advantage of last weekend's sweep would be gone if they did not hold their own in the next four games. It was up to Bruce Kison to stop Mike Schmidt and company. He responded by limiting the Phillies to just two hits in the first seven innings. Bill Robinson took charge offensively, belting a two-run triple in the fourth and scoring one out later on Bill Madlock's double. Harrelson led off the Phils' eighth with a walk and when McBride tripled, Tanner switched to Enrique Romo, but he was unable to put out the fire, allowing singles to Greg Gross and Pete Rose. With the lead cut to a run, Romo fanned Unser but with Bob Boone up, Tanner decided to bring in Tekulve. The Phils catcher hammered the first pitch right at Rennie Stennett. Stennett threw to Foli, who got the relay throw away just before he was leveled by Rose. The throw beat Boone to first and the threat had ended. With two out in the ninth, pinch hitters Luzinski and McCarver singled but Tekulve induced McBride to hit a grounder to Stennett and the Pirates came away with a split.

If Philadelphia had lost any incentive after the second game loss, they quickly regained it by pouncing on Jim Rooker for two runs in the second inning on Saturday. Greg Luzinski's two run homer doubled the Philadelphia lead. Rooker's problems were compounded when Moreno dropped a fly ball allowing Garry Maddox to reach second. It was just not Rooker's day as he walked Mike Anderson and he was mercifully removed after Larry Bowa's single gave the Phillies a 5-0 advantage. The next pitcher was Joe Coleman who had absorbed a terrible beating in the 15-2 game at Chicago on Tuesday. Before the veteran pitcher got out of the inning, the Phillies had scored thrice more on a wild pitch and RBI hits by Rose and Trillo.

After that shaky start, Coleman settled down and held Philadelphia where they were while the Pirates launched a comeback in the fifth. Omar Moreno put the Bucs on the scoreboard with a lead-off homer off Dickie Noles and after an infield single by Foli and a walk to Parker, Willie Stargell drove in a second run and Danny Ozark yanked the rookie in favor of Saucier. The Philadelphia reliever was making his third straight appearance and was unable to stem the tide. Milner's single brought in Parker with the third run. Madlock's double cut the deficit to four. When Ed Ott beat out a grounder, scoring Milner with the fifth run of the inning, a desperate Ozark changed pitchers again, bringing in Eastwick who whiffed Phil Garner to retire the side. The rally stalled in the sixth but was reignited in the eighth by Parker's leadoff homer. Eastwick got Stargell and Milner but Madlock singled and Ott moved him to second with another hit. Garner completed the comeback by ripping a double down the leftfield line, scoring Madlock and Ott with the tying runs. With the season and job slipping away, Ozark called on his beleaguered bullpen ace Tug McGraw to get out of the inning. Kent Tekulve was the scheduled hitter so Tanner called on Mike Easler. It was somewhat odd for the Bucs manager to send up a lefthanded hitter to face a lefthanded pitcher but Tanner knew that McGraw had trouble with lefthanders. Easler justified the strategy with a single to bring Garner home with the go-ahead run. McGraw got Moreno to retire the side, but the Bucs put him back on the ropes in the eighth with a single by Stargell and a double by Milner. With Madlock up and Ott on deck, McGraw intentionally walked Mad Dog to load the bases for the lefthanded hitting catcher. The strategy worked perfectly—for the Pirates—Ott slammed a towering drive high over the right field fence to give Pittsburgh an insurmountable 13-8 lead. The Phillies were done in. Sunday's game was mercifully rained out and the Buccaneers finished the carnage with a one-sided 7-1 rout on Monday.

The Pirates returned home to face the West coast teams for the second time with a two and a half game lead over the second place Expos.

Pitching was indeed the name of the game against San Diego as John Candelaria and

Bert Blyleven hurled back to back complete games, limiting the Padres to a total of ten hits in the 7-1, 5-1 victories. When the Bucs finally got to Gaylord Perry, tagging the veteran for five runs in five innings and holding on for their sixth straight win, the lead over Montreal had bulged to four games. The Pirates had won 24 of 34 games since the All-Star break and, having dispensed of the Phillies, it seemed to be only a matter of time before they wrapped up the division. John Milner had recovered from his June slump and was batting .413 with nine homeruns and 26 RBIs since the midsummer classic while the other half of the left field platoon, Bill Robinson, was batting .278 and led the team in homers with 23. The restructured infield of Madlock, Foli, Garner, and Stargell had produced over 300 runs with a combined average of .298 while providing Pittsburgh with its best interior defense since Bill Mazeroski was in his prime. Moreno had passed the 50 mark in both stolen bases and RBIs while quickly gaining recognition as one of baseball's premier center fielders. If there was a disappointment, it was in Dave Parker whose average had dipped under .300. Parker had been hitting consistently but had not yet put together a streak resembling his 1978 finish when he carried the club in August and September. Once Parker got hot, it would simply be a matter of finishing off the rest of the division.

The Pirates were brought back to earth by Dodger centerfielder Gary Thomasson on August 17. The .250 hitter slammed a three-run homer off Jim Bibby and a two-run double off Dave Roberts as Los Angeles rolled out to a 7-2 lead after four and a half innings. When knuckleballer Charlie Hough hit Tim Foli and walked Parker and Milner, the Bucs were ready to comeback. Bill Robinson fanned but Madlock's single drove in a pair and Ed Ott's hit scored Milner and moved Madlock to third as Ott took second on the throw. Tom Lasorda had seen enough of Hough and brought in Dave Patterson who gave up a sacrifice fly to Garner before getting pinch hitter Mike Easler to end the inning. Tekulve held the Dodgers at bay and the Pirates launched one more rally in the eighth. After Manny Sanguillen fanned as a pinch hitter, Omar Moreno singled to right. Omar tried to move into scoring position but was cut down trying to steal by Steve Yeager. A walk to Tim Foli and Dave Parker's single finished Patterson and Bobby Castillo was summoned to face John Milner. Milner also received a free pass, bringing Bill Robinson up with the bases loaded for the second time in the game. Bill was unable to deliver and Castillo's strikeout ended the Pirate's final threat. Pittsburgh went past the magic million mark in attendance the following night, but old friend Jerry Reuss scattered nine hits as Dusty Baker and Thomasson homered in a 5-1 Dodger triumph. The final game of the series was a classic pitchers' duel as John Candelaria duelled Bert Hooton through eight innings. Tekulve replaced Candelaria in the ninth but Hooton was still on as the Bucs came to bat in the bottom of the inning. Dave Parker led-off with a vicious liner which would have cleared the centerfield fence for a game-winning homer if Hooton had not grabbed it in self defense. Milner hammered a double to right but Lasorda stayed with his starter and he responded by fanning Robinson for the second out. Bill Madlock finally delivered the knock out punch, driving a game-ending homer over the fence in right center to salvage the final game of the series.

The San Francisco Giants came to Pittsburgh, beset by problems both internal and external. The Giants had not been able to challenge for first in the Western Division as they were supposed to, but were able to give the Pirates all kinds of problems. It took the Bucs nearly seven hours to defeat the Giants on Monday due in large part to a three hour and 42 minute rain delay. Pinch runner Alberto Lois scored on a wild pitch in the eighth and Tekulve recorded his 23rd save in preserving a 6-5 win on August 20. Bob Knepper held Pittsburgh to six hits for an easy win on Tuesday and the Bucs ended the homestand with a seesaw 8-6 win highlighted by Dave Parker's 1,000 career hit and Tim Foli's two-run eighth-inning single which put the Bucs ahead for good.

The Pirates lead was back down to two games as they arrived in San Diego and a repeat of their earlier success on the coast was necessary with the Expos just waiting for the Bucs to falter.

On August 24, the Pirates opened in San Diego with Candelaria squaring off against Randy Jones. Both teams scored unearned runs in the third and the game remained tied through seven innings. In the eighth, after Jones had retired 13 men in order, he yielded a home run to Parker. In the bottom of the eighth, Candelaria, who had pitched well but was plagued by poor defensive play, gave up an infield hit to Gene Tenace. Kurt Bevacqua sacrificed pinch runner Dan Briggs to second and Candelaria was relieved by Romo. Romo got the second out but after pinch hitter Jerry Turner walked, another pinch hitter, Jay Johnstone, singled to tie the game. Tanner went to Jackson and Roger Craig went to yet another pinch hitter. This time, Gene Richards singled to score Turner with the go-ahead run. Mark Lee closed out the ninth as the Padres won 3-2. The next night, Gaylord Perry was back in the saddle again and again tied up the Pirate bats for eight innings. The Padres had built a 2-0 lead and it looked as if the West Coast nightmare was going to happen again. But 1979 was not like previous years. Perry gave up a one out double to Parker and after getting Stargell, walked Milner, who was replaced by Matt Alexander. Madlock singled home Parker and both runners advanced on the throw to the plate. Fingers relieved Perry and his first pitch to Ott got past Bill Fahey, allowing Alexander to score the tying run. After walking Garner, Fingers was replaced by Mark Lee who struck out pinch hitter Bill Robinson.

In the bottom of the ninth, Tekulve survived an error by Foli to open the inning and the game went into extra innings.

In the 12th inning, Moreno singled home Garner who had doubled. In the bottom of the 12th, the Padres put runners on first and second with two outs. Richards delivered with a single to right and when Parker had trouble coming up with the ball, Winfield scored the tying run.

In the bottom of the 16th inning, Dave Roberts came in to pitch and was greeted with a lead-off single by Johnstone who went to second on Turner's sacrifice and to third on Fahey's ground out to second. Winfield and Fred Kendall were both intentionally passed to load the bases and bring up John D'Acquisto. Roberts' first three pitches to his mound opponent were all wide. As Roberts stepped off the mound to catch his breath, he glanced back at Winfield, who was standing on second giving him the "choke" sign. Roberts, failing to be intimidated, came back to strike out D'Acquisto on three pitches. In the 17th, Smith bunted for a single and Paul Dade followed with a single to left. Gonzalez was intentionally passed to load the bases. Roberts stiffened again and struck out Johnstone, got Turner to bounce to Foli who turned the play on Smith at the plate, and got Fahey to ground out to end the inning.

In the 19th, Robinson hit a two-out double to right field and scored the winning run when Foli lined an 0-2 pitch into right.

The win and the pitching by Roberts gave the Bucs a lift and they went out and stomped the Padres the following afternoon. With a run in and the bases loaded in the bottom of the second, Kison drove a ball into the left field pavilion for a grand slam. The Pirates went on to win 9-2. Kison pitched seven innings before giving way to Romo to close out the series and keep the momentum rolling.

Leading 2-1 in the ninth in Los Angeles, Tekulve got Joe Ferguson to fly out to left. Thomasson and pinch hitter Von Joshua singled. Romo came in to relieve and got Derrel Thomas to fly to center, but then the Dodger Stadium jinx struck again in the form of Dusty Baker's homer over the left field wall.

This loss could have touched off another West Coast disaster, but John Candelaria picked up the club by pitching a four-hitter the next night. On August 29, Jerry Reuss and Bert Blyleven were tied up in another pitching duel. Steve Garvey's third inning home run had provided the only run through the first seven innings. But in the eighth, with one out, Nicosia doubled and pinch hitter Willie Stargell tied the game with a rap up the middle. After Moreno walked to put runners on first and second, Garner, playing for the injured Foli, doubled to right to give the Bucs a 3-1 lead. Ken Brett came in and retired Parker but Robinson singled to give the Pirates a three run cushion. Tekulve put down a mild Dodger uprising in the eighth and went on to pick up the save.

In San Francisco, with both Foli and Parker injured, the Pirates jumped to an early 5-0 lead and managed to hang on for a 6-4 win. The following day the Pirates fell behind early in the first game of a doubleheader when the Giants scored three unearned runs in the first. The Bucs came back by getting a run in the fourth and Dale Berra cut the Giant margin to one with a homer to right. Stargell then tied the game with a giant-size homer to the upper deck in right. One out later, Mike Easler singled and Altobelli brought in Gary Lavelle. Pinch runner Matt Alexander stole second and moved to third on Ed Ott's infield single. Then Berra came through again with a fly to center, scoring Alexander with the lead run. Stargell's second round tripper in the eighth gave the Bucs a two-run margin. Tekulve came on to pitch the last two innings and after retiring the first batters in the ninth, gave up a single. At this point, Tanner trotted out of the dugout to talk to umpire Doug Harvey. After a short discussion with Harvey, Tanner went to the mound and called for Grant Jackson. This move in itself was not surprising with the lefthanded Darrell Evans due up. What did raise some eyebrows was the fact that Tekulve did not head for the dugout or even the rightfield clubhouse but to the Pirates' bullpen down the left field line. It was immediately apparent to any one with any baseball sense that Teke was going to play left field. The reason for this was that if Jackson didn't get Evans, Tekulve could come back to face righthanded hitting Mike Ivie. In the Pirate tradition, nothing came easy. Evans lifted a fly to left that Tekulve staggered under and squeezed for the last out.

In the nightcap, Jim Bibby didn't leave any room for doubt. He simply pitched a five hitter and with the support from Lee Lacy, who had a homer and three RBIs, coasted to a 7-2 victory.

The Pirates became the first team ever to sweep a season series in Candlestick Park the following day on the pitching of Candelaria and the batting of Nicosia. Candelaria hurled the Bucs' second complete game and struck out ten. Nicosia had two hits, both doubles, and two RBIs to pace the Pirates to a 5-3 win.

Due to some questionable scheduling, the Pirates came off the West Coast trip for a one day homestand, a Labor Day afternoon doubleheader with Philadelphia, before heading out on another week-long trip with stops in St. Louis and New York.

After an all-night plane ride from California, the tired and injured Pirates were no match for Lefty Carlton. For seven innings, all the Bucs could muster was a sixth inning double by Nicosia. McGraw finished the game without allowing a base runner as the Phils won 2-0.

In the nitecap, Jim Rooker made his first start since coming off the disabled list in another attempt to gain his 100th victory. Young Dale Berra helped the veteran capture the elusive win with his third home run and three RBIs in a 7-2 win to split the twinbill.

When the team left for St. Louis they were still two and a half games ahead of the now red hot Expos. The Cardinals were on the brink of elimination but felt a sweep of the two game series would put them right back in the race. Tony Scott's two run-two out double put the Redbirds in front in the third, but solo homers by Garner and Stargell tied the game in the fourth. St. Louis regained the lead in the fifth and were two up in the eighth when the Pirates scored three times to go back on top. Enrique Romo was entrusted with the lead and retired the first two batters in the eighth before walking Ken Oberkfell. Dane Iorg came off the bench to hit for Mark Littell and delivered a double to bring Oberkfell around with the tying run. The Bucs threatened to end the game in the tenth and Omar Moreno's double put the Pirates in business in the 11th. With one out, Parker was intentionally walked and Bill Robinson's infield single loaded the bases for John Milner. Veteran reliever Darold Knowles came on to face the Hammer. Before he went after Milner, Knowles fired a pick off attempt to first. As Robinson retreated to the bag, the throw struck his elbow and bounced down the right field line, scoring two runs and breaking the Cardinal's backs.

St. Louis was all but buried now and Pittsburgh began to finish things the next night, jumping to a 3-0 lead in the second. The lead seemed safe with Jim Bibby on the hill but Jim was far off form. He quickly lost the lead and left the game in the third, trailing 4-3.

Grant Jackson came on and gave up another run in the fourth before Jerry Mumphrey hit a grounder to Phil Garner who booted the ball, allowing two more runs to score and giving St. Louis an insurmountable 7-2 lead. The Bucs made it close but ended up losing 8-6 and moved on to New York with a two game lead over Montreal.

The Mets were battling Atlanta for the worst record in the league, but you would never know it by the way they played the Pirates. On September 7, the Pirates went in front twice but the Mets battled back and took a 4-3 lead in the fifth when Frank Taveras tripled home two runs. Pittsburgh drew even in the eighth on singles by Parker and Stargell, followed by Milner's run scoring grounder to first. Craig Swan and Tekulve held firm through ten innings when Tanner called on Joe Coleman. Lee Mazzilli greeted the new pitcher with a single and moved to third when Coleman threw John Stearns' bunt into right field. With runners on second and third, Joel Youngblood was intentionally passed and Bill Madlock turned Alex Trevino's grounder on Mazzilli and forced him at the plate. When Joe Torre sent Ed Kranepool up to pinch hit, Tanner went to Grant Jackson and Torre followed suit by exchanging Gil Flores for Kranepool. Flores came through with a fly to center but it was so shallow that Stearns dared not advance. Then Doug Flynn lined to Parker and the Pirates still had a chance. That chance came in the 14th inning when Garner worked Neil Allen for a walk. Scrap Iron then stole second but Nicosia and Moreno failed to move him up. Tim Foli then hit a ball right at Richie Hebner, who knocked it down but could not make the play, leaving runners at first and third with Dave Parker due up. Parker hit a bouncer to the right side and when Stearns could not make the play, Garner scored what proved to be the winning run. Jackson finished an outstanding performance by retiring New York three up and three down in the bottom of the 14th.

On Saturday, Bert Blyleven and Kevin Kobel matched goose eggs for five innings until Kranepool tagged the Dutchman with a two-run homer in the sixth. Kobel was working on a one hitter in the eighth when Ed Ott singled and Willie Stargell came off the bench with a hit moving Ott to second. Omar Moreno's single brought Ott home from second and Joe Torre out to remove Kobel in favor of Ed Glynn. After Moreno stole second, Tim Foli lifted a fly to right which was deep enough to bring in pinch runner Alberto Lois and tie the game. Once again the two teams battled into extra innings. The Bucs squandered scoring opportunities in the 11th, 13th, and 15th. The Pirates ran into trouble in the bottom of the 15th, when Lee Mazzilli led off with a double to center. Jim Rooker retired the next two hitters before Tanner brought in Jim Bibby. After Bibby intentionally walked Joel Youngblood, Stearns hit a liner to left and Lee Lacy was unable to make the diving catch as Mazzilli came home to end the game.

Sunday's series finale was another game in which the Pirates fell behind early and bolted back in the late innings to pull out a win. The Mets jumped off Bruce Kison for three runs in the first and after Milner's homer, added another in the second for a 4-1 lead. The Bucs started their comeback in the seventh when pinch hitter Lee Lacy singled home Ed Ott. Pittsburgh took the lead in the eighth when Parker hit a lead-off double off Andy Hassler. After Stargell and Milner went down, Madlock came through with a run-scoring single to right. Ott was walked and Lois ran for him. Torre lifted Hassler and brought in Tom Hausman. Garner hit a grounder to Taveras who threw high to first. When Madlock saw this while going to third, he headed home and scored on a head-first slide under the tag of catcher Stearns. On the play, Lois went to third where he scored on Bill Robinson's pinch-hit single to third. The Mets tied the game in the bottom of the inning when pinch-hitter Ron Hodges drove in Youngblood with a single to right. With one out in the ninth, Parker ripped a ball into the right field corner, and regardless of his sore knee, hustled in to third with a triple. Stargell followed with another line shot into right to score Parker with the winning run. Tekulve set the Mets up and down in order in the ninth to preserve the win.

It was a weary group of players that boarded the plane for the flight to Pittsburgh. The club had just finished a stretch that saw them playing from coast-to-coast with 15 of 17 games on the road. The Pirates were tired but happily confident that they had met

179

their greatest challenge and still managed to cling to first place. Even though the team had not played its best ball and had to fight and scratch for every game, they had still won 12 of 16.

Even though the Pirates were playing .750 ball they were still losing ground to the Expos, who had lost only once in their last 13 games. The truly disheartening thing was not so much that Montreal was winning daily but that they were winning games that they should have lost. The Expos were winning games in the last inning; something that a young team going through the pressures of a pennant race was not expected to do.

As the two teams went into the final three weeks, here's how they stood:

|            | W  | L  | PCT  | GB |
|------------|----|----|------|----|
| Pittsburgh | 85 | 57 | .598 | —  |
| Montreal   | 81 | 55 | .596 | 1  |

At this point, Montreal had six games in hand.

As the Pirates took the field to play the Cards on September 11, Montreal had already a commanding 5-1 lead in the first game of the doubleheader over the Cubs in Montreal. The Pirates were unable to do anything with John Denny for four innings while the Cards took a 2-0 lead on Ted Simmons' single and back-to-back doubles by Jerry Mumphrey and Ken Reitz. In the fifth, Milner led off with a double and Denny hit Madlock with a pitch. Ott moved both runners into scoring position with a sacrifice. Then, with Phil Garner batting, Denny uncorked a wild pitch that scored Milner. Garner then walked. Tanner pinch hit Easler for Don Robinson. Easler tied the score with a single to center. Romo came in to pitch in the sixth but couldn't get anyone out. The Cards regained a one-run lead before Dave Roberts put out the fire. In the Pirates' sixth. Parker led off with a single and Stargell followed with yet another dramatic home run. The Pirates added three more runs in the inning to go on to win 7-3.

Back at Olympic Stadium, the Cubs had scored four times in the eighth to pull back to within a run, but Montreal scored a run in the bottom of the eighth and went on to win 6-4. In the second game, the Expos broke out of a 2-2 tie in the fifth and defeated Bill Caudill.

The Pirates had won but still dropped out of first place by .0002.

The following night, the Pirates built a two-run lead on RBI singles by Ott in the second and Garner in the fifth. Candelaria was working on a four-hit shutout into the ninth when Mumphrey led off with a single. With one out, Simmons lined a shot to the gap in left. Mumphrey took a big turn at third and fell down. Garner was unable to react in time and Mumphrey scrambled back to the base. Tekulve came in to pitch and Lou Brock came up to pinch hit. Brock never took the bat off his shoulder and Teke struck him out. Tony Scott bounced out to second to end the game and give Tekulve his 27th save.

In Montreal the Cubs had blown a three-run lead as the Expos tied the game in the seventh. With bullpen ace Bruce Sutter pitching in the eighth, pitcher Steve Rogers drew a walk, Dave Cash singled and Tony Perez smashed a two-out, two-run double to break the game open.

On the 13th, after a lengthy rain delay, the Pirate-Card game was postponed and the attention swung to Montreal. With the Cubs leading 3-2 in the ninth, Gary Carter and Ellis Valentine singled off Rick Reuschel to start the inning. Sutter relieved and walked Scott to load the bases. Pinch hitter Rusty Staub hit a ball that took a bad hop over first baseman Larry Bittner's head for the win. Montreal was now tied in the standings and .003 points ahead.

The troublesome Mets once again gave the Pirates all they could handle for two games. On September 15, the Mets jumped on Bert Blyleven for two runs in the first. The Bucs tied the game in the third by manufacturing two runs on three singles, a stolen base, a sacrifice hit, and a sacrifice fly. The Pirates moved ahead in the fifth when

Moreno singled, stole second (his second of the game), and scored on Foli's single. Foli went to second on the play and went to third on a wild pitch. He then scored on Robinson's ground out to short. Blyleven held the lead until the seventh, when Mazzilli tied the game with a two-out two-run single. Roberts stopped the rally and in the bottom of the inning the Pirates took the lead again. Moreno and Foli drew back to back one-out walks. Parker forced Foli at second but Bill Robinson singled to center to score Moreno and give the Pirates a 5-4 win.

In Montreal, the Expos and the Cardinals split their doubleheader. The Expos won the first game in 11 innings by a 2-1 score but dropped the second game 4-1. This put the Pirates back in first place by a half a game.

On Sunday, the Pirates were shutout by Pete Falcone for the second time this season. But In Montreal, the Cards won the first game 4-3 and fought the Expos into the tenth with a 1-1 tie. In the bottom of the tenth, Montreal loaded the bases and pinch hitter Dave Cash smashed his first homer of the season for the win.

Before the two teams met for a two game series in Montreal, the race looked like this:

| | W | L | PCT | GB |
|---|---|---|---|---|
| Montreal | 87 | 57 | .604 | — |
| Pittsburgh | 88 | 58 | .603 | ½ |

Olympic Stadium was filled with 54,609 loyal believers in their Expos for the Monday night game on September 17th. The match up was Don Robinson going against Steve Rogers. First place was on the line.

Omar Moreno led off the Pirate third with a single, stole second, and moved to third on Foli's sacrifice. Parker singled to right to score Moreno and give Pittsburgh a 1-0 lead. The Bucs made it 2-0 in the fifth when Don Robinson singled with one out. After Moreno popped out, Foli and Parker each singled to drive in Robinson. Meanwhile, Robinson was in the process of outpitching their ace. Robinson had allowed three hits over the first four innings. After giving up a run in the fifth, he retired the last 14 men in order and finished with a six hitter.

The next night, the Pirates jumped to a three-run lead in the first when Moreno led off the game with a single off Bill Lee. Foli followed with a single but was erased on Parker's ground out. Robinson singled to center, scoring Moreno, and when Andre Dawson misplayed the ball, Parker scored. Stargell reached on Tony Scott's error. Robinson stole third and scored on Madlock's infield hit. Montreal came back in the third. Scott doubled. Lee doubled and went to third when Parker had trouble handling the ball in right. Warren Cromartie's sacrifice fly scored Lee and made the score 3-2.

The game was protested by manager Dick Williams in the bottom of the fifth when the umpires delayed the game because of rain for nine minutes and then resumed play with the rain still falling. This was the inning that Montreal loaded the bases with one out and couldn't score.

After a two-hour and 54 minute rain delay following the fifth inning, Romo replaced Kison. Perez was the first batter to face Romo and he singled. Carter sacrificed Perez to second. He scored on Larry Parish's hit to center to tie the game.

The game remained tied until the 11th inning when Mike Easler rapped a pinch hit single to left field. Stargell did it again with a game-winning home run over the right center field wall.

After the sweep of the Expos, the Pirates were now two games ahead and one game ahead in the loss column. The Expos traveled to New York for a pair of doubleheaders. The Pirates went to Philadelphia for a Wednesday, September 19, doubleheader and a single game on Thursday.

In the first game in Philadelphia, the Phils had a 2-0 lead in the fifth when Tim Foli hit his first home run in exactly a year off of Nino Espinosa. After the great comebacks against Philadelphia in August, no lead was considered safe by the Phillies, and when Dave Parker walked with two out in the seventh, manager Dallas Green replaced Espinosa with Kevin Saucier. Saucier struck out Stargell and was then lifted for pinch hitter Del Unser in the bottom of the inning. Unser led off with an infield single and moved to second when Rose walked. The Bucs responded to Manny Trillo's sacrifice by walking Bake McBride but Mike Schmidt spoiled the strategy with a grand slam home run over the left field fence.

With Tug McGraw on the hill in the eighth, memories of those great comebacks were evoked when John Milner, Madlock, Ott, and Garner singled to produce one run and load the bases for pinch hitter Lee Lacy. Lee's fly to left was too shallow to advance the runners, but Madlock came home when Moreno bounced into a fielder's choice. Trailing by three, Moreno took off for second, and when Dave Rader's throw carromed off Trillo's glove, Ott scored the third run of the inning.

The score was still 7-4 when Parker opened the ninth with a double over Greg Gross in center. Stargell's single to left cut the Phillies lead to two and after Milner bounced out, McGraw was replaced by Rawley Eastwick. Bill Madlock singled home pinch runner Matt Alexander who had stolen second, then moved up with another stolen base against Rader. Eastwick got Phil Garner for out number two and Tanner called on Manny Sanguillen to hit for Tekulve. "Sangy" had not recorded a hit since September 1 but came through with a slicing liner in the gap in left center field, scoring Madlock and Ott who had been intentionally walked. The final score was 9-7.

While the Pirates were rallying, they learned that Montreal had already beaten New York in the first game of their doubleheader and knew they had to keep the pressure on the Expos. They did just that by scoring three runs in the first inning of the second game to provide Jim Bibby with a working margin. Jim took charge from there, retiring the first nine Phillies before Rose singled to open the fourth and came around to score on singles by McBride and Schmidt. The Bucs countered that run with a tally in the fifth but Bibby was slipping fast and rookie Moreland's single tied the game at five in the sixth and the tie was broken when pinch hitter Tim McCarver bounced into a forceout, scoring Gross. The Pirates were unable to do anything against Saucier. The disappointing defeat was compounded when the Bucs learned that Montreal had completed a sweep of the Mets with a 4-1 win in their second game.

Philadelphia continued to play the spoiler role on Thursday and Randy Lerch took a 2-1 lead to the ninth inning. The Mets were providing almost no opposition for Montreal and the Pirates were in danger of losing first place when Bill Madlock opened the inning with a double to left. With one out, Steve Nicosia lined a single to left, but Madlock had to hold at third and Tanner again chose Manny Sanguillen as his pinch hitter. Sangy hit the first pitch right at Manny Trillo, who started a game-ending double play.

The disappointment of two straight losses in Philadelphia turned to gloom when Montreal completed another sweep at Shea Stadium and then to downright despair when Lynn McGlothen held the Bucs to four hits at Wrigley Field on Friday. With only two runs to show for their last 22 innings, the Pirates fell a game behind the Expos who were rained out in Philadelphia. If the team was virtually inactive on the field, the front office had no trouble keeping busy. Pete Peterson eliminated the problem of Tim Foli's possible free agency at the end of the season by signing the shortstop to a five-year contract. Foli's signing was a foregone conclusion, but the purchase of pitcher Doc Ellis came as a complete surprise. True, John Candelaria and Don Robinson were shelved with injuries, but Ellis was having a terrible season with the Mets. If the purchase was a surprise, it was total shock when Tanner announced that Ellis would be the starting pitcher against the Cubs on Sunday.

Before that game, the Pirates met Chicago on Saturday and faced a rookie pitcher named George "Heater" Riley. The controversy was obvious. The Pirates were getting a break in facing the first year hurler after the Expos had finished their season series with Chicago. In point of fact, it was probably a bad break. The Pirates had consistently lost key games to unknown pitchers in stretch drives of past years. Today was different as they literally pounded Riley in the second when Nicosia smashed a grounder off the pitcher's glove following Bill Madlock's lead-off single. Riley got another chance when Garner dropped a bunt to the left of the mound but Heater fell down and Madlock scored the first run. Garner got another hit at Riley's expense in the fifth to spark a two-run rally before Bill Buckner and Madlock traded homers to complete the scoring. Later, the Bucs finally got some good news from out of town, when the Phillies shook off a four-run Expos rally in the eighth, tied the game in the ninth, and won in the tenth on Mike Schmidt's single. That dropped Montreal into a tie with the Bucs, but an 8-2 romp in the second game put them a half game ahead going into Sunday's action.

Tanner decided to hold Ellis back until Monday's doubleheader with Montreal and started Jim Bibby instead. Big Jim has rarely pitched better than he did against the Cubs, spacing out three hits and not allowing a runner past second in a 6-0 romp over the Cubs in the last road game of the regular season. The offense finally exploded in the second inning against an injured Rick Reuschel, scoring five runs and sending 11 men to the plate. The Expos also won and both teams converged on Three Rivers Stadium for a twi-night doubleheader on September 24.

This is how the two teams stood, entering the last week of the season:

|            | W  | L  | PCT  | GB  |
|------------|----|----|------|-----|
| Montreal   | 93 | 60 | .608 | —   |
| Pittsburgh | 93 | 61 | .604 | ½   |

The Pirates had the four games with Montreal, three with the Cubs, and a make-up game scheduled for Thursday against St. Louis. While the Pirates met the Cardinals, the Expos would go to Atlanta for a make-up doubleheader, before meeting Philadelphia for three games at Olympic Stadium.

When the Pirates left Montreal the week before, it looked like the Expos would come to Pittsburgh needing three wins to win the division. The Pirate losses in Philadelphia and Chicago now had the Pirates needing three wins to regain first place.

The Pirates had beaten Montreal in five of their last six meetings, but the Expos jumped on Bert Blyleven for two runs in the first inning on four straight hits by Cash, Dawson, Perez, and Carter. Blyleven settled down after that but Dan Schatzeder was retiring 13 in a row after Madlock's double in the second. With one out in the sixth, Dave Parker walked and Bill Robinson lined a shot toward left field. Warren Cromartie never moved as the ball soared over the fence and the game was suddenly tied. The homer was Robby's first since August 13th and when Schatzeder walked Stargell on four pitches and followed with a ball to Madlock, Dick Williams quickly replaced the lefthander with veteran Stan Bahnsen. Madlock forced Stargell at second and then put the pressure on Montreal's defense by trying to steal second. When Gary Carter heaved the ball into centerfield, Mad Dog moved 90 feet closer to home with the go-ahead run. With Madlock bouncing back and forth off third, Nicosia hit a dribbler back to the mound. The thoroughly flustered Bahnsen could not pick up the ball and the error put the Pirates in front. Garner hit the next pitch through the left side and, sensing the kill, Tanner lifted Blyleven for pinch hitter Mike Easler. Bahnsen recovered to strike out Easler. Kent Tekulve came on to pitch the seventh. Teke was just about perfect, allowing only a lead-off single to Cromartie in the eighth which was immediatelyu erased on a doubleplay and single runs in the seventh and eighth wrapped up the first game.

The Bucs were in command now and ready to finish these upstart Expos in the second game. With one out, Foli and Parker singled and Bill Robinson's double gave the Pirates a 1-0 lead with runners at second and third. Rudy May fanned Stargell, walked Madlock intentionally and retired Nicosia on a fly to right to keep the Bucs from breaking the game open. It did not take Montreal long to tie the game. Cromartie led off with a double and Carter singled him in with two out. Dock Ellis, pitching with guile and brains more than talent, held the Expos at bay until the fourth when Gary Carter homered to give Montreal the lead. Dock was scheduled to lead off the fifth but four good innings were all Tanner expected from Ellis and Sanguillen pinch-hit for the pitcher. Sangy hit a fly ball that fell in the gap between Valentine and Dawson for a double and the Bucs went for the tie. Alberto Lois came in to run and Moreno moved him to third with a sacrifice bunt. The Expos brought the infield in but Foli hit a fly to center and Dawson's throw was not in time to keep Lois from tying the game again.

May had been in trouble in three of the first four innings and back-to-back hits by Stargell and Madlock had him on the ropes with nobody out in the fifth. Nicosia hit a double play ball to Parrish, but the third baseman knocked the ball down and had to settle for one out as Stargell and Madlock moved up. With Garner up and relief pitcher Enrique Romo on deck, May walked Scrap Iron intentionally, forcing Tanner to bat for Romo with Lee Lacy. The wheels continued to turn. Williams brought in Bahnsen again and Tanner called back Lacy and sent up John Milner. The strategy favored Montreal when Milner hit a grounder to Dave Cash. Cash was thinking about a doubleplay and, in his anxiety, fumbled the ball and got no one as Stargell scored the go-ahead run. The Bucs added another run when Moreno bounced out and broke the game open, and Foli lined a single to center scoring Garner and Milner.

Dave Roberts became the new Pirate pitcher but a single by Dawson, a walk to Staub, and a single by Duffy Dyer, who had replaced an injured Gary Carter, kayo'd Roberts and brought on Joe Coleman. Coleman got Valentine to hit into a double play and retired the side with no further damage. Coleman pitched well until Staub and Dyer worked him for walks with one out in the eighth. With that, Tanner brought in Tekulve to work his late inning magic. But this was one of the rare times Teke was ineffective. After Valentine forced Dyer at second, Parrish singled, and third string catcher John Tamargo delivered a pinch two-run double to tie the game. Grant Jackson got out of the inning but allowed a leadoff single to Cash in the ninth. Dawson struckout and Nicosia threw out Cash trying to steal second but Staub walked for the fourth time in the game. Dyer got another hit and Valentine singled home Staub with the winning run and split.

After letting the second game slip out of their hands, the Pirates were up against the wall. They were still a game behind and two more games had been played. The Expos had not shown Pittsburgh much in games between the two clubs until last night, but now had to be taken seriously. Montreal could split the next two games and leave town in first place. The Expos were now believing in themselves. The Pirates had still been the team to beat, the experienced team, the team that could handle the pressure. Montreal's second game win made them the team to beat and the Pirates had to regain that advantage; they began attacking as soon as they came to bat.

They came to bat in the first inning of the third game of the series. With one out, Tim Foli singled and moved to second on Parker's fly to deep center. With two out, it was up to Willie Stargell and the captain went one better with a drive over the fence in right center. The Expos were not about to quit this late in the season and came back with a run in the third. When Larry Parrish homered off Rooker in the fourth, the game was tied. Captain Willie came through again, hitting the first pitch from Scott Sanderson over the right field fence to give Pittsburgh a 3-2 lead. The fans gave Willie a standing ovation but the Expos refused to take a back seat to Stargell's magnificent performance. With two out in the fifth, Dawson singled, Perez walked, and Valentine's single tied the score once more. There were two out in the Pirates' fifth when they launched another attack. Again Stargell was the catalyst, drawing a walk. Bill Madlock singled and John Milner drew another free pass to load the bases for Ed Ott. Ed jumped on a hanging curve and lined it into centerfield, scoring Stargell and Milner, and knocking Sanderson out of the game. Phil Garner's single off Bill Atkinson increased the Bucs' lead to three but the Expos cut it back with a run on three hits in the sixth, finishing Rooker and bringing in Romo. Ross Grimsley was the Expos' new pitcher in the sixth and the Pirates came out swinging. Singles by Moreno, Foli, and Parker plated another run. With one out, John Milner hit a grounder to shortstop Rodney Scott. Scott kicked the ball into left field and the error opened the floodgates. Foli scored on the play and two more runs gave the Pirates a commanding 10-4 lead. The Expos were finally out of rallies. Romo gave up only one more hit and the Bucs were back in first.

The pressure was back on Montreal Wednesday night and the Pirates took full advantage. Bruce Kison was in complete control from the beginning as the Pirates scored a run in the first and two more in the fourth. Nobody could stop the Bucs now and they pounded four Expo pitchers for four more runs in the sixth. For the first time since August, the Pirates had a laugher on their hands. Three more runs in the seventh made the score 10-1 and the Expos were a thoroughly beaten team as they left for Atlanta.

With four games left against two noncontenders, the Pirates could only beat themselves as they faced St. Louis Thursday afternoon. But the Pirates were out of pitchers. Dave Roberts was pulled out of the bullpen to face the Cardinals. Roberts did not pitch badly but Omar Moreno's error helped St. Louis to a 3-0 lead and Tanner lifted him for a pinch hitter in the third. John Candelaria became the new pitcher but was obviously bothered by the rib-cage injury and left after giving up three hits in a third of an inning. Don Robinson was the next pitcher to test his arm and gave up three hits before leaving after the fifth. Ellis, Tekulve and Romo finished up as the Cardinals took a 9-5 decision. In Atlanta, it rained and rained and rained until the doubleheader had to be called off. The teams were now even in the loss column and the pennant picture was more confused than ever. If Montreal and Pittsburgh both won all their remaining games, Montreal would go to Atlanta for another attempt to get in the two games. If Montreal won there, they would return home for a one-game playoff with the Pirates. If either team lost, the other could win the division by winning all their remaining games.

On Friday night, Jim Bibby put on a repeat performance of last Sunday's game. He did give up one more hit and lost his shutout on a wild pitch in the eighth, but the game had been decided long before then. The Bucs scored once in the first and twice in the second before Dave Parker belted a two-run homer to put the game on ice. In Montreal, the pressure continued to affect the Expos. Two errors in the 11th inning resulted in a 3-2 loss and the Pirates' magic number was two.

Saturday, September 29, was a perfect atmosphere for a dramatic ball game. It was cold, damp, and a little foggy when Steve Ontiveros booted Omar Moreno's leadoff grounder. Tim Foli walked, Dave Parker had an infield single, and the Captain singled home two runs. Bill Madlock's sacrifice fly gave the Bucs a three-run head start. The score was 3-1 in the sixth and Bert Blyleven had only given up two hits when he walked Scot Thompson and Bill Buckner lined a double inside the first base line. Dave Kingman's high bouncer over Madlock got a run home and after Larry Bittner flied to center, Ontiveros doubled to right center and Kingman's run put the Cubs in front. A frustrated crowd at Three Rivers Stadium booed Chuck Tanner as he replaced Bert Blyleven, who had given those writers who said he could not win the big game even more fuel for their fires. Enrique Romo allowed two more hits before retiring the side with Pittsburgh trailing 5-3. The Pirates knew that Montreal had a 2-0 lead at Olympic Stadium when Madlock opened the bottom of the sixth with a double. Ed Ott ripped a single up the middle but Madlock had to wait for the ball to go through and could only move to third. Bill Buckner appeared to make a running catch on Garner's shallow fly to right but dropped the ball and had to settle for a force of Ott at second while Madlock scored.

The Expos lead over Philadelphia had been cut to a run in the ninth when Foli singled and Parker followed with his fourth hit of the game to start the seventh. Willie Stargell was the batter but Bruce Sutter's split finger fast ball prevented any more heroism as the Captain struck out. Sutter's bread-and-butter pitch got past Barry Foote to move the runners up and Milner pulled the Bucs within a run with a sacrifice fly to right field as Parker held at second. Bill Madlock shot a liner to left and Parker tore around third to score the tying run as Kingman chased the ball down in left. The frenzied crowd errupted moments later when the scoreboard flashed a tie score in Montreal. While

Sutter was retiring the Pirates with no further damage, the Expos had runners at first and third when Dave Cash singled over a drawn in outfield to win their game in the bottom of the ninth. The Pirates and Cubs went into extra innings. They were still tied in the 13th and the Cubs, Mick Kelleher, was at second with Jerry Martin batting. Martin hit a chopper to Madlock who looked Kelleher back to second and threw to first. Then Kelleher took off for third and Stargell's throw back to third sailed over both Madlock and Foli, down the left field foulline as Kelleher scored. The crowd was stunned, but the Bucs battled back. With two out, Foli singled and Parker hit a smash off the pitcher's leg. Ivan DeJesus could not make a play and Stargell was up with the tying run at second. Once again the Captain struck out.

All the bright optimism from the Montreal series had disappeared with the loss to Chicago. The Bucs were faced with another must-win situation. A win would clinch a tie and the Expos would determine what happened after that. If Montreal lost and Pittsburgh won, the Pirates would head for Cincinnati and the start of the playoffs. Otherwise, the Pirates would fly to Montreal for a possible sudden death encounter. In Pittsburgh, Bruce Kison would face Lynn McGlothen. Steve Carlton opposed Steve Rogers at Olympic Stadium.

Sunday, September 30, was Prize Day in Pittsburgh. The biggest prize was the Eastern Division title. Pittsburgh scored in the first on Stargell's sacrifice fly. The Phillies scored first in Montreal and led 1-0 after three innings. The Bucs scored again in the fourth and led 2-0 in the fifth when Willie Stargell came to bat. The Captain put the icing on the cake with a line drive that shot over the rightfield fence and nearly tore down the outer stadium wall. Stargell's blast brought an outpouring of love and appreciation from the Pittsburgh crowd in the form of a long, loud, standing ovation that would not end until Stargell emerged from the dugout to accept their applause.

The score in Montreal was still 1-0, but Steve Carlton was pitching a masterpiece and the Expos were running out of time.

The Cubs did not quit. "Kong" Kingman hit a towering home run to knock out Kison in the fourth and Chicago scored again in the fifth off Tekulve.

When Stargell came to bat again in the seventh, he was bypassed to load the bases for Bill Robinson. Pittsburgh's other elder statesman came through with a single to right for two runs and a 5-2 lead.

It was 5-3 and Dick Tidrow was warming up for Chicago to start the eighth, when the final report came from Montreal. Carlton had pitched a three hitter, striking out 12 and shutting out the Expos 2-0. The magic number was one and the celebration began instantaneously.

Three Rivers Stadium was rocking when Bruce Kimm faced Tekulve with two out in the ninth. Kimm popped a high fastball up above third base. Bill Madlock settled under the ball and grabbed the Eastern Division title. All the frustrations of '78 and '77 and '76 were forgotten as the Pirate family celebrated the end of a long, victorious season.

### The 1979 Championship Playoffs

After getting a day to come down from their celebrations of the division-clinching game of Sunday, the Pirates traveled to Cincinnati for the opening of the Championship Series. The Pirates and Reds were meeting for the fourth time in post-season play. Pittsburgh had never beaten Cincinnati in the three previous attempts and had managed to win only two games of the 11 played between the two clubs. But 1979 proved to be a special year.

The pitching match-ups for the first game saw Tom Seaver and John Candelaria going head-to-head. Seaver had struggled early in the year, suffering from injuries, but came on strong as the season ended. Candelaria, like Seaver, suffered with injuries. His chronic back ailment and sore arm had limited his effectiveness through the last two weeks of the season.

186

The game was everything a fan could expect. With one out in the bottom of the second, Johnny Bench tripled to left center but "Candy" struck out Ray Knight and Dan Driessen to end the inning. Pittsburgh responded to the strong pitching in the third when Garner drove a ball over the right field wall. Moreno later tripled to right and scored on Foli's sacrifice fly. Candy struggled in the fourth as Dave Concepcion singled and George Foster drilled a ball over the centerfield wall to tie the score. Bench followed with an infield hit but Candy got Knight to bounce into a doubleplay and Driessen to bounce out to end the inning. After Moreno's hit in the third, Seaver held the Pirates to just two more hits until he left the game for a pinch hitter in the eighth. Meanwhile, Candelaria held the Reds hitless for the fifth, sixth, and seventh before leaving the game after seven innings. The Reds threatened in the eighth. Romo struck out Rock Auerback, but Dave Collins singled and Joe Morgan walked. Tekulve then came in to get Concepcion to ground into an inning-ending double play. Tom Hume put the Bucs up and down in the ninth and Tekulve did the same to the Reds. In the tenth, Garner singled with one out but pinch hitter Mike Easler flied out and Moreno fanned. Jackson retired the Reds by getting Driessen to ground out to first and striking out Heity Cruze and Hume. The Pirates won the game in the eleventh when Foli and Parker opened the inning with singles and Stargell, like he had so many times during the regular season, homered deep to right center. The Reds didn't go quietly in the bottom of the inning. With two outs, Concepcion singled and Foster walked. Robinson came in and walked Bench to load the bases and put the winning run up to bat in the person of Ray Knight. Robinson struck out Knight but not without some excitement. On the third strike, Ott dropped the ball and instead of just stepping on home to end the game, threw to first to nip Knight.

Game Two was just as exciting as the first. The Reds opened the scoring in the second when Driessen singled, went to third on Knight's single and scored on Frank Pastore's sacrifice fly. After that, Jim Bibby held the Reds to just two hits until he was removed from the game in the seventh. Meanwhile, the Bucs had tied the game in the fourth on singles by Foli, Parker, and Stargell. However, on Stargell's single, Foli had held third and Stargell was easily caught off first. Milner was then intentionally passed to load the bases. Madlock followed with a grounder to short to force Milner but "Mad Dog" beat the play, at first allowing Foli to score. Pittsburgh took the lead in the fifth when Garner singled on a disputed call in right. The right fielder, Dave Collins, thought he had caught Garner's dying liner, but the second base umpire ruled that it had been trapped. Garner went to second on Bibby's sacrifice and scored on Foli's double to left. The game remained the same until the ninth when Cruz hit a pinch hit double to center and Collins doubled to right to tie the game at 2-2. Roberts came in and walked Morgan but Robinson was brought in and struck out Concepcion and got Foster to ground out to Garner. In the Pirate tenth, with Doug Bair pitching, Moreno led-off with a single and went to second on Foli's sacrifice. Parker then scored Moreno on a single to left. Robinson retired the Reds in order in the bottom of the tenth to pick up his second win in two days.

Game Three was back in Pittsburgh and the outcome was never in doubt. The Pirates jumped on starter Mike LaCoss for a run in the first when Moreno led-off with a walk, stole second, and was safe at third when Concepcion tried to throw him out on Foli's grounder. Parker delivered with a sacrifice fly. The Bucs added a run in the second when Garner tripled to right and scored on Foli's sacrifice fly to center. That was all for LaCoss and Fred Norman was called upon to end the inning. Stargell led-off the third by hitting a 1-2 pitch over the right field wall to make it 3-0. After Milner fouled out, Madlock hit Norman's first offering over the left field wall to give the Bucs run number four. In the fourth, Blyleven singled and went to second on Moreno's sacrifice. Foli flied out to right and Parker walked. Stargell chased Norman with a double to right to make the score 6-0. While all this was going on, Blyleven was on his way to a complete game, allowing one run on eight hits and striking out nine, including Cesar Geronimo in the ninth, to end the series.

## The 1979 World Series

After defeating Cincinnati with surprising ease, it was back to Baltimore, the scene of the Bucs last World Series triumph.

It was much like 1971. The Birds had the great pitching and the Pirates had the hitting. In '71, it was Mike Cuellar, Pat Dobson, Dave McNally and Jim Palmer on the hill and it was Clemente, Hebner, Oliver, Robertson, and Stargell with the bats. In '79, Palmer and Stargell were both back but they were surrounded by a different supporting cast. Baltimore had Mike Flanagan (23-9), Scott McGregor (13-6) and Denny Martinez (15-16). Pittsburgh had Parker, Madlock, Garner, and Moreno.

The Orioles had the better defense and pitching. They had run away with their division' and were the favorites.

The first game, scheduled for October 8, was rained-out. This was the first time an opening game of a Series had been postponed. During the night the temperature dropped under the freezing point, giving Baltimore its earliest recorded snowfall.

Game One was still in doubt until the late afternoon when Commissioner Bowie Kuhn ruled that the field was in playable condition. But the weather was more suited for a game between the Steelers and the Colts than the Bucs and the Birds.

The Pirates are a notoriously poor cold-weather team and Game One proved that out. With the temperatures in the low 40s and falling fast, Kison immediately got into trouble by giving up a lead-off hit to Al Bumbry and walking the light-hitting Mark Belanger on four pitches. When Ken Singleton hit a smash back to the box, Kison had a chance to get out of the mess. Because of the cold, Bruce could only knock the ball down and make the play at first. With first base open, Kison pitched carefully to power-hitting Eddie Murray and finally walked him. The Bucs had a chance to end the inning when John Lowenstein hit a doubleplay ball to Garner. But in the cold, Garner bobbled the ball. Bad went to terrible, as Garner couldn't grip the ball and ended up throwing it into left center allowing two runs to score. Kison then wild-pitched a run home and when Doug DeCinces drove a non-sinking sinker into the left field seats, it was 5-0. Billy Smith followed DeCinces with a single to right. Tanner had seen enough of Kison. Old Jim Rooker came in and closed the door and held the Orioles scoreless while the Pirates went to work on Flanagan.

In the fourth, Foli singled, went to third on Parker's single and scored on Stargell's ground out to Smith. In the sixth, Parker and Robinson led-off with singles, Stargell struck out, and Madlock flied out to right. Nicosia hit a 3-1 chop to DeCinces, who booted the ball all the way to second, to load the bases. Garner came up with a chance to atone for his disastrous error in the first. Garner fell behind in the count, but hung tough and took full advantage of the situation with a single through the left side to drive in two runs. Lacy pinch-hit for the pitcher and hit an easy hopper that DeCinces played off his chest. DeCinces made a futile swipe at Nicosia sliding into third and the bases were loaded for Moreno. Omar popped to center on the first pitch to end the inning. In the eighth, Stargell put the Bucs back to within a run when he hit a flat curveball on a 2-2 pitch into the seats in right. Pittsburgh had a final chance in the ninth, as after Foli ground out, Parker hit Flanagan's first pitch up the middle for a single. Flanagan smelled out an attempted steal and threw behind Parker at first. Parker went barreling into second, kicked the ball out of Belanger's glove and the tying run was in scoring position. Bill Robinson's grounder to second put Parker on third and left it up to Stargell. Stargell got under a 2-1 pitch and popped it into shallow left. Belanger made the catch and the Pirates were down one game to none.

With the exception of the first inning, the Pirates had out-played Baltimore. They out-hit the Birds eleven to six and out-scored them four to nothing over the last eight innings. Mike Flanagan hadn't been overly impressive and he was supposed to be Baltimore's best. Pittsburgh came to Baltimore needing a split and were confident that they would get it in Game Two.

Jim Palmer was pitted against Bert Blyleven. Palmer had struggled through an injury-plagued year while Blyleven had finally rid himself of the "choke" label by pitching a great game in the third game of the playoffs.

In 1971, Palmer won the second game by a 11-3 margin. This year it looked as though the Pirates were going to return the favor in the second inning. Stargell ripped a single to right, Milner shot a ball up the middle, and Madlock followed with a run-scoring single to right center. Ott scored Milner from third with a drive just short of the track in left center. But they let Palmer off the hook when Madlock was caught stealing and Garner grounded out to short.

After Murray caught a high changeup and drove it into the second level in right, the two pitchers settled down and the game went into the bottom of the sixth with the score still 2-1.

In the sixth, Murray was the batter again, after Singleton had led-off with a bloop single to left. Blyleven seemed to be tiring when Murray nailed him again—this time for an RBI double to left center. Romo and Jackson started to loosen at this point, but Blyleven got DeCinces to dribble such a weak bouncer to short that Foli had to make a great charging pick-up to get the out. On the play, Murray moved to third where a fly ball could give the Birds the lead. There was a light rain falling as Lowenstein came to the plate. The Orioles' left fielder hit a line drive through the mist into right field. Parker took the ball on the run, putting himself in perfect position to make a throw to the plate. The play wasn't close. Murray's only chance was to bowl over Ott, but the Pirate catcher held on allowing Blyleven to escape with a 2-2 tie.

DeCinces opened the door for the Bucs in the seventh with his pratfall and aerial circus. DeCinces fell down after fielding Madlock's grounder and then added to his misery by heaving the ball into the photographers' area. Ott struck out for the second out. Weaver then tried to force Tanner's hand by intentionally walking Garner. Tanner had Easler bat for Blyleven. Palmer looked as if he had Easler struckout but the home plate umpire, Bob Engle, called the pitch low for ball four. This brought up Moreno who had stranded six runners in the first game and again Omar fanned.

The Orioles threatened by loading the bases on walks in the seventh, but Robinson pitched his way out of that jam. In the eighth Baltimore had runners on first and second with no outs but Foli managed to turn an awkward 6-4-5-4 doubleplay.

In a driving rain in the ninth, Bill Robinson led-off with a single off Tippy Martinez. Weaver went to Don Stanhouse and Tanner ran for Robinson with Matt Alexander. Everyone knew Alexander was going to run and he wasted no time, going on the first pitch. Rick Dempsey's throw was right on the money and Alexander was gone. Madlock flied out to left center. Ott got a bad hop single off the glove of Billy Smith at second. Stanhouse walked Garner on four pitches to put runners on first and second. Tanner called on Sanguillen to pinch hit. Manny, not the hitter he was in '71, delivered with a shot to right. Singleton, playing shallow, had a play at the plate. Singleton's throw was on line but Murray cut it off. Ott beat Murray's relay with a beautiful hook slide under Dempsey's tag. In the last of the ninth, Tekulve got his first chance to face the Birds and retired them one-two-three.

The Bucs had gotten the split and were still not impressed with Baltimore. The Orioles' defense was questionable and would surely suffer on the fast turf in Three Rivers. Their offense was less than awesome and had only produced two runs in the last 17 innings.

The Pirates returned to Pittsburgh and a crowd of 50,848 jammed Three Rivers Stadium to watch their Bucs move a step closer to the title. Chuck Tanner had the one pitcher he wanted in a must game starting, John Candelaria. Omar Moreno led off the game and with no one on base, lined a double to rightfield. National League umpire Terry Tata called a balk on Scott McGregor and Dave Parker's sacrifice fly put the Bucs ahead 1-0. Singles by Stargell and Nicosia preceeded a Garner double and the Pirates had a three-run lead. Everything was going according to plan until the third inning. Kiko Garcia walked and Benny Ayala, a National League castoff, tagged the Candy Man with a two-run homer to left center. Singleton followed with a single. Eddie

Murray walked and Gary Roenicke singled with two out. Only Bill Robinson's throw to cut down Singleton at the plate kept Candelaria in the game. Then the rains came. The game was delayed 67 minutes. When it resumed there was concern that Candelaria, plagued throughout his career by a chronic back problem, would not be able to continue pitching. Tanner stuck with his ace and Candelaria took the mound in the fourth. He did not retire a batter. Rich Dauer doubled, Dempsey singled, and even the pitcher McGregor reached base when Foli fumbled his grounder. Kiko Garcia batted with the bases loaded and unloaded a triple to center. Enrique Romo came in but the tide was irreversible. Al Bumbrey batted for Ayala and was hit by a pitch. Singleton's hit and DeCinces grounder sent two more runs across the plate and Baltimore led 7-3. McGregor settled down and silenced the Pirate bats. A Stargell double and Madlock's single gave the Bucs a fourth run but the Orioles' lefthander retired the final eleven batters he faced and Baltimore had a two games to one lead in the series.

Down by a game, the pressure was on the Pirates. They had been beaten by players no one had heard of. A trip back to Baltimore was necessary and the Bucs had to win the next two at home. There were still excuses. The rain delay had stifled the Pirates momentum. Denny Martinez started for Baltimore and Willie Stargell took charge. The Captain led off the second inning with a home run over the centerfield fence. Before the inning was over, Martinez was gone and the Bucs led 4-0. Sloppy baserunning which resulted in Ott and Moreno being thrown out on the bases prevented an early runaway. The Orioles took advantage of the Pirates' mercy and scored three runs on "Babe" Garcia's two run double and another two base hit by Singleton in the third. Jim Bibby settled down after that and the Bucs added two more runs to take a comfortable 6-3 lead into the eighth. Grant Jackson had come on in the seventh to put down a mild Oriole threat and Don Robinson came in to pitch the eighth. He immediately pitched himself into trouble. Belanger and Singleton singled and DeCinces walked to load the bases with one out. Tanner pulled Robinson and called on his ace, Kent Tekulve to put out the fire. Earl Weaver went to his bench and sent Lowenstein up to hit for Roenicke. Teke threw a sinker that did not sink. Lowenstein lined it past Stargell into the rightfield corner and the Bucs lead was a run. Weaver went to his bench and found Billy Smith to bat for Dauer. With first base open, Smith was walked intentionally. Weaver went to his bench again and produced Terry Crowley, another National League reject who had found a home with the Orioles. Tekulve pitched carefully to Crowley and Crowley fought off Teke's best sinkers until the pitcher hung another one. Crowley lined it down the right field line and Baltimore was in front. The Orioles were jubilant, the Pirates defeated. Relief pitcher Tim Stoddard in recording his first hit as a professional, singled home another run over a drawn-in infield and Bumbry's high bouncer gave Baltimore a 9-6 lead. The big righthander, a college basketball standout, returned to the mound, retired Pittsburgh in the eighth and had two down in the ninth with Stargell at first when Madlock singled to center. The Pirates were still alive, with Ed Ott representing the tying run. He struck out.

Now a trip to Baltimore might not be necessary. It was bad enough that the Bucs were one game from elimination. Even worse was the fact that the Pirates knew they had a better team but now recognized the Orioles' talent. Weaver was outmanaging Tanner, and everything he did seemed to work. Still there was hope in Pittsburgh. The Bucs were inexplicably flat. They stranded too many men on base, the starters could not hold a lead and the relief ace, Kent Tekulve, had been thoroughly beaten. If the Pirates could start playing their best baseball, there was still a chance. Pittsburgh played best with their backs against the wall. They only had to win three games, two on the road, but the Pirates were the best road club in baseball. The claims were all true but they rang hollow in view of the situation. Win or lose, it had been a good year but the Pirates had to show the world the kind of baseball they were capable of playing. The game would be played for pride.

The Orioles went for the kill, starting with their ace Mike Flanagan. The Pirates were looking for Kison to start, but Bruce complained of numbness in his pitching arm.

Tanner turned to the gutty Jim Rooker. Rooker had pitched well in the first game and at times during the season. It was a calculated risk. If Rooker struggled, the rest of the staff would be called on.

All the intricacies of the situation suddenly seemed insignificant when it was learned that Chuck Tanner's mother had died early in the morning. Tanner's grief was shared by the whole club. But Tanner buried the pain deep inside himself and refused to let it affect the game. The character shown by Tanner was an inspiration to everyone. The tragedy had taken the players' minds off the game but it still had to be played.

After four innings Flanagan had limited the Bucs to two hits. But Rooker hadn't allowed any hits. Jim was pitching easily, mixing his pitches and keeping the Orioles off balance. The only base runner for Baltimore came in the fourth when Ayala walked on five pitches. In the fifth, Roenicke broke up the no-hitter with a double to left center. DeCinces lined a ball just over Garner's glove at second. Roenicke could only go to third. Roenicke scored when Dauer bounced in to a double play giving the Birds the lead. Rooker was not out of trouble as Dempsey lined a single to left and Flanagan drew a walk. Rooker was fading fast but managed to get out of the inning when Garcia bounced into a force play.

With the Pirates down a run, with a man on and two outs in the fifth, Tanner batted for his pitcher. Rooker had done his job. A surprise starter, Rooker held the Orioles close and in a regular season game would have remained. This was a do-or-die game so Tanner went to Blyleven.

Flanagan had held the Bucs in check through five, but in the sixth, the Bucs scratched out two runs. Foli led-off with a walk and Parker followed with a shot to center. The Pirates clean-up hitter, Bill Robinson, laid down a perfect bunt to put two runners in scoring position for Stargell. Captain Willie had stranded numerous runners in the previous games but tied this game with a long fly to Bumbry in the right center. Madlock gave the Bucs the lead with a sharp single to center to score Parker.

Blyleven was pitching well. He put the Birds down without a hit in the sixth and had two outs in the seventh when Dempsey hit a double to Moreno in right center. Weaver went to his bench at this point, calling on Pat Kelly to hit for Flanagan. Blyleven went 2-0 on Kelly and then came back to strike him out.

Weaver brought in Stoddard. This time Stoddard wasn't as successful as he had been the day before. Garner beat out a chop to short but was retired at second when Blyleven failed to sacrifice. Again Moreno failed to produce and forced Blyleven at second on a grounder to short. With Moreno on first and two outs, there was still a flicker of hope for the Pirate offense. Moreno, unable to do anything on the bases in the Series, had Stoddard so preoccupied that he finally threw the ball away on a pickoff attempt. This allowed Omar to get to second. Foli followed with a triple between the outfielders in right center. Weaver went to the lefty Tippy Martinez, to face Parker. David greeted Martinez with a drive to the gap in left center to score Foli. The Pirates were now playing the kind of ball that had won them the N. L. flag.

That was all Blyleven needed to close out the game. The Bucs added three more in the eighth just for good measure. Baltimore put together a mild rally in the ninth when, with two outs, DeCinces singled but even Weaver's lefthanded pinch hitters couldn't save them from defeat.

The Pirates had out-hit, out-pitched and out-played the Orioles and the series was going back to Baltimore and decent weather.

Game Six was supposed to be for the Orioles. Pittsburgh had fun in the fifth game but this time Baltimore had the veteran Jim Palmer and the home crowd to wrap it up. The Pirates had used up all their healthy starters when Blyleven went the game before and John Candelaria got the call. "Candy" had suffered from a pulled muscle in his rib cage in addition to the chronic back injury.

The Bucs came out of the clubhouse swinging. Moreno singled to open the game. Foli followed with a double on a chop off the glove of DeCinces. Parker jumped on the first pitch and ripped a shot to third that DeCinces made an excellent stop of and just nipped

Parker at first. Stargell also went after the first pitch and popped out to DeCinces in foul ground. Palmer got out of the inning by getting Milner to hit a bouncer back to the mound.

The Orioles also threatened in the first. Garcia led-off with a single. After Ayala flied out to center, Singleton singled past Foli in to left. Candelaria then ended the threat by getting Murray to bounce into a double play. The two pitchers settled down after the first and exchanged goose eggs through six innings. The Pirates had only gotten four hits, two after the first, going into the seventh. The Orioles had collected six hits, but other than the two in the first, they couldn't bunch them. The Pirates had a threat in the fourth when they loaded the bases without getting a hit. Palmer struckout Candelaria to end the inning.

The Pirates were trying to make something happen in the seventh. Tanner pinch-hit Lacy for Candelaria who had pitched a strong six innings and had gone as far as he could. Lacy failed but Moreno followed with a base hit just past Murray. Moreno's presence put added pressure on the O's defense. Moreno, still trying to make something happen, broke for second. Foli made contact on an 0-2 pitch and hit a chopper up the middle. It just hopped over Palmer and under Garcia, putting runners on first and second. The Orioles infield was tested again on Parker's grounder to second. The ball jumped past Dauer to score Moreno and put Foli on third. Stargell then hit a long fly to left to score Foli and put the Bucs ahead 2-0.

Tekulve came in and had to prove himself after the poor outing in Game Four. Tekulve mowed down the Birds. Teke had the sinker working, not like Saturday when the sinker stayed high. In the final three innings, the only man to get on base was pinch hitter Billy Smith who singled in the seventh. Teke struck out four, including Singleton to lead-off the ninth and DeCinces to end the game. When DeCinces waved at Tekulve's final sinker, the Bucs were back.

The Pirates were now playing their kind of baseball. They were getting good pitching, timely hitting and were forcing things to happen. Baltimore's pitching had been good but they weren't getting any offense. The Orioles defense was starting to show signs of cracking. The O's had had the Pirates down and could have ended it twice but they had let the Bucs battle back and that was fatal.

A seventh game of a World Series needs no build-up. The whole season comes down to one game; 25 men, healthy or not, are ready to be thrown into action.

Scott McGregor got the call for the Birds and Jim Bibby for the Bucs. McGregor was coming back on four days rest and Bibby had just three. McGregor's off-speed pitches were matched against Bibby's fastball.

Bibby continued the Pirates' pattern of attacking the Baltimore batters. Big Bibby kept everything around the plate and just used the curve to set up a fast ball. Jim was virtually unhittable, until Dauer led-off the third. The second baseman got around on a fast ball and hit it into the seats in left.

The lead did nothing to improve the O's defensive play. DeCinces staggered under Stargell's pop in short left for a double. Garcia then threw the ball wildly to third in an effort to get Stargell on Madlock's grounder.

With the crowd cheering on every pitch, McGregor got out of the trouble and put the Bucs up and down in order in the fifth. He was making the slim lead look bigger and bigger with every passing batter.

In the Orioles' fifth, Don Robinson gave up a lead-off single to DeCinces and two outs later, walked McGregor. Tanner went to Grant Jackson who got Bumbry to end the threat.

After Parker ground out weakly to second, Bill Robinson got a bad hop single through the left side to set the stage for Stargell. On the first pitch from McGregor, Stargell caught a low fastball and hit a towering drive that Singleton tracked to the 375 foot mark in right center. Singleton leaped as high as he could at the fence but with the rooting of the Buc bullpen members, the ball landed a few feet past Singleton's glove.

Stargell's two-run homer put the Pirates twelve outs away from the World Championship. Jackson got the next seven in a row. But the Birds were not dead yet. With one out in the eighth, Lee May, pinch-hitting for McGregor, walked. Belanger then went in to run for May. Jackson then walked Bumbry on a 3-2 pitch. Tanner summoned his ace, Kent Tekulve. Teke got pinch hitter Terry Crowley to bounce out to second and the Birds had two runners in scoring position. Singleton was intentionally walked to load the bases and get to Murray who was hitless in his last 20 at-bats. Murray followed with a high fly to right. The ball didn't appear to be trouble but Parker stumbled in the soft turf before finally gloving the ball just as he went on to the track. The Bucs had fought off the Birds charge and were now ready to put the game away.

With Stoddard now pitching, Garner took the first pitch in the ninth and doubled into the left field corner. After Tekulve failed to sacrifice, Weaver ran through his bullpen in an effort to stop the Buc momentum. It was to no avail as Moreno singled home Garner and later scored the fourth run when Robinson was hit by a pitch.

It came to Tekulve in the ninth with a three-run lead. Tekulve struck out Roenicke on four pitches and got DeCinces to chase a pitch a foot off the plate for the second out. Tekulve then induced pinch hitter Pat Kelly to fly out to Moreno on the first pitch and the Bucs were World Champions.

Winning the World Championship and in the style that they did, was befitting the Pirates. The Pirates had battled all season. They came back from a slow start and battled the Expos right down to the last day of the season. They continued by battling the Orioles. The Pirates never led in the Series until the sixth inning of the seventh game. The Pirates never quit; they may have lost some games but they were never defeated.

It wasn't just success for the 25-man team, it was success for the entire organization. It took the tireless work of so many people to put it all together. The Pirate theme song, "We Are Family," sums up the feeling of each person involved. It was all worth it.

## 5. STATISTICS

### Seasonal Leaders—Offensive

| RBIs (plus all players with 100 or more) | | RUNS SCORED (plus all players with 100 or more) | | DOUBLES (plus all players with 20 or more) | | TRIPLES (plus all players with 10 or more) | | HOMERUNS (plus all players with 20 or more) | | YEAR |
|---|---|---|---|---|---|---|---|---|---|---|
| Parker | 94 | Moreno | 110 | Parker | 45 | Moreno | 12 | Stargell | 32 | 79 |
| | | Parker | 109 | Garner | 32 | | | Parker | 25 | |
| | | | | Foli | 23 | | | B. Robinson | 24 | |
| | | | | Moreno | 21 | | | | | |
| | | | | Ott | 20 | | | | | |
| Parker | 117 | Parker | 102 | Parker | 32 | Parker | 12 | Parker | 30 | 78 |
| | | | | Taveras | 32 | | | Stargell | 28 | |
| | | | | B. Robinson | 26 | | | | | |
| | | | | Garner | 25 | | | | | |
| B. Robinson | 104 | Parker | 107 | Parker | 44 | Garner | 10 | B. Robinson | 26 | 77 |
| | | | | Garner | 35 | Taveras | 10 | Parker | 21 | |
| | | | | B. Robinson | 32 | | | | | |
| | | | | Oliver | 29 | | | | | |
| | | | | Stennett | 20 | | | | | |
| | | | | Taveras | 20 | | | | | |
| Parker | 90 | Zisk | 91 | Zisk | 35 | Parker | 10 | B. Robinson | 21 | 76 |
| | | | | Stennett | 31 | | | Zisk | 21 | |
| | | | | Parker | 28 | | | Stargell | 20 | |
| | | | | B. Robinson | 22 | | | | | |
| | | | | Oliver | 22 | | | | | |
| | | | | Hebner | 21 | | | | | |
| | | | | Stargell | 20 | | | | | |

*Led league.

193

| RBIs | | RUNS SCORED | | DOUBLES | | TRIPLES | | HOMERUNS | | YEAR |
|---|---|---|---|---|---|---|---|---|---|---|
| Parker | 101 | Oliver | 90 | Oliver | 39 | Parker | 10 | Parker | 25 | 75 |
| | | | | Parker | 35 | | | Stargell | 22 | |
| | | | | Stargell | 32 | | | Zisk | 20 | |
| | | | | Zisk | 27 | | | | | |
| | | | | Stennett | 25 | | | | | |
| | | | | Sanguillen | 24 | | | | | |
| Zisk | 100 | Hebner | 97 | Oliver | 38 | Oliver | 12 | Stargell | 25 | 74 |
| | | | | Stargell | 37 | | | | | |
| | | | | Zisk | 30 | | | | | |
| | | | | Stennett | 29 | | | | | |
| | | | | Sanguillen | 21 | | | | | |
| | | | | Hebner | 21 | | | | | |
| Stargell | 119* | Stargell | 106 | Stargell | 43 | Oliver | 7 | Stargell | 44 | 73 |
| | | | | Oliver | 38 | Zisk | 7 | Hebner | 25 | |
| | | | | Hebner | 28 | Sanguillen | 7 | Oliver | 20 | |
| | | | | Sanguillen | 26 | | | | | |
| | | | | Zisk | 23 | | | | | |
| | | | | Cash | 21 | | | | | |
| Stargell | 112 | Oliver | 88 | Stargell | 28 | | | Stargell | 33 | 72 |
| | | | | Oliver | 27 | | | | | |
| | | | | Hebner | 24 | Sanguillen | 8 | | | |
| | | | | Cash | 22 | | | | | |
| Stargell | 125 | Stargell | 104 | Oliver | 31 | Hebner | 8 | Stargell | 48* | 71 |
| | | | | Clemente | 29 | Clemente | 8 | Robertson | 26 | |
| | | | | Stargell | 26 | | | | | |
| | | | | Sanguillen | 26 | | | | | |
| Stargell | 85 | M. Alou | 97 | Oliver | 33 | Clemente | 10 | Stargell | 31 | 70 |
| | | | | Hebner | 24 | | | Robertson | 27 | |
| | | | | Clemente | 22 | | | | | |
| | | | | M. Alou | 21 | | | | | |
| Stargell | 92 | M. Alou | 105 | M. Alou | 41* | Clemente | 12* | Stargell | 29 | 69 |
| | | | | Stargell | 31 | | | | | |
| | | | | Hebner | 23 | | | | | |
| | | | | Sanguillen | 21 | | | | | |
| Clendenon | 87 | Wills | 76 | M. Alou | 28 | Clemente | 12 | Stargell | 24 | 68 |
| | | | | Clendenon | 20 | | | | | |
| | | | | Alley | 20 | | | | | |
| Clemente | 110 | Clemente | 103 | Clemente | 26 | Clemente | 10 | Clemente | 23 | 66 |
| | | | | Mazeroski | 25 | | | Stargell | 20 | |
| | | | | Alley | 25 | | | | | |
| | | | | M. Alou | 21 | | | | | |
| Clemente | 119 | Clemente | 105 | Clemente | 31 | Clemente | 11 | Stargell | 33 | 67 |
| Stargell | 102 | | | Stargell | 30 | Alley | 10 | Clemente | 29 | |
| | | | | Alley | 28 | Clendenon | 10 | Clendenon | 28 | |
| | | | | Mazeroski | 22 | | | | | |
| | | | | Clendenon | 22 | | | | | |
| | | | | Pagliaroni | 20 | | | | | |
| Stargell | 107 | Clemente | 91 | Clendenon | 32 | Clemente | 14 | Stargell | 27 | 65 |
| | | | | Balley | 28 | Clendenon | 14 | | | |
| | | | | Stargell | 25 | | | | | |

| RBIs | | RUNS SCORED | | DOUBLES | | TRIPLES | | HOMERUNS | | YEAR |
|---|---|---|---|---|---|---|---|---|---|---|
| | | | | Virdon | 22 | | | | | |
| | | | | Alley | 21 | | | | | |
| | | | | Clemente | 21 | | | | | |
| Clemente | 87 | Clemente | 95 | Clemente | 40 | Clendenon | 8 | Stargell | 21 | 64 |
| | | | | Bailey | 25 | Mazeroski | 8 | | | |
| | | | | Clendenon | 23 | | | | | |
| | | | | Mazeroski | 22 | | | | | |
| | | | | Schofield | 22 | | | | | |
| Clemente | 76 | Clemente | 77 | Clendenon | 28 | Clemente | 8 | Clemente | 17 | 63 |
| | | | | Clemente | 23 | | | | | |
| | | | | Mazeroski | 22 | | | | | |
| | | | | Virdon | 22 | | | | | |
| Mazeroski | 81 | Clemente | 95 | Groat | 34 | Virdon | 10* | Skinner | 20 | 62 |
| | | | | Skinner | 29 | | | | | |
| | | | | Clemente | 28 | | | | | |
| | | | | Virdon | 27 | | | | | |
| | | | | Mazeroski | 24 | | | | | |
| Stuart | 117 | Clemente | 100 | Clemente | 30 | Clemente | 10 | Stuart | 35 | 61 |
| | | | | Stuart | 28 | | | Clemente | 23 | |
| | | | | Hoak | 27 | | | | | |
| | | | | Groat | 25 | | | | | |
| | | | | Virdon | 22 | | | | | |
| | | | | Mazeroski | 21 | | | | | |
| | | | | Skinner | 20 | | | | | |
| Clemente | 94 | Hoak | 97 | Skinner | 33 | Hoak | 9 | Stuart | 23 | 60 |
| | | | | Groat | 26 | Virdon | 9 | | | |
| | | | | Hoak | 24 | | | | | |
| | | | | Clemente | 22 | | | | | |
| | | | | Mazeroski | 21 | | | | | |
| Stuart | 78 | Skinner | 78 | Hoak | 29 | Groat | 7 | Stuart | 27 | 59 |
| | | | | Burgess | 28 | Clemente | 7 | | | |
| | | | | Virdon | 24 | | | | | |
| | | | | Groat | 22 | | | | | |
| Thomas | 109 | Skinner | 93 | Groat | 36 | Virdon | 11 | Thomas | 35 | 58 |
| | | | | Skinner | 33 | Clemente | 10 | | | |
| | | | | Thomas | 26 | | | | | |
| | | | | Mazeroski | 24 | | | | | |
| | | | | Virdon | 24 | | | | | |
| Thomas | 89 | Thomas | 72 | Groat | 30 | Virdon | 11 | Thomas | 23 | 57 |
| | | | | Thomas | 30 | | | | | |
| | | | | Virdon | 28 | | | | | |
| | | | | Mazeroski | 27 | | | | | |
| Long | 91 | Walls | 76 | Clemente | 30 | Walls | 11 | Long | 27 | 56 |
| | | | | Thomas | 24 | Virdon | 10 | Thomas | 25 | |
| | | | | Virdon | 21 | | | | | |
| | | | | Walls | 20 | | | | | |
| | | | | Long | 20 | | | | | |
| Long | 79 | Thomas | 72 | Groat | 28 | Long | 13* | Thomas | 25 | 55 |
| | | | | Clemente | 23 | Clemente | 11 | | | |
| | | | | Freese | 21 | | | | | |

| RBIs | | RUNS SCORED | | DOUBLES | | TRIPLES | | HOMERUNS | | YEAR |
|---|---|---|---|---|---|---|---|---|---|---|
| Thomas | 94 | Thomas | 81 | Thomas | 32 | Skinner | 9 | Thomas | 23 | 54 |
| | | | | Cole | 22 | | | | | |
| Thomas | 102 | O'Connell | 88 | O'Connell | 26 | Bernier | 8 | Thomas | 30 | 53 |
| | | | | Thomas | 22 | O'Connell | 8 | | | |
| Kiner | 87 | Kiner | 90 | Bell | 21 | Bell | 5 | Kiner | 37* | 52 |
| | | | | Merson | 20 | | | | | |
| Kiner | 109 | Kiner | 124* | Kiner | 31 | Bell | 12* | Kiner | 42* | 51 |
| | | | | Bell | 27 | | | | | |
| | | | | Metkovich | 21 | | | | | |
| Kiner | 118 | Kiner | 112 | Hopp | 24 | Bell | 11 | Kiner | 47* | 50 |
| | | | | Bell | 22 | | | Westlake | 24 | |
| | | | | Kiner | 21 | | | | | |
| | | | | Murtaugh | 20 | | | | | |
| Kiner | 127* | Kiner | 116 | Westlake | 24 | Westlake | 8 | Kiner | 54* | 49 |
| Westlake | 104 | | | Castiglione | 20 | | | Westlake | 23 | |
| Kiner | 123 | Kiner | 104 | Rojek | 27 | Hopp | 12 | Kiner | 40* | 48 |
| | | | | Murtaugh | 21 | | | | | |
| Kiner | 127 | Kiner | 118 | Cox | 30 | Russell | 8 | Kiner | 51* | 47 |
| | | Gustine | 102 | Gustine | 30 | | | | | |
| | | | | Kiner | 23 | | | | | |
| | | | | Russell | 21 | | | | | |
| Kiner | 81 | Fletcher | 72 | Russell | 29 | Fletcher | 8 | Kiner | 23* | 46 |
| | | | | Elliott | 25 | | | | | |
| | | | | Fletcher | 25 | | | | | |
| | | | | Gustine | 23 | | | | | |
| | | | | Cox | 22 | | | | | |
| Elliott | 108 | Barrett | 97 | Elliott | 36 | Gionfriddo | 9 | Barrett | 15 | 45 |
| | | | | Barrett | 29 | | | | | |
| | | | | Gustine | 27 | | | | | |
| | | | | Russell | 24 | | | | | |
| | | | | Dahlgren | 24 | | | | | |
| Elliott | 108 | Russell | 109 | Russell | 34 | Barrett | 19* | Dahlgren | 12 | 44 |
| Dahlgren | 101 | | | Coscarart | 30 | Elliott | 16 | | | |
| | | | | Dahlgren | 28 | Russell | 14 | | | |
| | | | | Elliott | 28 | | | | | |
| | | | | Barrett | 24 | | | | | |
| | | | | V. DiMaggio | 20 | | | | | |
| Elliott | 101 | Fletcher | 91 | V. DiMaggio | 41 | Elliott | 12 | V. DiMaggio | 15 | 43 |
| | | | | Elliott | 30 | Russell | 11 | | | |
| | | | | Fletcher | 24 | | | | | |
| | | | | Custine | 21 | | | | | |
| Elliott | 89 | Fletcher | 86 | Elliott | 26 | Elliott | 7 | V. DiMaggio | 15 | 42 |
| | | | | V. DiMaggio | 22 | | | | | |
| | | | | Fletcher | 22 | | | | | |

| RBIs | RUNS SCORED | DOUBLES | TRIPLES | HOMERUNS | YEAR |
|---|---|---|---|---|---|
| V. DiMaggio 100 | Fletcher 95 | Fletcher 29<br>V. DiMaggio 27<br>Gustine 24<br>Elliott 24<br>Van Robays 23<br>Vaughan 20 | Fletcher 13<br>Elliott 10 | V. DiMaggio 21 | 41 |
| Van Robays 116<br>Fletcher 104 | Vaughan 113* | Vaughan 40<br>Elliott 34<br>Gustine 32<br>Van Robays 27<br>V. DiMaggio 26<br>Garms 23<br>Fletcher 22 | Vaughan 15<br>Elliott 11 | V. DiMaggio 19 | 40 |
| Fletcher 71 | Vaughan 97 | Vaughan 30<br>P. Waner 30<br>Fletcher 23<br>Rizzo 23<br>Brubaker 23 | Vaughan 11 | Fletcher 12 | 39 |
| Rizzo 111 | Rizzo 97 | Young 36<br>Suhr 35<br>Vaughan 35<br>P. Waner 31<br>Rizzo 31<br>L. Waner 25<br>Handley 25 | Suhr 14 | Rizzo 23 | 38 |
| Suhr 97 | P. Waner 94 | P. Waner 30<br>Suhr 28<br>L. Waner 23<br>W. Jensen 23<br>Handley 21<br>Brubaker 20<br>Young 20 | Vaughan 17*<br>Suhr 14 | Young 9 | 37 |
| Suhr 118<br>Brubaker 102 | Vaughan 122*<br>Suhr 111<br>P. Waner 104 | P. Waner 53<br>W. Jensen 34<br>Suhr 33<br>Vaughan 30<br>Brubaker 27<br>Young 23 | Suhr 12<br>Vaughan 11<br>Young 10<br>W. Jensen 10 | Suhr 11 | 36 |
| Vaughan 99 | Vaughan 108 | Vaughan 34<br>Suhr 33<br>P. Waner 29<br>W. Jensen 28<br>Young 25<br>L. Waner 22 | L. Waner 14<br>P. Waner 12<br>Suhr 12<br>Young 10<br>Vaughan 10 | Vaughan 19 | 35 |
| Suhr 103 | P. Waner 122*<br>Vaughan 115 | Vaughan 41<br>Suhr 36<br>P. Waner 32<br>L. Waner 27<br>Lindstrom 24<br>Traynor 22 | P. Waner 16<br>Suhr 13<br>Vaughan 11<br>Traynor 10 | P. Waner 14 | 34 |
| Vaughan 97 | P. Waner 101 | Lindstrom 39<br>P. Waner 38 | Vaughan 19*<br>P. Waner 16 | Suhr 10 | 33 |

| RBIs | | RUNS SCORED | | DOUBLES | | TRIPLES | | HOMERUNS | | YEAR |
|---|---|---|---|---|---|---|---|---|---|---|
| | | | | Suhr | 31 | Suhr | 11 | | | |
| | | | | Vaughan | 29 | Lindstrom | 10 | | | |
| | | | | Traynor | 27 | | | | | |
| | | | | Piet | 21 | | | | | |
| Piet | 85 | P. Waner | 107 | P. Waner | 62 | Suhr | 16 | P. Waner | 8 | 32 |
| | | | | Suhr | 31 | L. Waner | 11 | Grace | 8 | |
| | | | | L. Waner | 27 | P. Waner | 10 | | | |
| | | | | Traynor | 27 | Traynor | 10 | | | |
| | | | | Piet | 25 | Vaughan | 10 | | | |
| | | | | Barbee | 22 | | | | | |
| P. Traynor | 103 | Grantham | 91 | Traynor | 37 | Traynor | 15 | | | 31 |
| | | | | P. Waner | 35 | L. Waner | 13 | | | |
| | | | | Grantham | 26 | P. Waner | 10 | Grantham | 10 | |
| Comorosky | 119 | Grantham | 120 | Comorosky | 47 | Comorosky | 23* | Grantham | 18 | 30 |
| Traynor | 119 | P. Waner | 117 | Grantham | 34 | P. Waner | 18 | | | |
| Suhr | 107 | Comorosky | 112 | Bartell | 32 | Suhr | 14 | | | |
| | | | | P. Waner | 32 | Grantham | 14 | | | |
| | | | | Suhr | 26 | Bartell | 13 | | | |
| | | | | Traynor | 22 | Traynor | 11 | | | |
| Traynor | 108 | L. Waner | 134 | P. Waner | 43 | L. Waner | 20* | P. Waner | 15 | 29 |
| P. Waner | 101 | P. Waner | 131 | Bartell | 40 | P. Waner | 15 | | | |
| | | Bartell | 101 | L. Waner | 28 | Bartell | 13 | | | |
| | | | | Traynor | 27 | Traynor | 12 | | | |
| | | | | Comorosky | 26 | Comorosky | 11 | | | |
| | | | | Grantham | 23 | Grantham | 10 | | | |
| | | | | Sheely | 22 | | | | | |
| Traynor | 124 | P. Waner | 142* | P. Waner | 50* | P. Waner | 19 | Grantham | 10 | 28 |
| | | L. Waner | 121 | Traynor | 38 | L. Waner | 14 | | | |
| | | | | L. Waner | 22 | Traynor | 12 | | | |
| | | | | Grantham | 24 | | | | | |
| | | | | Wright | 20 | | | | | |
| P. Waner | 131* | L. Waner | 133* | P. Waner | 40 | P. Waner | 17* | P. Waner | 9 | 27 |
| Traynor | 106 | P. Waner | 113 | Grantham | 33 | Grantham | 11 | Wright | 9 | |
| Wright | 105 | | | Traynor | 32 | | | | | |
| | | | | Harris | 27 | | | | | |
| | | | | Wright | 26 | | | | | |
| | | | | Barnhart | 25 | | | | | |
| Cuyler | 92 | Cuyler | 113* | P. Waner | 35 | P. Waner | 22* | Cuyler | 8 | 26 |
| | | P. Waner | 101 | Cuyler | 31 | Traynor | 17 | Grantham | 8 | |
| | | | | Grantham | 27 | Cuyler | 15 | P. Waner | 8 | |
| | | | | Traynor | 25 | Wright | 15 | Wright | 8 | |
| | | | | | | Grantham | 13 | | | |
| Wright | 121 | Cuyler | 144* | Cuyler | 43 | Cuyler | 26* | Cuyler | 18 | 25 |
| Barnhart | 114 | Traynor | 114 | Traynor | 39 | Traynor | 14 | Wright | 18 | |
| Traynor | 106 | Carey | 109 | Carey | 39 | Carey | 13 | | | |
| Cuyler | 102 | Moore | 106 | Barnhart | 32 | Barnhart | 11 | | | |
| | | | | Wright | 32 | Wright | 10 | | | |
| | | | | Moore | 29 | | | | | |
| | | | | Grantham | 24 | | | | | |
| | | | | Smith | 22 | | | | | |
| Wright | 111 | Carey | 113 | Maranville | 33 | Maranville | 20 | Cuyler | 9 | 24 |
| | | | | Carey | 30 | Wright | 18 | | | |
| | | | | Wright | 28 | Cuyler | 16 | | | |

| RBIs | | RUNS SCORED | | DOUBLES | | TRIPLES | | HOMERUNS | | YEAR |
|---|---|---|---|---|---|---|---|---|---|---|
| | | | | Cuyler | 27 | Traynor | 13 | | | |
| | | | | Traynor | 26 | Grimm | 12 | | | |
| | | | | Grimm | 25 | Barnhart | 11 | | | |
| Traynor | 101 | Carey | 120 | Carey | 32 | Traynor | 19* | Traynor | 12 | 23 |
| | | Traynor | 108 | Grimm | 29 | Carey | 19* | | | |
| | | | | Barnhart | 25 | Grimm | 13 | | | |
| | | | | | | Barnhart | 13 | | | |
| Bigbee | 99 | Carey | 140 | Bigbee | 29 | Bigbee | 15 | Russell | 12 | 22 |
| | | Maranville | 115 | Carey | 28 | Maranville | 15 | | | |
| | | Bigbee | 113 | Grimm | 28 | Tierney | 14 | | | |
| | | | | Tierney | 26 | Grimm | 13 | | | |
| | | | | Maranville | 26 | Traynor | 12 | | | |
| | | | | | | Carey | 12 | | | |
| Grimm | 71 | Bigbee | 100 | Carey | 34 | Bigbee | 17 | | | 21 |
| | | | | Maranville | 25 | Grimm | 17 | Grimm | 7 | |
| | | | | Bigbee | 23 | Barnhart | 13 | Carey | 7 | |
| | | | | Whitted | 23 | Maranville | 12 | Whitted | 7 | |
| | | | | Tierney | 22 | | | | | |
| | | | | Grimm | 21 | | | | | |
| Whitted | 74 | Bigbee | 78 | Bigbee | 19 | Bigbee | 15 | Bigbee | 4 | 20 |
| | | | | | | Southworth | 13 | Nicholson | 4 | |
| | | | | | | Whitted | 12 | | | |
| Cutshaw | 51 | Bigbee | 61 | Cutshaw | 15 | Southworth | 14* | Stengel | 4 | 19 |
| | | | | | | Stengel | 10 | Southworth | 4 | |
| Cutshaw | 68 | Carey | 70 | Cutshaw | 16 | Cutshaw | 10 | Cutshaw | 5 | 18 |
| Carey | 51 | Carey | 82 | Carey | 21 | Carey | 12 | Fischer | 3 | 17 |
| Hinchman | 76 | Carey | 90 | Carey | 23 | Hinchman | 16* | Carey | 7 | 16 |
| | | | | | | Carey | 11 | | | |
| | | | | | | Johnston | 10 | | | |
| Wagner | 78 | Carey | 76 | Hinchman | 33 | Wagner | 17 | Wagner | 6 | 15 |
| | | | | Wagner | 32 | Hinchman | 14 | | | |
| | | | | Carey | 26 | Johnston | 12 | | | |
| | | | | Baird | 26 | Baird | 12 | | | |
| Voix | 57 | Carey | 76 | Carey | 25 | Carey | 17 | Konetchy | 4 | 14 |
| | | | | Konetchy | 23 | | | | | |
| Miller | 90 | Carey | 99* | Viox | 32 | Miller | 20 | Byrne | 10 | 13 |
| | | | | Miller | 24 | Wilson | 14 | | | |
| | | | | Carey | 23 | Carey | 10 | | | |
| | | | | Byrne | 22 | | | | | |
| Wagner | 102* | Carey | 114 | Wagner | 35 | Wilson | 36* | Wilson | 11 | 12 |
| | | | | Miller | 33 | Wagner | 20 | | | |
| | | | | Byrne | 31 | Miller | 12 | | | |
| | | | | Carey | 23 | Byrne | 11 | | | |
| Wilson | 107* | Byrne | 96 | Wilson | 34 | Byrne | 17 | Wilson | 12 | 11 |
| | | | | Clarke | 25 | Wagner | 16 | | | |

| RBIs | | RUNS SCORED | | DOUBLES | | TRIPLES | | HOMERUNS | | YEAR |
|---|---|---|---|---|---|---|---|---|---|---|
| | | | | Byrne | 24 | Clarke | 13 | | | |
| | | | | Wagner | 23 | Wilson | 12 | | | |
| | | | | | | Carey | 10 | | | |
| Wagner | 81 | Byrne | 101 | Byrne | 43* | Wilson | 13 | Flynn | 6 | 10 |
| | | | | Wagner | 34 | Byrne | 12 | | | |
| | | | | Leach | 24 | Miller | 10 | | | |
| | | | | Clarke | 23 | | | | | |
| | | | | Gibson | 22 | | | | | |
| Wagner | 100* | Leach | 126* | Wagner | 39* | Miller | 13 | Leach | 6 | 09 |
| | | | | Miller | 31 | Wilson | 12 | | | |
| | | | | Leach | 29 | Clarke | 11 | | | |
| | | | | Gibson | 25 | Wagner | 10 | | | |
| | | | | Wilson | 22 | Abstein | 10 | | | |
| | | | | Abstein | 20 | | | | | |
| Wagner | 109* | Wagner | 100 | Wagner | 39* | Wagner | 19* | Wagner | 10 | 08 |
| | | | | Leach | 24 | Leach | 16 | | | |
| | | | | | | Clarke | 15 | | | |
| | | | | | | Thomas | 10 | | | |
| Abbaticchio | 82 | Leach | 102 | Wagner | 38* | Wagner | 14 | Wagner | 6 | 07 |
| Wagner | 82 | | | | | Clarke | 13 | | | |
| | | | | | | Leach | 12 | | | |
| Nealon | 83* | Wagner | 103* | Wagner | 38* | Clarke | 13* | Nealon | 3 | 06 |
| | | | | Nealon | 21 | Nealon | 12 | | | |
| | | | | Ritchey | 21 | | | | | |
| Wagner | 101 | Wagner | 114 | Wagner | 32 | Clarke | 15 | Wagner | 6 | 05 |
| | | | | Ritchey | 29 | Wagner | 14 | | | |
| | | | | | | Leach | 14 | | | |
| Wagner | 75 | Beaumont | 97 | Wagner | 44* | Wagner | 14 | Wagner | 4 | 04 |
| | | Wagner | 97 | Ritchey | 22 | Beaumont | 12 | | | |
| | | | | | | Leach | 12 | | | |
| | | | | | | Ritchey | 12 | | | |
| | | | | | | Clarke | 11 | | | |
| Wagner | 101 | Beaumont | 137* | Clarke | 32* | Wagner | 19* | | | 03 |
| | | | | Wagner | 30 | Leach | 17 | Beaumont | 7 | |
| | | | | Beaumont | 30 | Clarke | 15 | Leach | 7 | |
| | | | | Ritchey | 28 | Sebring | 13 | | | |
| | | | | Bransfield | 23 | Ritchey | 10 | | | |
| Wagner | 91* | Clarke | 104 | Wagner | 33* | Leach | 20 | Leach | 6* | 02 |
| | | Beaumont | 101 | Clarke | 27 | Wagner | 16 | | | |
| | | | | Bransfield | 21 | Clarke | 14 | | | |
| | | | | Beaumont | 21 | | | | | |
| | | | | Leach | 21 | | | | | |
| Wagner | 126* | Clarke | 118 | Wagner | 39* | Bransfield | 17 | Beaumont | 8 | 01 |
| | | Beaumont | 118 | Clarke | 26 | Clarke | 14 | | | |
| | | | | Bransfield | 26 | Leach | 13 | | | |
| | | | | Ritchey | 20 | Davis | 11 | | | |
| | | | | | | Wagner | 10 | | | |
| Wagner | 100 | Wagner | 107 | Wagner | 45* | Wagner | 22* | Williams | 5 | 00 |
| | | Beaumont | 105 | T. O'Brien | 22 | Clarke | 12 | | | |

| RBIs | | RUNS SCORED | | DOUBLES | | TRIPLES | | HOMERUNS | | YEAR |
|---|---|---|---|---|---|---|---|---|---|---|
| | | | | | | Williams | 11 | | | |
| | | | | | | Zimmer | 10 | | | |
| Williams | 116 | Williams | 126 | Williams | 28 | Williams | 27* | Williams | 9 | 99 |
| | | McCarthy | 108 | McCarthy | 22 | McCarthy | 17 | | | |
| | | | | McCreery | 21 | Bowerman | 10 | | | |
| | | | | | | Clarke | 10 | | | |
| McCarthy | 78 | Donovan | 112 | Donovan | 16 | McCarthy | 12 | McCarthy | 4 | 98 |
| Ely | 74 | E. Smith | 99. | Ely | 20 | H. Davis | 28* | E. Smith | 6 | 97 |
| | | | | | | E. Smith | 17 | | | |
| | | | | | | Padden | 10 | | | |
| E. Smith | 94 | E. Smith | 121 | Stenzel | 26 | E. Smith | 14 | E. Smith | 6 | 96 |
| | | Donovan | 113 | Lyons | 25 | Stenzel | 14 | | | |
| | | Stenzel | 104 | E. Smith | 22 | | | | | |
| | | | | Donovan | 20 | | | | | |
| Beckley | 110 | Donovan | 114 | Stenzel | 38 | Beckley | 20 | Stenzel | 7 | 95 |
| | | Stenzel | 114 | Beckley | 30 | Cross | 13 | | | |
| | | E. Smith | 109 | | | E. Smith | 13 | | | |
| | | Beckley | 104 | | | Stenzel | 13 | | | |
| | | | | | | Bierbauer | 11 | | | |
| Stenzel | 121 | Stenzel | 148 | Stenzel | 39 | Stenzel | 20 | Stenzel | 13 | 94 |
| Beckley | 120 | Donovan | 145 | Beckley | 36 | E. Smith | 19 | | | |
| | | E. Smith | 128 | E. Smith | 33 | Beckley | 17 | | | |
| | | Beckley | 121 | Donovan | 21 | Bierbauer | 13 | | | |
| Beckley | 106 | Van Haltren | 129 | Beckley | 32 | E. Smith | 23 | E. Smith | 7 | 93 |
| Lyons | 105 | E. Smith | 121 | E. Smith | 26 | Beckley | 19 | | | |
| E. Smith | 103 | Donovan | 114 | | | Lyons | 16 | | | |
| | | Beckley | 108 | | | Bierbauer | 11 | | | |
| | | Lyons | 103 | | | Van Haltren | 11 | | | |
| Beckley | 96 | G. Miller | 103 | Beckley | 21 | Beckley | 19 | Beckley | 10 | 92 |
| | | Beckley | 102 | Bierbauer | 20 | E. Smith | 14 | | | |
| | | | | | | Shugart | 14 | | | |
| | | | | | | Farrell | 13 | | | |
| | | | | | | G. Miller | 12 | | | |
| Beckley | 73 | Beckley | 94 | Beckley | 20 | Beckley | 20 | Beckley | 4 | 91 |
| | | | | | | | | F. Carroll | 4 | |
| G. Miller | 66 | G. Miller | 85 | G. Miller | 24 | Hecker | 9 | Decker | 5 | 90 |
| | | | | LaRoque | 20 | | | | | |
| Beckley | 97 | Beckley | 91 | G. Miller | 25 | F. Carroll | 11 | Beckley | 9 | 89 |
| | | | | Beckley | 24 | Beckley | 10 | | | |
| | | | | Fields | 22 | Hanlon | 10 | | | |
| | | | | Kuehne | 20 | | | | | |
| Kuehne | 62 | Sunday | 69 | Kuehne | 22 | Kuehne | 11 | C. Smith | 4 | 88 |
| F. Carroll | 54 | J. Coleman | 75 | F. Carroll | 24 | F. Carroll | 15 | F. Carroll | 6 | 87 |
| J. Coleman | 54 | | | J. Coleman | 21 | Kuehne | 15 | | | |
| C. Smith | 54 | | | | | J. Coleman | 11 | | | |

## Seasonal Leaders—Offensive

| Batting Average (plus all .300 hitters with 350 at bats) | | Strikeouts (plus all players with 75 or more) | | Bases-on-Balls (plus all players with 50 or more) | | Hits (plus all players with 175 or more) | | Stolen bases (plus all players with 20 or more) | | Year |
|---|---|---|---|---|---|---|---|---|---|---|
| Parker | .310 | Stargell | 105 | Parker | 67 | Moreno | 196 | Moreno | 77 | 79 |
| | | Moreno | 104 | Garner | 55 | Parker | 193 | Madlock | 21 | |
| | | Parker | 101 | Milner | 51 | | | Parker | 20 | |
| | | | | Moreno | 51 | | | | | |
| Parker | .334 | B. Robinson | 105 | Moreno | 81 | Parker | 194 | Moreno | 71 | 78 |
| | | Moreno | 104 | Garner | 66 | Taveras | 182 | Taveras | 46 | |
| | | Stargell | 93 | Parker | 57 | | | Garner | 27 | |
| | | Parker | 92 | Stargell | 50 | | | Parker | 20 | |
| Parker | .338 | Parker | 107 | Parker | 58 | Parker | 215 | Taveras | 70 | 77 |
| Stennett | .326 | Moreno | 102 | Garner | 55 | Oliver | 175 | Moreno | 53 | |
| Oliver | .308 | B. Robinson | 92 | Dyer | 54 | | | Garner | 32 | |
| B. Robinson | .304 | | | | | | | Stennett | 28 | |
| Oliver | .323 | Stargell | 101 | Zisk | 52 | Parker | 168 | Taveras | 58 | 76 |
| Parker | .313 | Zisk | 96 | Stargell | 50 | Stennett | 168 | | | |
| | | Parker | 80 | | | Zisk | 168 | | | |
| | | Taveras | 79 | | | | | | | |
| Sanguillen | .328 | Stargell | 109 | Zisk | 68 | Oliver | 176 | Taveras | 17 | 75 |
| Parker | .308 | Zisk | 109 | Stargell | 58 | | | | | |
| | | Parker | 89 | | | | | | | |
| Oliver | .321 | Stargell | 106 | Stargell | 87 | Oliver | 198 | Clines | 14 | 74 |
| Zisk | .313 | Zisk | 91 | Zisk | 65 | Stennett | 196 | | | |
| Stargell | .301 | | | Hebner | 60 | | | | | |
| | | | | Kirkpatrick | 51 | | | | | |
| Stargell | .299 | Stargell | 129 | Stargell | 80 | Oliver | 191 | Clines | 8 | 73 |
| | | Robertson | 77 | Hebner | 56 | | | | | |
| | | | | Robertson | 55 | | | | | |
| Davalillo | .318 | Stargell | 129 | Stargell | 65 | Oliver | 176 | Davalillo | 14 | 72 |
| Clemente | .312 | Robertson | 84 | Hebner | 52 | | | | | |
| Oliver | .312 | | | | | | | | | |
| Hebner | .300 | | | | | | | | | |
| Clemente | .341 | Stargell | 154* | Stargell | 83 | Clemente | 178 | Clines | 15 | 71 |
| Sanguillen | .319 | Robertson | 101 | | | | | | | |
| Clemente | .352 | Stargell | 119 | Robertson | 51 | M. Alou | 201 | M. Alou | 19 | 70 |
| Sanguillen | .325 | Robertson | 98 | | | | | | | |
| Clemente | .345 | Stargell | 120 | Stargell | 61 | M. Alou | 231* | M. Alou | 22 | 69 |
| M. Alou | .331 | Patek | 86 | Clemente | 56 | Clemente | 175 | | | |
| Stargell | .307 | | | Hebner | 53 | | | | | |
| Sanguillen | .303 | | | Patek | 53 | | | | | |
| Hebner | .301 | | | | | | | | | |

| Batting Average | | Strikeouts | | Bases-on-Balls | | Hits | | Stolen bases | | Year |
|---|---|---|---|---|---|---|---|---|---|---|
| M. Alou | .332 | Clendenon | 163* | Clemente | 51 | M. Alou | 185 | Wills | 52 | 68 |
| | | Stargell | 105 | | | | | | | |
| | | Alley | 78 | | | | | | | |
| | | Clemente | 77 | | | | | | | |
| Clemente | .357* | Clendenon | 107 | Stargell | 67 | Clemente | 209* | Wills | 29 | 67 |
| M. Alou | .338 | Clemente | 103 | | | M. Alou | 186 | | | |
| Wills | .302 | Stargell | 103 | | | Wills | 186 | | | |
| M. Alou | .342* | Clendenon | 142 | Clendenon | 52 | Clemente | 202 | M. Alou | 23 | 66 |
| Clemente | .317 | Clemente | 109 | Pagliaroni | 50 | M. Alou | 183 | | | |
| Stargell | .315 | Stargell | 109 | | | | | | | |
| Clemente | .329* | Clendenon | 128 | Bailey | 70 | Clemente | 194 | Bailey | 10 | 65 |
| | | Stargell | 127 | | | Clendenon | 184 | | | |
| | | Bailey | 93 | | | | | | | |
| | | Pagliaroni | 84 | | | | | | | |
| | | Alley | 82 | | | | | | | |
| | | Clemente | 78 | | | | | | | |
| Clemente | .339* | Clendenon | 96 | Schofield | 54 | Clemente | 211* | Clendenon | 12 | 64 |
| | | Stargell | 92 | Clemente | 51 | | | | | |
| | | Clemente | 87 | | | | | | | |
| | | Bailey | 78 | | | | | | | |
| Clemente | .320 | Clendenon | 136* | Schofield | 69 | Clemente | 192 | Clendenon | 22 | 63 |
| | | Bailey | 98 | Bailey | 58 | | | | | |
| | | Stargell | 85 | | | | | | | |
| | | Schofield | 83 | | | | | | | |
| Burgess | .328 | Stuart | 94 | Skinner | 76 | Groat | 199 | Clendenon | 16 | 62 |
| Clemente | .312 | Skinner | 89 | | | | | | | |
| Skinner | .302 | | | | | | | | | |
| Clemente | .351* | Stuart | 121* | Hoak | 73 | Clemente | 201 | Christopher | 6 | 61 |
| Stuart | .301 | | | Skinner | 51 | | | | | |
| Groat | .325* | Stuart | 107 | Hoak | 74 | Groat | 186 | Skinner | 11 | 60 |
| Clemente | .314 | | | Skinner | 59 | Clemente | 179 | | | |
| Stuart | .297 | Stuart | 86 | Hoak | 71 | Hoak | 166 | Skinner | 10 | 59 |
| Burgess | .297 | Hoak | 75 | Skinner | 67 | | | | | |
| | | | | Virdon | 55 | | | | | |
| Skinner | .321 | Thomas | 79 | Skinner | 58 | Groat | 175 | Skinner | 12 | 58 |
| Groat | .300 | Stuart | 75 | Virdon | 52 | | | | | |
| Groat | .315 | Virdon | 69 | Thomas | 44 | Thomas | 172 | Fondy | 11 | 57 |
| Skinner | .305 | | | | | | | | | |
| Virdon | .334 | Long | 85 | Long | 54 | Virdon | 170 | Clemente | 6 | 56 |
| Clemente | .311 | Walls | 83 | Walls | 50 | Clemente | 169 | Virdon | 6 | |
| Long | .291 | Thomas | 76 | Thomas | 60 | Groat | 139 | Freese | 5 | 55 |

## Seasonal Leaders—Offensive (continued)

| Batting Average | | Strikeouts | | Bases-on-Balls | | Hits | | Stolen bases | | Year |
|---|---|---|---|---|---|---|---|---|---|---|
| Gordon | .306 | Allie | 84 | Gordon<br>Allie<br>Roberts<br>Thomas | 67<br>56<br>55<br>51 | Thomas | 172 | Roberts | 6 | 54 |
| O'Connell | .294 | Thomas | 93 | Abrams<br>O'Connell<br>Bernier<br>Thomas | 58<br>57<br>51<br>50 | O'Connell | 173 | Bernier | 15 | 53 |
| Groat | .284 | Kiner | 77 | Kiner | 110* | Kiner | 126 | Del Greco | 6 | 52 |
| Kiner | .309 | Strickland | 83 | Kiner | 137* | Bell | 164 | Reiser<br>Strickland<br>Garagiola | 4<br>4<br>4 | 51 |
| Murtaugh | .294 | Kiner<br>Westlake | 79<br>78 | Kiner | 122 | Kiner | 149 | Hopp<br>O'Connell | 7<br>7 | 50 |
| Kiner<br>Hopp | .310<br>.318 | Westlake | 69 | Kiner<br>Rojek | 117*<br>50 | Kiner | 170 | Hopp | 9 | 49 |
| D. Walker | 3.16 | Gustine | 62 | Kiner<br>Rojek<br>Murtaugh<br>Walker | 112<br>61<br>60<br>52 | Rojek | 186 | Rojek | 24 | 48 |
| Kiner | .313 | Kiner | 81 | Greenberg<br>Kiner<br>Russell<br>Gustine | 104<br>98<br>63<br>63 | Gustine<br>Kiner | 183<br>177 | Cox<br>Gustine<br>Westlake | 5<br>5<br>5 | 47 |
| Cox | .290 | Kiner | 109* | Fletcher<br>Kiner<br>Russell<br>Elliott | 111<br>74<br>67<br>64 | Russell | 143 | Russell | 11 | 46 |
| Elliott | .290 | Barrett | 68 | Barrett<br>Russell<br>Elliott<br>Gionfriddo<br>Coscarart<br>Dahlgren<br>Salkeld | 79<br>71<br>64<br>60<br>55<br>51<br>50 | Elliott | 157 | Barrett | 25 | 45 |
| Russell | .312 | V. DiMaggio | 83* | Barrett<br>Russell<br>Elliott | 86<br>79<br>75 | Russell | 181 | Barrett | 28* | 44 |
| Elliott | .315 | V. DiMaggio | 126* | Fletcher<br>Russell<br>V. DiMaggio<br>Elliott | 95<br>77<br>70<br>56 | Elliott | 183 | Gustine<br>Russell | 12<br>12 | 43 |
| Elliott | .296 | V. DiMaggio | 87* | Fletcher | 105 | Elliott | 166 | Barrett | 10 | 42 |

## Seasonal Leaders—Offensive (continued)

| Batting Average | | Strikeouts | | Bases-on-Balls | | Hits | | Stolen bases | | Year |
|---|---|---|---|---|---|---|---|---|---|---|
| | | | | Elliott | 52 | | | V. DiMaggio | 10 | |
| | | | | V. DiMaggio | 52 | | | | | |
| Vaughan | .316 | V. DiMaggio | 100 | Fletcher | 118* | Fletcher | 150 | Elliott | 13 | 41 |
| | | | | Vaughan | 88 | | | | | |
| Garms | .355* | V. DiMaggio | 83 | Fletcher | 119* | Vaughan | 178 | Elliott | 13 | 40 |
| Vaughan | .300 | | | Vaughan | 88 | | | | | |
| P. Waner | .328 | Brubaker | 51 | Vaughan | 70 | Vaughan | 182 | Handley | 17* | 39 |
| Vaughan | .306 | | | | | | | | | |
| Fletcher | .303 | | | | | | | | | |
| Vaughan | .322 | Young | 64 | Vaughan | 104 | L. Waner | 194 | Vaughan | 14 | 38 |
| L. Waner | .313 | | | Suhr | 87 | P. Waner | 175 | | | |
| Rizzo | .301 | | | Rizzo | 54 | | | | | |
| | | | | Handley | 53 | | | | | |
| P. Waner | .354 | Young | 63 | Suhr | 83 | P. Waner | 219 | Vaughan | 7 | 37 |
| L. Waner | .330 | | | P. Waner | 63 | L. Waner | 177 | | | |
| Vaughan | .322 | | | Vaughan | 54 | | | | | |
| Todd | .307 | | | | | | | | | |
| P. Waner | .373* | Brubaker | 96* | Vaughan | 118* | P. Waner | 218 | Suhr | 8 | 36 |
| Vaughan | .335 | | | Suhr | 95 | Jensen | 197 | | | |
| L. Waner | .321 | | | P. Waner | 74 | Vaughan | 190 | | | |
| Suhr | .312 | | | Brubaker | 50 | Suhr | 182 | | | |
| Vaughan | .385* | Young | 59 | Vaughan | 97* | Jensen | 203 | Jensen | 9 | 35 |
| Jensen | .324 | | | Suhr | 70 | Vaughan | 192 | | | |
| P. Waner | .321 | | | P. Waner | 61 | P. Waner | 176 | | | |
| L. Waner | .309 | | | | | | | | | |
| P. Waner | .362* | Berger | 65 | Vaughan | 94* | P. Waner | 217* | Vaughan | 10 | 34 |
| Vaughan | .333 | | | P. Waner | 68 | Vaughan | 186 | | | |
| Traynor | .309 | | | Suhr | 66 | | | | | |
| Piet | .323 | Suhr | 52 | Suhr | 72 | P. Waner | 191 | Piet | 12 | 33 |
| Vaughan | .314 | | | Vaughan | 64 | Traynor | 190 | | | |
| Lindstrom | .310 | | | P. Waner | 60 | Vaughan | 180 | | | |
| P. Waner | .309 | | | | | | | | | |
| Traynor | .304 | | | | | | | | | |
| P. Waner | .341 | Piet | 56 | Suhr | 63 | P. Waner | 215 | Piet | 19 | 32 |
| L. Waner | .333 | | | P. Waner | 56 | L. Waner | 188 | | | |
| Traynor | .329 | | | | | | | | | |
| Vaughan | .318 | | | | | | | | | |
| P. Waner | .322 | Grantham | 50 | P. Waner | 73 | L. Waner | 214 | Comorosky | 11 | 31 |
| L. Waner | .314 | | | Grantham | 71 | Traynor | 183 | | | |
| Grantham | .305 | | | Traynor | 54 | P. Waner | 180 | | | |
| P. Waner | .368 | Grantham | 66 | Grantham | 81 | P. Waner | 217 | P. Waner | 18 | 30 |
| Traynor | .366 | | | Suhr | 80 | Comorosky | 187 | | | |
| Grantham | .342 | | | P. Waner | 57 | Traynor | 182 | | | |
| Bartell | .320 | | | Comorosky | 51 | Grantham | 179 | | | |
| Comorosky | .313 | | | | | | | | | |

| Batting Average | | Strikeouts | | Bases-on-Balls | | Hits | | Stolen bases | | Year |
|---|---|---|---|---|---|---|---|---|---|---|
| Traynor | .356 | Grantham | 38 | Grantham | 93 | L. Waner | 234 | Comorosky | 19 | 29 |
| L. Waner | .353 | | | P. Waner | 89 | P. Waner | 200 | | | |
| P. Waner | .336 | | | Sheely | 75 | Traynor | 192 | | | |
| Comorosky | .321 | | | | | Bartell | 184 | | | |
| Bartell | .302 | | | | | | | | | |
| P. Waner | .370 | Wright | 53 | P. Waner | 77 | P. Waner | 223 | Traynor | 12 | 28 |
| Traynor | .337 | | | Adams | 64 | L. Waner | 221 | | | |
| L. Waner | .335 | | | Grantham | 59 | Traynor | 192 | | | |
| Grantham | .323 | | | | | | | | | |
| Wright | .310 | | | | | | | | | |
| P. Waner | .380* | Wright | 46 | Grantham | 74 | P. Waner | 237 | Cuyler | 20 | 27 |
| L. Waner | .355 | | | P. Waner | 60 | L. Waner | 223 | | | |
| Traynor | .342 | | | | | Traynor | 196 | | | |
| Harris | .326 | | | | | | | | | |
| Barnhart | .310 | | | | | | | | | |
| Grantham | .305 | | | | | | | | | |
| P. Waner | .336 | Cuyler | 66 | P. Waner | 66 | Cuyler | 197 | Cuyler | 35* | 26 |
| Cuyler | .321 | | | Grantham | 60 | Traynor | 182 | | | |
| Grantham | .318 | | | Cuyler | 50 | P. Waner | 180 | | | |
| Traynor | .317 | | | | | | | | | |
| Wright | .308 | | | | | | | | | |
| Cuyler | .357 | Cuyler | 56 | Moore | 73 | Cuyler | 220 | Carey | 49* | 25 |
| Carey | .343 | | | Carey | 66 | Traynor | 189 | Cuyler | 41 | |
| Grantham | .326 | | | Barnhart | 59 | Wright | 189 | | | |
| Barnhart | .325 | | | Cuyler | 58 | Carey | 186 | | | |
| Traynor | .320 | | | Traynor | 52 | Barnhart | 175 | | | |
| Wright | .308 | | | Grantham | 50 | | | | | |
| Cuyler | .354 | Cuyler | 62 | Carey | 58 | Carey | 178 | Carey | 49* | 24 |
| | | | | | | Wright | 177 | Cuyler | 32 | |
| | | | | | | | | Traynor | 24 | |
| Grimm | .345 | Grimm | 43 | Carey | 73 | Traynor | 208 | Carey | 51* | 23 |
| Traynor | .338 | | | | | Grimm | 194 | Traynor | 28 | |
| Barnhart | .324 | | | | | Carey | 188 | | | |
| Carey | .308 | | | | | | | | | |
| Bigbee | .350 | Maranville | 43 | Carey | 80* | Bigbee | 215 | Carey | 51* | 22 |
| Tierney | .345 | | | Maranville | 61 | Carey | 207 | Bigbee | 24 | |
| Carey | .329 | | | Bigbee | 56 | Maranville | 198 | Maranville | 24 | |
| Gooch | .329 | | | | | | | | | |
| Cutshaw | .340 | Maranville | 58 | Carey | 70 | Bigbee | 204 | Carey | 37 | 21 |
| Bigbee | .323 | Grimm | 38 | | | Maranville | 180 | Maranville | 24 | |
| Carey | .309 | | | | | | | Bigbee | 21 | |
| Carey | .289 | Grimm | 40 | Carey | 59 | Southworth | 155 | Carey | 52* | 20 |
| | | | | Southworth | 52 | | | | | |
| Southworth | .280 | Stengel | 35 | Bigbee | 37 | Bigbee | 132 | Cutshaw | 36 | 19 |
| | | | | | | | | Bigbee | 31 | |
| | | | | | | | | Southworth | 23 | |

## Seasonal Leaders—Offensive (continued)

| Batting Average | | Strikeouts | | Bases-on-Balls | | Hits | | Stolen bases | | Year |
|---|---|---|---|---|---|---|---|---|---|---|
| Cutshaw | .285 | Carey | 25 | Carey | 62* | Cutshaw | 132 | Carey | 58* | 18 |
| Carey | .296 | King | 58 | Carey | 58 | Carey | 174 | Carey | 46* | 17 |
| Hinchman | .315 | Hinchman | 61 | Carey | 59 | Hinchman | 175 | Carey | 63* | 16 |
| | | | | Hinchman | 54 | | | Baird | 20 | |
| Hinchman | .307 | Baird | 88* | Voix | 63 | Hinchman | 177 | Carey | 36* | 15 |
| | | Hinchman | 75 | Carey | 57 | | | Baird | 29 | |
| | | | | | | | | Johnson | 26 | |
| | | | | | | | | Wagner | 22 | |
| Voix | .265 | Kelly | 59 | Voix | 63 | Carey | 144 | Carey | 38 | 14 |
| | | | | Carey | 59 | | | Wagner | 23 | |
| | | | | Wagner | 51 | | | Kelly | 21 | |
| | | | | | | | | Konetchy | 20 | |
| Voix | .317 | Carey | 67 | Voix | 64 | Carey | 172 | Carey | 61* | 13 |
| Wagner | .300 | | | Carey | 55 | | | Wagner | 21 | |
| | | | | | | | | Miller | 20 | |
| Wagner | .324 | Carey | 79 | Carey | 61 | Wagner | 181 | Carey | 45 | 12 |
| Carey | .302 | | | Wagner | 59 | Carey | 177 | Wagner | 26 | |
| Wilson | .300 | | | Byrne | 54 | Wilson | 175 | Byrne | 20 | |
| Wagner | .334* | Carey | 75 | Byrne | 67 | Wilson | 163 | Carey | 27 | 11 |
| Clarke | .324 | | | Wagner | 67 | | | Byrne | 23 | |
| Wilson | .300 | | | Clarke | 53 | | | Wagner | 20 | |
| | | | | Miller | 51 | | | | | |
| Wagner | .320 | Wilson | 68 | Byrne | 66 | Wagner | 178* | Byrne | 36 | 10 |
| | | | | Wagner | 59 | Byrne | 178* | Wagner | 24 | |
| | | | | Clarke | 53 | | | | | |
| Wagner | .339* | | | Clarke | 80* | Wagner | 168 | Wagner | 35 | 09 |
| | | | | Leach | 66 | | | Clarke | 31 | |
| | | | | Wagner | 66 | | | Leach | 27 | |
| Wagner | .354* | | | Clarke | 65 | Wagner | 201* | Wagner | 53* | 08 |
| | | | | Abbaticchio | 58 | | | Leach | 24 | |
| | | | | Wagner | 54 | | | Clarke | 24 | |
| | | | | Leach | 54 | | | Abbaticchio | 22 | |
| Wagner | .350 | | | Anderson | 80 | Wagner | 180 | Wagner | 61* | 07 |
| Leach | .303 | | | Clarke | 68 | | | Leach | 43 | |
| | | | | Abbaticchio | 65 | | | Clarke | 37 | |
| | | | | | | | | Abbaticchio | 35 | |
| | | | | | | | | Anderson | 27 | |
| Wagner | .339 | | | Ritchey | 68 | Wagner | 175 | Wagner | 53 | 06 |
| Clarke | .309 | | | Wagner | 58 | | | Leach | 21 | |
| | | | | Nealon | 53 | | | | | |
| Wagner | .363 | | | Clarke | 55 | Wagner | 199 | Wagner | 57 | 05 |
| Beaumont | .328 | | | Wagner | 54 | | | Clark | 24 | |
| | | | | Ritchey | 51 | | | Clymer | 23 | |
| | | | | | | | | Beaumont | 21 | |

207

## Seasonal Leaders—Offensive (continued)

| Batting Average | | Strikeouts | | Bases-on-Balls | | Hits | | Stolen bases | | Year |
|---|---|---|---|---|---|---|---|---|---|---|
| Wagner | .349* | | | Ritchey | 59 | Beaumont | 185* | Wagner | 53* | 04 |
| Beaumont | .301 | | | Wagner | 59 | | | Beaumont | 28 | |
| | | | | | | | | Leach | 23 | |
| Wagner | .355* | | | Ritchey | 55 | Beaumont | 209* | Wagner | 46 | 03 |
| Clarke | .351 | | | | | Wagner | 182 | Beaumont | 23 | |
| Beaumont | .341 | | | | | | | Leach | 22 | |
| | | | | | | | | Clarke | 21 | |
| | | | | | | | | Sebring | 20 | |
| Beaumont | .357* | | | Ritchey | 53 | Beaumont | 194* | Wagner | 43* | 02 |
| Wagner | .329 | Clarke | 51 | Wagner | 177 | Clarke | 34 | | | |
| Clarke | .321 | | | | | | | Beaumont | 33 | |
| Bransfield | .308 | | | | | | | Leach | 29 | |
| | | | | | | | | Bransfield | 24 | |
| Wagner | .350 | | | Davis | 56 | Wagner | 196 | Wagner | 48* | 01 |
| Beaumont | .328 | | | Clarke | 51 | Beaumont | 182 | Beaumont | 32 | |
| Clarke | .316 | | | | | | | Bransfield | 28 | |
| | | | | | | | | Clarke | 22 | |
| | | | | | | | | Davis | 22 | |
| Wagner | .381* | | | Clarke | 51 | Wagner | 201 | Wagner | 38 | 00 |
| | | | | | | | | Beaumont | 27 | |
| | | | | | | | | Clarke | 21 | |
| Williams | .355 | | | Williams | 60 | Williams | 219 | Beaumont | 31 | 99 |
| Beaumont | .352 | | | | | | | McCarthy | 28 | |
| McCreery | .323 | | | | | | | Donovan | 26 | |
| McCarthy | .305 | | | | | | | Williams | 26 | |
| Donovan | .302 | | | Padden | 35 | Donovan | 184 | Donovan | 41 | 98 |
| Donovan | .322 | | | E. Smith | 70 | Donovan | 154 | Donovan | 34 | 97 |
| E. Smith | .310 | | | | | | | E. Smith | 25 | |
| Davis | .305 | | | | | | | | | |
| E. Smith | .362 | | | E. Smith | 74 | Donovan | 183 | Stenzel | 57 | 96 |
| Stenzel | .361 | | | Lyons | 67 | E. Smith | 175 | Donovan | 48 | |
| Donovan | .319 | | | | | | | E. Smith | 33 | |
| Lyons | .307 | | | | | | | | | |
| Stenzel | .374 | | | Stenzel | 57 | Stenzel | 192 | Stenzel | 53 | 95 |
| Beckley | .328 | | | E. Smith | 55 | | | Cross | 39 | |
| | | | | | | | | Donovan | 36 | |
| | | | | | | | | E. Smith | 35 | |
| | | | | | | | | Beckley | 20 | |
| E. Smith | .356 | | | Stenzel | 75 | Stenzel | 185 | Stenzel | 61 | 94 |
| Stenzel | .354 | | | E. Smith | 65 | Beckley | 183 | Donovan | 41 | |
| Beckley | .343 | | | | | | | E. Smith | 33 | |
| Donovan | .302 | | | | | | | Beckley | 21 | |
| E. Smith | .346 | | | Lyons | 97 | E. Smith | 179 | Donovan | 46 | 93 |
| Van Haltren | .338 | | | E. Smith | 77 | Van Haltren | 179 | Van Haltren | 37 | |

## Seasonal Leaders—Offensive (continued)

| Batting Average | Strikeouts | Bases-on-Balls | Hits | Stolen bases | Year |
|---|---|---|---|---|---|
| Donovan .317 | | Van Haltren 75 | | E. Smith 26 | |
| Lyons .306 | | Beckley 54 | | | |
| Beckley .303 | | | | | |
| E. Smith .274 | | E. Smith 82 | G. Miller 158 | G. Miller 28 | 92 |
| | | G. Miller 69 | | Shugart 28 | |
| | | | | Farrell 20 | |
| Beckley .292 | | G. Miller 59 | Beckley 162 | Hanlon 54 | 91 |
| | | | | G. Miller 35 | |
| | | | | F. Carroll 22 | |
| | | | | Shugart 21 | |
| | | | | Reilly 20 | |
| G. Miller .273 | | G. Miller 68 | G. Miller 150 | G. Miller 32 | 90 |
| | | | | LaRoque 27 | |
| Beckley .301 | | F. Carroll 85 | Beckley 157 | Hanlon 53 | 89 |
| | | Hanlon 58 | | Sunday 47 | |
| | | | | Dunlap 21 | |
| G. Miller .277 | | F. Carroll 32 | Kuehne 123 | Sunday 71 | 88 |
| | | | | C. Smith 37 | |
| | | | | Kuehne 34 | |
| | | | | G. Miller 27 | |
| | | | | Dunlap 24 | |
| | | | | Beckley 20 | |
| F. Carroll .328 | | Whitney 55 | J. Coleman 139 | G. Miller 33 | 87 |
| | | | | C. Smith 30 | |
| | | | | Dalrymple 29 | |
| | | | | J. Coleman 25 | |
| | | | | F. Carroll 23 | |

## Seasonal Leaders—Pitching

| WINS (plus all 20 game winners) | | STRIKEOUTS | | APPEARANCES (plus all pitchers with 40 or more) | | INN. PITCHED (plus all pitchers with 250 or more) | | YEAR |
|---|---|---|---|---|---|---|---|---|
| Candelaria | 14-9 | Blyleven | 172 | Tekulve | 94* | | | 79 |
| | | | | Romo | 84 | Blyleven | 237 | |
| | | | | Jackson | 72 | | | |
| D. Robinson | 14-6 | Blyleven | 182 | Tekulve | 91* | Blyleven | 244 | 78 |
| Blyleven | 14-10 | | | Jackson | 60 | | | |
| | | | | Whitson | 43 | | | |
| Candelaria | 20-5 | Gossage | 151 | Tekulve | 72 | Candelaria | 231 | 77 |
| | | | | Gossage | 72 | | | |
| | | | | Jackson | 49 | | | |
| Candelaria | 16-7 | Candelaria | 138 | Tekulve | 64 | Candelaria | 220 | 76 |

## Seasonal Leaders—Pitching (continued)

| WINS | | STRIKEOUTS | | APPEARANCES | | INN. PITCHED | | YEAR |
|---|---|---|---|---|---|---|---|---|
| | | | | Moose | 53 | | | |
| | | | | Giusti | 40 | | | |
| Reuss | 18-11 | Reuss | 131 | Giusti | 61 | Reuss | 237 | 75 |
| | | | | Hernandez | 46 | | | |
| | | | | Demery | 45 | | | |
| Reuss | 16-11 | Rooker | 139 | Giusti | 64 | Rooker | 263 | 74 |
| | | | | Hernandez | 58 | Reuss | 260 | |
| | | | | Kison | 40 | | | |
| Briles | 14-13 | Ellis | 122 | Giusti | 67 | Briles | 219 | 73 |
| | | Rooker | 122 | Hernandez | 59 | | | |
| | | | | Johnson | 50 | | | |
| | | | | Rooker | 41 | | | |
| Blass | 19-8 | Moose | 144 | Giusti | 54 | Blass | 250 | 72 |
| | | | | Hernandez | 53 | | | |
| Ellis | 19-9 | Ellis | 137 | Giusti | 58 | Blass | 240 | 71 |
| | | | | Grant | 42 | | | |
| Walker | 15-6 | Veale | 178 | Giusti | 66 | Ellis | 202 | 70 |
| | | | | Walker | 42 | Veale | 202 | |
| | | | | Dal Canton | 41 | | | |
| | | | | Gibbon | 41 | | | |
| Blass | 16-10 | Veale | 213 | Dal Canton | 57 | Veale | 226 | 69 |
| | | | | Hartenstein | 56 | | | |
| | | | | Moose | 44 | | | |
| Blass | 18-6 | Veale | 171 | Kline | 56 | Veale | 245 | 68 |
| | | | | Face | 43 | | | |
| Veale | 16-8 | Veale | 179 | Face | 61 | Sisk | 208 | 67 |
| | | | | McBean | 51 | | | |
| | | | | Pizzaro | 50 | | | |
| Veale | 16-12 | Veale | 229 | Mikkelsen | 71 | Veale | 268 | 66 |
| | | | | Face | 54 | | | |
| | | | | McBean | 47 | | | |
| Law | 17-9 | Veale | 276 | McBean | 62 | Veale | 266 | 65 |
| Veale | 17-12 | | | Schwall | 43 | | | |
| Veale | 18-12 | Veale | 250* | McBean | 58 | Veale | 280 | 64 |
| | | | | Face | 55 | | | |
| | | | | Sisk | 42 | | | |
| | | | | Veale | 40 | | | |
| Friend | 17-16 | Friend | 144 | Sisk | 57 | Friend | 269 | 63 |
| | | | | Face | 56 | | | |
| | | | | McBean | 55 | | | |
| | | | | Haddix | 49 | | | |

## Seasonal Leaders—Pitching (continued)

| WINS | | STRIKEOUTS | | APPEARANCES | | INN. PITCHED | | YEAR |
|---|---|---|---|---|---|---|---|---|
| Friend | 18-14 | Friend | 144 | Face | 63 | Friend | 262 | 62 |
| | | | | Olivo | 62 | | | |
| | | | | Sturdivant | 49 | | | |
| | | | | Lamabe | 46 | | | |
| Friend | 14-19 | Gibbon | 145 | Face | 62 | Friend | 236 | 61 |
| | | | | Labine | 56 | | | |
| | | | | Shantz | 43 | | | |
| | | | | Friend | 41 | | | |
| Law  20-9 | | Friend | 183 | Face | 68* | Friend | 276 | 60 |
| | | | | Green | 45 | Law | 272 | |
| Face | 18-1 | Haddix | 149 | Face | 57 | Law | 266 | 59 |
| Law | 18-9 | | | | | | | |
| Friend | *22-14 | Friend | 135 | Face | 57 | Friend | 274 | 58 |
| | | | | Gross | 40 | | | |
| Friend | 14-18 | Friend | 143 | Face | 59 | Friend | 277* | 57 |
| | | | | Arroyo | 54 | | | |
| | | | | Purkey | 48 | | | |
| | | | | Friend | 40 | | | |
| | | | | Kline | 40 | | | |
| Friend | 17-17 | Friend | 166 | Face | 68* | Friend | 314* | 56 |
| | | | | Friend | 49 | Kline | 264 | |
| | | | | Kline | 44 | | | |
| Friend | 14-9 | Friend | 98 | Friend | 44 | Law | 201 | 55 |
| | | | | Law | 43 | | | |
| | | | | Face | 42 | | | |
| Littlefield | 10-11 | Littlefield | 92 | Hetki | 58 | Surkont | 208 | 54 |
| Dickson | 10-19 | Lindell | 102 | Hetki | 54 | Dickson | 201 | 53 |
| | | | | Dickson | 45 | | | |
| | | | | Face | 41 | | | |
| Dickson | 14-21 | Dickson | 112 | Main | 48 | Dickson | 278 | 52 |
| | | | | Wilks | 44 | | | |
| | | | | Dickson | 43 | | | |
| Dickson | 20-16 | Queen | 123 | Werle | 59 | Dickson | 289 | 51 |
| | | | | Wilks | 48 | | | |
| | | | | Dickson | 45 | | | |
| Chambers | 12-15 | Chambers | 93 | Dickson | 51 | Chambers | 249 | 50 |
| | | | | Werle | 48 | | | |
| Chambers | 13-7 | Werle | 106 | Dickson | 44 | Dickson | 224 | 49 |
| Chesnes | 14-6 | Higbe | 86 | Higbe | 56 | Chesnes | 194 | 48 |

## Seasonal Leaders—Pitching (continued)

| WINS | | STRIKEOUTS | | APPEARANCES | | INN. PITCHED | | YEAR |
|---|---|---|---|---|---|---|---|---|
| Ostermuller | 12-10 | Higbe | 46 | Higbe | 99 | Higbe | 225 | 47 |
| Ostermuller | 13-10 | Hallett | 64 | Hallett | 35 | Ostermuller | 193 | 46 |
| | | | | Gerheauser | 35 | | | |
| Strincevich | 16-10 | Roe | 148* | Rescigno | 44 | Roe | 235 | 45 |
| Sewell | 21-12 | Roe | 88 | Rescigno | 48 | Sewell | 286 | 44 |
| | | | | Strincevich | 40 | | | |
| Sewell | 21-9 | Sewell | 65 | Gornicki | 42 | Sewell | 265 | 43 |
| | | Klinger | 65 | | | | | |
| Sewell | 17-15 | Sewell | 69 | Sewell | 48 | Sewell | 248 | 42 |
| | | | | Dietz | 40 | | | |
| Butcher | 17-12 | Heintzelman | 81 | Sewell | 39 | Sewell | 249 | 41 |
| Sewell | 16-5 | Brown | 73 | Brown | 48 | Sewell | 190 | 40 |
| | | | | Lanahan | 45 | | | |
| Klinger | 14-17 | Brown | 71 | Sewell | 52 | Klinger | 225 | 39 |
| | | | | Brown | 47 | | | |
| Brown | 15-9 | Bauers | 117 | Brown | 51* | Bauers | 243 | 38 |
| | | | | Tobin | 40 | | | |
| | | | | Bauers | 40 | | | |
| Blanton | 14-12 | Blanton | 143 | Brown | 50 | Blanton | 243 | 37 |
| Swift | 16-16 | Blanton | 127 | Brown | 47 | Swift | 262 | 36 |
| | | | | Swift | 45 | | | |
| | | | | Blanton | 44 | | | |
| Blanton | 18-13 | Blanton | 142 | Bush | 41 | Blanton | 254 | 35 |
| Hoyt | 15-6 | Hoyt | 105 | French | 49 | French | 264 | 34 |
| | | | | Hoyt | 48 | | | |
| | | | | Birkofer | 41 | | | |
| French | 18-13 | French | 88 | French | 47 | French | 291 | 33 |
| French | 18-16 | French | 72 | French | 47* | French | 274 | 32 |
| Meine | *19-13 | French | 73 | French | 39 | Meine | 284* | 31 |
| | | | | | | French | 276 | |
| Kremer | *20-12 | French | 90 | French | 42 | Kremer | 276* | 30 |
| | | | | Spencer | 41 | French | 275 | |

212

| WINS | | STRIKEOUTS | | APPEARANCES | | INN. PITCHED | | YEAR |
|---|---|---|---|---|---|---|---|---|
| Kremer | 18-10 | Brame | 68 | Swetonic | 41 | Grimes | 233 | 29 |
| Grimes | *25-14 | Grimes | 97 | Grimes | 48* | Grimes | 331 | 28 |
| Hill | 22-11 | Hill | 95 | Hill<br>Meadows | 43<br>40 | Meadows<br>Hill | 299<br>278 | 27 |
| Kremer<br>Meadows | *20-6<br>*20-9 | Kremer | 74 | Kremer<br>Yde | 37<br>37 | Kremer | 231 | 26 |
| Meadows | 19-10 | Aldridge | 88 | Morrison<br>Kremer | 44*<br>40 | Meadows | 255 | 25 |
| Cooper | 20-14 | Morrison | 85 | Morrison<br>Kremer | 41*<br>41* | Cooper<br>Kremer | 269<br>259 | 24 |
| Morrison | 25-13 | Morrison | 114 | Morrison | 42 | Morrison<br>Cooper | 302<br>295 | 23 |
| Cooper | 23-14 | Cooper | 129 | Morrison<br>Cooper | 45<br>41 | Cooper<br>Morrison | 295<br>286 | 22 |
| Cooper | *22-14 | Cooper | 134 | Cooper | 38 | Cooper | 327* | 21 |
| Cooper | 24-15 | Cooper | 114 | Cooper | 44 | Cooper<br>Adams | 327<br>263 | 20 |
| Cooper | 19-13 | Cooper | 106 | Cooper | 35 | Cooper<br>Adams | 287<br>263 | 19 |
| Cooper | 19-14 | Cooper | 117 | Cooper | 38 | Cooper | 273 | 18 |
| Cooper | 17-11 | Cooper | 99 | Cooper | 40 | Cooper | 298 | 17 |
| Mamaux | 21-15 | Mamaux | 163 | Mamaux<br>Cooper | 45<br>42 | Mamaux | 310 | 16 |
| Mamaux | 21-8 | Mamaux | 152 | Adams | 40 | Harmon<br>Mamaux | 270<br>252 | 15 |
| Cooper | 16-15 | Cooper | 102 | McQuillan<br>Cooper<br>Adams | 45<br>40<br>40 | Adams<br>Cooper<br>McQuillan | 283<br>267<br>259 | 14 |
| Adams | 21-10 | Adams | 144 | Adams<br>Robinson<br>Hendrix | 43<br>43<br>42 | Adams | 314 | 13 |
| Hendrix | 24-9 | Hendrix | 176 | Camnitz | 41 | Hendrix | 289 | 12 |

## Seasonal Leaders—Pitching (continued)

| WINS | | STRIKEOUTS | | APPEARANCES | | INN. PITCHED | | YEAR |
|---|---|---|---|---|---|---|---|---|
| Camnitz | 22-12 | | | | | Camnitz | 277 | |
| | | | | | | O'Toole | 275 | |
| Adams | 22-12 | Camnitz | 139 | Leifield | 42 | Leifield | 318 | 11 |
| Camnitz | 20-15 | | | Camnitz | 40 | Adams | 293 | |
| | | | | Adams | 40 | Camnitz | 268 | |
| Adams | 18-9 | Camnitz | 120 | Leifield | 40 | Camnitz | 260 | 10 |
| Camnitz | 25-6 | Camnitz | 133 | Camnitz | 41 | Willis | 290 | 09 |
| Willis | 22-11 | | | | | Camnitz | 283 | |
| Maddox | 23-8 | Camnitz | 118 | Willis | 41 | Willis | 305 | 08 |
| Willis | 23-11 | | | | | Maddox | 261 | |
| Willis | 22-11 | Leifield | 112 | Leifield | 40 | Willis | 293 | 07 |
| Leifield | 20-16 | | | | | Leifield | 286 | |
| Willis | 22-13 | Willis | 124 | Willis | 41 | Willis | 322 | 06 |
| Leever | 22-7 | | | | | Leever | 260 | |
| | | | | | | Leifield | 256 | |
| Phillippe | 22-13 | Phillippe | 133 | Phillippe | 38 | Phillippe | 279 | 05 |
| Flaherty | 19-9 | Lynch | 95 | Leever | 34 | Leever | 253 | 04 |
| Leever | 25-7 | Phillippe | 123 | Leever | 36 | Phillippe | 289 | 03 |
| Phillippe | 24-9 | | | Phillippe | 36 | Leever | 284 | |
| Chesbro | *28-6 | Chesbro | 136 | Chesbro | 35 | Chesbro | 286 | 02 |
| Tannehill | 20-6 | | | | | Phillippe | 272 | |
| Phillippe | 20-9 | | | | | | | |
| Phillippe | 22-12 | Chesbro | 129 | Phillippe | 37 | Phillippe | 296 | 01 |
| Chesbro | 21-10 | | | | | Chesbro | 288 | |
| | | | | | | Tannehill | 252 | |
| Tannehill | 20-6 | Waddell | 130* | Tannehill | 43 | Tannehill | 247 | 00 |
| Tannehill | 24-14 | Leever | 121 | Tannehill | 41 | Tannehill | 333 | 99 |
| Leever | 20-23 | | | | | | | |
| Tannehill | 25-13 | Tannehill | 93 | Tannehill | 43 | Tannehill | 327 | 98 |
| | | | | | | Rhines | 258 | |
| Hawley | 18-18 | Killen | 99 | Killen | 42 | Killen | 337 | 97 |
| | | | | Hawley | 40 | Hawley | 311 | |
| Killen | *30-18 | Hawley | 137 | Killen | 52* | Killen | 432 | 96 |
| Hawley | 22-21 | | | Hawley | 49 | Hawley | 378 | |

## Seasonal Leaders—Pitching (continued)

| WINS | | STRIKEOUTS | | APPEARANCES | | INN. PITCHED | | YEAR |
|------|------|------|------|------|------|------|------|------|
| Hawley | 31-22 | Hawley | 142 | Hawley | 56* | Hawley | 444 | 95 |
| Gumbert | 15-14 | Gumbert | 65 | Gumbert | 37 | Gumbert | 269 | 94 |
| Killen | *35-14 | Killen | 99 | Killen | 55 | Killen | 415 | 93 |
| Baldwin | 26-27 | Baldwin | 157 | Baldwin | 56 | Baldwin | 440 | 92 |
| Baldwin | 22-28 | Baldwin | 197 | Baldwin | 53 | Baldwin | 438 | 91 |
| Hecker | 18-8 | Baker | .76 | Baker | 25 | Baker | 178 | 90 |
| Staley | 21-26 | Staley | 159 | Staley | 49 | Staley | 420 | 89 |
| Morris | 29-24 | Morris | 135 | Morris | 55* | Morris | 480 | 88 |
| Morris | 14-22 | Morris | 91 | Morris | 38 | Morris | 318 | 87 |

## Seasonal Leaders—Pitching

### ERA Leaders (since 1912)

| Year | Player | ERA | | Year | Player | ERA |
|------|--------|------|---|------|--------|------|
| 1979 | Kison | 3.14 | | 1955 | Friend | 2.84 |
| 1978 | Blyleven | 3.02 | | 1954 | Littlefield | 3.60 |
| 1977 | Candelaria | 2.34* | | 1953 | Dickson | 4.52 |
| 1976 | Kison | 3.08 | | 1952 | Dickson | 3.56 |
| 1975 | Reuss | 2.54 | | 1951 | Dickson | 4.02 |
| 1974 | Rooker | 2.77 | | 1950 | Chambers | 4.30 |
| 1973 | Briles | 2.84 | | 1949 | Dickson | 3.29 |
| 1972 | Blass | 2.84 | | 1948 | Riddle | 3.49 |
| 1971 | Blass | 2.85 | | 1947 | Higbe | 3.72 |
| 1970 | Walker | 3.04 | | 1946 | Ostermuller | 2.84 |
| 1969 | Moose | 2.91 | | 1945 | Roe | 2.87 |
| 1968 | Veale | 2.06 | | 1944 | Ostermuller | 2.72 |
| 1967 | Sisk | 3.33 | | 1943 | Sewell | 2.48 |
| 1966 | Veale | 3.02 | | 1942 | Sewell | 3.41 |
| 1965 | Law | 2.16 | | 1941 | Butcher | 3.05 |
| 1964 | Veale | 2.73 | | 1940 | Sewell | 2.79 |
| 1963 | Friend | 2.34 | | 1939 | Klinger | 4.36 |
| 1962 | Friend | 3.06 | | 1938 | Klinger | 3.00 |
| 1961 | Gibbon | 3.32 | | 1937 | Bauers | 2.87 |
| 1960 | Friend | 3.00 | | 1936 | Lucas | 3.17 |
| 1959 | Law | 2.98 | | 1935 | Blanton | 2.59 |
| 1958 | Kline | 3.53 | | 1934 | French | 3.58 |
| 1957 | Law | 2.86 | | 1933 | French | 2.72 |
| 1956 | Kline | 3.38 | | 1932 | Swetonic | 2.87 |

## Seasonal Leaders—Pitching (continued)

| | | | | | | |
|---|---|---|---|---|---|---|
| 1931 | Meine | 2.98 | 1921 | Adams | 2.65 |
| 1930 | French | 4.35 | 1920 | Adams | 2.16 |
| 1929 | Grimes | 3.13 | 1919 | Adams | 1.98 |
| 1928 | Grimes | 2.99 | 1918 | Cooper | 2.11 |
| 1927 | Kremer | 2.47* | 1917 | Cooper | 2.36 |
| 1926 | Kremer | 2.61* | 1916 | Cooper | 1.87 |
| 1925 | Aldridge | 3.63 | 1915 | Mamaux | 2.03 |
| 1924 | Yde | 2.83 | 1914 | Cooper | 2.12 |
| 1923 | Meadows | 3.01 | 1913 | Adams | 2.15 |
| 1922 | Cooper | 3.18 | 1912 | Robinson | 2.26 |

## Seasonal Leaders—Pitching

### LEADING RELIEF PITCHERS SINCE 1960

| | | Wins | Saves | Total |
|---|---|---|---|---|
| 1979 | Tekulve | 10 | 31 | 41 |
| 1978 | Tekulve | 8 | 31 | 39 |
| 1977 | Gossage | 11 | 26 | 37 |
| 1976 | Tekulve | 9 | 5 | 14 |
| 1975 | Giusti | 5 | 17 | 22 |
| 1974 | Giusti | 6 | 12 | 18 |
| 1973 | Giusti | 9 | 20 | 29 |
| 1972 | Giusti | 7 | 15 | 22 |
| 1971 | Giusti | 5 | 30 | 35* |
| 1970 | Giusti | 9 | 26 | 35 |
| 1969 | Hartenstein | 10 | 5 | 15 |
| 1968 | Kline | 4 | 12 | 16 |
| 1967 | Face | 7 | 15 | 22 |
| 1966 | Face | 6 | 16 | 22 |
| 1965 | McBean | 5 | 18 | 23 |
| 1964 | McBean | 8 | 18 | 26* |
| 1963 | McBean | 11 | 9 | 20 |
| 1962 | Face | 8 | 23 | 31* |
| 1961 | Face | 6 | 13 | 19 |
| 1960 | Face | 10 | 15 | 25 |

## Manager's Records

### (Listed Alphabetically)

| MANAGER | YEARS | GAMES | WON | LOST | PCT |
|---|---|---|---|---|---|
| Hugo Bezdek | 1917-19 | 356 | 166 | 187 | .470 |
| Bobby Bragan | 1956-57 | 261 | 102 | 155 | .397 |
| Al Buckenberger | 1892-94 | 339 | 189 | 146 | .564 |
| Tom Burns | 1892 | 56 | 25 | 30 | .455 |
| Bill Burwell | 1947 | 1 | 1 | 0 | 1.000 |
| Donie Bush | 1927-29 | 427 | 246 | 178 | .580 |
| Nixey Callahan | 1916-17 | 218 | 85 | 129 | .397 |

## Manager's Records (continued)

| Manager | Years | Games | Won | Lost | Pct |
|---|---|---|---|---|---|
| Fred Clarke | 1900-15 | 2424 | 1422 | 969 | .595 |
| Spud Davis | 1946 | 3 | 1 | 2 | .333 |
| Patsy Donovan | 1897-98 | 264 | 128 | 128 | .500 |
| Fred Dunlap | 1889 | 16 | 7 | 9 | .438 |
| Jewel Ens | 1929-31 | 344 | 176 | 167 | .513 |
| Frankie Frisch | 1940-46 | 1085 | 539 | 528 | .505 |
| George Gibson | 1920-22, 32-34 | 669 | 401 | 330 | .549 |
| Alex Grammas | 1969 | 5 | 4 | 1 | .800 |
| Fred Haney | 1953-55 | 462 | 163 | 299 | .353 |
| Ned Hanlon | 1899, 91 | 125 | 57 | 66 | .463 |
| Guy Hecker | 1890 | 138 | 23 | 113 | .169 |
| Billy Herman | 1947 | 155 | 61 | 92 | .399 |
| Connie Mack | 1894-96 | 288 | 149 | 134 | .527 |
| Bill McGunnigle | 1891 | 59 | 24 | 33 | .421 |
| Bill McKechnie | 1922-26 | 707 | 409 | 293 | .583 |
| Billy Meyer | 1948-52 | 774 | 317 | 452 | .412 |
| Danny Murtaugh | 1957-64, 67, 70-71, 73-76 | 2068 | 1115 | 950 | .540 |
| Horace Phillips | 1887-89 | 334 | 149 | 180 | .453 |
| Larry Shepard | 1968-69 | 320 | 164 | 155 | .514 |
| Chuck Tanner | 1977- | 486 | 282 | 203 | .581 |
| Pie Traynor | 1934-39 | 867 | 457 | 406 | .530 |
| Bill Virdon | 1972-73 | 291 | 163 | 128 | .560 |
| Honus Wagner | 1917 | 5 | 1 | 4 | .200 |
| Harry Walker | 1965-67 | 409 | 224 | 184 | .549 |
| Bill Watkins | 1898-99 | 177 | 80 | 92 | .465 |

## Batting Records

### PIRATE INDIVIDUAL BATTING RECORDS

| | Season | | | Career | |
|---|---|---|---|---|---|
| Years, League | — | | 18 | H. Wagner, W. Stargell, R. Clemente | |
| Games | 163 | B. Mazeroski, 1967 | 2,433 | R. Clemente | |
| Games, Consec. | — | | 822 | G. Suhr | |
| At Bats | 698 | M. Alou, 1969 | 9,454 | R. Clemente | |
| Runs | 148 | J. Stenzel, 1894 | | | |
| | 144 | H. Cuyler, 1925 | 1,520 | H. Wagner | |
| Runs, Games | 6 | C. Beaumont, 7/22/99 | | | |
| Hits | 237 | P. Waner, 1927 | 3,000 | R. Clemente | |
| Hits, 9 inning game | 7 | R. Stennett, 9/6/75 | — | | |
| Hits, Consec. | — | | 10 | H. Cuyler, 1925 | |
| Singles | 198 | L. Waner, 1927 | 2,154 | R. Clemente | |
| Doubles | 62 | P. Waner, 1932 | 556 | H. Wagner, P. Waner | |
| Triples | 36 | O. Wilson, 1912 | 231 | H. Wagner | |
| Homeruns, RH | 54 | R. Kiner, 1949 | 301 | R. Kiner | |
| Homeruns, LH | 48 | W. Stargell, 1971 | 461 | W. Stargell | |

|  | | Season | | Career |
|---|---|---|---|---|
| Homeruns, Home | 31 | R. Kiner, 1948 | | |
| Homeruns, Road | 26 | F. Thomas, 1958 | | |
| Homeruns, Rookie | 23 | J. Rizzo, 1938;<br>R. Kiner, 1946 | | — |
| Homeruns, Consec.<br> Games | 8 | D. Long, 1956 | | — |
| Grandslams | 4 | R. Kiner, 1949 | 11 | R. Kiner,<br>W. Stargell |
| Homeruns, Pinch-hit | 3 | Hyatt, Skinner, Stuart,<br>Pagan | | — |
| Homeruns, Month | 16 | R. Kiner, Sept., 1949 | | — |
| Homeruns, Game | 3 | By several players | | — |
| RBI's | 131 | P. Waner, 1927 | 1,476 | W. Stargell |
| Consec. Games,<br> 1 or More RBI's | 10 | W. Stargell, 1971<br>R. Zisk, 1974 | | — |
| Total Bases | 366 | H. Cuyler, 1925 | 4,492 | R. Clemente |
| Long Hits | 90 | W. Stargell, 1973 | 920 | W. Stargell |
| Long Hits, Game | 5 | W. Stargell, 8/1/70 | | — |
| Extra Bases on<br> Long Hits | 191 | R. Kiner, 1949 | 1947 | W. Stargell |
| Sacrifice Hits | 35 | R. Ganley, 1906 | | — |
| Sacrifice Flies | 12 | F. Thomas, 1957 | | — |
| Stolen Bases | 77 | O. Moreno, 1979 | 678 | M. Carey |
| Caught Stealing | 25 | B. Southworth, 1920<br>F. Taveras, 1978 | | — |
| Bases on Balls | 137 | R. Kiner, 1951 | 909 | P. Waner |
| Strikeouts | 163 | D. Clendenon, 1968 | 1851 | W. Stargell |
| Strikeouts, Fewest | 10 | P. Traynor, 1928 | | — |
| Hit by Pitch | 14 | A. Oliver, 1970 | | — |
| GIDP | 25 | A. Todd, 1938 | | — |
| GIDP, Fewest | 4 | F. Taveras, 1978 | | — |
| Batting Average | .385 | A. Vaughan, 1935 | .340 | P. Waner |
| Slugging Pct., RH | .658 | R. Kiner, 1949 | .567 | R. Kiner |
| Slugging Pct., LH | .607 | A. Vaughan, 1935 | .532 | W. Stargell |
| Consec. Game Hitting<br> Streak, LH | 25 | C. Grimm, 1923 | | — |
| Consec. Game Hitting<br> Streak, RH | 26 | D. O'Connell, 1953 | | — |

## PIRATE CLUB BATTING RECORDS

|  | | Game | Season | |
|---|---|---|---|---|
| Games | | — | 163 | 1965, 1967,<br>1968, 1979 |
| At Bats | | — | 5,724 | 1967 |
| Runs | 27-11 | vs. Boston, 6/6/94 | 912 | 1925 |
|  | 24-6 | vs. St. Louis, 6/22/25 | | |
| Runs, Inning | 12 | vs. St. Louis, 4/22/92 | | |
|  | 12 | vs. Boston, 6/6/94 | | |
|  | 11 | vs. St. Louis, 9/7/42 | | |

|  | | Game | Season | |
|---|---|---|---|---|
| Hits | 27 | vs. Phila., 8/8/22 | 1,698 | 1922 |
| Singles | | | 1,297 | 1922 |
| Doubles | | | 316 | 1925 |
| Triples | 8 | vs. St. Louis, 5/30/25 | 129 | 1912 |
| Homeruns | 7 | vs. Boston, 6/8/94 | 158 | 1966 |
| | 7 | vs. St. Louis, 8/16/47 | | |
| Homeruns, Inning | 4 | 1894 | — | |
| Grandslams | 2 | vs. St. Louis, 6/22/25 | 7 | 1978 |
| | 2 | vs. Phila., 5/1/33 | | |
| Pinch-hit Homeruns | 1 | | 8 | 1944 |
| RBI's | 20 | vs. St. Louis, 6/22/25 | 844 | 1930 |
| Total Bases | 47 | vs. Atlanta, 8/1/70 | 2,430 | 1966 |
| Long Hits | 14 | vs. Atlanta, 8/1/70 | 498 | 1925 |
| Sacrifice Hits | | — | 190 | 1906 |
| Sacrifice Flies | | — | 58 | 1954 |
| Stolen Bases | | — | 264 | 1907 |
| Bases on Balls | | — | 607 | 1947 |
| Strikeouts | | — | 1,011 | 1966 |
| Strikeouts, Few | | — | 326 | 1922 |
| Hit by Pitch | 5 | vs. Cleve., 4/23/90 | 46 | 1917, 1969 |
| Batting Average | | — | .309 | 1928 |
| Slugging Pct. | | — | .449 | 1930 |
| Most .300 Hitters | | — | 9 | 1928 |
| Wins | — | | 110 | 1909 |
| Consec. Wins | | — | 16 | 1909 |
| Consec. Wins. Start of Season | | — | 10 | 1962 |
| Losses | | — | 113 | 1890; |
| | | | 112 | 1952 |
| Consec. Losses | | | 23 | 1890; |
| | | — | 12 | 1939 |
| Won/Lost Pct. | | — | .741 | 1902 |

## Pitching Records

### PIRATE INDIVIDUAL PITCHING RECORDS

| | | Season | | Career |
|---|---|---|---|---|
| Years, League | | — | 18 | C. Adams |
| Games, LH | 72 | G. Jackson, 1979 | 469 | W. Cooper |
| Games, RH | 94 | K. Tekulve, 1979 | 802 | E. Face |
| Games Started | 42 | B. Friend, 1956 | 477 | B. Friend |
| Complete Games | 32 | V. Willis, 1906 | 263 | W. Cooper |
| Games Finished | 67 | K. Tekulve, 1979 | 547 | E. Face |
| Shutouts | 8 | J. Chesbro, 1902; | 46 | C. Adams |
| | | A. Leifield, 1906; | | |
| | | A. Mamaux, 1915; | | |
| | | C. Adams, 1920 | | |
| Innings Pitched | 331 | B. Grimes, 1928 | 3,481 | B. Friend |
| Wins | 34 | F. Killen, 1893; | | |
| | 28 | J. Chesbro, 1902 | 202 | W. Cooper |

## Individual Pitching Records (continued)

|  | Season | | Career | |
|---|---|---|---|---|
| Wins in Succession, Starter | 13 | C. Phillippe, 1910; D. Ellis, 1971 | — | |
| Wins in Succession, Relief | 17 | E. Face, 1959 | — | |
| Years Winning 20 or More | — | | 4 | C. Phillippe, V. Willis, J. Tannehill, W. Cooper |
| Losses | 21 | M. Dickson, 1952 | 218 | B. Friend |
| Consec. Losses | 13 | B. Grimes, 1917 | — | |
| Won/Lost Pct. | 947 | E. Face, 1959 | .665 | S. Leever |
| Homeruns | 32 | M. Dickson, 1951 | — | |
| Saves | 31 | K. Tekulve, 1978, 1979 | — | |
| Bases on Balls | 159 | M. O'Toole, 1912 | 869 | B. Friend |
| Strikeouts | 276 | B. Veale, 1965 | 1,682 | B. Friend |
| Hit Batters | 21 | J. Chesbro, 1902 | — | |
| Wild Pitches | 18 | B. Veale, 1964 | — | |
| ERA | 187 | W. Cooper, 1916 | — | |

## PIRATE CLUB PITCHING RECORDS

|  | Game | | Season |
|---|---|---|---|
| Complete Games | — | | 133 | 1904 |
| Shutouts | — | | 26 | 1906 |
| Consec. Shutouts | — | | 6 | 1903 |
| Consec. Shutout Innings | — | | 56 | 1903 |
| Bases on Balls | — | | 244 | 1901 |
| Strikeouts | 16 | B. Veale vs. Phila., 6/1/65 | 1,124 | 1969 |
| Hit Batters | — | | 85 | 1895 |
| ERA, Lowest | — | | 2.07 | 1909 |
| 20-Game Winners | — | | 3 | 1902 |

## PIRATE CLUB FIELDING RECORDS

|  | Game | | Season |
|---|---|---|---|
| Assists | 28 | vs. N.Y., 6/7/11 | 2,089 | 1905 |
| Chances | 55 | vs. N.Y., 6/7/11 | 6,462 | 1968 |
| Errors | — | | 291 | 1904 |
| Errors, Fewest | — | | 132 | 1949 |
| Consec. Errorless Games | — | | 8 | 1958, 1963 |
| Double Plays | 6 | vs. St. Louis, 9/6/48 | 215 | 1966 |
| Highest Fielding Ave. | — | | .979 | 1968, 1970, 1971, 1979 |
| Putouts | | | 4,480 | 1979 |

Longest Game, Home      2i innings, lost 1-3 to NY 7/17/14
Longest Game, Road      22 innings, lost 5-6 to Bkl. 8/22/17

**Pirate Top 10 Records**

TOP 10 BATTING

GAMES
| | |
|---|---|
| Roberto Clemente | 2,433 |
| Honus Wagner | 2,432 |
| Willie Stargell | 2,181 |
| Max Carey | 2,171 |
| Bill Mazeroski | 2,163 |
| Paul Waner | 2,154 |
| Pie Traynor | 1,941 |
| Lloyd Waner | 1,803 |
| Tommy Leach | 1,548 |
| Fred Clarke | 1,442 |

AT-BATS
| | |
|---|---|
| Roberto Clemente | 9,454 |
| Honus Wagner | 9,046 |
| Paul Waner | 8,429 |
| Max Carey | 8,406 |
| Bill Mazeroski | 7,755 |
| Willie Stargell | 7,592 |
| Pie Traynor | 7,559 |
| Lloyd Waner | 7,256 |
| Tommy Leach | 5,909 |
| Fred Clarke | 5,471 |

RUNS
| | |
|---|---|
| Honus Wagner | 1,520 |
| Paul Waner | 1,492 |
| Roberto Clemente | 1,416 |
| Max Carey | 1,414 |
| Pie Traynor | 1,183 |
| Willie Stargell | 1,159 |
| Lloyd Waner | 1,151 |
| Fred Clarke | 1,017 |
| Tommy Leach | 1,007 |
| Arky Vaughan | 936 |

HITS
| | |
|---|---|
| Roberto Clemente | 3,000 |
| Honus Wagner | 2,970 |
| Paul Waner | 2,868 |
| Max Carey | 2,416 |
| Pie Traynor | 2,416 |
| Lloyd Waner | 2,317 |
| Willie Stargell | 2,145 |
| Bill Mazeroski | 2,016 |

| | |
|---|---|
| Arky Vaughan | 1,709 |
| Fred Clarke | 1,638 |

SINGLES
| | |
|---|---|
| Roberto Clemente | 2,154 |
| Honus Wagner | 2,101 |
| Paul Waner | 2,018 |
| Lloyd Waner | 1,906 |
| Max Carey | 1,827 |
| Pie Traynor | 1,823 |
| Bill Mazeroski | 1,522 |
| Tommy Leach | 1,229 |
| Willie Stargell | 1,225 |
| Arky Vaughan | 1,218 |

DOUBLES
| | |
|---|---|
| Honus Wagner | 556 |
| Paul Waner | 556 |
| Roberto Clemente | 440 |
| Willie Stargell | 405 |
| Max Carey | 375 |
| Pie Traynor | 371 |
| Bill Mazeroski | 294 |
| Arky Vaughan | 291 |
| Al Oliver | 276 |
| Gus Suhr | 276 |

TRIPLES
| | |
|---|---|
| Honus Wagner | 231 |
| Paul Waner | 186 |
| Roberto Clemente | 166 |
| Pie Traynor | 164 |
| Fred Clarke | 155 |
| Max Carey | 148 |
| Tommy Leach | 137 |
| Arky Vaughan | 116 |
| Jacob P. Beckley | 114 |
| Lloyd Waner | 114 |

HOMERUNS
| | |
|---|---|
| Willie Stargell | 461 |
| Ralph Kiner | 301 |
| Roberto Clemente | 240 |
| Frank Thomas | 163 |
| Bill Mazeroski | 138 |

## Top 10 Batting Records (continued)

### HOME RUNS

| | |
|---|---|
| Al Oliver | 135 |
| Dave Parker | 122 |
| Richie Hebner | 121 |
| Dick Stuart | 117 |
| Paul Waner | 108 |

### TOTAL BASES

| | |
|---|---|
| Roberto Clemente | 4,492 |
| Honus Wagner | 4,234 |
| Paul Waner | 4,120 |
| Willie Stargell | 4,041 |
| Pie Traynor | 3,289 |
| Max Carey | 3,285 |
| Lloyd Waner | 2,898 |
| Bill Mazeroski | 2,848 |
| Arky Vaughan | 2,484 |
| Fred Clarke | 2,286 |

### RUNS BATTED IN

| | |
|---|---|
| Willie Stargell | 1476 |
| Honus Wagner | 1,475 |
| Roberto Clemente | 1,305 |
| Pie Traynor | 1,273 |
| Paul Waner | 1,177 |
| Bill Mazeroski | 853 |
| Ralph Kiner | 801 |
| Gus Suhr | 789 |
| Arky Vaughan | 764 |
| Al Oliver | 717 |

### EXTRA-BASE HITS

| | |
|---|---|
| Willie Stargell | 920 |
| Honus Wagner | 869 |
| Paul Waner | 850 |
| Roberto Clemente | 846 |
| Pie Traynor | 593 |
| Max Carey | 589 |
| Bill Mazeroski | 494 |
| Arky Vaughan | 491 |
| Ralph Kiner | 486 |
| Al Oliver | 467 |
| Gus Suhr | 467 |

### BATTING AVERAGE

| | |
|---|---|
| Paul Waner | .340 |
| Kiki Cuyler | .336 |
| E. E. (Mike) Smith | .328 |
| Honus Wagner | .328 |
| Matty Alou | .327 |
| Arky Vaughan | .324 |
| Clarence Beaumont | .321 |
| Pie Traynor | .320 |
| Lloyd Waner | .319 |
| Roberto Clemente | .317 |
| Dave Parker | .317 |

### STOLEN BASES

| | |
|---|---|
| Max Carey | 678 |
| Honus Wagner | 639 |
| Fred Clarke | 261 |
| Tommy Leach | 249 |
| Omar Moreno | 217 |
| Frank Taverus | 206 |
| Carson Bigbee | 182 |
| Ginger Beaumont | 169 |
| Pie Traynor | 158 |
| Kiki Cuyler | 130 |

## TOP 10 PITCHING

### STRIKEOUTS—Pitcher

| | |
|---|---|
| Bob Friend | 1,682 |
| Bob Veale | 1,652 |
| Wilbur Cooper | 1,191 |
| Vernon Law | 1,092 |
| Babe Adams | 1,036 |
| Steve Blass | 896 |
| Dock Ellis | 868 |
| Deacon Phillippe | 853 |
| Sam Leever | 845 |
| Roy Face | 842 |

### INNINGS PITCHED

| | |
|---|---|
| Bob Friend | 3,481 |
| Wilbur Cooper | 3,201 |
| Babe Adams | 2,991 |
| Vernon Law | 2,673 |
| Sam Leever | 2,645 |
| Deacon Phillippe | 2,283 |
| Rip Sewell | 2,108 |
| Ray Kremer | 1,955 |
| Bob Veale | 1,869 |
| Howie Camnitz | 1,754 |

WINS

| | |
|---|---|
| Wilbur Cooper | 202 |
| Sam Leever | 194 |
| Babe Adams | 194 |
| Bob Friend | 191 |
| Deacon Phillippe | 165 |
| Vernon Law | 162 |
| Rip Sewell | 143 |
| Ray Kremer | 143 |
| Bob Veale | 116 |
| Howie Camnitz | 115 |

GAMES—Pitcher

| | |
|---|---|
| Elroy Face | 802 |
| Bob Friend | 568 |
| Vernon Law | 483 |
| Babe Adams | 483 |
| Wilbur Cooper | 469 |
| Dave Giusti | 410 |
| Sam Leever | 388 |
| Rip Sewell | 385 |
| Kent Tekulve | 363 |
| Bob Veale | 340 |

## Pirate Hall of Famers

| Player | Yr. Inducted | Pos. | Lifetime Bat. Ave. | Years with Pitt. as Player |
|---|---|---|---|---|
| Honus Wagner | 1936 | SS | .328 | 1900-1917 |
| Fred Clarke | 1945 | OF | .315 | 1900-1915 |
| Pie Traynor | 1948 | 3B | .320 | 1920-1937 |
| Paul Waner | 1952 | OF | .333 | 1926-1940 |
| Max Carey | 1961 | OF | .285 | 1910-1926 |
| Bill McKechnie | 1962 | Pirate Manager | | 1922-1926 |
| Lloyd Waner | 1967 | OF | .316 | 1927-1941 |
| Branch Rickey | 1967 | Pirate General Mgr. | | 1951-1955 |
| "Kiki" Cuyler | 1968 | OF | .321 | 1921-1927 |
| Roberto Clemente | 1973 | OF | .317 | 1955-1972 |
| Ralph Kiner | 1975 | OF | .279 | 1946-1953 |

## OTHER HALL OF FAMERS WHO SPENT PART OF THEIR CAREER AS PIRATES

| | | |
|---|---|---|
| Jake Beckley | Billy Herman | Connie Mack |
| Jack Chesbro | Waite Hoyt | Heinie Manush |
| Joe Cronin | Joseph Kelley | Rabbit Maranville |
| James "Pud" Galvin | George Kelly | Casey Stengel |
| Burleigh Grimes | Fred Lindstrom | Arthur "Dazzy" Vance |
| | Al Lopez | |

## General Information

### RETIRED UNIFORM NUMBERS

No. 1   Billy Meyer

No. 20  Pie Traynor-3/3/71

No. 21  Roberto Clemente-4/6/73

No. 33  Honus Wagner

No. 40 Danny Murtaugh-4/7/77

# CLUB PRESIDENTS

| President | Years |
|---|---|
| William A. Nimick | 1887-1890 |
| J. Palmer O'Neill | 1891 |
| William C. Temple | 1892 |
| Albert C. Buckenberger | 1893 |
| William W. Kerr | 1894-1897 |
| William H. Watkins | 1898 |
| William W. Kerr | 1899 |
| Barney Dreyfuss | 1900-1932 |
| William E. Benswanger | 1932-8/8/46 |
| Frank E. McKinney | 8/8/46-1950 |
| John W. Galbreath | 1951-1969 |
| Daniel M. Galbreath | 1970-present |

## CLUB GENERAL MANAGERS*

| Manager | Year |
|---|---|
| Ray L. Kennedy | 1946 |
| H. Roy Harmey | 1947-1951 |
| Branch Rickey | 1951-1956 |
| Joe L. Brown | 1956-1976 |
| Joseph M. O'Toole (Vice President, Business Administration) and Harding Peterson (Vice President, Player Personnel) | 1976-1979 |
| Harding Peterson | 1979-present |

*Prior to 1946 the club presidents performed the current duties of general manager.

## AWARDS

The Sporting News Most Valuable Player (1929-45)
  Arky Vaughan 1935
The Sporting News Player, Pitcher of the Year (1948-present)
  Ralph Kiner 1950
  Dick Groat 1960
  Vern Law 1960
  Roberto Clemente 1966
  Dave Parker 1978
The Sporting News Fireman of the Year (1960-present)
  Roy Face 1962
  Al McBean 1964
  Dave Giusti 1971
The Sporting News Rookie Awards (1946-present)
  Don Robinson 1978
The Sporting News Major League Executive of the Year (1936-present)
  Joe L. Brown 1958
The Sporting News Manager of the Year (1936-present)
  Billy Meyer 1948
  Danny Murtaugh 1960
  Danny Murtaugh 1970
The Sporting News Major League Player of the Year (1936-present)

224

## Awards (continued)

Bill Mazeroski 1960
Willie Stargell 1979
The Sporting News Man of the Year
Willie Stargell 1979
The Baseball Writers' Association Most Valuable Player Award (1931-present)
Dick Groat 1960
Roberto Clemente 1966
Dave Parker 1978
Willie Stargell (with Keith Hernandez) 1979
The Baseball Writers' Association Cy Young Memorial Award (1956-present)
Vern Law 1960

## PIRATES IN THE ALL-STAR GAME

1933    Pie Traynor, Paul Waner
1934    Pie Traynor, Paul Waner, Arky Vaughan
1935    Paul Waner, Arky Vaughan
1936    Arky Vaughan, Gus Suhr
1937    Paul Waner, Arky Vaughan, Cy Blanton
1938    Arky Vaughan, Lloyd Waner, Mace Brown
1939    Arky Vaughan
1940    Arky Vaughan
1941    Arky Vaughan, Bob Elliott, Al Lopez
1942    Bob Elliott
1943    Vince DiMaggio, Rip Sewell
1944    Bob Elliott, Vince DiMaggio, Rip Sewell
1946    Rip Sewell, Frankie Gustine
1947    Frankie Gustine
1948    Frankie Gustine, Ralph Kiner, Elmer Riddle
1949    Ralph Kiner
1950    Ralph Kiner
1951    Ralph Kiner
1952    Ralph Kiner
1953    Murry Dickson
1954    Frank Thomas
1955    Frank Thomas
1956    Bob Friend, Dale Long
1957    Hank Foiles
1958    Bob Friend, Frank Thomas, Bill Mazeroski, Bob Skinner
1959    Bill Mazeroski, Smoky Burgess, Elroy Face, Dick Groat
1960    Bill Mazeroski, Smoky Burgess, Elroy Face, Dick Groat, Roberto Clemente
        Vern Law, Bob Skinner, Bob Friend
1961    Smoky Burgess, Elroy Face, Roberto Clemente, Dick Stuart
1962    Bill Mazeroski, Dick Groat, Roberto Clemente
1963    Bill Mazeroski, Roberto Clemente
1964    Bill Mazeroski, Roberto Clemente, Smokey Burgess, Willie Stargell
1965    Roberto Clemente, Willie Stargell, Bob Veale
1966    Roberto Clemente, Willie Stargell, Bob Veale
1967    Roberto Clemente, Bill Mazeroski, Gene Alley
1968    Gene Alley, Matty Alou
1969    Roberto Clemente, Matty Alou

1970    Roberto Clemente
1971    Roberto Clemente, Willie Stargell, Dock Ellis, Manny Sanguillen
1972    Roberto Clemente, Willie Stargell, Manny Sanguillen, Al Oliver, Steve Blass
1973    Willie Stargell, Dave Giusti
1974    Ken Brett
1975    Manny Sanguillen, Al Oliver, Jerry Reuss
1976    Al Oliver
1977    Dave Parker, John Candelaria
1978    Dave Parker (replaced by Willie Stargell due to injury)
1979    Dave Parker

## 6. NICKNAMES

Definition: "A descriptive name given instead of, or in addition to, the one belonging to the person, place, or thing." Nicknames are usually complimentary and some of them—Bambino, Big Train, Brown Bomber, Joltin' Joe, Iron Horse, Cobra—recall a vivid picture of the man to the sports fan. "Fan" is a nickname of sorts being short for fanatic. Lefty, Shorty, Skinny, Red, Blackie, Fats, and Pudge are our pals. These names given in childhood often stick for life even if the physique changes.

Baseball players, great and not so great, have been given nicknames by fans, sportswriters, and sportscasters. These names give the fans a handle and bring them closer to their heroes. The Pirates have had their share of nicknames and the following is an alphabetical listing. The given name, or name by which the player is usually known, is followed by the nickname.

| | |
|---|---|
| Bill Abstein | Big Bill |
| Ed Albosta | Rube |
| Luis Arroyo | Yo-Yo |
| Jim Bagby Sr. | Sarge |
| Walter Barbare | Dinty |
| Clyde Barnhart | Pooch |
| Frank Barrett | Red |
| Dick Bartell | Rowdy Richard |
| Eddie Basinski | Fiddler |
| Jake Beckley | Eagle Eye |
| Bill Bell | Ding Dong |
| Fern Bell | Danny |
| Fred Bennett | Red |
| Claude Berry | Admiral |
| Carson Bigbee | Skeeter |
| Lyle Bigbee | Al |
| Ralph Birkofer | Lefty |
| Homer Blankenship | Si |
| Ernie Bonham | Tiny |
| Luke Boone | Danny |
| Frank Bowerman | Mike |
| Nelson Briles | Nellie |
| Earl Brown | Snitz |
| George Brunet | Lefty |
| Jimmy Burke | Sunset Jimmy |
| Guy Bush | The Mississippi Mudcat |

| | |
|---|---|
| Joe Bush | Bullet Joe |
| Howie Camnitz | Red |
| John Candelaria | The Candy Man |
| Max Carey | Scoops |
| Leon Chagnon | Shag |
| Cliff Chambers | Lefty |
| Jack Chesbro | Happy Jack |
| Fred Clarke | Cap |
| Willie Clark | Wee Willie |
| Roberto Clemente | Bob |
| Pete Compton | Bash |
| Ralph Comstock | Commy |
| Duff Cooley | Sir Richard |
| Dan Costello | Dashing Dan |
| George Cutshaw | Clancy |
| Harry Davis | Jasper |
| Frank Delahanty | Pudgie |
| Walt Dickson | Hickory |
| Mike Donlin | Turkey Mike |
| Bill Duggleby | Frosty Bill |
| Fred Dunlap | Sure Shot |
| Erv Dusak | Four Sack |
| Billy Earle | The Little Globetrotter |
| Roy Ellam | Whitey, Slippery |
| Bob Ferguson | Death to Flying Things |
| Ira Flagstead | Pete |
| Les Fleming | Moe |
| Gene Freese | Augie |
| George Freese | Bud |
| Bob Friend | Warrior |
| Frankie Frisch | The Fordham Flash |
| Fred Fussell | Moonlight Ace |
| Pud Galvin | Gentle Jeems, The Little Steam Engine |
| Phil Garner | Scrap Iron, Scraps |
| Johnny Gee | Whiz |
| Frank Genius | Frenchy |
| Wally Gerber | Spooks |
| Al Gerheauser | Lefty |
| Gus Getz | Gee-Gee |
| George Gibson | Moon |
| Jack Gilbert | Jackrabbit |
| Jack Glasscock | Pebbly Jack |
| Jack Gorman | Stooping Jack |
| George Grantham | Boots |
| Hank Greenberg | Hammerin' Hank |
| Burleigh Grimes | Ol' Stubblebeard |
| Charlie Grimm | Jolly Cholly |
| Al Grunwald | Stretch |
| Harry Gambert | Gunboat |
| Harvey Haddix | The Kitten |
| Luke Hamlin | Hot Potato |
| Lee Handley | Jeep |
| Bob Harmon | Hickory Bob |

| | |
|---|---|
| Ray Harrell | Cowboy |
| Joe Harris | Moon |
| Chuck Hartenstein | Twiggy |
| Fred Hartman | Dutch |
| Wally Hebert | Preacher |
| Art Herring | Sandy |
| Carmen Hill | Specs, Bunker |
| Chuck Hiller | Iron Hands |
| Don Hoak | Tiger |
| Bill Hoffer | Wizard |
| Solly Hofman | Circus Solly |
| Johnny Hopp | Hippity |
| Elmer Horton | Herky Jerky |
| Waite Hoyt | Schoolboy |
| Jim Hughey | Cold Water Jim |
| Bert Husting | Pete |
| Charlie Jackson | Lefty |
| Grant Jackson | Buck |
| Sam Jethroe | Jet |
| Davy Jones | Kangaroo |
| Henry Jones | Baldy |
| Ken Jungels | Curly |
| John Kelty | Chief |
| Frank Killen | Lefty |
| Ed Kinsella | Rube |
| Ted Kluszewski | Klu, Big Klu |
| Otto Knabe | Dutch |
| Fred Kommers | Bugs |
| Ed Konetchy | Big Ed, Koney |
| George Kopacz | Sonny |
| Clem Koshorek | Scooter |
| Bill Koski | T-Bone |
| Danny Kravitz | Dusty, Beak |
| Ray Kremer | Wiz |
| Otto Krueger | Oom Paul |
| Earl Kunz | Pinch |
| Bob Kuzava | Sarge |
| Johnny Lanning | Tobacco Chewin' Johnny |
| Paul LaPalme | Lefty |
| Vern Law | Deacon |
| Sam Leever | The Goshen Schoolmaster |
| Ed Lennox | Eggie |
| Fred Lindstrom | Lindy |
| Hans Lobert | Honus |
| Johnny Logan | Yatcha |
| Bobby Lowe | Link |
| Red Lucas | The Nashville Narcissus |
| Bill Luhrsen | Wild Bill |
| Pop Lytle | Dad |
| Danny MacFayden | Deacon Danny |
| Connie Mack | The Tall Tactician |
| Bill Madlock | Mad Dog |
| Roy Mahaffey | Popeye |

| | |
|---|---|
| Luis Marquez | Canenal |
| Gene Mauch | Skip |
| Al Maul | Smiling Al |
| Bill Mazeroski | Maz |
| Sam McDowell | Sudden Sam |
| Bill McKechnie | Deacon |
| Cal McLish | Buster |
| Lee Meadows | Specs |
| George Medich | Doc |
| Heine Meine | The Count of Luxemburg |
| Mike Menosky | Leaping Mike |
| Gene Michael | Stick |
| Johnny Miljus | Big Serb |
| Frank Miller | Bullet |
| George Miller | Foghorn, Calliope, Doggie |
| Roscoe Miller | Roxy, Rubberlegs |
| John Milner | The Hammer |
| Fritz Mollwitz | Zip |
| Felipe Montemayor | Monty |
| Gene Moore | Blue Goose |
| Lew Moren | Hicks |
| Ed Morris | Cannonball |
| Johnny Morrison | Jughandle Johnny |
| Walt Moryn | Moose |
| Ray Mueller | Iron Man |
| Hugh Mulcahy | Losing Pitcher |
| Eddie Murphy | Honest Eddie |
| Judge Nagle | Lucky |
| John O'Brien | Chewing Gum |
| Tommy O'Brien | Obie |
| Jack O'Connor | Peach Pie |
| Billy O'Dell | Digger |
| Al Oliver | Mr. Scoop |
| Wayne Osborne | Ossie |
| Joe Page | Fireman, The Gay Reliever |
| Jim Pagliaroni | Pag |
| Frank Papish | Pap |
| Dave Parker | The Cobra, The Franchise |
| Tom Parsons | Long Tom |
| Freddie Patek | The Flea, Moochie |
| Paul Pettit | Lefty |
| Jesse Petty | The Silver Fox |
| Jack Pfiester | Jack the Giant Killer |
| Babe Phelps | Blimp |
| Bill Phillips | Whoa Bill, Silver Bill |
| Jack Phillips | Stretch |
| Bill Pierro | Wild Bill |
| Johnny Podgajny | Specs |
| Pedro Ramos | Pete |
| Xavier Rescigno | Mr. X |
| Charlie Reilly | Princeton Charlie |
| Pete Reiser | Pistol Pete |
| Dino Restelli | Dingo |

| | |
|---|---|
| Bobby Rhawn | Rocky |
| Hal Rice | Hoot |
| Joe Rickert | Diamond Joe |
| Marv Rickert | Twitch |
| Johnnie Riddle | Mutt |
| Claude Ritchey | Little All Right |
| Hank Robinson | Rube |
| Andre Rogers | Andy |
| Roy Sanders | Butch, Pep |
| Fritz Scheeren | Dutch |
| Dick Schofield | Ducky |
| Fred Schulte | Fritz |
| Bob Schultz | Bill |
| Joe Schultz | Germany |
| Joe Schultz Jr. | Dode |
| Bill Schuster | Broadway |
| Earl Sheely | Whitey |
| John Shovlin | Brode |
| Elmer Singleton | Smoky |
| Earl Smith | Oil |
| Hal Smith | Cura |
| Willie Stargell | Pops, Captain Willie |
| Ray Starr | Iron Man |
| Casey Stengel | The Old Professor |
| Ed Stevens | Big Ed |
| George Strickland | Bo |
| Nick Strincevich | Jumbo |
| Bill Stuart | Chauncey |
| Dick Stuart | Dr. Strangeglove |
| Tom Sturdivant | Snake |
| Billy Sunday | The Evangelist |
| George Susce | Good Kid |
| Harry Swacina | Swats |
| Kent Tekulve | Teke |
| Fresco Thompson | Tommy |
| Jim Tobin | Abba Dabba |
| Harry Truby | Bird Eye |
| Terry Turner | Cotton |
| Bob Vail | Doc |
| Maurice Van Robays | Bomber |
| Honus Wagner | The Flying Dutchman |
| Dixie Walker | The People's Cherce |
| Lloyd Waner | Little Poison |
| Paul Waner | Big Poison |
| Jim Weaver | Big Jim |
| Bill Werle | Bugs |
| Kirby White | Redbuck |
| Burgess Whitehead | Whitey |
| Ted Wilks | Cork |
| Jimmy Williams | Buttons |
| Claude Willoughby | Weeping Willie |

| | |
|---|---|
| Art Wilson | Dutch |
| Owen Wilson | Chief |
| George Witt | Red |
| Roy Wood | Woody |
| Glenn Wright | Buckshot |
| Harley Young | Cy the Third |
| Irv Young | Young Cy, Cy the Second |

In many cases nicknames have completely replaced the players given names. This is a representative list of Pirates who were known almost exclusively by the names listed which are nicknames.

| | |
|---|---|
| Babe Adams | Whammy Douglas |
| Sparky Adams | Bad Bill Eagan |
| Goat Anderson | Truck Eagan |
| Jap Barbeau | Stump Edington |
| Ginger Beaumont | Jewel Ens |
| Boom Boom Beck | Nanny Fernandez |
| Sheriff Blake | Steamer Flanagan |
| Kitty Bransfield | Gussie Gannon |
| Kid Camp | Mudcat Grant |
| King Cole | Howdie Grosskloss |
| Ripper Collins | Mule Haas |
| Zip Collins | Pink Hawley |
| Wid Conroy | Ducky Hemp |
| Cookie Cuccurulla | Babe Herman |
| Kiki Cuyler | Bonnie Hollingsworth |
| Spud Davis | Dixie Howell |
| Cozy Dolan | Spook Jacobs |
| Jiggs Donahue | Doc Johnston |
| Bubber Jonnard | Steamboat Straus |
| Brickyard Kennedy | Pie Traynor |
| Rimp Lanier | Dazzy Vance |
| Tacks Latimer | Peak-a-boo Veach |
| Cookie Lavagetto | Coot Veal |
| Watty Lee | Rube Waddell |
| Buckshot May | Piggy Ward |
| Moon McCormick | Hooks Warner |
| Chappie McFarland | Mule Watson |
| Irish McIlveen | Farmer Weaver |
| Stuff McInnis | Deacon White |
| Catfish Metkovich | Possum Whitted |
| Vinegar Bend Mizell | Kaiser Wilhelm |
| Cholly Naranjo | Snake Wiltse |
| Preacher Roe | Spades Wood |
| Doc Scanlan | Chief Yellowhorse |
| Crazy Schmidt | Chief Zimmer |
| Wildfire Schulte | |
| Phenomenal Smith | |

# 7.  THE WORLD SERIES AND PLAYOFFS

Playing in a World Series is the dream for everyone who has played baseball. It separates a player from the rest of the crowd. He knows that for the next week or so, every time he steps onto the field his every move will be viewed by the entire baseball world. He will be placed on the center-stage, directly in the spotlight. For that week he'll be chased by hundreds of reporters asking for "just a couple of minutes." All the reporters have a different style; but they all ask almost the same questions, and always expect a new and interesting answer.

With all the attention comes the pressure of knowing that he and his teammates can be the best in their profession; they can become champions. But there is also the pressure of knowing that no one can help; a team must win or lose on their own. There's no more scoreboard watching or comparisons of schedules. Everything depends on the team. Then there's the pressure of knowing that you may fail.

Every player reacts differently to this pressure. Some thrive on it and play their best in games that mean the most. These are the players who want to come to bat with the bases loaded and two outs. These are the players who want the ball hit to them when their team needs a big out. Others become cautious. They try to become too perfect and fail to play their normal game.

This section is about the players and the teams who have been there. These men have had the talent and the luck to step into the winner's circle.

The Pirates have played in seven World Series' and have been able to walk away with the crown five times. In each of these five times, the series has gone down to the very last game. The Battlin' Bucs have the distinction of being the only club to come back twice and win after trailing three games to one. The Pirates have never lost a seventh game.

## In the Beginning

In the winter of 1899-1900, Pirate history took a dramatic turn for the better. It was in that winter that Louisville owner Barney Dreyfuss got wind of a plan to eliminate four of the National League's 12 teams. This plan, proposed by Andy Freeman, owner of the New York Giants, would chop off Cleveland, Washington, Baltimore and Louisville, the so-called "dead wood" of the circuit.

A fast thinking Dreyfuss learned that W. W. Kerr and his associate Phil Auten, owners of the Pirates, were tired of throwing money away on a losing proposition in Pittsburgh. In December 1899, Kerr and Dreyfuss reached an agreement that would give Dreyfuss half ownership of the Bucs provided he would bring his best players with him. (This has often been called a merger of the two clubs but in actuality the transaction was a form of a trade since Louisville was not officially dropped from the league. See the section on trades.)

The Pirates, led by newcomers Honus Wagner, Fred Clarke, Tommy Leach, Deacon Phillippe, and Claude Ritchey, were transformed from a disappointing seventh place team in '99 to a second place club in '00. The 1900 club made up 21 games in the standings, finishing just four and a half games off the pace. In what would later become the team's trademark, the Bucs finished strong, winning 31 and losing 19 in the last two months of the season.

Baseball entered a new era in 1901. Ban Johnson, president of the Western League (baseball's top minor league in 1900), organized franchises in the abandoned cities of Cleveland, Baltimore, and Washington. With an expanded league, Johnson decided that his league needed a new name. He felt that his circuit should be called the American League, showing the country-wide appeal that it had. Johnson then made a bold move. Backed by all American League owners, he withdrew from the National Agreement, which bound his league to a minor league status and declared his league to be a full major league. Johnson invaded the National League strongholds of Philadelphia and Boston and the war between the two leagues was soon in full scale.

232

The Pirates won their first championship that year. The Bucs started slow but gathered momentum and took hold of the number one spot on June 15 to coast under the wire with a seven and a half lead over the second place Phillies. In that initial glory year, the *Spalding Guide* pointed out that the Pirates were "more harmonious as a team than its adversaries and did less kicking, the latter being a weakness that characterized every team in the league in 1901."

With the N.L.-A.L. war raging and almost every team suffering heavy casualties, Barney Dreyfuss and his manager, Fred Clarke, were able to keep their champions intact. The 1902 Bucs could have won in any year, but in a weakened league, the race was over in May. The Pirates finished 27 games ahead of the rest of the pack. The Pirates were led by 28-game winner Jack Chesbro and 20-game winners Jesse Tannehill and Deacon Phillippe. Also on this team (possibly the greatest in N.L. history) was the league's batting leader Ginger Beaumont, who batted .357. The legendary Honus Wagner, who batted .329, led the league in runs scored (105), doubles (33), RBIs (91), stolen bases (43) and slugging percentage (.487), and the tiny Tommy Leach was the surprising home run leader with a total of six.

Peace came to the baseball world in the winter of 1903. Dreyfuss, a member of the National League committee, met with Johnson and other American League representatives. In the constant give-and-take of negotiations, both sides had to make some concessions. The N.L. agreed to recognize the Americans as a full-fledged league if the A.L. would agree to set-up a joint committee to determine the status of disputed contracts of the raided players. The A.L. won the right to place a team in New York and the N.L. and Dreyfuss had the promise of Johnson to keep out of Pittsburgh.

The Pirates made it three in a row in 1903 and on September 1 agreed to meet the Boston Pilgrims, the A.L. champs, in a best-of-nine series at the end of the season. Some National League owners were opposed to a World Series but the public demanded it and Dreyfuss saw the benefit it would bring to baseball.

The Bucs won the third pennant easily. Honus Wagner won his second batting title by hitting .355. With the help of Clarke's .351 average and Beaumont's .341 average, the Pirates held the top spot from June 19 through the end of the season.

Unfortunately, the Pirates entered the World Series with an injured pitching staff. Sam Leever, the Bucs' top pitcher, led the league with a 2.06 ERA but was ineffective in the Series due to a nagging shoulder injury. Nine-game winner Brickyard Kennedy was bothered by a hip injury and Ed Doheny, a 16-game winner, suffered a mental breakdown. Deacon Phillippe threw himself into the breech by pitching five complete games.

Jimmy Sebring was the Series' batting star. He batted .367 with 11 hits including the Series first home run. Jake Stahl (.303) was the only other player to hit over .300. Beaumont and Clarke each hit .265. Wagner batted .222 and had only one hit in his last 14 at-bats.

On the other side, Boston's pitching was the key. Cy Young won two games and had a 1.59 ERA and Bill Dineen won three games (two shutouts) and had a 2.06 ERA.


## 1903 WORLD SERIES


Game 1    at Boston 10/1/03

| | | |
|---|---|---|
| Pitt. | 4 0 1  1 0 0  1 0 0—7 | 12 2 |
| Bos. | 0 0 0  0 0 0  2 0 1—3 | 6 4 |

The Pirates jumped on 28-game winner Cy Young for four runs with two out in the first, including the first series hit, a Tommy Leach triple. Tommy had four hits on the afternoon. Jimmy Sebring tagged the initial series home run in the seventh and totaled four RBIs on three hits. Deacon Phillippe went the distance for Pittsburgh and struck out 10.

Game 2   at Boston   10/2/03

| | | |
|---|---|---|
| Pitt. | 0 0 0   0 0 0   0 0 0—0 | 3 2 |
| Bos. | 2 0 0   0 0 1   0 0 x—3 | 8 0 |

Patsy Dougherty's leadoff inside-the-park home run was all the offense Boston needed. Pirates' starter Sam Leever was forced to leave after one inning with a sore shoulder. Bill Dineen struckout 11 for Boston. The Bucs only threat came in the fourth with runners at second and third with one out. Honus Wagner lined to second baseman Hobe Ferris who tagged Fred Clarke for the unassisted doubleplay.

Game 3   at Boston   10/3/03

| | | |
|---|---|---|
| Pitt. | 0 1 2   0 0 0   0 1 0—4 | 7 1 |
| Bos. | 0 0 0   1 0 0   0 1 0—2 | 4 2 |

Deacon Phillipe, pitching with just a day's rest, scattered four hits for his second series victory. The Bucs knocked out Tom Hughes in the third when a walk to Ginger Beaumont, Fred Clarke's double, and Leach's single gave the Pirates a 2-0 lead. Young relieved and hit Wagner to load the bases. Cy got two outs but Freddy Parent bobbled Sebring's grounder and Clarke scored the Pirates' third run. Boston scored on Parent's sacrifice fly in the fourth but Claude Ritchie's run-scoring single in the eighth revived the three-run edge. Boston scored on a two out double by Jimmy Collins and Chick Stahl's single. Phillippe then retired the last four batters in order to send the series to Pittsburgh with the Bucs a game up.

Game 4   at Pittsburgh   10/6/03

| | | |
|---|---|---|
| Bos. | 0 0 1   0 1 0   0 0 2—4 | 9 1 |
| Pitt. | 1 0 0   0 1 0   3 0 x—5 | 12 1 |

Game four was delayed one day by rain after a travel day, so Clarke was able to send Philippe back to the mound for his third start. Deacon limited the Pilgrims to one run on four hits through the first eight innings while the Pirates built a 5-2 lead. Two out hits by Wagner and Kitty Bransfield scored Clarke with the first run. Boston tied the game when Candy LaChance scored with two out on Lou Criger's single. The Pirates reclaimed the lead when Ginger Beaumont tripled and Leach drove him home with a two-out single off starter Bill Dineen. The Pirates seemed to wrap up the game in the seventh when Leach blasted a two-run triple to rightfield, and scored when Wagner singled to center. Phillippe tired in the ninth and allowed three straight hits, scoring one run and leaving runners on first and third. Deacon got Parent to bounce into a force at second but LaChance and Ferris followed with singles to load the bases. Duke Ferrell pinch-hit for Criger and hit a sacrifice fly to left, cutting the Pirates lead to a run. With two out, Jack O'Brien popped out to Ritchey and the Pirates had a two-game lead in the best of nine series.

Game 5   at Pittsburgh   10/7/03

| | | |
|---|---|---|
| Bos. | 0 0 0   0 0 6   4 1 0—11 | 14 2 |
| Pitt. | 0 0 0   0 0 0   0 2 0— 2 | 6 4 |

Clarke was out of first line pitchers and sent nine-game winner Brickyard Kennedy against Cy Young. Kennedy battled Young on even terms for five inings before succumbing in the sixth with the help of errors by Clarke and Wagner. Young lost his shutout in the eighth when Leach rapped another triple after Parent's two-out error.

Game 6   at Pittsburgh   10/8/03

| | | |
|---|---|---|
| Bos. | 0 0 3   0 2 0   1 0 0—6 | 10 1 |
| Pitt. | 0 0 0   0 0 0   3 0 0—3 | 10 3 |

With two out in the third, Dineen singled, Patsy Dougherty walked, Jimmy Collins singled home Dineen, and Jake Stahl singled home Dougherty. When Tommy Leach could not handle Buck Freeman's grounder, Eddie Phelps singled to start the inning.

Leever's grounder moved the runners up and Beaumont's hit to center put the Bucs on the board. Clarke followed with a double to bring in Phelps and Beaumont. A shaken Dineen got Leach on a fly to right but Clarke stole third, and walks to Wagner and Bransfield loaded the bases with two out. Ritchey could only produce a grounder to Parent who forced Bransfield at second. The Bucs did not seriously threaten again and the series was tied.

| Game 7 at Pittsburgh 10/10/03 | | | | | | | | | | | |
| Bos. | 2 0 0 | 2 0 2 | 0 1 0—7 | 11 | 4 |
| Pitt. | 0 0 0 | 1 0 1 | 0 0 1—3 | 10 | 3 |

Phillippe got another extra day of rest when the game was postponed by cold weather. Once again errors plagued the Pirates. Boston led 1-0 in the first when Stahl tripled into the crowd scoring Collins who had also tripled. When Freeman grounded to Ritchey, Claude threw home to get Stahl. The throw was in time but Phelps could not hold it and Boston led by two. They scored twice in the fourth on triples by Freeman and Ferris before the Pirates reached Young for a run on Bransfield's triple and Ritchey's ground out. The Bucs rallied again in the ninth and had a run in with two men on and the top of the order due up. Young retired Beaumont, Clarke, and Leach in order to bring Boston within a win from the first series victory.

| Game 8 at Boston 10/13/03 | | | | | | |
| Pitt. | 0 0 0 | 0 0 0 | 0 0 0—0 | 4 | 0 |
| Bos. | 0 0 0 | 2 0 1 | 0 0 x—3 | 8 | 0 |

Once again, Phillippe gained an extra day of rest but the tired pitcher could not match Bill Dineen. The game was scoreless when Leach walked and Wagner singled him to third with none out in the fourth. The Bucs tried to manufacture a run with a double steal. Criger threw to third, trapping Leach off base. Tommy tried to score but Collins nailed him at the plate. Boston responded with two runs on Ferris' single and Dineen took charge from there. He fanned Wagner to end the game and bring the first World's Championship to Boston.

In 1909, the Pirates closed out the century's first decade where they started, in first place. The '09 Bucs won 110 games, the most ever by a Pittsburgh team and the second-most ever in the National League.

The Pirates were led once again by Honus Wagner who won his fourth consecutive batting title by hitting .339. Wagner also led the league with 100 RBIs, 39 doubles, and a .489 slugging percentage. Tommy Leach also contributed by leading the league with 126 runs scored.

As a team, the Pirates scored more runs (701), hammered out more hits (1332), doubles (218), and triples (92) than any other N.L. club. The Bucs were also best with a .260 batting average and a .353 slugging percentage.

The pitching staff was led by a pair of right-handers, Howie Camnitz (25-6, 1.62 ERA) and Vic Willis (22-11, 2.23 ERA). Also on the staff were a couple of 37-year-olds named Phillippe and Leever. Both contributed eight wins, with Phillippe losing three and Leever dropping just one.

The Series was hailed as a duel between Wagner and the A.L. batting champ, Ty Cobb. The Dutchman proved to be the better of the two. He batted .333 and stole six bases while Cobb batted a low .231 with only two steals.

The real star of this series, which was the first to go seven games, was the Pirates' rookie pitcher, Babe Adams. Adams pitched and won three complete games including a six-hit shutout in Game 7. In the regular season, Adams was 12-3 with a 1.11 ERA in 130 innings.

After the Series, Dreyfuss released first baseman Bill Abstein, who struck out nine times and committed five errors.

Game 1   at Pittsburgh   10/8/09
```
Det.                    1 0 0  0 0 0  0 0 0—1  6  4
Pitt.                   0 0 0  1 2 1  0 0 x—4  5  0
```
Clarke chose 12-game winner Babe Adams to start the series over 20-game winners Vic Willis and Howie Camnitz. Adams opponent was 29-game winner George Mullin. Walks to Davy Jones and Ty Cobb followed by Jim Delahanty's two out single gave Detroit the lead. Clarke's homer tied the score and two unearned runs gave the Bucs all the offense they needed. Adams allowed only two singles over the final four innings.

Game 2   at Pittsburgh   10/9/09
```
Det.                    0 2 3  0 2 0  0 0 0—7  9  3
Pitt.                   2 0 0  0 0 0  0 0 0—2  5  1
```
Pittsburgh took the lead on a walk to Bobby Byrne and doubles by Leach and Dots Miller. Two out singles by George Moriarty, Tom Jones, and Boss Schmidt's two-run double tied the game in the second. Delahanty's two-run double knocked Camnitz out in the third. With Cobb on third and Willis pitching in relief, the Georgia Peach stole home with the Tigers fifth run. Wild Bill Donovan allowed only three hits after the first inning to even the series.

Game 3   at Detroit   10/11/09
```
Pitt.                   5 1 0  0 0 0  0 0 2—8  10  2
Det.                    0 0 0  0 0 0  4 0 2—6  10  5
```
The Bucs hit and ran their way to five first inning runs, disposing of 19-game winner Ed Summers in the process. Pittsburgh's lead was cut to two in the seventh when Bill Abstein's error allowed three unearned runs to score with two out. Clarke's sacrifice fly and Wagner's RBI single gave the Bucs two insurance runs which proved to be the margin of victory. Another Abstein error, Donie Bush's infield hit and Cobb's double cut the Pirates' lead to three. Sam Crawford's grounder scored Bush and Nick Maddox retired Delahanty to end his complete game victory.

Game 4   at Detroit   10/12/09
```
Pitt.                   0 0 0  0 0 0  0 0 0—0  5  6
Det.                    0 2 0  3 0 0  0 0 0—5  8  0
```
Mullin recovered from his first game defeat to pitch a five hit complete game and strike out ten. The Tigers scored twice in the second on only one hit, Oscar Stanage's single scoring Moriarty and Tom Jones. The Pirates threatened in the third on Byrne's double, a walk to Leach and a double steal as Clarke struck out. Wagner was called out on strikes and the Bucs did not get another runner as far as second base.

Game 5   at Pittsburgh   10/13/09
```
Det.                    1 0 0  0 0 2  0 1 0—4  6  1
Pitt.                   1 1 1  0 0 0  4 1 x—8  10  2
```
Again, Adams allowed a first inning run, on Davy Jones' leadoff homer. A bases-loaded walk to Abstein tied the score after an inning. Summers wild pitched George Gibson home to put the Bucs in front and Clarke's walk, Wagner's single and Miller's ground out gave Pittsburgh a 3-1 lead. Cobb's single and Crawford's double cut the Pirate lead to a run and when Wagner threw away Delahanty's grounder, Crawford scored the tying run. Manager Clarke took charge and broke the game open with a three-run homer, his second of the series. Adams went the distance for his second series victory.

Game 6    at Detroit    10/14/09
Pitt.                          3 0 0    0 0 0    0 0 1—4   6   2
Det.                           1 0 0    2 1 1    0 0 x—5  10   2

The Pirates opened the game with four straight singles for three runs. A walk to Bush and Crawford's double put the Tigers on the board and RBIs by Moriarty and Tom Jones tied the game in the fourth. Delahanty's two out double in the fifth scored Bush with the go-ahead run and Cobb's RBI double in the sixth off Camnitz gave the Tigers an insurance run. Miller and Abstein opened the Pirates ninth with back to back singles. Owen Wilson was called on to bunt. Wilson popped the attempt toward Tom Jones and then collided with the Tigers' first baseman. Jones dropped the ball and had to be carried off on a stretcher. Miller scored on the play, Abstein moved to third and Gibson was safe at first. Gibson hit a grounder to Jones' replacement, Sam Crawford, who got Abstein at the plate for the first out. With runners on first and second, Clarke sent Ed Abbaticchio up for reliever Phillippe. Mullin fanned Abby and Schmidt cut down Wilson trying to steal third to end the game.

Game 7    at Detroit    10/16/09
Pitt.                          0 2 0    2 0 3    0 1 0—8   7   0
Det.                           0 0 0    0 0 0    0 0 0—0   6   3

Babe Adams, making his third start, gained a record-tying third victory and brought Pittsburgh its first World's Championship. Ham Hyatt's sacrifice fly scored Abstein with the only run Babe needed but the Bucs added another on Clarke's bases loaded walk, the second of four the manager drew in the game. Two more runs scored on Miller's two-run single off Mullin in the fourth. Adams scattered six hits and held Ty Cobb hitless in four at-bats.

### The Middle Years

It was 16 years before the Pirates were able to hang bunting around Forbes Field in preparation for the Fall Classic. The Bucs won the 1925 pennant with ease, finishing eight and a half games ahead of the second-place Giants. As a club, the Bucs batted .307, scored 912 runs, collected 1651 hits, and stole 159 bases. Pittsburgh had eight players bat over .300 with two others batting .298.

This team featured an outfield of Kiki Cuyler (.357, 144 runs, 43 doubles, 26 triples, and 41 stolen bases), Max Carey (.343, 104 runs, 39 doubles, and 46 stolen bases), and Clyde Barnhart (.325 and 144 RBIs). Pie Traynor and Glenn Wright were on the left side of the infield. Eddie Moore and George Grantham were on the right side. Earl Smith and Johnny Gooch shared the catching duties.

The Pirates didn't have a 20-game winner that year but did have Lee Meddows with 19 wins, Remy Kremer, Johnny Morrison, and Emil Yde with 17 apiece, and Vic Aldridge with 15.

In the Series, the Pirates faced the Washington Senators who had become World Champions the year before by defeating the Giants in seven games. The Senators were led by a pair of 20-game winners, Walter Johnson and Stan Coveleski. Also on that club was Roger Peckinpaugh, the A.L. MVP, Sam Rice, who batted .350 and scored 111 runs, and Goose Goslin, who scored 116 runs and drove in 113 more.

Things looked bad for the Bucs after being shutout by Johnson in Game 4. The Pirates now trailed three games to one and had to look forward to facing Coveleski in Game 5 and Johnson again in Game 7. But the Pirates did it. They beat Coveleski and Johnson and became the first team to win three in a row after losing three of the first four games.

A look at the Series' stats show that Carey led all hitters with a .458 average. Smith batted .350, and Traynor hit .346. For the Senators, Joe Harris batted .440, Rice .364, and Goslin .308.

Game 1   at Pittsburgh   10/7/25
Was.                                010  020  001—4  8  1
Pitt.                               000  010  000—1  5  0

Walter Johnson held the National League's best hitting club to five hits and fanned ten en route to his first series victory. Pie Traynor's fifth-inning homer broke the Big Train's shutout bid. Joe Harris put Washington in front with a homer off Lee Meadows in the second. Three straight singles by Harris, Ossie Bluege, and Roger Peckinpaugh loaded the bases in the fifth and Sam Rice's base hit gave the Senators their margin of victory. The A.L. champs added a run off Johnny Morrison when Bluege drove home Goose Goslin from second.

Game 2   at Pittsburgh   10/8/25
Was.                                010  000  001—2  8  2
Pitt.                               000  100  02x—3  7  0

Kiki Cuyler's two-run eighth inning homer put the Pirates in front and the Bucs held off a Washington rally to even the series. The Senators jumped in front in the second on a Joe Judge home run but Glenn Wright's blast tied the score after four innings. Vic Aldridge pitched out of a bases loaded, none out situation in the fifth and dueled Senators 20 game winner Stan Coveleski until Cuyler broke the tie in the eighth. Harris and Buddy Myer singled, Peckinpaugh walked and again the bases were loaded in the ninth. Bobby Veach pinch-hit for Muddy Ruel and brought Harris home with a fly to Max Carey in center. Bucky Harris sent Dutch Reuther up for Coveleski. Aldridge fanned him for the second out. Sam Rice's grounder to second ended the Senators' rally and evened the series.

Game 3   at Washington   10/10/25
Pitt.                               010  101  000—3  8  3
Was.                                001  001  20x—4  10  1

Glenn Wright's sacrifice fly gave Pittsburgh the lead, scoring Traynor who had led off with a triple against starter Alex Ferguson. After Washington tied the game, Cuyler doubled and Clyde Barnhart's single put the Bucs back in front. An unearned run gave the Pirates a 3-1 lead but Goslin's sixth inning homer kept Washington close going into the seventh. A walk to pinch hitter Nemo Leibold and infield hits by Harris and Goslin loaded the bases with one out. Joe Judge drove in the tying run with a fly to Carey in center and Joe Harris singled to left, scoring Bucky Harris with the lead run. Firpo Marberry came on in relief for Washington and started by striking out Wright and George Grantham. Earl Smith came up and hit a fly ball to very deep right center field. Rice went back to the fence, jumped, and disappeared into the stands. He emerged with the ball and Smith was ruled out. The Pirates protested to no avail and the controversy continued until Rice's death in 1974 when a letter written by him, to be opened upon his death, started that he did in fact catch the ball.

Game 4   at Washington   10/11/25
Pitt.                               000  000  000—0  6  1
Was.                                004  000  00x—4  12  0

Walter Johnson held the Pirates to six singles and the Senators took a three-games-to-one lead in the series. Home runs by Goslin and Joe Harris accounted for Washington's scoring. Goslin tagged starter Emil Yde for a three-run blast and Harris followed immediately with a drive into the leftfield bleachers. The Bucs threatened to score in the second, advancing runners to second and third before Yde bounced out to end the inning. Johnson did not allow another Pirate past second.

Game 5    at Washington    10/12/25

| Pitt. | 0 0 2   0 0 0   2 1 1—6 13   0 |
|-------|-------------------------------|
| Was.  | 1 0 0   1 0 0   1 0 0—3  8   1 |

The Senators scored first when Goslin drove in Rice with a bloop double. Walks to Carey and Cuyler off Coveleski preceeded Barnhart's single to tie the game. Traynor's sacrifice fly put the Bucs in front. Joe Harris hit a solo homer in the fourth but the Pirates took the lead for good on hits by Carey, Cuyler, and Barnhart following a walk to Eddie Moore. The Senators came back again and had runners at first and third with two out in the seventh. Aldridge ended the threat, retiring Joe Harris on a fly to Cuyler in right. Vic set the Senators down in order over the last two innings for his second complete game victory.

Game 6    at Pittsburgh    10/13/25

| Was.  | 1 1 0   0 0 0   0 0 0—2 6 2 |
|-------|-----------------------------|
| Pitt. | 0 0 2   0 1 0   0 0 x—3 7 1 |

Goslin's third home run of the series put Washington in front. A single by Judge and a double by Peckinpaugh gave the Senators a two-run margin. Moore led off the third by working Ferguson for a walk. When Peckinpaugh failed to touch second on Carey's bouncer over the mound, both runners were safe. Cuyler's sacrifice moved the runners up and Barnhart's grounder to third scored Moore with the Pirates' first run. With two out, Traynor singled up the middle to tie the game. Moore again led off in the third and drove Ferguson's pitch over the temporary fence in left field to give the Bucs a 3-2 lead. After leaving a runner at third in the eighth, the Senators came alive in the ninth on Joe Harris' one out double. Harris held as Judge popped to Wright at shortstop. When Ossie Bluege grounded to Traynor, Remy Kremer had the win and the Bucs had evened the series.

Game 7    at Pittsburgh    10/15/25

| Was.  | 4 0 0   2 0 0   0 1 0—7  7 2 |
|-------|------------------------------|
| Pitt. | 0 0 3   0 1 0   2 3 x—9 15 2 |

Aided by a day of rain, Fred Clarke sent Vic Aldridge to the mound with two days rest to face Walter Johnson who had three days between starts. Aldridge only retired one batter and the Senators took advantage of a shaky Pirate defense to build a four-run lead. A bases-loaded walk to Judge and Bluege's one run single finished Aldridge for the series. Morrison got Peckinpaugh to bounce into a force out but all runners were safe when interference was ruled against Earl Smith. Moore's error allowed the fourth Washington run to cross the plate. Johnson was not nearly as sharp as in Game Four but stifled Pirate scoring threats in the first and second. Morrison batted for himself in the third and blooped a single to center. He scored moments later on Moore's double. Carey singled, cutting the Senators' lead to two runs. After Cuyler bounced out, Barnhart's hit cut the difference to one. With runners on second and third and two out in the fourth, Joe Harris doubled home his fifth and sixth runs of the series, giving Johnson a three run lead to work with. It began to rain at Forbes Field when Carey and Cuyler doubled for the Pirates' fourth run. The rain was falling even harder in the seventh when Moore hit a pop into shallow leftfield. Peckinpaugh was unable to make the play and was charged with his seventh error of the series. Carey's third double of the game scored Moore and Cuyler moved Carey to third with a sacrifice bunt. Barnhart's groundball to second could not bring Carey home but Traynor tied the game with a triple to right center. Pie tried to score on the play but was thrown out and the game remained tied. With one out in the eighth, Peckinpaugh went from goat to hero with a home run off Kremer to reclaim the lead. Johnson was four outs from victory when Smith doubled. Yde came in to run for the catcher and Carson Bigbee ripped a double over Goslin's head in leftfield. Yde scored and the game was tied again. Johnson remained in the game and walked Moore. Carey hit a grounder to Peckinpaugh and the American League's Most Valuable Player threw wildly to second. Everybody was safe. Peckinpaugh reacquired the goats horns when Cuyler hit a shot to right field that wound up amongst the overflowing crowd. Everybody came around to score, but the hit was ruled a double and the Pirates took a two run lead to the top of the ninth. Red Oldham made his only series appearance in the ninth and retired the Senators one-two-three to return the Championship to Pittsburgh after a sixteen year absence.

After a disappointing third place finish in 1926, the Bucs regrouped in '27 to win their sixth N.L. flag. The Bucs led early, holding the number one spot from May 22 to June 6, but fell behind the Cubs in early June. Pittsburgh regained the lead on September 1, by beating Chicago 4-3 at Forbes Field. The Pirates fought off late charges by the Giants and the Cardinals to finally clinch the pennant on October 1, the next to last game of the year.

The Pirates again had a potent hitting attack. The Bucs led the N.L. with a .305 batting average and 1648 hits. Paul Waner, in only his second year, had a great season. He led the league with a .380 average, 237 hits, 17 triples, and 131 RBIs. Brother Lloyd, in his first year, batted .355 and led the league with 133 runs scored. Pie Traynor played a brilliant third base and batted .342.

The Pirate pitching corps was spear-headed by Carmen Hill, who won 22 and Remy Kremer, who won 19 and had the best ERA (2.47) in the league. Lee Meadows and Vic Aldridge again won 19 and 15 games respectively.

In the Series, the Bucs had the misfortune to run into one of the greatest teams ever. The 1927 Yankees topped the American League in every offensive category except doubles and stolen bases. But who needed stolen bases when Ruth and Gehrig combined for 107 homeruns and the team hit 158 homers total. Their pitching wasn't to be overlooked either. The Yanks 11 shutouts and 3.25 ERA were both best in the A.L. Waite Hoyt's 22 wins and Wilcy Moore's 2.28 ERA were both best in the league.

The wide-spread belief is that the Pirates were intimidated by this awesome club. But a look at the scores shows that the Bucs were in every game except one and lost two one-run decisions. The Waners both had a good series at the plate with Lloyd batting .400 and Paul hitting .333. George Grantham also chipped in with a .364 average. For the Yankees, Mark Koenig had nine hits for a .500 average. Ruth batted .400 and had the only two homers in the series. Gehrig added two doubles and two triples with a .308 batting average.


## 1927 WORLD SERIES


Game 1   at Pittsburgh   10/5/27
N.Y.        1 0 3  0 1 0  0 0 0—5  6  1
Pitt.        1 0 1  0 1 0  0 1 0—4  9  2

The Yankees scored first with two out on Babe Ruth's single and Lou Gehrig's blooper which got past Paul Waner and went for a triple. Waite Hoyt hit Lloyd Waner, the Pirates' lead-off hitter, who went to third on his brother's double and scored on Glenn Wright's sacrifice fly. George Grantham's error opened the gates for two unearned runs to score on a bases loaded walk to Bob Meusel and Tony Lazzeri's force out. Earl Smith had Gehrig picked off third but could not handle Traynor's throw in the rundown, allowing a third run to score. Kremer's double and Paul Waner's single cut the New York lead to two but Gehrig's sacrifice fly scored Mark Koenig with their fifth run. Lloyd Waner's double and Barnhart's single made the score 5-3 after five innings. When Wright and Traynor singled with one out in the eighth, Miller Huggins called on Wilcy Moore to replace Hoyt. Moore retired Grantham on a force play but Joe Harris' hit scored Wright and moved Grantham to third. He was stranded there when Smith grounded to Gehrig.

Game 2   at Pittsburgh   10/6/27

| N.Y. | 0 0 3   0 0 0   0 3 0—6 11 0 |
|---|---|
| Pitt. | 1 0 0   0 0 0   0 1 0—2 7 2 |

The Bucs took a lead on Lloyd Waner's triple and Barnhart's sacrifice fly off George Pipgras. Hits by Earle Combs and Koenig, Lloyd Waner's error, and a sacrifice fly by Ruth gave the Yankees a 2-1 lead against Vic Aldridge. Gehrig's double, Meusel's infield single, and Lazzeri's sacrifice fly gave New York a third run. They knocked Aldridge out in the eighth and the Pirates could only scratch out one more run on Paul Waner's sacrifice fly, scoring brother Lloyd.

Game 3   at New York   10/7/27

| Pitt. | 0 0 0   0 0 0   0 1 0—1 3 1 |
|---|---|
| N.Y. | 2 0 0   0 0 0   6 0 x—8 9 0 |

Gehrig's two-run triple put the Yankees in front but again the story was New York's pitching. Herb Pennock retired the first 21 batters he faced. Murderers' Row broke the game open with six runs on four hits including a three-run homer by Ruth, the Yankees' first homer of the series. The attention returned to Pennock who retired Wright for out number 22. Pie Traynor broke the suspense with a single to left and Barnhart's double broke up Pennock's shutout.

Game 4   at New York   10/8/27

| Pitt. | 1 0 0   0 0 0   2 0 0—3 10 1 |
|---|---|
| N.Y. | 1 0 0   0 2 0   0 0 1—4 12 2 |

Wright's two out RBI single put the Bucs on top but hits by Combs, Koenig, and Ruth tied the game after one inning. Ruth clubbed a two-run homer in the fifth but errors by Gehrig and Lazzeri, an RBI single by Barnhart, and Paul Waner's fly to center knotted the game at 3-3. It was still tied in the bottom of the ninth when Combs walked and Koenig bunted for a hit. A wild pitch moved the runners up but Johnny Miljus fanned Gehrig and Meusel after intentionally walking Ruth. With a one strike count on Lazzeri, Miljus' pitch got past Johnny Gooch and Combs scored the series' ending run.

It took 33 long and often frustrating years before the N.L. pennant again flew over Forbes Field. The 1960 season saw the Pirates grab the lead in the middle of May and successfully fight off challenges from Milwaukee and St. Louis to win by seven games.

The Bucs fielded a solid club. The N.L. MVP, Dick Groat, was at short and another All-Star, Bill Mazeroski, was at second. The outfield featured Roberto Clemente in right, Bill Virdon in center and Bob Skinner in left. The pitching staff was headed by 20-game winner, Vern Law and 19-game winner, Bob Friend. Out of the bullpen came the Cy Young award winner, Elroy Face, whose 68 appearances were the most of any pitcher in the league.

The Bucs of 1960 had a team of 25 stars. Some shone brighter than others, but every player was counted on to contribute when called upon. The Pirates came to be known as a team that could come back from any deficit and win in the late innings.

Their opponents in the Series were once again the New York Yankees. The Yanks were again a strong team. Mickey Mantle had 40 homers in the regular season, Roger Maris hit 39 and the club smashed a record 193 round-trippers. However, the Yankee pitching was not as formidable as in '27. Art Ditmar topped the staff with a 15-9 record, Jim Coates won 13, and Whitey Ford won 12.

In the Series, the Bucs avenged their loss in 1927 by winning the wildest series of all time. The Yankees came into the Classic with a 15-game winning streak and after a loss in Game 1, they looked as if they were going to win 15 more as they bombarded Pirate pitching for 26 runs in Games 2 and 3. The Yankees shattered all kinds of records. As a team they batted .338 on 91 hits and scored 55 runs with 10 home runs. Individually, it was Elston Howard batting .462, Mickey Mantle .400, Bill Skowron .375, and Bobby Richardson .367. Richardson drove in 12 runs and Mantle 11.

241

The Pirates were not as offensive. They had a team average of only .256. Bill Mazeroski was the Bucs' individual leader with a .320 average. Roberto Clemente (.310) was the only other regular to bat over .300. Powerwise, the Bucs only hit four home runs, but three of them came in the last game. Clemente hit safely in all seven games.

## 1960 WORLD SERIES

Game 1    at Pittsburgh    10/5/60

| | | |
|---|---|---|
| N.Y. | 1 0 0  1 0 0  0 0 2—4 | 13  2 |
| Pitt. | 3 0 0  2 0 1  0 0 x—6 | 8  0 |

*Ditmar,* Coates (1), Maas (5), Duren (7) and Berra
*Law,* Face (7) and Burgess

Roger Maris gave the Yanks a 1-0 lead with a two-out, upper-deck homer in the top of the first but the Pirates jumped on starter Art Ditmar for three runs as Bill Virdon led off with a walk, stole second, and went to third when nobody covered the base as Yogi Berra's throw sailed into center. Dick Groat followed with a double to right and Bob Skinner singled to center scoring Groat. Skinner stole second and scored on Roberto Clemente's single to center. In the fourth, Roger Maris singled and Mickey Mantle walked. Berra then drove a ball to deep rightcenter forcing Virdon to make a great leaping catch at the 420-foot mark. On the play, Maris went to third where he was able to score on Bill Skowron's single. The Pirates answered with two runs of their own when Bill Mazeroski singled, was sacrificed to second, and scored on Virdon's double off the screen in right. The Yankees attempted a comeback in the ninth when with one out, and a man on first, pinch-hitter Elston Howard homered to the seats in right. Tony Kubek followed with a single but was retired when Hector Lopez grounded into a game-ending doubleplay, Mazeroski to Groat to Stuart.

Game 2    at Pittsburgh    10/6/60

| | | |
|---|---|---|
| N.Y. | 0 0 2  1 2 7  3 0 1—16 | 19  1 |
| Pitt. | 0 0 0  1 0 0  0 0 2— 3 | 13  1 |

*Turley,* Shantz (9) and Howard.
*Friend,* Green (5), Labine (6), Witt (6), Gibbon (7), Cheney (9) and Burgess.

The Yankees scored two runs in the third when Richardson walked, went to second on Bob Turley's sacrifice and scored when Kubek singled to center. Kubek later scored on Gil McDougald's double inside the third base line. They scored a run in the fourth, two in the fifth and put the game out of sight with seven tallies in the sixth. Mantle smashed two home runs (including a three-run, 475 ft. blast in the 7th) and drove in five. Richardson and Kubek each had three hits and scored three times. As a team the Yankees had 19 hits, good for 30 total bases.

Game 3    at New York    10/8/60

| | | |
|---|---|---|
| Pitt. | 0 0 0  0 0 0  0 0 0— 0 | 4  0 |
| N.Y. | 6 0 0  4 0 0  0 0 x—10 | 16  1 |

*Mizell,* Labine (1), Green (1), Witt (4), Cheney (6), Gibbon (8) and Smith.
*Ford* and Howard.

The Yanks picked up where they had left off the game before scoring six in the first, highlighted by Richardson's grand slam just inside the leftfield foul pole. In the fourth inning, Mantle hit his third homer of the series, a two-out shot into the leftfield bullpen. Later in the same inning, Richardson singled home two runs to set a series record for six RBIs in a game. Whitey Ford sailed with a four-hit shutout.

Game 4    at New York    10/9/60

| | | |
|---|---|---|
| Pitt. | 0 0 0  0 3 0  0 0 0—3 | 7  0 |
| N.Y. | 0 0 0  1 0 0  1 0 0—2 | 8  0 |

*Law,* Face (7) and Burgess, Oldis (9).

*Terry,* Shantz (7), Coates (8) and Berra.

Vernon Law won his second game, this time with both his arm and his bat. Law scattered eight hits (eight less than the Yankees had the day before) and struck out five in six and one-third innings. With the lumber, he went two-for-three, driving in a run and scoring what proved to be the winning run. But he did have some help. Trailing 1-0 in the fifth (Skowron homered to right), Gino Cimoli singled to right, Smokey Burgess bounced to first but both runners were safe when Skowron was late with his throw to second. Don Hoak and Mazeroski both popped-out. Law then delivered with a double into the leftfield corner, scoring Cimoli. Virdon followed with a single to center. Burgess scored and so did Law, just ahead of Mantle's peg to the plate. Virdon saved the game in the seventh when with one out, one run in and runners on first and second, Bob Cerv drove a ball to the 400-foot sign in right-center where Virdon made an outstanding leaping stab. Elroy Face picked up his second save by pitching two and two-thirds perfect innings.

Game 5    at New York    10/10/60

| | | |
|---|---|---|
| Pitt. | 0 3 1  0 0 0  0 0 1—5 10 2 |
| N.Y. | 0 1 1  0 0 0  0 0 0—2  5 2 |

*Haddix,* Face (7) and Burgess, Oldis (9)

*Ditmar,* Arroyo (2), Stafford (3), Duren (8) and Howard, Berra (9)

The Pirates jumped to an early lead, getting three runs in the second when Stuart lead-off with a single. He was forced out at second when Cimoli bounced to Richardson. Burgess then doubled into the rightfield corner, moving Cimoli to third. Hoak bounced to Kubek, who threw to third trying to get Burgess, but McDougald dropped the ball and Hoak scampered into second. Mazeroski followed with a double down the leftfield line scoring Burgess and Hoak. The Yankees got on the board when Howard doubled to right and scored when Richardson and Kubek grounded out to the right side. Both teams scored single runs in the fourth. Groat doubled and scored on Clemente's single to left. Maris drilled a homer into the third deck of the right field stands. Harvey Haddix was pitching a three hitter into the seventh until Kubek and Lopez each singled. Danny Murtaugh called in Face, who put out the fire and finished the game without allowing a hit. Going back to the last inning of Game 1, Face retired 18 of 19 batters.

Game 6    at Pittsburgh    10/12/60

| | |
|---|---|
| N.Y. | 0 1 5  0 0 2  2 2 0—12 17 1 |
| Pitt. | 0 0 0  0 0 0  0 0 0— 0  7 1 |

*Ford* and Howard, Blanchard (3).

*Friend,* Cheney (3), Mizell (4), Green (6). Labine (6), Witt (9) and Smith.

The Pirates came home looking for a quick finish to the series but what they got was another humiliating defeat. Leading 1-0. Kubek was hit by a pitch to lead-off the third. Maris doubled off the screen in right and both runners scored on Mantle's single to right. Berra singled to right center, putting runners on the corners. That was all for Friend but not for the Yanks. Skowron greeted Tom Cheney with a sacrifice fly scoring Mantle, then Johnny Blanchard singled to center. Richardson tripled off the scoreboard in left, scoring Berra and Blanchard and setting a new series record with 11 RBIs. Richardson later extended his record with his second triple in the seventh driving in Blanchard. Ford went the distance for his second complete shutout of the series.

Game 7    at Pittsburgh    10/13/60

| | |
|---|---|
| N.Y. | 0 0 0  0 1 4  0 2 2— 9 13 1 |
| Pitt. | 2 2 0  0 0 0  0 5 1—10 11 0 |

Turley, Stafford (2), Shantz (3), Coates (8), *Terry (8)* and Blanchard.

Law, Face (6), Friend (9), *Haddix (9)* and Burgess, Smith (8).

The Pirates jumped to an early lead, scoring two in the first when, with two outs,

Skinner walked and Rocky Nelson homered into the rightfield seats. The Bucs added two more in the second as Burgess singled over first, Hoak drew a walk from reliever Bill Stafford, and Mazeroski beat out a bunt down the third base line to load the bases. Law failed to help himself as he bounced into a doubleplay, Stafford to Blanchard to Skowron. Fortunately, Virdon delivered with a single to right, scoring Hoak and Mazeroski. The Yankees scored in the fifth on Skowron's solo-homer. New York took the lead in the sixth as Richardson singled and Kubek walked. Face came and got Maris to pop to Hoak, but Mantle singled to center, scoring Richardson and moving Kubek to third. Berra followed with a three-run homer down the right field line into the upper-deck. New York increased its lead to three in the eighth when with two outs, Berra walked. Skowron beat out a chopper to third, Blanchard singled to right, scoring Berra, with Skowron going to third. Clete Boyer drove in Skowron with a double into the left field corner. The Pirates came back in the bottom of the eighth as Cimoli, batting for Face, singled to right. Virdon then hit a shot to short that took a bad hop and hit Kubek in the throat. Both runners were safe and Kubek was forced to leave the game. Groat singled past third, scoring Cimoli and putting Virdon on second. Casey Stengel brought in Coates who almost got out of the inning. Skinner made the first out as he sacrificed the runners into scoring position. Nelson flied out to right and both runners had to hold their bases. Clemente tapped a slow roller down the first base line and was safe as he beat Skowron to the bag. On the play, Virdon scored from third.

Then with a 2-2 count, Hal Smith homered over the left field wall to give the Bucs a 9-7 lead. But the Yankees weren't finished yet. Richardson led off the ninth with a single to left. Pinch hitter Dale Long singled to right. Murtaugh went to Haddix who got Maris to foul out to Smith for the first out. Mantle singled to center, scoring Richardson and moving Long to Third. With Berra coming to bat, McDougald ran for Long and represented the tying run. Berra hit a grounder to Nelson, who realizing the possibility of a series-ending doubleplay stepped on first and turned to throw to second. But as he did, Mantle saw that the force had been removed and dove back into first under Nelson as McDougald crossed the plate. Haddix then got Skowron to bounce to short to end the inning. In the ninth, Mazeroski sent Ralph Terry's second pitch over the left field wall and the city into ecstasy.

### The Era of "the Family"

After losing Donn Clendenon, Manny Mota and Maury Wills to Montreal and Al McBean, Dave Roberts and Ron Slocum to San Diego, the Pirates went to their farm system and came up with players that would form the core of the club for the 70s. Coming to the club in this period were catcher Manny Sanguillen, first baseman Bob Robertson, second baseman Dave Cash, third baseman Richie Hebner, and outfielder Al Oliver. Add those youngsters to veterans Roberto Clemente, Bill Mazeroski, Willie Stargell, Matty Alou, and Gene Alley and it's easy to see that the Bucs fielded a formidable team.

Success came to Pittsburgh again in 1970 when the Bucs fought off the Cubs and the Mets to win their first Eastern Division Championship by six games. Clemente batted .352, Sanguillen batted .325, and Stargell contributed 31 homers and 85 RBIs to the offense. Luke Walker was the winningest pitcher with 15 and Dave Giusti saved 26.

In the Championship Series, the Pirates lost three hard-fought games to the Cincinnati Reds. Stargell led all batters with six hits and a .500 average. Clemente was held to three hits and a .214 average.


1970 CHAMPIONSHIP SERIES

Game 1    at Pittsburgh    10/3/70

Cin.        0 0 0    0 0 0    0 0 0    3—3    9    0
Pitt.       0 0 0    0 0 0    0 0 0    0—0    8    0

Dock Ellis and Gary Nolan matched goose eggs for nine innings until pinch hitter Ty Cline tripled to right center and scored on Pete Rose's broken bat single to right in the top of the tenth. The Reds added two more runs and Clay Carroll finished the shutout. Ellis allowed nine hits in nine and two-thirds innings and Nolan allowed eight hits in nine innings. The Pirates' best scoring threat came in the third when Hebner singled and two outs later Alou doubled. Cash then whistled a one-hopper to second baseman Tommy Helms' right. The ball looked like a sure hit, but Helms speared the ball as he was falling down and managed to throw out Cash at first.

Game 2   at Pittsburgh   10/4/70
Cin.                         0 0 1   0 1 0   0 1 0—3   8   1
Pitt.                        0 0 0   0 0 1   0 0 0—1   5   2

Cincinnati opened the scoring in the third when Bobby Tolan singled, stole second and went to third when Sanguillen's throw sailed into center. Tolan later scored when Luke Walker uncorked a wild pitch. The lead went to two runs in the fifth when Tolan blasted a two-out homer to center. The Bucs countered with a run in the sixth when Cash doubled, and Clemente and Sanguillen singled. With the Pirates threatening, Don Gullett got Stargell to end the inning. Cincinnati added an insurance run in the eighth which wasn't needed as Gullett held the Bucs hitless for the last three innings.

Game 3   at Cincinnati   10/5/70
Pitt.                        1 0 0   0 1 0   0 0 0—2   10   0
Cin.                         2 0 0   0 0 0   0 1 x—3   5   0

The Pirates scored a run in the first but the lead didn't last long. In the bottom of the first, Tony Perez and Johnny Bench hit back-to-back homers. Pittsburgh tied the game in the fifth when Alou singled, went to second on a wild pitch, and scored on Stargell's single. In the eighth, Ty Cline walked, and Pete Rose singled. Joe Gibbon came in to pitch to Tolan and had him down 0-2. Tolan then singled to left to score Cline with the winning run. The Bucs tried to come back in the ninth when Clemente and Stargell singled but Oliver bounced to Helms to end the series.

The following year, the Pirates jumped to an early lead and put down a late season charge by St. Louis to win by seven games.

The Pirates were carried by the big bat of Willie Stargell who clubbed 48 home runs and drove in 125 runs. Clemente added a .341 average and Sanguillen hit .319. The pitching staff was headed by Dock Ellis with 19 wins and Steve Blass with a 2.85 ERA. Dave Giusti set a Pirate record with 30 saves.

In the N.L.C.S., Bob Robertson was the batting hero with four home runs, six RBIs and a .438 average. Dave Cash had eight hits and a .421 average. Dave Giusti was the pitching star, appearing in all four games, and saving three.

## 1971 CHAMPIONSHIP SERIES

Game 1   at San Francisco   10/2/71
Pitt.                        0 0 2   0 0 0   2 0 0—4   9   0
S.F.                         0 0 1   0 4 0   0 0 x—5   7   2

Steve Blass had fanned nine Giants in the first four innings and a tired, injured San Francisco club seemed to be no match for the Pirates. Chris Speier led off the Giants fifth with a single and light hitting Tito Fuentes suddenly put San Francisco ahead with a home run. Blass walked Willie Mays and Willie McCovey followed with a tremendous blast into the right field stands, putting the Giants ahead 5-2. The Bucs rallied in the seventh on hits by Dave Cash and Gene Alley, followed by a walk to Roberto Clemente. Al Oliver singled home two runs but Gaylord Perry retired Bob Robertson to end the threat.

Game 2   at San Francisco   10/3/71

| Pitt. | 0 1 0   2 1 0   4 0 1—9 15 0 |
|---|---|
| S.F. | 1 1 0   0 0 0   0 0 2—4 9 0 |

Pittsburgh had trouble with nine-game winner John Cumberland through the first three innings and trailed 2-1. San Francisco took a 1-0 lead on Mays' double to score Fuentes. The Giants might have blown the game open but left the bases loaded in the first. Bob Robertson began a fantastic afternoon by doubling in the second. Manny Sanguillen singled Bob home with the tying run. The Giants were leading 2-1 on Ken Henderson's RBI single when the Pirates first baseman came to bat again in the fourth. Robertson hit a long fly ball to left field. Henderson went back, jumped, and deflected the ball into the seats for a home run. When Sanguillen singled, manager Charlie Fox replaced Cumberland with Jim Barr. Manny stole second and Jackie Hernandez broke the tie with another single. Gene Clines' homer in the fifth put the Bucs ahead 4-2 and a double by Cash and hits by Oliver and Clemente gave the Bucs a three-run margin. After Stargell fanned, Robertson put the icing on the cake with his second homer. Just for good measure, Bobby slammed another home run in the ninth. Willie Mays' two run shot in the ninth did nothing to dim Robertson's performance and the series moved to Pittsburgh.

Game 3   at Pittsburgh   10/5/71

| S.F. | 0 0 0   0 0 1   0 0 0—1 5 2 |
|---|---|
| Pitt. | 0 1 0   0 0 0   0 1 x—2 4 1 |

Nellie Briles was scheduled to pitch the first game at Pittsburgh but pulled a hamstring muscle while warming up. His replacement was Bob Johnson, a disappointment in the regular season after being acquired from Kansas City. Johnson responded to the challenge with eight strong innings. Hebner's throwing error brought Henderson home with the Giants only run, equalizing Bob Robertson's home run in the second. Juan Marichal allowed only four hits but two were homers. Hebner atoned for his error with a blast over the rightfield fence to put the Pirates in front. Dave Giusti retired the Giants in the ninth.

Game 4   at Pittsburgh   10/6/71

| S.F. | 1 4 0   0 0 0   0 0 0—5 10 0 |
|---|---|
| Pitt. | 2 3 0   0 0 4   0 0 x—9 11 2 |

Neither Blass nor Perry was effective in the rematch of the first game. Blass was plagued by the long ball again. Chris Speier's drive and another blast by McCovey gave San Francisco a 5-2 lead. When Sanguillen and Bill Mazeroski singled, Perry was in trouble. Hebner delivered with a home run to tie the game. Bruce Kison came on to stop the Giants and Perry settled down until the sixth. Cash was on second with two out when Clemente singled to break the tie. Jerry Johnson came on to face lefthanded hitters Stargell, and Oliver. A passed ball moved Clemente to second and forced Johnson to walk Stargell intentionally. Oliver slammed a three-run homer into the right field seats and the Pirates were on their way to Baltimore.

The Orioles were defending world champs. They came into the series with four 20-game winners and the same club that had won the A.L. championship three years in a row.

This Series belonged to Clemente. He hit safely in all seven games, running his World Series streak to 14 games. Overall, he batted .414 with four RBIs. Of his 12 hits, five went for extra-bases, including two homers. Clemente's fielding and hustle were inspirational. He was named the MVP for leading the Bucs to the championship.

Other stars were Sanguillen with a .379 average and Bob Robertson with two home runs and five RBIs. Brooks Robinson was the only Oriole to bat over .300 as he had seven hits and a .318 average.

Steve Blass was the pitching star, winning two complete games and giving up only two runs and seven hits in 18 innings. Bruce Kison, Dave Giusti, Nellie Briles, and Bob Moose combined to hold the Birds scoreless for 22 consecutive innings from Game 4 through Game 6. After allowing 16 runs in the first two games, Pirate pitching allowed only seven runs in the last five. For the 0's, Dave McNally won two and lost one in four games and finished with a 1.98 ERA. Mike Cuellar lost twice and Pat Dobson had a 4.05 ERA in three games.

## 1971 CHAMPIONSHIP SERIES

Game 1   at Baltimore   10/9/71

| | | | | | | |
|---|---|---|---|---|---|---|
| Pitt. | 0 3 0 | 0 0 0 | 0 0 0—3 | 3 | 0 |
| Balt. | 0 1 3 | 0 1 0 | 0 0 x—5 | 10 | 3 |

The Pirates posted an early 3-0 lead with the help of some shaky Baltimore defense. In the second, Robertson led off with a walk and went to second on a wild pitch. Sanguillen then bounced to Mark Belanger whose throw to third hit Robertson and bounced into the Baltimore dugout. Robertson scored and Sanguillen went to second. Jose Pagan bounced back to McNally, advancing Sangy to third. Hernandez laid down a perfect squeeze bunt. Sangy scored when Elrod Hendricks dropped the throw from McNally. On the play, Hernandez went to second. After Ellis struck out, Cash singled to right center scoring Hernandez.

The Orioles rebounded with a Frank Robinson homer. In the third, Belanger singled and went to second when Don Buford singled on the right side of the infield. Merv Rettenmund followed with a home run over the leftcenter field wall.

After the Bucs scored in the second, they had only one real threat. It came in the third when Clemente singled to start the inning and Stargell followed with a walk. At this point, McNally toughened. He struck out Robinson and Sanguillen and got Pagan to fly to left. After Stargell's walk, McNally retired 19 consecutive batters until Sanguillen reached on Belanger's error in the ninth.

Game 2   at Baltimore   10/11/71

| | | | | | | |
|---|---|---|---|---|---|---|
| Pitt. | 0 0 0 | 0 0 0 | 0 3 0— 3 | 8 | 1 |
| Balt. | 0 1 0 | 3 6 1 | 0 0 x—11 | 14 | 1 |

Following a day of rain, Baltimore clubbed the Pirates by scoring three runs in the fourth, and six in the fifth. The batting stars in this game were Brooks Robinson (3-for-3 with 3 RBIs) and Frank Robinson (3-for-4). The Orioles scored 11 runs without an extra-base hit.

The Pirates scored all their runs in the eighth on a Hebner three-run homer into the right field seats.

Game 3   at Pittsburgh   10/12/71

| | | | | | | |
|---|---|---|---|---|---|---|
| Balt. | 0 0 0 | 0 0 0 | 1 0 0—1 | 3 | 3 |
| Pitt. | 1 0 0 | 0 0 1 | 3 0 x—5 | 7 | 0 |

The Pirates drew first blood when Cash led off the bottom of the first with a double down the left field line. Cash went to third when Boog Powell threw wildly to Cuellar on Oliver's ground ball. Clemente forced Oliver at second, Johnson to Belanger, as Cash scored. The Bucs took a two-run lead in the sixth when Sanguillen doubled and scored on Pagan's single. Frank Robinson put the Birds on the board with a lead-off homer into the second level of the left field seats. The Pirates put the game away in the bottom of the seventh when Clemente reached first on Cuellar's error, Stargell walked (third time in the game and sixth in the first three games), and Robertson missed a bunt sign but homered to right center. Blass pitched superbly, allowing only three hits.

Game 4   at Pittsburgh   10/13/71

| | | | | | | |
|---|---|---|---|---|---|---|
| Balt. | 3 0 0 | 0 0 0 | 0 0 0—3 | 4 | 1 |
| Pitt. | 2 0 1 | 0 0 0 | 1 0 x—4 | 14 | 0 |

Paul Blair opened the game with a single and before the prime time TV audience could get settled into their easy chairs, the O's had a 3-0 lead. After Blair's single, Belanger and Rettenmund followed with infield hits. Then with Frank Robinson the batter, Sanguillen let a ball get past him scoring Blair and putting runners on second and third. Frank Robinson was then intentionally walked. Brooks Robinson scored Belanger with a sacrifice fly to center, with all the runners advancing. Powell did the same, scoring Rettenmund. Kison was brought in to pitch and retired Dave Johnson to end the inning. The Bucs battled back in the bottom of the first as Cash drew a lead-off walk, and after Hebner popped out and Clemente struck out, Stargell doubled, scoring Cash. Blair then misplayed Oliver's drive to center allowing Stargell to score. The Pirates tied the game in the third when, with one out, Hebner and Clemente singled, Stargell popped to short center and Oliver drove in Hebner with a single to right. The winning run was scored in the seventh. With one out, Robertson and Sanguillen singled, Vic Davalillo, batting for Hernandez, flied to center but was safe when Blair dropped the ball. Robertson went to third but Sanguillen overran second and was thrown out. Rookie Milt May looped a pinch hit single into right center to drive in Robertson. The star of the game was rookie pitcher Bruce Kison. He pitched six and two-thirds and allowed only one hit. Kison set a record by hitting three Bird batters.

Game 5   at Pittsburgh   10/14/71

| | | | | | | | |
|---|---|---|---|---|---|---|---|
| Balt. | 000 | 000 | 000—0 | 2 | 1 |
| Pitt. | 021 | 010 | 0 x 0—4 | 9 | 0 |

This game belonged to Nellie Briles. He shutout the Orioles on two hits and two walks. With the help of two doubleplays, Briles faced only two over the 27 batter limit. The game was decided in the second when Robertson led off with a home run over the right field fence. Sanguillen followed with a single and stole second. Pagan and Hernandez struckout, but Briles delivered with a single to center, scoring Sanguillen. The Pirates added two more insurance runs but the Orioles never threatened and never had two base runners in the same inning.

Game 6   at Baltimore   10/16/71

| | | | | | |
|---|---|---|---|---|---|
| Pitt. | 011 | 000 | 000 0—2 | 9 | 1 |
| Balt. | 000 | 001 | 100 1—3 | 8 | 0 |

Back in Baltimore, the Bucs were hoping for a quick ending. It looked good as the Pirates took a lead in the second when Oliver doubled and scored on Robertson's single. Clemente homered over the right field fence to put the Bucs ahead 2-0 after three. But the Orioles refused to fold. Buford hit a solo-home run into the rightfield seats in the sixth. The Orioles tied the game in the seventh as Belanger singled, stole second, and scored on Dave Johnson's single to left. The game went into extra-innings with the score remaining the same and both teams had chances to win. The Orioles put runners on second and third with two outs in the ninth but Johnson grounded out to short to end the threat. The Pirates had their chance in the tenth as Cash singled, Clemente was intentionally passed and Stargell drew a walk. With two outs, McNally was called upon to face Oliver and got the Buc slugger to fly to center. Baltimore finally scratched out a run in the bottom of the inning when Frank Robinson walked and went to third on Rettenmund's single. Robinson scored when Brooks Robinson flied to shallow center and Davalillo's throw took a high hop between the mound and home allowing him to slide under Sanguillen's tag.

Game 7   at Baltimore   10/17/71

| | | | | | |
|---|---|---|---|---|---|
| Pitt. | 000 | 100 | 010—2 | 6 | 1 |
| Balt. | 000 | 000 | 010—1 | 4 | 0 |

After three scoreless innings, Clemente put the Pirates ahead with a two-out home run over the left field wall. Blass and Cuellar matched out for out and the game remained 1-0 through seven innings. In the eighth, Stargell led-off with a single to left.

Pagan drilled a ball off the left center field fence and when Rettenmund bobbled the ball for just a second, Stargell headed for home. On the relay, Belanger's throw skipped under Powell's glove and rolled to the plate allowing Stargell to slide in just ahead of the tag. The Orioles rallied in the bottom of the eighth with Hendricks and Belanger hitting singles. Tom Shopay, batting for Cuellar, sacrificed both runners into scoring position. Buford grounded to first scoring Hendricks and putting the tying run just ninety feet away. Blass then got Johnson to ground to deep short where Hernandez, who had been critized by Earl Weaver before the series, made an excellent play ending the Birds' chances. In the ninth, Powell grounded to Cash and Frank Robinson popped to short. The O's were down to an out with Rettenmund the batter. He hit a ball up the middle where Hernandez made a gliding stop behind second and threw to Robertson to give the Bucs their fourth World Championship.

Pittsburgh won its third Eastern Divisional Title in 1972. The Bucs had an easy time of it in the regular season, finishing 11 games ahead of the second place Cubs. The club was basically the same team that had won the World Championship the year before. Roberto Clemente batted .312 and collected his 3,000 hit on September 30, off Jon Matlack. Al Oliver also batted .312. Vic Davalillo, playing part-time in left, batted .318. Willie Stargell, playing first base for the injured Bob Robertson, batted .293 and had 33 home runs and 112 RBIs. Steve Blass, Dock Ellis, Nellie Briles, and Bob Moose again formed the core of the pitching staff with Dave Giusti and Ramon Hernandez in the bullpen.

As in 1970, the Bucs met the Reds in the Championship Series. This time the series went the full five games with the teams exchanging wins through the first four games. This was possibly the most exciting Championship in N.L. history as the pennant wasn't decided until the last batter in the last inning of the last game.

The clubs were evenly matched. Pittsburgh featured strong hitting with good, consistent pitching and the Reds were much the same. Their hitting came from Pete Rose, Joe Morgan, Johnny Bench, and Tony Perez. The pitching was supplied by Gary Nolan, Ross Grimsley, Tom Hall, and Clay Carroll.


## 1972 CHAMPIONSHIP SERIES


Game 1    at Pittsburgh    10/7/72

| | | | | | |
|---|---|---|---|---|---|
| Cin. | 1 0 0 | 0 0 0 | 0 0 0—1 | 8 | 0 |
| Pitt. | 3 0 0 | 0 2 0 | 0 0 x—5 | 6 | 0 |

After the Reds took a 1-0 lead in the top of the first, the Pirates answered with three of their own in the home half of the first. The Bucs scored three runs on a single by Rennie Stennett, a triple by Al Oliver, a double by Willie Stargell, and a single by Richie Hebner. Pittsburgh added two runs in the fifth on a home run by Al Oliver that cleared the 385 ft. mark in right center. Steve Blass pitched eight and a third innings, scattered eight hits, and won his fourth consecutive game in post-season play.

Game 2    at Pittsburgh    10/8/72

| | | | | | |
|---|---|---|---|---|---|
| Cin. | 4 0 0 | 0 0 0 | 0 1 0—5 | 8 | 1 |
| Pitt. | 0 0 0 | 1 1 1 | 0 0 0—3 | 7 | 1 |

Cincinnati scored four runs in the first off starter Bob Moose. Pete Rose and Joe Morgan both singled. Bobby Tolan doubled down the left field line on a ball that the Pirates claimed to have hit at least a foot foul. But none the less, two runs scored. Johnny Bench followed with a double to right center moving Tolan to third. Tony Perez then doubled down the right field line, scoring Tolan and Bench. The Pirates chipped away at the Cincinnati lead, by scoring single runs in each of the middle three innings. With the Bucs rallying in the eighth, Tom Hall struck out Stargell to end the Pirates' chances.

Game 3    at Cincinnati    10/9/72

| Pitt. | 0 0 0   0 1 0   1 1 0—3   7   0 |
|-------|--------------------------------|
| Cin.  | 0 0 2   0 0 0   0 0 0—2   8   1 |

The Reds jumped in front in the third inning by scoring two runs and looked as if they were going to add to the lead in the fourth but great fielding plays by Gene Alley and Rennie Stennett stopped the Reds and turned the tide in the Pirates favor. In that fourth inning, Bench tripled to left. Perez popped to shallow left center where Alley made an outstanding, twisting, leaping catch. On the play, Bench went to third. Cesar Geronimo then flied to Stennett in left who threw out Bench at the plate. In the fifth, Sanguillen homered to left center. Pittsburgh tied the game in the seventh when Hebner was hit by a pitch and Sanguillen singled. Alley sacrificed both runners into scoring position. Davalillo was then intentionally walked and Stennett delivered with an infield single to score Hebner. Cash flied out and Davalillo was caught off second to end the rally. The Pirates took the lead in the eighth when, with one out, Stargell walked, Oliver doubled, and Hebner walked. After the Oliver double, Gene Clines ran for Stargell and scored when Sanguillen beat out an infield hit to Darrell Chaney at short. The Reds threatened in the bottom of the eighth, but with one out and Rose on second, Giusti got Morgan to ground out and struck out Tolan on four pitches.

Game 4    at Cincinnati    10/10/72

| Pitt. | 0 0 0   0 0 0   1 0 0—1   2   3 |
|-------|--------------------------------|
| Cin.  | 1 0 0   2 0 2   2 0 x—7  11   1 |

Ross Grimsley was the star of the game. He limited the Pirates to one run on two hits. The only run came on a Roberto Clemente homer in the seventh inning. Grimsley didn't walk a man while fanning five. The Reds took the lead in the first again. With two outs and Tolan on first, Bench singled, advancing Tolan to third. Tolan scored when Sanguillen, attempting to throw out Bench at second, threw the ball into center field. Cincinnati added two runs in the fourth. Bench singled and stole second. Two outs later, Geronimo lifted a pop into shallow left. This time Alley could not make the play. Bench scored and when Alley threw the ball away, Geronimo went to third. Geronimo scored when Chaney beat out a bunt. The Reds added four more runs but for the Pirates, it was too much Grimsley.

Game 5    at Cincinnati    10/11/72

| Pitt. | 0 2 0   1 0 0   0 0 0—3   8   0 |
|-------|--------------------------------|
| Cin.  | 0 0 1   0 1 0   0 0 2—4   7   1 |

For the first time in the series, the Pirates scored first, getting two runs in the second as Sanguillen singled, and scored on Hebner's double to right. Hebner went to third when the relay got away from Chaney. He later scored on Cash's single. In the third, the Reds scored when Cline singled and went to second on Gullett's sacrifice. Rose then hit a ball that took a bad hop at first base and went over Stargell's head and into the right field corner for a double. Pittsburgh took a two-run lead again in the fourth on singles by Sanguillen, Hebner, and Cash. Geronimo made it a one-run game by homering in the fifth. The game score remained the same through eight and a half innings. Then in the bottom of the ninth, Bench homered off Giusti. Perez singled and was then replaced by pinch runner George Foster. Denis Menke followed with a single after he was unable to sacrifice. Giusti then went to an 2-0 count on Geronimo and Virdon went to Moose. Moose got Geronimo to fly out to Clemente, but Foster went to third. Chaney then popped out to short. Hal McRae pinch-hit for Clay Carroll. Moose had the count at a ball and a strike but his third pitch skipped past Sanguillen and Foster scored from third with the winning run.

After the game the Pirates clubhouse was quiet. The players were staring into their lockers or looking at the floor. Clemente then shouted from the center of the room, "Quit hanging your heads. We had a great year. Start thinking about next February when we'll all be together again. We'll come back and do it again only next time we're going all the way."

Sadly, the Pirates weren't all together the next year. The team suffered the loss of Clemente and also the puzzling ineffectiveness of Steve Blass and finished third behind the Mets and the Cubs. The '74 season looked like a repeat of the year before as the Bucs were stuck in last place on June 7. But the Pirates came on strong and took possession of first place on August 25. The rest of the season was a dog-fight with the Cardinals. The team slipped in and out of the top spot until the final day of the season when the Bucs beat the Cubs by scoring two runs with two out in the ninth as Steve Swisher dropped Bob Robertson's third strike and then threw wildly, allowing the final rally. Al Oliver led the team with 198 hits and his .321 average was second in the N.L. Richie Zisk batted .313 with 17 home runs and 100 RBIs. Stargell batted .301 with 25 homers and 96 RBIs. The pitching staff was headed by a couple of newcomers. Ken Brett won 13 and Jerry Reuss won 16. Jim Rooker finished with a 15-11 record and a 2.77 ERA, eighth best in the League.

In the Championship Series the Pirates took on the Dodgers and lost in four games. Stargell was the only Buc to do much offensively. He batted .400 with two home runs. For the Dodgers, Bill Russell batted .389, Ron Cey batted .313, and Steve Garvey had two homers and five RBIs.

## 1974 CHAMPIONSHIP SERIES

Game 1   at Pittsburgh   10/5/74

| | | | | | | | | | |
|---|---|---|---|---|---|---|---|---|---|
| L.A. | 0 1 0 | 0 0 0 | 0 0 2—3 | 9 | 2 |
| Pitt. | 0 0 0 | 0 0 0 | 0 0 0—0 | 4 | 0 |

Don Sutton pitched a four hitter and just waited for his teammates to get some runs. He got a one run lead in the second when Davey Lopes walked on a 3-2 pitch with the bases loaded. The score remained the same until the Dodgers put the game on ice with two runs in the ninth.

Game 2   at Pittsburgh   10/6/74

| | | | | | |
|---|---|---|---|---|---|
| L.A. | 1 0 0 | 1 0 0 | 0 3 0—5 | 12 | 0 |
| Pitt. | 0 0 0 | 0 0 0 | 2 0 0—2 | 8 | 3 |

The Dodgers jumped on Jim Rooker for a run in the first as Lopes walked and scored on singles by Bill Buckner and Garvey. Ron Cey gave Andy Messersmith a two-run lead with a home run in the fourth. The Pirates finally scored in the seventh when Paul Popovich and Zisk singled. Stennett sacrificed both runners into scoring position. Popovich scored when Hebner grounded out to first. Oliver got an RBI when he chopped a single off Cey's glove at third. It was then a battle of the bullpen aces, with Giusti going against Mike Marshall. There was no contest. Giusti couldn't get an out. Cey led off with a double and went to third when Russell bunted and Sanguillen was late with his throw to Hebner. Willie Crawford scored Cey with a pinch-hit single. Sanguillen committed his second error of the inning when his attempted pick-off throw of Russell at second sailed into center. With runners at second and third, Manny Mota singled to make the score 4-2. Giusti was replaced by Larry Demery who wild-pitched Crawford home to set the score at 5-2. Marshall retired the last six batters in order.

Game 3   at Los Angeles   10/8/74

| | | | | | |
|---|---|---|---|---|---|
| Pitt. | 5 0 2 | 0 0 0 | 0 0 0—7 | 10 | 0 |
| L.A. | 0 0 0 | 0 0 0 | 0 0 0—0 | 4 | 5 |

The Pirates, with their pride badly damaged, erupted for five runs in the first inning on home runs by Stargell and Hebner. Kison pitched six and two-thirds innings and allowed only two hits. Ramon Hernandez finished out the game and completed the four-hit shutout.

Game 4    at Los Angeles    10/9/74

| | | | | |
|---|---|---|---|---|
| Pitt. | 0 0 0 | 0 0 0 | 1 0 0— 1 | 3 1 |
| L.A. | 1 0 2 | 0 2 2 | 2 3 x—12 | 12 0 |

The Dodgers also had some pride. They also had a solid team and a pitcher named Sutton. Sutton hurled a three hitter and missed the shutout on a home run by Stargell. Meanwhile, the Dodger bats exploded for 12 runs highlighted by a pair of two-run homers by Steve Garvey. Russell added three RBIs and the game was never in doubt.

Pittsburgh won its fifth divisional title in six years in 1975. This year the Bucs took the lead on June 6th and had to fight off a challenge from their cross-state rivals in Philadelphia. The Phils managed to draw even with the Bucs on August 15 but the Pirates spurted for 25 wins in their next 39 games to wrap up the Eastern Championship on September 22. Dave Parker had his first big year, batting .308 with 25 homers and 101 RBIs. Stargell batted .295, blasted 22 home runs, and drove in 90 runs. Sanguillen contributed a .328 average and Zisk knocked in 75 runs with 20 home runs and a .290 average. Jerry Reuss led the pitchers with an 18-11 record and joining the club on June 6 was a youngster named John Candelaria.

Candelaria finished the regular season with a record of 8-6 but will always be remembered for his outstanding pitching in Game 3 of the Championship Series against the Reds. Unfortunately, Candy's pitching was wasted as the Reds won in three games. This was the third time the Pirates and Reds had met in championship play and each time the Reds had come out on top. Cincinnati had an overall record of 9-2 against the Pirates.

## 1975 CHAMPIONSHIP SERIES

Game 1    at Cincinnati    10/4/75

| | | | | |
|---|---|---|---|---|
| Pitt. | 0 2 0 | 0 0 0 | 0 0 1—3 | 8 0 |
| Cin. | 0 1 3 | 0 4 0 | 0 0 x—8 | 11 0 |

Between Don Gullett's pitching and Don Gullett's hitting, the Pirates didn't stand a chance in the series opener. After getting to Gullett for two runs in the second on a walk to Parker, a double by Hebner, and a single by Frank Taveras, Pittsburgh was held to two hits until the eighth inning. Gullett put the Reds on the board in the bottom of the second. George Foster and Dave Concepcion both walked and after Ken Griffey struck out and Geronimo flied out, Guillett delivered with a single to left to score Foster. The Reds took the lead in the third as Morgan and Bench led-off with walks and Perez followed with an RBI single to center. After Foster and Concepcion flied out to right, Griffey doubled to score Bench and Perez. Cincinnati broke the game open in the fifth with a four-run inning highlighted by Gullett's two run homer to left.

Game 2    at Cincinnati    10/5/75

| | | | | |
|---|---|---|---|---|
| Pitt. | 0 0 0 | 1 0 0 | 0 0 0—1 | 5 0 |
| Cin. | 2 0 0 | 2 0 1 | 1 0 x—6 | 12 1 |

Cincinnati took a two-run lead in the first on a two-out home run by Perez. The little lefty, Fred Norman, held the Bucs in check for the first three innings but allowed a run in the fourth when Stargell doubled, went to third on a wild pitch and scored when Hebner grounded out. Norman allowed Pittsburgh just four hits in the first six innings before giving way to Rawly Eastwick in the seventh. Eastwick retired the Pirates in order except for a lead-off double in the ninth by Zisk.

Game 3    at Pittsburgh    10/7/75

| | | | | | |
|---|---|---|---|---|---|
| Cin. | 0 1 0  0 0 0  0 2 0  2—5 | 6 | 0 |
| Pitt. | 0 0 0  0 0 2  0 0 1  0—3 | 7 | 2 |

John Candelaria started the third game and struck out the first four men he faced. Foster then flied out and Concepcion homered over the left center field wall. Candy struck out Griffey to end the second and fanned Geronimo and Nolan in the third. For the Reds, Gary Nolan had allowed only one hit, a first inning single by Hebner, through the first four innings. In the fifth, Candelaria retired the Reds in order for the third consecutive inning, striking out Concepcion for his ninth of the game (Kench fanned in the fourth). In the fifth, the Pirates staged a minor rally when with one out, Zisk and Sanguillen singled but Taveras fouled out and Candelaria struck out. In the sixth, Geronimo and Nolan struck out for numbers 10 and 11. With one out in the sixth, Hebner singled off Nolan's glove and Oliver followed with a blast over the center field wall to put Pittsburgh ahead 2-1. Candelaria still had a one hitter in the seventh but Cincinnati got two base runners on an error by Taveras and a walk. Candy got Perez to strike out and Concepcion to bounce out to end the threat. The game remained 2-1 through seven full innings when Candelaria struck out Griffey and Geronimo giving him a total of 14 for the game but then pinch hitter Rettenmund walked and Rose followed with a home run over the left field fence to give the Reds a 3-2 lead. Giusti came in to end the inning. In the bottom of the ninth, Stargell singled and was replaced by Willie Randolph. Parker struck out and Zisk singled. Sanguillen popped out to third. Pinch hitter Bob Robertson walked to load the bases. Duffy Dyer was chosen to pinch hit for the reliever Giusti. Dyer worked relief pitcher Eastwick for a walk to tie the game. The Reds scored twice in the tenth. Griffey beat out a bunt and was given second on a balk call. He went to third on Geronimo's ground out and scored on Ed Armbrister's sacrifice fly. The second run came on a Rose single and a double by Morgan. The Pirates had run out of comebacks and it was once again close but no prize.

## 8.   CLEMENTE—THE GREAT ONE

In 1971, Roberto Clemente reached center stage. For the first time since 1960, the Pirates had won the National League championship and headed for the World Series. Clemente was in the spotlight, in baseball's biggest event. Sixty million television viewers, the national media and the fans in Baltimore would finally see the kind of baseball Roberto Clemente played. It was a kind of baseball they had never seen before. Clemente opened with a double to deep right center off Dave McNally in the first game. He finished with a home run over the left-centerfield fence off Mike Cuellar in game seven. In between, he played at "something close to perfection," according to writer Roger Angell. In the field, he played with reckless abandon, catching everything within reach and throwing with a power and accuracy that had Oriole runners constantly looking over their shoulders. At the plate, he attacked every pitch, spraying line drives to every part of Memorial and Three Rivers Stadiums. On the bases, he ran with a controlled fury, arms flying, feet pumping, head bobbing. He resembled a raging cyclone as he slid into second or third or home. When Baltimore won the second game 11-3, Clemente's amazing throw from rightfield to third base was the topic of conversation. After game four, the first night game in World Series history, Roberto's rocket shot off the stadium wall, just foul, was most discussed. When Steve Blass won his second game to capture the championship, it was Clemente's overall play was considered the highlight of the series. When it was over, everybody agreed that it was a once-in-a-lifetime performance. Clemente said, "this is the way I play all the time. All season, every season. I gave everything I had to this game." After 17 years, Roberto Clemente had shown the world what kind of player he was.

Roberto came to Pittsburgh in 1955, a combination of luck and excellent scouting. His purchase from Brooklyn's AAA team at Montreal could be compared to the purchase of Manhattan, except that the Dodgers knew what they were losing. Roberto came to a Pirate club that was the laughing stock of baseball. His success was not instant, but there were immediate signs of the form that would mark his future greatness. He played the tricky rightfield corner at Forbes Field like an instrument, taking a carrom off the fence and gunning down one runner after another. At the plate, the bat was his weapon. He would stand deep in the batters' box, jump on a pitch, and pull it or wait and drive it to the opposite field. Almost every hit was either a line drive or a hard grounder. Every day, he put on a performance for the Pittsburgh fans who had starved for this kind of baseball. Those fans paid Roberto's salary and he felt a responsibility to them. When he played, he would give everything he had and more. When he could not play, he would not.

Clemente was an artist. He would not cheat the paying customers by playing something less than he expected from himself. Today, his occasional absences from the lineup would hardly be noticed. In the fifties and sixties, a player was supposed to play with pain, to keep playing until it was absolutely impossible. Roberto was already separated from his teammates and manager by race and nationality. His philosophy was considered arrogant. Players and writers did not believe he was injured. They called him a hypochondriac.

Hypochondriac. The tag followed Clemente like a shadow throughout his career. Despite a severe back injury suffered in 1954, an arm injury in 1959, and an attack of malaria in 1965, he played in 140 or more games in eight straight seasons and yet the tag remained affixed. Clemente knew what was best for him. He knew when not to play, and he told people. His teammates were angered. Players were not supposed to talk about their injuries. Clemente did not suffer from the American "Macho" image, that the players adhered to. Roberto came from Puerto Rico where there was nothing wrong with being hurt. The writers ridiculed him, never giving him the respect and recognition he deserved. Clemente had a tremendous pride in his work and he was angered by the lack of recognition. He was insulted by the press in 1960. The Pirates had won the World's Championship for the first time in 35 years and the heroes were many. Roberto felt he was surely one of the most valuable players. The baseball writers voted Dick Groat as the league's Most Valuable Player. Don Hoak was second. Clemente, a distant eighth. Roberto never wore his 1960 World Series ring because of the anger of being snubbed by the writers. He wore instead, the 1961 All-Star game ring. He had driven in the winning run and those that saw him knew he was great.

Anybody that watched Clemente play saw his greatness, but many were deprived of seeing the Great One at his prime. The Pirates slipped drastically after 1960 and Roberto was a superstar with a second rate team. He was trapped in Pittsburgh, Pennsylvania, away from the giant media centers of New York and Los Angeles. He was trapped in Forbes Field, a park that punished the home run swinger and rewarded the line drive hitter. In the power crazy era of the sixties, he could not compete with Mays and Mantle and Aaron.

His records are many and have been well documented but they deserve to be noted again.

Lifetime batting average: .317
Batting Champion: 1961, 64, 65, 67
*Sporting News* All-Star team: 1961, 64, 65, 66, 67, 70
All-Star team member: 1960-67, 69-72
*Sporting News* All-Star Fielding Team: 1961-72

Led National League in assists five times
Recorded 10 hits in two consecutive games, August 22-23, 1970
His feats were unequalled by all the other stars that gained the recognition he deserved.

Slowly, the problems began to recede and the recognition came. The veterans whom Clemente had fought for attention had been traded; Groat to St. Louis, Hoak to Philadelphia, Dick Stuart to Boston. They were replaced by young players, many of them black. Roberto was the elder statesman now and these players treated him with respect. In 1964, Danny Murtaugh was forced to resign as manager because of a heart condition. Murtaugh had been one of Roberto's chief antagonists but the new manager, Harry Walker, was immediately pro-Clemente. Walker told anybody who would listen that Roberto was the game's greatest player. Clemente responded with his third batting title but the Pirates finished third.

In 1966, Walker asked Clemente to try to hit for power, to challenge Forbes Field. Roberto responded with a career high 29 home runs and 109 RBIs. He almost single-handedly led the Pirates into the pennant race. Again the Pirates finished third, through no fault of Clemente's. He had carried the team and would finally be recognized. He did not lead the league in any of the three major batting categories, his team did not win the pennant, yet Roberto Clemente was named the Most Valuable Player in the National League. Recognition had been achieved.

Even the MVP award was limited satisfaction to Clemente. It was an indication of his talent but not an actual display. He put on the display in October of 1971 and the recognition was complete. The World Series performance would stand out in the memory of every person who had seen it, but there had to be lasting recognition, a mark that would stand out in the record books forever, 3,000 hits.

On September 29, 1972, Clemente topped a Tom Seaver pitch over the mound and beat Ken Boswell's throw by a step. The official scorer immediately charged Boswell with an error. A little topper was not fitting for Roberto's 3,000th hit. It should be a line drive. It came the next day, a blast to the left centerfield power alley off Jon Matlack. It was Roberto's last hit of the season, 3,000, exactly. The team went on to the playoffs, losing the fifth game to Cincinnati on a wild pitch. The defeat was crushing but the season was over and Clemente returned home.

The people that only saw Roberto Clemente as a baseball player missed an equally important facet of the man: Clemente the humanitarian. Roberto loved his family, his fans, and his country of Puerto Rico more than anything else. He always wanted to be someone the youth of Puerto Rico could look up to. When he was named Most Valuable Player in 1966, he became their Babe Ruth. He wanted to build a Sports City for the young Puerto Ricans. He gave them pride because he cared. It showed in the way he played baseball and in his actions off the field. When the country of Nicaragua was ravaged by an earthquake, Clemente was made honorary chairman of the relief drive. This did not mean making speeches and attending dinners. For Clemente, it meant going door to door for supplies and making sure they reached the victims of the disaster. It meant a trip to Managua.

Suddenly he was gone. The plane carrying supplies to Managua had crashed. There were no survivors. It was unbelievable. The people who had finally come to know his greatness were stunned. His friends and family and the fans who had followed him through his career were grief stricken. The team which had come to depend on him was decimated. Within days, the Baseball Writers of America waived the five year waiting period and inducted Roberto Clemente into the Hall of Fame.

The Pirates have recovered and are again World Champions. His friends and family and fans have accepted the loss and continue living with fond memories of the past. Memories of a game played as it had never been played before or will be played again. The memories of Clemente are of a man who gave everything he had on and off the field. That is how he would want to be remembered.

# 9.   CAPTAIN WILLIE

Willie Stargell epitomizes the one salient trait in human civilization that has sustained itself for the last two thousand years. Stargell has a respect for all human beings in all walks of life. It is his ability to manifest kindness and humility that has endeared him to the people in Pittsburgh and the tri-state area.

When Stargell was named the Most Valuable Player in both the National League Championship Series and the World Series, it seemed to be a fitting tribute to the man who has come to represent baseball in Pittsburgh. Stargell is the Pirates' leader, he is a tower of strength that the other players can draw from. And to the community Stargell is one of them. He works hard for what he gets and is not afraid to scratch and claw for what he wants. He is proud of his accomplishments but even if he should fail he still holds his head high. People nurtured in the steel mills and the coal mines have no aversions to a rough and tumble guy. They are proud of their work and understand the problems of making a living.

It wasn't always easy for Stargell. As an 18-year-old from Oakland, California, Stargell didn't understand the prejudice and hatred he found his first year in Roswell, Texas.

Nellie King, former Pirate pitcher and broadcaster and now sports information director at Duquesne University, recalls that in Stargell's first year, he was two weeks away from being sent home when his manager, Al Kubski, and the Pirates' Branch Rickey, Jr., sat him down and reassured him that life would get better and that he had the ability to play in the majors.

Stargell finished the season with a .274 average and 87 RBIs, but not without further problems. One day a man came to Stargell and threatened, "If you play tonight, I'll blow your brains out." Stargell did play and collected several hits. He felt that if he didn't play he would be cheating himself; but although he was only 18, Stargell realized that he may have hated that man, but to hate an entire race would put him in the gutter with the rest of those idiots.

Stargell came to Pittsburgh in 1962 and played solid ball throughout the '60s. He played without a lot of fanfare and never cried for recognition. But the fans who watched Stargell knew his greatness. He played left field without the hoopla of diving for a ball thirty feet away, to lay there while the center fielder chased it down. There were no histrionics after a strikeout, and no bickering with umpires. Fans could not fault his genuine efforts.

I remember an incident that occurred in 1968. The city of Johnstown was sponsoring a Black Arts Festival at the local arena. The first half of the evening featured exhibits and demonstrations by local artists, and the second half consisted of an African dance exhibition by a national company. It had been rumored that Stargell was going to make an appearance that night, but through the first half of the evening no one had seen him. After the lights had been turned down and the dancing program had begun, I saw the biggest man I had ever seen. Stargell came and sat down, four chairs away from my family. He had just settled into his seat when he noticed two elderly ladies standing behind him. Stargell offered the ladies his chair and went to get two more. My father, noticing that his 11-year-old son was much more interested in his favorite ball player than cultural dancing, leaned to me and said, "That's how a gentleman acts. That shows you are thoughtful."

Stargell shows a sensitivity toward people. Perhaps he has been injured from the discriminations that he has suffered. He, like all black players, has suffered the ignominy of being called "nigger," or having to eat in second rate restaurants. He taught himself how to control his rage at these insults, and this self-control helped him to become a better player. Stargell has learned how to make people feel at ease in a tense situation. His ability to see both sides of a problem has given him the ability to evaluate situations. He has learned to take the tension and form it into a type of concentration that allows him to meet the challenge at hand. Evidence of this came in the seventh game of the 1979 World Series. Trailing by one run, with a man on in the sixth inning, Stargell hit Scot McGregor's first pitch into the right field bullpen to give the Pirates the win. Yet he is able to see the humor in life. Nellie King relates the following story:

During the civil-rights turmoil in '68 or '69, after Martin Luther King had been shot, the racial tension in the country was high. There were riots in Detroit and other cities. There were no problems on the team, we all traveled together and about the only racial tensions we saw were in the newspapers. One day we traveled to St. Louis and were just checking into our rooms at the Chase Hotel. Mazeroski and I were the first to get on the elevator with a typical midwestern couple, and they seemed very proper. Then in comes this sea of black faces, about six or seven players crowded on the elevator. The couple probably had never seen this many blacks at one time and were visibly nervous. We went up about six floors and no one said a word. The elevator stopped and Maz got off, but as he did he held the doors and said, "How come you guys have flat noses?" The poor couple's mouths just about dropped to the floor; they must have thought we were going to have a riot right there on the elevator. Stargell got off the elevator, put his arm around Maz's shoulder and said, "By God, those guys do have flat noses!"

Stargell is able to maintain a certain perspective. He doesn't try to embarrass people with his accomplishments. If he hit 40 home runs in a year, he would never brag to the media or say that he was better than another player. This attitude has projected itself to all members of the team; they don't allow themselves to get too high after a victory or too low after a defeat. This motivates them to excell, and to perform to the best of their abilities. An example of this level-headed approach to each situation came in the past World Series. Phil Garner didn't let his error in the first inning of the first game shatter his confidence. He was able to overcome that mistake and have a great series.

After Clemente died in 1972, the consensus was that Stargell would assume the mantle of leadership. However, Stargell showed his humility. He was not the type of person who would stand up in the middle of the clubhouse and say "if you have any problems, come to me," but he would, in his own easy-going manner, let every player on the team know that he was willing to listen. He earned the respect of his fellow players on the field. He motivated them by his actions. In 1973, he had his best year. He led the league on six categories, including home runs with 44 and RBIs with 119. This has carried on right through to the past season.

After his two shocking disappointments in 1971 and '73 when he was not elected the National League's Most Valuable Player, he finally received his just reward in 1979. But again, through the questionable genius of several baseball writers, he was denied the honor singularly. By now Stargell has learned that it's not the awards that a man receives that makes him great; it is the respect that he has earned from his peers. His playing excellence and humanitarianism has earned him that respect and the respect of the entire nation. *Sports Illustrated* named him co-Sportsman of the Year, along with Terry Bradshaw of the Pittsburgh Steelers. This honor is another testimony to his character and his leadership, as well as his ability.

## 10. BOX SCORES OF SOME MEMORABLE GAMES

### First National League Game for the Pittsburgh Alleghenies

| ALLEGHENIES | R | H | O | A | E |
|---|---|---|---|---|---|
| Dalrymple, l | 1 | 1 | 1 | 0 | 0 |
| Brown, m | 0 | 1 | 4 | 1 | 0 |
| Miller, c | 2 | 1 | 4 | 0 | 0 |
| Barkley, 2 | 0 | 0 | 4 | 3 | 0 |
| Coleman, r | 1 | 0 | 2 | 1 | 0 |
| McKinnon, l | 2 | 4 | 8 | 0 | 0 |
| Whitney, 3 | 0 | 2 | 3 | 0 | 0 |
| Smith, s | 0 | 1 | 0 | 5 | 0 |
| Galvin, p | 0 | 2 | 0 | 0 | 0 |
| Totals | 6 | 12 | 27 | 10 | 0 |

| CHICAGO | R | H | O | A | E |
|---|---|---|---|---|---|
| Sunday, m | 0 | 2 | 3 | 0 | 1 |
| Ryan, l | 0 | 1 | 0 | 1 | 0 |
| Sullivan, r | 1 | 1 | 0 | 0 | 0 |
| Anson, l | 1 | 2 | 7 | 0 | 1 |
| Pfeffer, 2 | 0 | 2 | 4 | 3 | 0 |
| Williamson, s | 0 | 0 | 1 | 1 | 0 |
| Burns, 3 | 0 | 2 | 3 | 2 | 0 |
| Daly, c | 0 | 0 | 9 | 2 | 1 |
| Clarkson, p | 0 | 0 | 0 | 6 | 0 |
| Totals | 2 | 10 | 27 | 15 | 3 |

```
Alleghenies    2 1 0   2 0 0   0 1 0—6
Chicago        0 0 0   0 0 0   1 0 1—2
```

Earned Runs: Alleghenies 3; Chicago 2
Two Base Hits: McKinnon, Ryan, Anson, Pfeffer
Three Base Hits: Dalrymple, McKinnon, Whitney, Sullivan
First Base On Balls: Miller, Smith, Burns
Total Bases: Alleghenies 19; Chicago 14
First Base On Errors: Alleghenies 1
Stolen Bases: Miller, Smith, Burns
Double Plays: Smith, Barkley and McKinnon
Hit By Pitched Ball: Coleman, Pfeffer
Passed Balls: Miller 2; Daly
Struck Out: Dalrymple, Brown 2, Barkley, Galvin, Sullivan, Williamson
Left On Bases: Alleghenies 4; Chicago 5
Time of Game: 1:35
Umpire: Joseph Quest

### World Series Box Scores

### 1ST WORLD SERIES GAME EVER

#### 1903—GAME 1

**Thursday, October 1—At Boston**

| Pittsburgh (N.L.) | AB | R | H | O | A | E |
|---|---|---|---|---|---|---|
| Beaumont, cf | 5 | 1 | 0 | 3 | 0 | 0 |
| Clarke, lf | 5 | 0 | 2 | 4 | 0 | 0 |
| Leach, 3b | 5 | 1 | 4 | 0 | 1 | 1 |
| Wagner, ss | 3 | 1 | 1 | 1 | 2 | 1 |
| Bransfield, 1b | 5 | 2 | 1 | 7 | 0 | 0 |
| Ritchey, 2b | 4 | 1 | 0 | 1 | 2 | 0 |
| Sebring, rf | 5 | 1 | 3 | 1 | 0 | 0 |
| Phelps, c | 4 | 0 | 1 | 10 | 0 | 0 |
| Phillippe, p | 4 | 0 | 0 | 0 | 2 | 0 |
| Totals | 40 | 7 | 12 | 27 | 7 | 2 |

| Boston (A.L.) | AB | R | H | O | A | E |
|---|---|---|---|---|---|---|
| Dougherty, lf | 4 | 0 | 0 | 1 | 1 | 0 |
| Collins, 3b | 4 | 0 | 0 | 2 | 3 | 0 |
| Stahl, cf | 4 | 0 | 1 | 2 | 0 | 0 |
| Freeman, rf | 4 | 2 | 2 | 2 | 0 | 0 |
| Parent, ss | 4 | 1 | 2 | 4 | 4 | 0 |
| LaChance, 1b | 4 | 0 | 0 | 8 | 0 | 0 |
| Ferris, 2b | 3 | 0 | 1 | 2 | 4 | 2 |
| Criger, c | 3 | 0 | 0 | 6 | 1 | 2 |
| aO'Brien | 1 | 0 | 0 | 0 | 0 | 0 |
| Young, p | 3 | 0 | 0 | 0 | 1 | 0 |
| bFarrell | 1 | 0 | 0 | 0 | 0 | 0 |
| Totals | 35 | 3 | 6 | 27 | 14 | 4 |

| Pittsburgh | 4 0 1   1 0 0   1 0 0—7 |
| Boston | 0 0 0   0 0 0   2 0 1—3 |

aStruck out for Criger in ninth. bGrounded out for Young in ninth. Three-base hits—Freeman, Parent, Leach 2, Bransfield. Home run—Sebring. Runs batted in—Sebring 4, Leach, Wagner, LaChance 2, Parent. Stolen bases—Wagner, Bransfield, Ritchey. Left on bases—Boston 6, Pittsburgh 9. Earned runs—Boston 2, Pittsburgh 3. Bases on balls—Off Young 3. Struck out—By Young 5, by Phillippe 10. Hit by pitcher—by Phillippe (Ferris). Passed ball—Criger. Umpires—O'Day (N.L.) and Connolly (A.L.). Time—1:55. Attendance—16,242.

## 1909—7TH GAME

### Saturday, October 16—At Detroit

| Pittsburgh (N.L.) | AB | R | H | O | A | E | Detroit (A.L.) | AB | R | H | O | A | E |
|---|---|---|---|---|---|---|---|---|---|---|---|---|---|
| Byrne, 3b | 0 | 0 | 0 | 0 | 0 | 0 | D. Jones, lf | 4 | 0 | 1 | 3 | 0 | 1 |
| Hyatt, cf | 3 | 1 | 0 | 0 | 0 | 0 | Bush, ss | 3 | 0 | 0 | 2 | 5 | 1 |
| Leach, cf-3b | 3 | 2 | 2 | 4 | 2 | 0 | Cobb, rf | 4 | 0 | 0 | 1 | 0 | 0 |
| Clarke, lf | 0 | 2 | 0 | 5 | 0 | 0 | Crawford, cf | 4 | 0 | 0 | 4 | 0 | 1 |
| Wagner, ss | 3 | 1 | 1 | 3 | 3 | 0 | Delahanty, 2b | 3 | 0 | 2 | 3 | 3 | 0 |
| Miller, 2b | 5 | 0 | 2 | 3 | 0 | 0 | Moriarty, 3b | 1 | 0 | 1 | 1 | 0 | 0 |
| Abstein, 1b | 4 | 1 | 1 | 10 | 0 | 0 | O'Leary, 3b | 3 | 0 | 0 | 1 | 1 | 0 |
| Wilson, rf | 4 | 1 | 0 | 0 | 0 | 0 | T. Jones, 1b | 4 | 0 | 1 | 9 | 0 | 0 |
| Gibson, c | 5 | 0 | 1 | 2 | 1 | 0 | Schmidt, c | 3 | 0 | 1 | 3 | 2 | 0 |
| Adams, p | 3 | 0 | 0 | 0 | 4 | 0 | Donovan, p | 0 | 0 | 0 | 0 | 1 | 0 |
|  |  |  |  |  |  |  | Mullin, p | 3 | 0 | 0 | 0 | 2 | 0 |
| Totals | 30 | 8 | 7 | 27 | 10 | 0 | Totals | 32 | 0 | 6 | 27 | 14 | 3 |

| Pittsburgh | 0 2 0   2 0 3   0 1 0—8 |
| Detroit | 0 0 0   0 0 0   0 0 0—0 |

Two-base hits—Leach, Gibson, Abstein, Moriarty, Delahanty, Schmidt. Three-base hit—Wagner. Runs batted in—Hyatt, Clarke, Wagner 2, Miller 2. Sacrifice hits—Leach, Clarke, Wilson, Adams. Sacrifice fly—Hyatt. Stolen bases—Clarke 1, Miller, Abstein. Double play—Bush, Schmidt and Delahanty. Earned runs—Pittsburgh 6, Detroit 0. Left on bases—Pittsburgh 11, Detroit 7. Struck out—Sy Adams 1, by Mullin 1. Bases on balls—Off Adams 1, off Donovan 6, off Mullin 4. Hit by pitcher—By Adams (Bush), by Donovan (Byrne). Hits—Off Donovan 2 in 3 innings, off Mullin 5 in 6 innings. Losing pitcher—Donovan. Umpires—O'Loughlin (A.L.), Johnstone (N.L.), Evans (A.L.) and Klem (N.L.). Time—2:10. Attendance—17,562.

## 1925—7TH GAME

### Thursday, October 15—At Pittsburgh

| Wash'ton (A.L.) | AB | R | H | O | A | E | Pittsburgh (N.L.) | AB | R | H | O | A | E |
|---|---|---|---|---|---|---|---|---|---|---|---|---|---|
| Rice, cf | 5 | 2 | 2 | 3 | 0 | 0 | Moore, 2b | 4 | 3 | 1 | 2 | 0 | 1 |
| S. Harris, 2b | 5 | 0 | 0 | 6 | 3 | 0 | Carey, cf | 5 | 3 | 4 | 4 | 0 | 0 |
| Goslin, lf | 4 | 2 | 1 | 2 | 0 | 0 | Cuyler, rf | 4 | 0 | 2 | 4 | 0 | 1 |
| J. Harris, rf | 3 | 1 | 1 | 1 | 1 | 0 | Barnhart, lf | 5 | 0 | 1 | 2 | 0 | 0 |
| Judge, 1b | 3 | 1 | 1 | 6 | 0 | 0 | Oldham, p | 0 | 0 | 0 | 0 | 0 | 0 |
| Bluege, 3b | 4 | 0 | 1 | 0 | 0 | 0 | Traynor, 3b | 4 | 0 | 2 | 1 | 3 | 0 |
| aPeckinpaugh, ss | 3 | 1 | 1 | 0 | 2 | 2 | Wright, ss | 4 | 0 | 1 | 1 | 3 | 0 |
| Ruel, c | 4 | 0 | 0 | 6 | 0 | 0 | McInnis, 1b | 4 | 0 | 2 | 7 | 0 | 0 |
| Johnson, p | 4 | 0 | 0 | 0 | 3 | 0 | Smith, c | 4 | 0 | 1 | 4 | 0 | 0 |
| Totals | 35 | 7 | 7 | 24 | 9 | 2 | cYde | 0 | 1 | 0 | 0 | 0 | 0 |
|  |  |  |  |  |  |  | Gooch, c | 0 | 0 | 0 | 2 | 0 | 0 |

## 1925 7th Game (continued)

| | | | | | | | |
|---|---|---|---|---|---|---|---|
| Aldrich, p | s | 0 | 0 | 0 | 0 | 0 | 0 |
| Morrison, p | | 1 | 1 | 1 | 0 | 0 | 0 |
| bGrantham | | 1 | 0 | 0 | 0 | 0 | 0 |
| Kremer, p | | 1 | 0 | 0 | 0 | 1 | 0 |
| dBigbee, lf | | 1 | 1 | 1 | 0 | 0 | 0 |
| Totals | | 38 | 9 | 15 | 27 | 7 | 2 |

```
Washington    4 0 0  2 0 0  0 1 0—7
Pittsburgh    0 0 3  0 1 0  2 3 *—9
```

aPeckinpaugh given base in first inning on Smith's interference. bFlied out for Morrison in fourth. cRan for Smith in eighth. dDoubled for Kremer in eighth. Runs batted in—Barnhart, Moore, Cuyler 3, Carey 2, Traynor, Bluege, Ruel, J. Harris 2, Bigbee, Peckinpaugh 2. Two-base hits—Carey 3, Moore, J. Harris, Cuyler 2, Smith, Bigbee. Three-base hit—Traynor. Home run—Peckinpaugh. Sacrifice hit—Cuyler. Stolen base—Carey. Double play—S. Harris and Judge. Left on bases—Pittsburgh 7, Washington 5, Earned runs—Washington 7, Pittsburgh 5. Struck out—By Morrison 2, by Kremer 1, by Oldham 2, by Johnson 3. Bases on balls—Off Aldridge 3, off Johnson 1. Wild pitches—Aldridge 2. Hits—Off Aldridge 2 in 1/3 inning, off Morrison 4 in 3 2/3 innings, off Kremer 1 in 4 innings, off Oldham 0 in 1 inning. Winning pitcher—Kremer. Umpires—McCormick (N.L.), Moriarty (A.L.), Rigler (N.L.) and Owens (A.L.). Time—2:31. Attendance—42,856.


## 1960—7TH GAME

### Thursday, October 13—At Pittsburgh

| New York (A.L.) | AB | R | H | O | A | E | Pittsburgh (N.L.) | AB | R | H | O | A | E |
|---|---|---|---|---|---|---|---|---|---|---|---|---|---|
| Richardson, 2b | 5 | 2 | 2 | 2 | 5 | 0 | Virdon, cf | 4 | 1 | 2 | 3 | 0 | 0 |
| Kubek, ss | 3 | 1 | 0 | 3 | 2 | 0 | Groat, ss | 4 | 1 | 1 | 3 | 2 | 0 |
| DeMaestri, ss | 0 | 0 | 0 | 0 | 0 | 0 | Skinner, lf | 2 | 1 | 0 | 1 | 0 | 0 |
| dLong | 1 | 0 | 1 | 0 | 0 | 0 | Nelson, 1b | 3 | 1 | 1 | 7 | 0 | 0 |
| eMcDougald, 3b | 0 | 1 | 0 | 0 | 0 | 0 | Clemente, rf | 4 | 1 | 1 | 4 | 0 | 0 |
| Maris, rf | 5 | 0 | 0 | 2 | 0 | 1 | Burgess, c | 3 | 0 | 2 | 0 | 0 | 0 |
| Mantle, cf | 5 | 1 | 3 | 0 | 0 | 0 | bChristopher | 0 | 0 | 0 | 0 | 0 | 0 |
| Berra, lf | 4 | 2 | 1 | 3 | 0 | 0 | Smith, c | 1 | 1 | 1 | 1 | 0 | 0 |
| Skowron, 1b | 5 | 2 | 2 | 10 | 2 | 0 | Hoak, 3b | 3 | 1 | 0 | 3 | 2 | 0 |
| Blanchard, c | 4 | 0 | 1 | 1 | 1 | 0 | Mazeroski, 2b | 4 | 2 | 2 | 5 | 0 | 0 |
| Boyer, 3b-ss | 4 | 0 | 1 | 0 | 3 | 0 | Law, p | 2 | 0 | 0 | 0 | 1 | 0 |
| Turley, p | 0 | 0 | 0 | 0 | 0 | 0 | Face, p | 0 | 0 | 0 | 0 | 1 | 0 |
| Stafford, p | 0 | 0 | 0 | 0 | 1 | 0 | cCimoli | 1 | 1 | 1 | 0 | 0 | 0 |
| aLopez | 1 | 0 | 1 | 0 | 0 | 0 | Friend, p | 0 | 0 | 0 | 0 | 0 | 0 |
| Shantz, p | 3 | 0 | 1 | 3 | 1 | 0 | Haddix, p | 0 | 0 | 0 | 0 | 0 | 0 |
| Coates, p | 0 | 0 | 0 | 0 | 0 | 0 | | | | | | | |
| Terry, p | 0 | 0 | 0 | 0 | 0 | 0 | | | | | | | |
| Totals | 40 | 9 | 13 | f24 | 15 | 1 | Totals | 31 | 10 | 11 | 27 | 6 | 0 |

```
New York      0 0 0  0 1 4  0 2 2— 9
Pittsburgh    2 2 0  0 0 0  0 5 1—10
```

aSingled for Stafford in third. bRan for Burgess in seventh. cSingled for Face in eighth. d Singled for DeMaestri in ninth. eRan for Long in ninth. fNone out when winning run scored. Runs batted in—Mantle 2, Berra 4, Skowron, Blanchard, Boyer, Virdon 2, Groat, Nelson 2, Clemente, Smith 3, Mazeroski. Two-base hit—Boyer. Home runs—Nelson, Skowron, Berra, Smith, Mazeroski. Sacrifice hit—Skinner. Double

260

plays—Stafford, Blanchard and Skowron; Richardson, Kubek and Skowron; Kubek, Richardson and Skowron. Left on bases—New York 6, Pittsburgh 1. Earned runs—New York 9, Pittsburgh 10, Bases on balls—Off Turley 1, off Stafford 1, off Shantz 1, off Law 1, off Face 1. Struck out—None. Pitching records—Off Turley 2 hits and 3 runs in 1 inning (pitched to one batter in second); off Stafford 2 hits and 1 run in 1 inning; off Shantz 4 hits and 3 runs in 5 innings (pitched to three batters in eighth); off Coates 2 hits and 2 runs in 2/3 inning; off Terry 1 hit and 1 run in 1/3 inning; off Law 4 hits and 3 runs in 5 innings (pitched to two batters in sixth); off Face 6 hits and 4 runs in 3 innings; off Friend 2 hits and 2 runs in 0 inning (pitched to two batters in ninth); off Haddix 1 hit and 0 runs in 1 inning. Winning pitcher—Haddix. Losing pitcher—Terry. Umpires—Jackowski (N.L.), Chylak (A.L.), Boggess (N.L.), Stevens (A.L.), Landes (N.L.), Honochick (A.L.). Time—2:36. Attendance—26,683.

Mazeroski's game.

## 1971—4TH GAME

### Wed., October 13—At Pittsburgh

| Baltimore (A.L.) | AB | R | H | O | A | E | Pittsburgh (N.L.) | AB | R | H | O | A | E |
|---|---|---|---|---|---|---|---|---|---|---|---|---|---|
| Blair, cf | 4 | 1 | 2 | 2 | 1 | 1 | Cash, 2b | 4 | 1 | 1 | 3 | 3 | 0 |
| Belanger, ss | 4 | 1 | 1 | 3 | 4 | 0 | Hebner, 3b | 5 | 1 | 1 | 1 | 1 | 0 |
| Rettenmund, lf | 4 | 1 | 1 | 1 | 0 | 0 | Clemente, rf | 4 | 0 | 3 | 0 | 0 | 0 |
| F. Robinson, rf | 2 | 0 | 0 | 2 | 0 | 0 | Stargell, lf | 5 | 1 | 2 | 1 | 0 | 0 |
| B. Robinson, 3b | 3 | 0 | 0 | 1 | 1 | 0 | Oliver, cf | 4 | 0 | 2 | 6 | 0 | 0 |
| Powell, 1b | 3 | 0 | 0 | 6 | 0 | 0 | Robertson, 1b | 4 | 1 | 1 | 11 | 0 | 0 |
| Johnson, 2b | 3 | 0 | 0 | 3 | 2 | 0 | Sanguillen, c | 4 | 0 | 2 | 4 | 0 | 0 |
| Etchebarren, c | 2 | 0 | 0 | 6 | 0 | 0 | Hernandez, ss | 3 | 0 | 1 | 1 | 2 | 0 |
| Dobson, p | 2 | 0 | 0 | 0 | 3 | 0 | bDavalillo | 1 | 0 | 0 | 0 | 0 | 0 |
| Jackson, p | 0 | 0 | 0 | 0 | 0 | 0 | Giusti, p | 0 | 0 | 0 | 0 | 0 | 0 |
| aShopay | 1 | 0 | 0 | 0 | 0 | 0 | Walker, p | 0 | 0 | 0 | 0 | 0 | 0 |
| Watt, p | 0 | 0 | 0 | 0 | 0 | 0 | Kison, p | 2 | 0 | 0 | 0 | 1 | 0 |
| Richert, p | 0 | 0 | 0 | 0 | 0 | 0 | cMay | 1 | 0 | 1 | 0 | 0 | 0 |
|  |  |  |  |  |  |  | dAlley, ss | 0 | 0 | 0 | 0 | 2 | 0 |
| Totals | 28 | 3 | 4 | 24 | 11 | 1 | Totals | 37 | 4 | 14 | 27 | 9 | 0 |

| | |
|---|---|
| Baltimore | 3 0 0   0 0 0   0 0 0—3 |
| Pittsburgh | 2 0 1   0 0 0   1 0 *—4 |

aGrounded into fielder's choice for Jackson in seventh. bReached first on Blair's error for Hernandez in seventh. cSingled for Kison in seventh. dRan for May in seventh. Runs batted in—B. Robinson, Powell, Stargell, Oliver 2, May. Two-base hits—Stargell, Oliver, Blair. Stolen bases—Sanguillen, Hernandez. Sacrifice flies—B. Robinson, Powell. Double plays—Hernandez, Cash and Robertson; Belanger, Johnson and Powell. Left on bases—Baltimore 4, Pittsburgh 13. Earned runs—Baltimore 3, Pittsburgh 4, Bases on balls—Off Dobson 3, off Jackson 1, off Walker 1. Struck out—By Dobson 4, by Watt 1, by Richert 1, by Kison 3, by Giusti 1. Pitching records—Off Dobson 3 runs and 10 hits in 5 1/3 innings; off Jackson 0 runs and 0 hits in 2/3 inning; off Watt 1 run and 4 hits in 1 1/3 innings; off Richert 0 runs and 0 hits in 2/3 inning; off Walker 3 runs and 3 hits in 2/3 innings; off Kison 0 runs and 1 hit in 6 1/3 innings; off Giusti 0 runs and 0 hits in 2 innings. Passed ball—Sanguillen. Hit by pitcher—By Kison 3 (Johnson, F. Robinson, Etchebarren). Winning pitcher—Kison. Losing pitcher—Watt. Save—Giusti. Umpires—Vargo (N.L.), Odom (A.L.), Kibler (N.L.), Chylak (A.L.), Sudol (N.L.) and Rice (A.L.). Time—2:48. Attendance—51,378.

First World Series Game under the lights.

## Sunday, October 17—At Baltimore

| Pittsburgh (N.L.) | AB | R | H | O | A | E | | Baltimore (A.L.) | AB | R | H | O | A | E |
|---|---|---|---|---|---|---|---|---|---|---|---|---|---|---|
| Cash, 2b | 4 | 0 | 0 | 4 | 3 | 0 | | Buford, lf | 3 | 0 | 1 | 0 | 0 | 0 |
| Clines, cf | 4 | 0 | 0 | 2 | 0 | 0 | | Johnson, 2b | 4 | 0 | 0 | 2 | 2 | 0 |
| Clemente, rf | 4 | 1 | 1 | 2 | 0 | 0 | | Powell, 1b | 4 | 0 | 0 | 12 | 0 | 0 |
| Robertson, 1b | 4 | 0 | 1 | 11 | 1 | 1 | | F. Robinson, rf | 4 | 0 | 0 | 3 | 0 | 0 |
| Sanguillen, c | 4 | 0 | 2 | 5 | 0 | 0 | | Rettenmund, cf | 4 | 0 | 0 | 2 | 0 | 0 |
| Stargell, lf | 4 | 1 | 1 | 0 | 0 | 0 | | B. Robinson, 3b | 2 | 0 | 0 | 1 | 5 | 0 |
| Pagan, 3b | 3 | 0 | 1 | 0 | 2 | 0 | | Hendricks, c | 3 | 1 | 2 | 7 | 0 | 0 |
| Hernandez, ss | 3 | 0 | 0 | 2 | 5 | 0 | | Belanger, ss | 3 | 0 | 1 | 0 | 3 | 0 |
| Blass, p | 3 | 0 | 0 | 1 | 2 | 0 | | Cuellar, p | 2 | 0 | 0 | 0 | 3 | 0 |
| | | | | | | | | aShopay | 0 | 0 | 0 | 0 | 0 | 0 |
| | | | | | | | | Dobson, p | 0 | 0 | 0 | 0 | 0 | 0 |
| | | | | | | | | McNally, p | 0 | 0 | 0 | 0 | 0 | 0 |
| Totals | 33 | 2 | 6 | 27 | 13 | 1 | | Totals | 29 | 1 | 4 | 27 | 13 | 0 |

```
Pittsburgh      0 0 0   1 0 0   0 1 0—2
Baltimore       0 0 0   0 0 0   0 1 0—1
```

aSacrificed for Cuellar in eighth. Runs batted in—Clemente, Pagan, Buford. Two-base hits—Hendricks, Pagan. Home run—Clemente. Sacrifice hit—Shopay. Caught stealing—Buford. Double play—Cash and Robertson. Left on bases—Pittsburgh 4, Baltimore 4. Earned runs—Pittsburgh 2, Baltimore 1. Bases on balls—Off Blass 2. Struck out—By Blass 5, by Cuellar 6, by Dobson 1. Pitching records—Off Blass 1 run and 4 hits in 9 innings; off Cuellar 2 runs and 4 hits in 8 innings; off Dobson 0 runs and 2 hits in 2/3 inning; off McNally 0 runs and 0 hits in 1/3 inning. Losing pitcher—Cuellar. Umpires—Chylak (A.L.), Sudol (N.L.), Rice (A.L.), Vargo (N.L.), Odom (A.L.) and Kibler (N.L.). Time—2:10. Attendance—47,291.

Bucs come back from 2-0 fefeat.

## Wednesday, October 17—At Baltimore

| Pittsburgh | AB | R | H | PO | A | E | | Baltimore | AB | R | H | PO | A | E |
|---|---|---|---|---|---|---|---|---|---|---|---|---|---|---|
| Moreno, cf | 5 | 1 | 3 | 4 | 0 | 0 | | Bumbry, cf | 3 | 0 | 0 | 0 | 0 | 0 |
| Foli, ss | 4 | 0 | 1 | 3 | 1 | 0 | | Garcia, ss | 3 | 0 | 1 | 0 | 5 | 1 |
| Parker, rf | 4 | 0 | 0 | 2 | 0 | 0 | | eAyala | 0 | 0 | 0 | 0 | 0 | 0 |
| B. Robinson, lf | 4 | 1 | 1 | 2 | 0 | 0 | | fCrowley | 1 | 0 | 0 | 0 | 0 | 0 |
| Stargell, 1b | 5 | 1 | 4 | 6 | 1 | 0 | | Stoddard, p | 0 | 0 | 0 | 0 | 1 | 0 |
| Madlock, 3b | 3 | 0 | 0 | 2 | 1 | 0 | | Flanagan, p | 0 | 0 | 0 | 0 | 0 | 0 |
| Nicosia, c | 4 | 0 | 0 | 6 | 1 | 0 | | Stanhouse, p | 0 | 0 | 0 | 0 | 0 | 0 |
| Garner, 2b | 3 | 1 | 1 | 1 | 2 | 0 | | T. Martinez, p | 0 | 0 | 0 | 0 | 0 | 0 |
| Bibby, p | 1 | 0 | 0 | 1 | 0 | 0 | | D. Martinez, p | 0 | 0 | 0 | 0 | 0 | 0 |
| aSanguillen | 1 | 0 | 0 | 0 | 0 | 0 | | Singleton, rf | 3 | 0 | 0 | 1 | 0 | 0 |
| D. Robinson, p | 0 | 0 | 0 | 0 | 0 | 0 | | Murray, 1b | 4 | 0 | 0 | 11 | 0 | 0 |
| Jackson, p | 1 | 0 | 0 | 0 | 0 | 0 | | Lowenstein, lf | 2 | 0 | 0 | 2 | 0 | 1 |
| Tekulve, p | 1 | 0 | 0 | 0 | 0 | 0 | | bRoenicke, lf | 2 | 0 | 0 | 1 | 0 | 0 |
| | | | | | | | | DeCinces, 3b | 4 | 0 | 2 | 3 | 3 | 0 |
| | | | | | | | | Dempsey, c | 3 | 0 | 0 | 3 | 0 | 0 |
| | | | | | | | | gKelly | 1 | 0 | 0 | 0 | 0 | 0 |
| | | | | | | | | Dauer, 2b | 3 | 1 | 1 | 4 | 2 | 0 |
| | | | | | | | | McGregor, p | 1 | 0 | 0 | 1 | 2 | 0 |
| | | | | | | | | cMay | 0 | 0 | 0 | 0 | 0 | 0 |
| | | | | | | | | dBelanger, ss | 0 | 0 | 0 | 1 | 1 | 0 |
| Totals | 36 | 4 | 10 | 27 | 6 | 0 | | Totals | 30 | 1 | 4 | 27 | 14 | 2 |

| Pittsburgh | 0 0 0　0 0 2　0 0 2—4 |
| Baltimore | 0 0 1　0 0 0　0 0 0—1 |

| PITTSBURGH | IP | H | R | ER | BB | SO |
|---|---|---|---|---|---|---|
| Bibby | 4 | 3 | 1 | 1 | 0 | 3 |
| D. Robinson | 2/3 | 1 | 0 | 0 | 1 | 0 |
| Jackson (Winner) | 2 2/3 | 0 | 0 | 0 | 2 | 1 |
| Tekulve (Save) | 1 2/3 | 0 | 0 | 0 | 1 | 2 |

| BALTIMORE | IP | H | R | ER | BB | SO |
|---|---|---|---|---|---|---|
| McGregor (Loser) | 8 | 7 | 2 | 2 | 2 | 2 |
| Stoddard | 1/3 | 1 | 1 | 1 | 0 | 0 |
| Flanagan | 0* | 1 | 1 | 1 | 0 | 0 |
| Stanhouse | 0* | 1 | 0 | 0 | 0 | 0 |
| T. Martinez | 0* | 0 | 0 | 0 | 0 | 0 |
| D. Martinez | 2/3 | 0 | 0 | 0 | 0 | 0 |

*Pitched to one batter in ninth.

Bases on balls—Off D. Robinson 1 (McGregor), off Jackson 2 (May, Brumbry), off Tekulve 1 (Singleton), off McGregor 2 (Garner, Madlock).

Strikeouts—By Bibby 3 (Murray 2, Lowenstein), by Jackson 1 (Roenicke), by Tekulve 2 (Roenicke, DeCinces), by McGregor 2 (Parker 2).

aGrounded out for Bibby in fifth. bStruck out for Lowenstein in seventh. cWalked for McGregor in eighth. dRan for May in eighth. eAnnounced as pinch hitter for Garcia in eighth. fGrounded out for Ayala in eighth. gFlied out for Dempsey in ninth. Runs batted in—Moreno, B. Robinson, Stargell 2, Dauer. Two-base hits—Stargell 2, Garner.

Home runs—Dauer, Stargell. Caught stealing—Garcia. Sacrifice hit—Foli. Hit by pitcher—By T. Martinez (Parker), by D. Martinez (B. Robinson). Double play—Belanger and Murray. Left on bases—Pittsburgh 10, Baltimore 6. Umpires—Neudecker (AL) plate, Engel (NL) first base, Goetz (AL) second base, Tata (NL) third base, McKean (AL) left field, Runge (NL) right field. Time—2:54. Attendance—53.733.

History repeats: Bucs come back from 3-1 deficit.

### All-Star Box Scores

### GAME OF 1944—FORBES FIELD, PITTSBURGH, JULY 11

| AMERICANS | AB | R | H | PO | A | E |
|---|---|---|---|---|---|---|
| Tucker (White Sox), cf | 4 | 0 | 0 | 4 | 0 | 0 |
| Spence (Senators), rf | 4 | 0 | 2 | 2 | 1 | 0 |
| McQuinn (Browns), 1b | 4 | 0 | 1 | 5 | 1 | 1 |
| Stephens (Browns), ss | 4 | 0 | 1 | 1 | 0 | 0 |
| Johnson (Red Sox), lf | 3 | 0 | 0 | 2 | 1 | 0 |
| Keltner (Indians), 3b | 4 | 1 | 1 | 0 | 4 | 0 |
| Doerr (Red Sox), 2b | 3 | 0 | 0 | 4 | 1 | 1 |
| Hemsley (Yankees), c | 2 | 0 | 0 | 2 | 0 | 0 |
| Hayes (Athletes), c | 1 | 0 | 0 | 3 | 0 | 1 |
| Borowy (Yankees), p | 1 | 0 | 1 | 0 | 0 | 0 |
| Hughson (Red Sox), p | 1 | 0 | 0 | 0 | 0 | 0 |
| Muncrief (Browns), p | 0 | 0 | 0 | 1 | 0 | 0 |
| cHiggins (Tigers) | 1 | 0 | 0 | 0 | 0 | 0 |
| Newhouse (Tigers), p | 0 | 0 | 0 | 0 | 1 | 0 |
| Newsom (Athletics), p | 0 | 0 | 0 | 0 | 0 | 0 |
| Totals | 32 | 1 | 6 | 24 | 9 | 3 |

| NATIONALS | AB | R | H | PO | A | E |
|---|---|---|---|---|---|---|
| Galan (Dodgers), lf | 4 | 1 | 1 | 2 | 0 | 0 |
| Cavarretta, (Cubs), 1b | 2 | 1 | 2 | 12 | 0 | 0 |

| | | | | | | |
|---|---|---|---|---|---|---|
| Musial (Cardinals), cf-rf | 4 | 1 | 1 | 2 | 1 | 0 |
| W. Cooper (Cardinals), c | 5 | 1 | 2 | 5 | 2 | 0 |
| Mueller (Reds), c | 0 | 0 | 0 | 0 | 0 | 0 |
| Walker (Dodgers), rf | 4 | 0 | 2 | 0 | 0 | 0 |
| DiMaggio (Pirates), cf | 0 | 0 | 0 | 0 | 0 | 0 |
| Elliott (Pirates), 3b | 3 | 0 | 0 | 0 | 0 | 0 |
| Kurowski (Cardinals), 3b | 1 | 0 | 1 | 0 | 1 | 0 |
| Ryan (Braves), 2b | 4 | 1 | 2 | 4 | 4 | 1 |
| Marion (Cardinals), ss | 3 | 1 | 0 | 2 | 3 | 0 |
| Walters (Reds), p | 0 | 0 | 0 | 0 | 1 | 0 |
| aOtt (Giants) | 1 | 0 | 0 | 0 | 0 | 0 |
| Raffensberger (Phils), p | 0 | 0 | 0 | 0 | 0 | 0 |
| bNicholson (Cubs) | 1 | 1 | 1 | 0 | 0 | 0 |
| Sewell (Pirates), p | 1 | 0 | 0 | 0 | 0 | 0 |
| dMedwick (Giants) | 0 | 0 | 0 | 0 | 0 | 0 |
| Tobin (Braves), p | 0 | 0 | 0 | 0 | 0 | 0 |
| Totals | 33 | 7 | 12 | 27 | 15 | 1 |

| | |
|---|---|
| American League | 0 1 0　0 0 0　0 0 0—1 |
| National League | 0 0 0　0 4 0　2 1 x—7 |

| AMERICANS | IP | H | R | ER | BB | SO |
|---|---|---|---|---|---|---|
| Borowy (Yankees) | 3 | 3 | 0 | 0 | 1 | 0 |
| Hughson (Red Sox) | 1 2/3 | 5 | 4 | 3 | 1 | 2 |
| Muncrief (Browns) | 1 1/3 | 1 | 0 | 0 | 0 | 1 |
| Newhouser (Tigers) | 1 2/3 | 3 | 3 | 2 | 2 | 1 |
| Newsome (Athletics) | 1/3 | 0 | 0 | 0 | 0 | 0 |

| NATIONALS | IP | H | R | ER | BB | SO |
|---|---|---|---|---|---|---|
| Walters (Reds) | 3 | 5 | 1 | 1 | 0 | 1 |
| Raffensberger (Phillies) | 2 | 1 | 0 | 0 | 0 | 2 |
| Sewell (Pirates) | 3 | 0 | 0 | 0 | 1 | 2 |
| Tobin (Braves) | 1 | 0 | 0 | 0 | 0 | 0 |

Winning pitcher—Raffensberger. Losing pitcher—Hughson.

aFlied out for Walters in third. bDoubled for Raffensberger in fifth. cGrounded out for Muncrief in seventh. dSacrificed for Sewell in eighth. Runs batted in—Kurowski 2, Nicholson, Galan, W. Cooper, Walker, Musial, Borowy. Two-base hits—Nicholson. Kurowski. Three-base hit—Cavarretta. Sacrifice hits—Marion, Musial, Medwick. Stolen base—Ryan. Double plays—Spence and Hemsley; Marion, Ryan and Cavaretta. Wild pitch—Muncrief. Left on bases—Nationals 9, Americans 5. Umpires—Barr and Sears (N.L.), Berry and Hubbard (A.L.). Time of game 2:11. Attendance—29,589.

---

## FIRST GAME OF 1959—FORBES FIELD, PITTSBURGH, JULY 7

| AMERICANS | AB | R | H | PO | A | E |
|---|---|---|---|---|---|---|
| Minoso (Indians), lf | 5 | 0 | 0 | 0 | 1 | 0 |
| Fox (White Sox), 2b | 5 | 1 | 2 | 2 | 0 | 0 |
| Kaline (Tigers), cf | 3 | 1 | 1 | 1 | 0 | 0 |
| Kuenn (Tigers), cf | 1 | 1 | 0 | 0 | 0 | 0 |
| Skowron (Yankees), 1b | 3 | 0 | 2 | 3 | 0 | 0 |
| Power (Indians), 1b | 1 | 1 | 1 | 3 | 0 | 0 |
| Colavito (Indians), rf | 3 | 0 | 1 | 1 | 0 | 0 |
| bWilliams (Red Sox) | 0 | 0 | 0 | 0 | 0 | 0 |
| cMcDougald (Yanks), ss | 0 | 0 | 0 | 0 | 0 | 0 |

| | AB | R | H | PO | A | E |
|---|---|---|---|---|---|---|
| Triandos (Orioles), c | 4 | 0 | 1 | 8 | 0 | 0 |
| fMantle (Yankees), rf | 0 | 0 | 0 | 0 | 0 | 0 |
| Killebrew (Senators), 3b | 3 | 0 | 0 | 0 | 1 | 0 |
| Bunning (Tigers), p | 0 | 0 | 0 | 0 | 0 | 0 |
| dRunnels (Red Sox) | 0 | 0 | 0 | 0 | 0 | 0 |
| eSievers (Senators) | 0 | 0 | 0 | 0 | 0 | 0 |
| Ford (Yankees), p | 0 | 0 | 0 | 0 | 1 | 0 |
| Daley (Athletics), p | 0 | 0 | 0 | 0 | 0 | 0 |
| Aparicio (White Sox), ss | 3 | 0 | 0 | 4 | 2 | 0 |
| gLollar (White Sox), c | 1 | 0 | 0 | 1 | 0 | 0 |
| Wynn (White Sox), p | 1 | 0 | 0 | 1 | 0 | 0 |
| Duren (Yankees), p | 1 | 0 | 0 | 0 | 0 | 0 |
| Malzone (Red Sox), 3b | 2 | 0 | 0 | 0 | 0 | 0 |
| Totals | 36 | 4 | 8 | 24 | 5 | 0 |

| NATIONALS | AB | R | H | PO | A | E |
|---|---|---|---|---|---|---|
| Temple (Reds), 2b | 2 | 0 | 0 | 1 | 3 | 0 |
| aMusial (Cardinals) | 1 | 0 | 0 | 0 | 0 | 0 |
| Face (Pirates), p | 0 | 0 | 0 | 0 | 0 | 0 |
| Antonelli (Giants), p | 0 | 0 | 0 | 0 | 0 | 0 |
| hBoyer (Cardinals), 3b | 1 | 1 | 1 | 1 | 0 | 0 |
| Mathews (Braves), 3b | 3 | 1 | 1 | 2 | 1 | 1 |
| iGroat (Pirates) | 0 | 0 | 0 | 0 | 0 | 0 |
| Elston (Cubs), p | 0 | 0 | 0 | 0 | 0 | 0 |
| Aaron (Braves), rf | 4 | 1 | 2 | 2 | 0 | 0 |
| Mays (Giants), cf | 4 | 0 | 1 | 2 | 0 | 0 |
| Banks (Cubs), ss | 3 | 1 | 2 | 1 | 2 | 0 |
| Cepeda (Giants), 1b | 4 | 0 | 0 | 6 | 0 | 0 |
| Moon (Dodgers), lf | 2 | 0 | 0 | 1 | 0 | 0 |
| Crandall (Braves), c | 3 | 1 | 1 | 10 | 0 | 0 |
| Drysdale (Dodgers), p | 1 | 0 | 0 | 0 | 0 | 0 |
| Burdette (Braves), p | 1 | 0 | 0 | 0 | 0 | 0 |
| Mazeroski (Pirates), 2b | 1 | 0 | 1 | 1 | 0 | 0 |
| Totals | 30 | 5 | 9 | 27 | 6 | 1 |

| | | |
|---|---|---|
| American League | 0 0 0   1 0 0   0 3 0—4 |
| National League | 1 0 0   0 0 0   2 2 x—5 |

| AMERICANS | IP | H | R | ER | BB | SO |
|---|---|---|---|---|---|---|
| Wynn (White Sox) | 3 | 2 | 1 | 1 | 1 | 3 |
| Duren (Yankees) | 3 | 1 | 0 | 0 | 1 | 4 |
| Bunning (Tigers) | 1 | 3 | 2 | 2 | 0 | 1 |
| Ford (Yankees) | 1/3 | 3 | 2 | 2 | 0 | 0 |
| Daley (Athletics) | 2/3 | 0 | 0 | 0 | 0 | 1 |

| NATIONALS | IP | H | R | ER | BB | SO |
|---|---|---|---|---|---|---|
| Drysdale (Dodgers) | 3 | 0 | 0 | 0 | 0 | 4 |
| Burdette (Braves) | 3 | 4 | 1 | 1 | 0 | 2 |
| Face (Pirates) | 1 2/3 | 3 | 3 | 3 | 2 | 2 |
| Antonelli (Giants) | 1/3 | 0 | 0 | 0 | 1 | 0 |
| Elston (Cubs) | 1 | 1 | 0 | 0 | 0 | 1 |

Winning pitcher—Antonelli. Losing pitcher—Ford.

aPopped out for Temple in sixth. bWalked for Colavito in eighth. cRan for Williams in eighth. dAnnounced as batter for Bunning in eighth. eWalked for Runnels in eighth.

fRan for Triandos in eighth. gHit into force play for Aparicio in eighth. hSingled for Antonelli in eighth. iSacrificed for Mathews in eighth. Runs batted in—Kaline, Power, Triandos 2, Mathews, Aaron, Mays, Crandall, Mazeroski. Two-base hits—Banks 2, Triandos. Three-base hit—Mays. Home runs—Mathews, Kaline. Sacrifice hit. Groat. Double play—Aparicio and Skowron. Left on bases—Americans 8, Nationals 4. Wild pitch—Elton. Umpires—Berlick, Donatelli and Crawford (N. L.), Runge, Paparella and Rice (A. L.). Time of game—2:33. Attendance—35,277.

## GAME OF 1974—THREE RIVERS STADIUM, PITTSBURGH, JULY 23

| AMERICANS | AB | R | H | RBI | PO | A |
|---|---|---|---|---|---|---|
| Carew (Twins), 2b | 1 | 1 | 0 | 0 | 0 | 1 |
| Grich (Orioles), 2b | 3 | 0 | 1 | 0 | 0 | 2 |
| Campaneris (Athletics), ss | 4 | 0 | 0 | 0 | 2 | 3 |
| Jacksen (Athletics), rf | 3 | 0 | 0 | 0 | 3 | 0 |
| Allen (White Sox), 1b | 2 | 0 | 1 | 1 | 2 | 0 |
| Yastrz'ski (Red Sox), 1b | 1 | 0 | 0 | 0 | 5 | 0 |
| Murcer (Yankees), cf | 2 | 0 | 0 | 0 | 0 | 0 |
| Hendrick (Indians), cf | 2 | 0 | 1 | 0 | 3 | 0 |
| Burroughs (Rangers), lf | 0 | 0 | 0 | 0 | 1 | 0 |
| Rudi (Athletics), lf | 2 | 0 | 0 | 0 | 1 | 0 |
| B. Robinson (Orioles), 3b | 3 | 0 | 0 | 0 | 0 | 0 |
| hMayberry (Royals) | 1 | 0 | 0 | 0 | 0 | 0 |
| Fingers (Athletics), p | 0 | 0 | 0 | 0 | 0 | 0 |
| Munson (Yankees), c | 3 | 1 | 1 | 0 | 7 | 0 |
| Perry (Indians), p | 0 | 0 | 0 | 0 | 0 | 0 |
| bKaline (Tigers) | 1 | 0 | 0 | 0 | 0 | 0 |
| Tiant (Red Sox), p | 0 | 0 | 0 | 0 | 0 | 0 |
| dF. Robinson (Angels) | 1 | 0 | 0 | 0 | 0 | 0 |
| Hunter (Athletics), p | 0 | 0 | 0 | 0 | 0 | 0 |
| Chalk (Angels), 3b | 1 | 0 | 0 | 0 | 0 | 0 |
| Totals | 30 | 2 | 4 | 1 | 24 | 6 |

| NATIONALS | AB | R | H | RBI | PO | A |
|---|---|---|---|---|---|---|
| Rose (Reds), lf | 2 | 0 | 0 | 0 | 1 | 0 |
| Brett (Pirates), p | 0 | 0 | 0 | 0 | 0 | 0 |
| cBrock (Cardinals) | 1 | 1 | 1 | 0 | 0 | 0 |
| Smith (Cardinals), rf | 2 | 1 | 1 | 1 | 2 | 0 |
| Morgan (Reds), 2b | 2 | 0 | 1 | 1 | 3 | 4 |
| gCash (Phillies), 2b | 1 | 0 | 0 | 0 | 0 | 1 |
| Aaron (Braves), rf | 2 | 0 | 0 | 0 | 0 | 0 |
| Cedeno (Astros), cf | 2 | 0 | 0 | 0 | 2 | 0 |
| Bench (Reds), c | 3 | 1 | 2 | 0 | 7 | 0 |
| Grote (Mets), c | 0 | 0 | 0 | 0 | 1 | 0 |
| Wynn (Dodgers), cf-rf | 3 | 1 | 1 | 0 | 0 | 0 |
| Matlack (Mets), p | 0 | 0 | 0 | 0 | 0 | 0 |
| Grubb (Padres), lf | 1 | 0 | 0 | 0 | 0 | 0 |
| Garvey (Dodgers), 1b | 4 | 1 | 2 | 1 | 6 | 2 |
| Cey (Dodgers), 3b | 2 | 0 | 1 | 2 | 0 | 0 |
| eSchmidt (Phillies), 3b | 0 | 1 | 0 | 0 | 0 | 1 |
| Bowa (Phillies), ss | 2 | 0 | 0 | 0 | 2 | 0 |
| fPerez (Reds) | 1 | 0 | 0 | 0 | 0 | 0 |
| Kessinger (Cubs), ss | 1 | 1 | 1 | 1 | 1 | 0 |

| | | | | | | |
|---|---|---|---|---|---|---|
| Messersmith (Dodgers), p | 0 | 0 | 0 | 0 | 2 | 1 |
| aGarr (Braves), lf | 3 | 0 | 0 | 0 | 0 | 0 |
| McGlothen (Cardinals), p | 0 | 0 | 0 | 0 | 0 | 0 |
| Marshall (Dodgers), p | 1 | 0 | 0 | 0 | 0 | 1 |
| Totals | 33 | 7 | 10 | 6 | 27 | 10 |

```
          Americans        0 0 2  0 0 0  0 0 0—2
          Nationals        0 1 0  2 1 0  1 2 x—7
```

| AMERICANS | IP | H | R | ER | BB | SO |
|---|---|---|---|---|---|---|
| Perry (Indians) | 3 | 3 | 1 | 1 | 0 | 4 |
| Tiant (Red Sox) | 2 | 4 | 3 | 2 | 1 | 0 |
| Hunter (Athletics) | 2 | 2 | 1 | 1 | 1 | 3 |
| Fingers (Athletics) | 1 | 1 | 2 | 2 | 1 | 0 |

| NATIONALS | IP | H | R | ER | BB | SO |
|---|---|---|---|---|---|---|
| Messersmith (Dodgers) | 3 | 2 | 2 | 2 | 3 | 4 |
| Brett (Pirates) | 2 | 1 | 0 | 0 | 1 | 0 |
| Matlack (Mets) | 1 | 1 | 0 | 0 | 1 | 0 |
| McGlothen (Cardinals) | 1 | 0 | 0 | 0 | 0 | 1 |
| Marshall (Dodgers) | 2 | 0 | 0 | 0 | 1 | 2 |

Winning pitcher—Brett. Losing pitcher—Tiant.

aStruck out for Messersmith in third. bFouled out for Perry in fourth. cSingled for Brett in fifth. dHit into force play for Tiant in sixth. eWalked for Cey in sixth. fStruck out for Bowa in sixth. gFlied out for Morgan in seventh. hGrounded out for B. Robinson in eighth. Errors—Bench, Munson. Double plays—None. Left on bases—Americans 8. Nationals 6. Two-base hits—Cey, Munson, Morgan, Garvey. Three-base hits—Kessinger. Home run—Smith. Stolen bases—Carew, Brock. Sacrifice hit—Perry. Sacrifice fly—Morgan. Wild pitch—Fingers. Bases on balls—Off Tiant 1 (Bench), off Hunter 1 (Schmidt), off Fingers 1 (Schmidt), off Messer-1 (Munson), off Marshall 1 (Yastrzemski). Strikeouts—By Perry 4 (Rose, Morgan, Bench, Garr), by Hunter 3 (Garvey, Perez, Cedeno), by Messersmith 4 (Campaneris 2, Jackson, Allen), by McGlothen 1 (Jackson), by Marshall 2 (Tudi, Chalk). Umpires—Sudol (NL) plate, Frantz (AL) first base, Vargo (NL) second base, Anthony (AL) third Sudol (NL) plate, Frantz (AL) first base, Vargo (NL) second base, Anthony (AL) third base, Kibler (NL) left field. Maloney (AL) right field. Time—2:37. Attendance—50,706.

Official scorers—Joe Heiting, Houston Post; Charley Feeney, Pittsburgh Post-Gazette; Luke Quay, McKeesport Daily News.

## NO-HIT GAME BOX SCORES

### Sept. 20, 1907   Brooklyn at Pittsburgh

| BROOKLYN | ab | r | b | p | a | e | PITTSBURGH | ab | r | b | p | a | e |
|---|---|---|---|---|---|---|---|---|---|---|---|---|---|
| Casey, 3b | 3 | 0 | 0 | 0 | 3 | 0 | Hallman, rf | 4 | 0 | 0 | 2 | 0 | 0 |
| Lewis, ss | 3 | 0 | 0 | 3 | 4 | 0 | Leach, cf | 4 | 0 | 0 | 1 | 0 | 0 |
| Jordan, 1b | 3 | 0 | 0 | 12 | 0 | 0 | Clarke, lf | 4 | 0 | 2 | 0 | 0 | 0 |
| Hummel, 2b | 4 | 0 | 0 | 1 | 3 | 0 | Wagner, ss | 3 | 1 | 0 | 3 | 3 | 1 |
| Batch, lf | 4 | 1 | 0 | 3 | 0 | 0 | Abbat'o, 2b | 3 | 0 | 0 | 0 | 4 | 0 |
| Burch, rf | 2 | 0 | 0 | 1 | 0 | 0 | Swaci'a, 1b | 2 | 1 | 0 | 14 | 0 | 0 |
| Maloney, cf | 2 | 0 | 0 | 4 | 0 | 0 | Storke, 3b | 0 | 0 | 0 | 1 | 2 | 0 |

| | | | | | | | | | | | | |
|---|---|---|---|---|---|---|---|---|---|---|---|---|
| Bergen, c | 3 | 0 | 0 | 0 | 0 | 0 | Gibson, c | 2 | 0 | 0 | 6 | 0 | 0 |
| Stricklett, p | 3 | 0 | 0 | 0 | 2 | 0 | Maddox, p | 3 | 0 | 0 | 0 | 1 | 1 |
| Totals | 27 | 1 | 0 | 24 | 12 | 0 | Totals | 25 | 2 | 2 | 27 | 10 | 2 |

```
Brooklyn      0 0 0   1 0 0   0 0 0—1
Pittsburgh    0 0 0   0 1 0   1 0 x—2
```

Two-base hit—Clarke. Sacrifice hits—Stroke, Gibson, Maloney. First on balls—Off Maddox 3, Stricklett 4. Hit by pitcher—Jordan. Struck out—By Maddox 5. Left on bases—Pittsburgh 5, Brooklyn 4. First on errors—Brooklyn 2. Time—1:30. Umpire—Klem. Attendance—2,380.

### May 6, 1951   Pittsburgh at Boston

#### PITTSBURGH

| | ab | r | h | tb | o | a | e |
|---|---|---|---|---|---|---|---|
| Dillinger, 3b | 5 | 0 | 1 | 1 | 0 | 1 | 0 |
| Metkovich, cf | 4 | 2 | 3 | 5 | 2 | 0 | 0 |
| Bell, rf | 4 | 0 | 1 | 1 | 2 | 0 | 0 |
| Kiner, 1b | 5 | 0 | 1 | 2 | 11 | 0 | 0 |
| Westlake, lf | 4 | 1 | 0 | 0 | 2 | 0 | 0 |
| Strickland, ss | 2 | 0 | 0 | 0 | 1 | 5 | 0 |
| Basgall, 2b | 3 | 0 | 1 | 1 | 4 | 2 | 0 |
| FitzGerald, c | 4 | 0 | 1 | 1 | 5 | 1 | 0 |
| Chambers, p | 4 | 0 | 1 | 1 | 0 | 2 | 0 |
| Totals | 35 | 3 | 9 | 12 | 27 | 11 | 0 |

#### BOSTON

| | ab | r | h | tb | o | a | e |
|---|---|---|---|---|---|---|---|
| Hartsfield, 2b | 1 | 0 | 0 | 0 | 3 | 3 | 0 |
| Jethroe, cf | 4 | 0 | 0 | 0 | 3 | 0 | 0 |
| Torgeson, 1b | 1 | 0 | 0 | 0 | 9 | 0 | 0 |
| Elliott, 3b | 4 | 0 | 0 | 0 | 1 | 3 | 0 |
| Gordon, rf | 3 | 0 | 0 | 0 | 4 | 0 | 0 |
| Cooper, c | 4 | 0 | 0 | 0 | 4 | 0 | 0 |
| Olmo, lf | 4 | 0 | 0 | 0 | 2 | 0 | 0 |
| Kerr, ss | 2 | 0 | 0 | 0 | 1 | 4 | 0 |
| Estock, p | 0 | 0 | 0 | 0 | 0 | 0 | 1 |
| *Marquez | 1 | 0 | 0 | 0 | 0 | 0 | 0 |
| Nichols, p | 0 | 0 | 0 | 0 | 0 | 0 | 0 |
| Totals | 24 | 0 | 0 | 0 | 27 | 10 | 1 |

*Fanned for Estock in eighth.

```
Pittsburgh    1 0 0   0 0 1   0 1 0—3
Boston        0 0 0   0 0 0   0 0 0—0
```

Runs batted in—Bell, Chambers, Basgall. Two-base hits—Metkovich 2, Kiner. Stolen base—Bell. Sacrifices—Estock, Hartsfield, Strickland. Double plays—Basgall and Kiner; Elliott, Hartsfield and Torgeson. Left on bases—Pittsburgh 11, Boston 7. Bases on balls—Off Estock 5, off Chambers 8. Struck out—By Estock 2, by Chambers 4. Pitching records—Off Estock 8 hits, 3 runs in 8 innings, off Nichols 1 hit, 0 runs in 1 inning. Wild pitch—Chambers. Winning pitcher—Chambers (3-2). Losing pitcher—Estock (0-1). Umpires—Dascoli, Goetz and Jorda. Time of game—2:01. Attendance—15,492.